The JOURNALS of SYLVIA PLATH

"...bring together all the incarnations of the poet and novelist we have known and allow us to see her as she must have been in life: complex, fascinating, cruel and kind, and, ultimately, enigmatic and elusive...a rare thing: a portrait of the artist as an adolescent girl, as a young woman, and as a wife and mother...Few lives blaze up as hers did, illuminating so much."
Chicago Sun-Times

"SO DAMNED BEAUTIFULLY
WRITTEN...
Sylvia Plath's jou
of love and the
deavor from one
voices of the Eng
Los Angeles ... .iner

The JOURNALS of SYLVIA PLATH

A publishing event hailed
by reviewers and critics
all over America...

The JOURNALS of SYLVIA PLATH

The JOURNALS of SYLVIA PLATH

The JOURNALS of SYLVIA PLATH

Foreword by Ted Hughes

Ted Hughes, Consulting Editor
and Frances McCullough, Editor

BALLANTINE BOOKS • NEW YORK

The editors are especially grateful to Ruth Mortimer of The Neilson Library at Smith College.

Library of Congress Catalog Card Number: 81-19435

ISBN 0-345-35168-1

This edition published by arrangement with Doubleday & Company, Inc.

Printed in Canada

First Ballantine Books Edition: August 1983
Fourth Printing: July 1987

delight in life. Ahead is a large array of blind
alleys. You are half-deliberately, half-desperately,
cutting off your grip on creative life. You are
becoming a neuter machine. You cannot love,
even if you knew how to begin to love. Every
thought is a devil, a hell — if you could do a lot of
things over again, ah, how differently you would do
them! You want to go home, back to the womb.
You watch the world being torn door after door in
your face, numbly, blindly. You have forgotten
the secret you knew, once, ah, once, of being
joyous, of laughing, of opening doors.

[15]
January 10, 1953: Look at that ugly
dead mask here and do not forget
it. It is a chalk mask with dead
dry poison behind it, like the death
angel. It is what I was this fall, and
what I never want to be again. The
pasting disconsolate mouth, the flat, bored,
numb, expressionless eyes: symptoms of the
foul decay within. Eddie wrote me after my
last honest letter saying I had better go to
get psychiatric treatment to root out the
sources of my trouble problems. I smile, now,
thinking: we all like to think we are

CONTENTS

EDITOR'S NOTE   *xi*

FOREWORD   *xiii*

PART I:
Smith College 1950–1955   *1*

PART II:
Cambridge 1955–1957
Smith College 1957–1958   *89*

PART III:
Boston 1958–1959
England 1960–1962   *237*

Chronology   *356*

Index   *359*

EDITOR'S NOTE

Sylvia Plath began keeping a diary when she was a child. She kept it right up until her death, and, next to her poems, it is her most important work. The journal had the usual functions of such documents—to chart a life, to pique memory, to confirm inner life and perhaps to dispel the doubt that one exists at all—but it was also vastly more than that. Plath at one point called it "a litany of dreams, directives and imperatives," and, more precisely, her "Sargasso," by which she meant a repository of imagination, a bringing forth from the unconscious of the urgent material that first saw the light of day in these pages. So here is not only her life—always seen as perilously short ("tick tock . . . a life is passing. My life. . . .")—but also the germs of most of her work. The interrelation is especially important in a writer whose work was so completely centered on her biographical details, though it's important to understand that the autobiography does not work in Plath as it does in the "confessional" writers, but rather in a mythological sense— as can be seen most clearly in Judith Kroll's critical study Chapters in a Mythology. *In the absence of a good biography, this journal offers something that no biography could—in its best passages the voice that speaks through these pages is as true and unique as the Plath of the poems.*

We have tried, in the cutting of the work, to stick to a few basic principles: to include what seem to us the most important elements relating to her work, her inner life, and her valiant struggle to find herself and her voice. This leaves a great deal of material by the road: countless numbers of sketches, prospective poems and stories, lists of characters' names, detailed descriptions of rooms, places, people, and other elements related to her work. Obviously there are also lots of missing pages of ordinary commentary that seemed not particularly relevant to any of the basic concerns of the book. Because it is very early—in terms of the ages of Plath's survivors—to release such a document, there has been special concern for those who must live out their lives as characters in this drama. There are quite a few nasty bits missing—Plath had a very sharp tongue and tended to use it on nearly everybody, even people of whom she was inordinately fond (Paul and Clarissa Roche, for instance, who take some tartness in this book and yet were very close to Plath right up until the end). So, some of the more devastating comments are missing—these are marked "[omission]" to distinguish them from ordinary cuts— and there are a few others cuts—of intimacies—that have the effect of diminishing Plath's eroticism, which was quite strong. In the later Smith College section and the Devon section a few names have been changed.

Commentary is at a minimum. Because of the cuts and gaps in Plath's own papers, the book doesn't always form a coherent narrative—in those cases there are notes to orient the reader. There are a couple of longer notes where it seemed important to place the material in some sort of perspective. The book is a treasure house of thousands of loose ends to be caught up in tracing images and ideas to the poems and stories and novel; in a few cases, the correspondences have been pointed out, but for the most part the reader is left to his own devices to interpret the material. The book these journals make is an enormously moving document, and it seems best simply to let it speak for itself.

Frances McCullough

FOREWORD

As records, Sylvia Plath's journals are different in kind from her stories, poems, essays and letters, and it is to be hoped that publishing them will serve a useful purpose.

Nearly all her earlier writings (and definitely all the prose she wrote for publication) suffered from her ambition to see her work published in particular magazines, and from her efforts to produce what the market seemed to require. The impulse to apprentice herself to various masters and to adapt her writing potential to practical, profitable use was almost an instinct with her. She went about it, as these journals show, with a relentless passion, and yet in a fever of uncertainty and self-doubt. This campaign of willful ideals produced everything in her work that seems artificial. Yet a sympathetic reader of these pages will be able to see that it was perhaps only one aspect — and one of the outermost — of a drive that was moving all the time in quite a different direction.

One can compare what was really going on in her to a process of alchemy. Her apprentice writings were like impurities thrown off from the various stages of the inner transformation, by-products of the internal work. One really can use these terms in her case. In spite of the care she devoted to each thing she wrote, as soon as it was well finished, she cast it behind her with something like contempt, sometimes with rage. Such things were not what she wanted at all. But what did she want? In a different culture, perhaps, she would have been happier. There was something about her reminiscent of what one reads of Islamic fanatic lovers of God—a craving to strip away everything from some ultimate intensity, some communion with spirit, or with reality, or simply with intensity itself. She showed something violent in this, something very primitive, perhaps very female, a readiness, even a need, to sacrifice everything to the new birth. With her, this was vividly formulated at every level of her being. The negative phase of it, logically, is suicide. But the positive phase (more familiar in religious terms) is the death of the old false self in the birth of the new real one. And this is what she finally did achieve, after a long and painful labor.

Ariel and the associated later poems give us the voice of that self. They are the proof that it arrived. All her other writings, except these journals, are the waste products of its gestation.

Sylvia Plath was a person of many masks, both in her personal life and in her writings. Some were camouflage cliché facades, defensive mechanisms, involuntary. And some were deliberate poses, attempts to find the keys to one style or another. These were the visible faces of her lesser selves, her false or provisional selves, the minor roles of her inner drama. Though I spent every day with her for six years, and was rarely separated from her for more than two or three hours at a time, I never saw her show her real self to anybody—except, perhaps, in the last three months of her life.

Her real self had showed itself in her writing, just for a moment, three years earlier, and when I heard it—the self I had married, after all, and lived with and knew well—in that brief moment, three lines recited as she went out through a doorway, I knew that what I had always felt must happen had now begun to happen, that her real self, being the real poet, would now speak for itself, and would throw off all those lesser and artificial selves that had monopolized the words up to that point, it was as if a dumb person suddenly spoke.

A real self, as we know, is a rare thing. The direct speech of a real self is rarer still. Where a real self exists it reveals itself, as a rule, only in the quality of the person's presence, or in actions. Most of us are never more than bundles of contradictory and complementary selves. Our real self, if our belief that we have one is true, is usually dumb, shut away beneath the to-and-fro conflicting voices of the false and petty selves. As if dumbness were the universal characteristic of the real self. When a real self finds language, and manages to speak, it is surely a dazzling event—as *Ariel* was.

But apart from its speech—that strange vital substance which its language seems to be—*Ariel* supplies little of the incidental circumstances or the crucial inner drama that produced it. Maybe it is this very bareness of circumstantial detail that has excited the wilder fantasies projected by others in Sylvia Plath's name. We respond to the speech, that fascinating substance, which is everywhere fully itself, nowhere diluted and ordinary—but we can only discuss it, or communicate our feelings about it, in terms of those externals, the drama of her psychological makeup, the accidents of her life.

This is where her journals demonstrate their difference in kind from all her other writings. Here she set down her day to day struggle with her warring selves, for herself only. This is her autobiography, far from complete, but complex and accurate, where she strove to see herself honestly and fought her way through the unmaking and remaking of herself. And the Sylvia Plath we can divine here is the closest we can now get to the real person in her daily life.

The journals exist in an assortment of notebooks and bunches of loose sheets. This selection contains perhaps a third of the whole bulk, which is now in The Neilson Library at Smith College. Two more notebooks survived for a while, maroon-backed ledgers like the '57–'59 volume, and continued the record from late '59 to within three days of her death. The last of these contained entries for several months, and I destroyed it because I did not want her children to have to read it (in those days I regarded forgetfulness as an essential part of survival). The other disappeared.

Ted Hughes

ONE

Smith College
1950 – 1955

Having bitten on life like a sharp apple
Or, playing it like a fish, been happy,

Having felt with fingers that the sky is blue,
What have we after that to look forward to?

Not the twilight of the gods but a precise dawn
of sallow and grey bricks, and newsboys crying war.

> —Louis MacNeice
> "Aubade"

We only begin to live when we conceive life as Tragedy. . . .

> —W. B. Yeats

Hold to the now, the here, through which all future plunges
to the past. . . .

> —James Joyce

These were epigraphs in Plath's original notebook.

Before she entered Smith in the fall, Plath had a summer job working in the fields at Lookout Farm in the Massachusetts countryside.

LOOKOUT FARM

July 1950. I may never be happy, but tonight I am content. Nothing more than an empty house, the warm hazy weariness from a day spent setting strawberry runners in the sun, a glass of cool sweet milk, and a shallow dish of blueberries bathed in cream. Now I know how people can live without books, without college. When one is so tired at the end of a day one must sleep, and at the next dawn there are more strawberry runners to set, and so one goes on living, near the earth. At times like this I'd call myself a fool to ask for more. . . .

Ilo asked me today in the strawberry field, "Do you like the Renaissance painters? Raphael and Michelangelo? I copied some of Michelangelo once. Ant what do you think of Picasso?... These painters who make a circle and a little board going down for a leg?" We worked side by side in the rows, and he would be quiet for a while, then suddenly burst out with conversation, speaking with his thick German accent. He straightened up, his tan, intelligent face crinkling up with laughter. His chunky, muscular body was bronzed, and his blond hair tucked up under a white handkerchief around his head. He said, "You like Frank Sinatra? So sendimendal, so romandic, so moonlight night, *ja*?"

A sudden slant of bluish light across the floor of a vacant room. And I knew it was not the streetlight, but the moon. What is more wonderful than to be a virgin, clean and sound and young, on such a night?... (Being raped.)*

Tonight was awful. It was the combination of everything. Of the play *Good-bye My Fancy*, of wanting, in a juvenile way, to be, like the heroine, a reporter in the trenches, to be loved by a man who admired me, who understood me as much as I understood myself. And then there was Jack, who tried so hard to be nice, who was hurt when I said all he wanted was to make out. There was the dinner at the country club, the affluence of money everywhere. And then there was the record... the one so good for dancing. I forgot that it was the one until Louie Armstrong began to sing in a voice husky with regret ["I Can't Get Started"]... Jack said: "Ever heard it before?" so I smiled. "Oh, yes." It was (with) Bob [another boyfriend]. That settled things for me... a crazy record, and it was our long talks, his listening and understanding. And I knew I loved him.

Today is the first of August. It is hot, steamy and wet. It is raining. I am tempted to write a poem. But I remember what it said on one rejection slip: After a heavy rainfall, poems titled "Rain" pour in from across the nation.

With me, the present is forever, and forever is always shifting, flowing, melting. This second is life. And when it is gone, it

---

*"(Being raped.)" is a later addition in a different ink; Plath was making fun of herself here.

is dead. But you can't start over with each new second, you have to judge by what is dead. It's like quicksand . . . hopeless from the start. A story, a picture, can renew sensation a little, but not enough, not enough. Nothing is real except the present, and already I feel the weight of centuries smothering me. Some girl a hundred years ago once lived as I do. And she is dead. I am the present, but I know I, too, will pass. The high moment, the burning flash come and are gone, continuous quicksand. And I don't want to die.

Some things are hard to write about. After something happens to you, you go to write it down, and either you overdramatize it or underplay it, exaggerate the wrong parts or ignore the important ones. At any rate, you never write it quite the way you want to. I've just got to put down what happened to me this afternoon. I can't tell Mother; not yet, anyway. She was in my room when I came home, fussing with clothes, and she didn't even sense that something had happened. She just kept scolding and chattering on and on. So I couldn't stop her and tell her. No matter how it comes out, I have to write it.

It rained all afternoon at the farm, and I was cold and wet, my hair under a silk print kerchief, my red ski jacket over my sweatshirt. I had worked hard on beans all afternoon and picked over three bushels. Since it was five o'clock, people were leaving, and I was waiting beside the cars for my ride home. Kathy had just come up, and as she got on her bike she called, "Here comes Ilo."

I looked, and sure enough, there he was, coming up the road in his old khaki shirt with his familiar white handkerchief tied around his head. I was on conversational terms with him since that day we worked together in the strawberry field. He had given me a pen-and-ink sketch of the farm, drawn with detail and assurance. Now he was working on a sketch of one of the boys.

So I called, "Have you finished John's picture?" "Oh, *ja, ja.*" He smiled. "Come and see. Your last chance." He had promised to show it to me when he was done, so I ran out and got in step with him on his way to the barn. That's where he lives.

On the way, we passed Mary Coffee. I felt her looking at me rather strangely. Somehow I couldn't meet her eyes. "Hullo,

Mary," Ilo said. "Hello, Ilo," Mary said in an oddly colorless voice.

We walked by Ginny, Sally, and a crowd of kids keeping dry in the tractor shed. A roar went up as we passed. A singsong, "Oh, Sylvia." My cheeks burned. "Why do they have to tease me?" I asked. Ilo just laughed. He was walking very fast. "We're going home in a little while," Milton yelled from the washroom.

I nodded and kept walking, looking at the ground. Then we were at the barn, a huge place, a giant high-ceilinged room smelling of horses and damp hay. It was dim inside; I thought I saw the figure of a person on the other side of the stalls, but I couldn't be sure. Without saying a word, Ilo had begun to mount a narrow flight of wooden stairs. "You live up there? All these stairs?" He kept walking up, so I followed him, hesitating at the top. "Come in, come in," he said, opening a door. The picture was there, in his room. I walked over the threshold. It was a narrow place with two windows, a table full of drawing things, and a cot, covered with a dark blanket. Oranges and milk were set out on a table with a radio. "Here." He held out the picture. It was a fine pencil sketch of John's head. "Why, how do you do it? With the side of the pencil?"

It seemed of no significance then, but now I remember how Ilo had shut the door, had turned on the radio so that music came out. He talked very fast, showing me a pencil. "See, here the lead comes out, any size." I was very conscious of his nearness. His blue eyes were startlingly close, looking at me boldly, with flecks of laughter in them. "I really have to go. They will be waiting. The picture was lovely."

Smiling, he was between me and the door. A motion. His hand closed around my arm. And suddenly his mouth was on mine, hard, vehement, his tongue darting between my lips, his arms like iron around me. "Ilo, Ilo!" I don't know whether I screamed or whispered, struggling to break free, my hands striking wildly, futilely against his great strength. At last he let me go, and stood back. I held my hand against my mouth, warm and bruised from his kiss. He looked at me quizzically with something like surprised amusement as he saw that I was crying, frightened. No one ever kissed me that way before, and I stood there, flooded with longing, electric, shivering.

"Why, why?" He made sympathetic, depreciating little noises. "I get you some water." He poured me out a glass, and I drank it. He opened the door, and I stumbled blindly downstairs, past Maybelle and Robert, the little colored children, who called my name in the corrupted way kids have of pronouncing things. Past Mary Lou, their mother, who stood there, a silent, dark presence.

And I was outdoors. A truck was going by. Coming from behind the barn. In it was Bernie . . . the horrible, short, muscular boy from the washroom. His eyes glittered with malicious delight, and he drove fast, so I could not catch up with him. Had he been in the barn? Had he seen Ilo shut the door, seen me come out? I think he must have. I walked up past the washroom to the cars. Bernie yelled out, "Why are you crying?" I wasn't crying. Kenny and Freddy came by on the tractor. A group of boys, going home, looked at me with a light flickering somewhere in their eyes. "Did he kiss you?" one asked, with a knowing smile.

I felt sick. I couldn't have spoken if someone had talked to me. My voice was stuck in my throat, thick and furry.

Mr. Tompkins came up to the pump to watch Kenny and Freddy run the old stock car. They were nice, but they knew. They all must know.

"There's cutie pie," Kenny said.

"Cutie pie and angel face," Freddy said.

So I stood there, arms folded, staring at the whirring engine, smiling as if I was all right, as if nothing had happened.

Milton sat in the rumble seat with me going home. David drove, and Andy was in front. They all looked at me with that dancing light in their eyes. David said in a stiff, strained voice, "Everybody in the washroom was watching you go into the barn and making wisecracks."

Milton asked about the picture. We talked a little about art and drawing. They were all so nice. I think they may have been relieved at my narrow escape; they may have expected me to cry. They knew, though, they knew.

So I'm home. And tomorrow I have to face the whole damn farm. Good Lord, it might have happened in a dream. Now I can almost believe it did. But tomorrow my name will be on the tip of every tongue. I wish I could be smart, or flip, but

I'm too scared. If only he hadn't kissed me. I'll have to lie and say he didn't. But they know. They all know. And what am I against so many . . . ?

This description of taking gas at the dentist's foreshadows writing of a much later period.

WELLESLEY

This morning I had my two left wisdom teeth out. At 9:00 A.M. I walked into the dentist's office. Quickly, with a heavy sense of impending doom, I sat in the chair after a rapid, furtive glance around the room for any obvious instruments of torture such as a pneumatic drill or a gas mask. No such thing. The doctor pinned the bib around my neck; I was just about prepared for him to stick an apple in my mouth and strew sprigs of parsley on my head. But no. All he did was ask, "Gas or novocaine?" (Gas or novocaine. Heh, heh! Would you like to see what we have on stock, madam? Death by fire or water, by the bullet or the noose. Anything to please the customer.) "Gas," I said firmly. The nurse sneaked up behind me, put a rubber oval over my nose, the tubes of it cutting pleasantly into my cheek. "Breathe easily." The gas sifted in, strange and sickeningly sweet. I tried not to fight it. The dentist put something in my mouth, and the gas began to come in in big gulps. I had been staring at the light. It quivered, shook, broke into little pieces. The whole constellation of little iridescent fragments started to swing in a rhythmic arc, slow at first, then faster, faster. I didn't have to try hard to breathe now; something was pumping at my lungs, giving forth an odd, breathy wheeze as I exhaled. I felt my mouth cracking up into a smile. So that's how it was . . . so simple, and no one had told me. I had to write it, to describe how it was, before I went under. I fancied my right hand was the tip of the arc, I curved up, but just as my hand got into position, the arc would swing the other way, gaining momentum. How clever of them, I thought. They kept the feeling all secret; they wouldn't even let you write it down. And then I was on a pirate ship, the captain's face peering at me from behind the wheel, as he swung it, steering. There were columns of black, and green leaves, and he was saying loudly, "All right, close down easily, easily." Then the sunlight burst into the room through the venetian blinds; I breathed hard, filling my lungs with air. I could see my feet, my arms; there I was. I tried hard to get back in my body again... it was such a long way to my feet. I lifted my hands to my head; they shook. It was all over... till next Saturday.

Emile. There it is; his name. And what can I say? I can say he called for me at nine Saturday night, that I was still weak from having two wisdom teeth out that morning. I can say that we went on a double date dancing at Ten Acres, that I drank five glasses, in the course of the evening, to the bottom of sparkling tawny ginger ale, while the others drank beer. But that's not it. Not at all. This is how it was. I dressed slowly, smoothing, perfuming, powdering. I sat upstairs in the moist gray twilight, with the rain trickling down outside, while the family talked and laughed with company down on the porch. This is I, I thought, the American virgin, dressed to seduce. I know I'm in for an evening of sexual pleasure. We go on dates, we play around, and if we're nice girls, we demure [sic] at a certain point. And so it goes. We walked into the bar and sat down, two by two. Emile and I had the initial strangeness to rub off. We began to talk... about the funeral he went to this morning, about his twenty-year-old cousin who broke his back and is paralyzed for life, about his sister who died of pneumonia at twelve years. "Good Lord, we're morbid tonight." He shuddered. And then, "You know something I've always liked... I mean wanted to like? Dark eyes and blond hair." So we talked about little things, how words lose their meaning when you repeat them over and over; how all people of the Negro race look alike until you get to know them individually; how we always liked the age we were at best. "I pity Warrie," he said, nodding at the other boy. "He's twenty-two, out of Amherst, and he has to work the rest of his life. When I figure... only two more years of college." "I know, I've always dreaded birthdays." "You don't look as young as you are." "I don't see," I said, "how people stand being old. Your insides all dry up. When you're young, you're so self-reliant. You don't even need much religion." "You're not by any chance a Catholic?" He asked as if it were quite unlikely. "No, you?" "Yes." He said it very low.

There was more small talk, more laughing, sidelong glances, more of the unspoken physical friction that makes each new conquest so delightful. In the air was the strong smell of masculinity which creates the ideal medium for me to exist in. There was something in Emile tonight, a touch of seriousness, a chemical magnetism, that met my mood the way two pieces of a child's puzzle fit together. He has a fine face, dark hair, and eyes with enormous black pupils; a straight nose, a one-sided flashing grin, a clean-cut chin. He is neatly made, with small, sensitive hands. I knew it would be the way it was. On the dance floor he held me close to him [omission] . . . my breasts aching firm against his chest. And it was like warm wine flooding through me, a sleepy, electric drowsiness. He nuzzled his face in my hair, kissed my cheek. "Don't look at me," he said. "I've just come out of a swimming pool, hot and wet." (God, I knew it would be like this.) He was looking at me intently, searchingly, and our eyes met. I went under twice; I was drowning; and he flicked his gaze away. On the way to Warrie's at midnight, Emile kissed me in the car, his mouth wet and gentle on mine. At Warrie's more ginger ale, more beer, and dancing with the dim light from the porch, Emile's body warm and firm against mine, rocking back and forth to the soft, erotic music. (Dancing is the normal prelude to intercourse. All the dancing classes when we are too young to understand, and then this.) "You know"—Emile looked at me— "we ought to sit down." I shook my head. "No?" he said. "How about some water, then. Feel all right?" (Feel all right. Oh, yes. Yes, thank you.) He steered me out to the kitchen, cool, smelling of linoleum, with the sound of the rain falling outside. I sat and sipped the water he brought me, while he stood looking down, his features strange in the half-light. I put the glass down. "That was quick," he said. "Should I have taken longer?" I stood up, and his face moved in, his arms about me. After a while I pushed him away. "The rain's rather nice. It makes you feel good inside, elemental, just to listen." I was backed against the sink; Emile was close, warm, his eyes glittering, his mouth sensuous and lovely. "You," I said deliberately, "don't give a damn about me except physically." Any boy would deny that, any gallant boy, any gallant liar. But Emile shook me, his voice was urgent. "You know, you shouldn't have said that. You know? You know?" "The truth always hurts." (Even clichés can come in handy.) He grinned. "Don't be bitter; I'm not. Come away from the sink, and watch." He stepped back, drawing me toward him, slapping my stomach away; he kissed me long and sweetly. At last he let go. "There," he said with a quiet smile. "The truth doesn't always hurt, does it?" And so we left. It was pouring rain. In the car he put his arm around me, his head against mine, and we watched the streetlights coming at us, blurred and fluid in the watery dark. As we ran up the walk in the rain, as he came in and had a drink of water, as he kissed me good night, I knew that something in me wanted him, for what I'm not sure: he drinks, he smokes, he's Catholic, he runs around with one girl after another, and yet . . . I wanted him. "I don't have to tell you it's been nice," I said at the door. "It's been marvelous." He smiled. "I'll call you. Take care." And he was gone. So the rain comes down hard outside my room, and like Eddie Cohen,* I say, ". . . fifteen thousand years . . . of what? We're still nothing but animals." Somewhere, in his room, Emile lies, about to sleep, listening to the rain. God only knows what *he's* thinking.

There are times when a feeling of expectancy comes to me, as if something is there, beneath the surface of my understanding, waiting for me to grasp it. It is the same tantalizing sensation when you almost remember a name, but don't quite reach it. I can feel it when I think of human beings, of the hints of evolution suggested by the removal of wisdom teeth, the narrowing of the jaw no longer needed to chew such roughage as it was accustomed to; the gradual disappearance of hair from the human body; the adjustment of the human eye to the fine print, the swift, colored motion of the twentieth century. The feeling comes, vague and nebulous, when I consider the prolonged adolescence of our species; the rites of birth, marriage

---

*Eddie Cohen was a pen pal of Plath's—one of the very few people with whom she shared her true feelings. He was the first to see the coming psychic break and advised her to seek psychiatric help to avoid it. The line of his she quotes here reappears in *The Bell Jar*.

and death; all the primitive, barbaric ceremonies streamlined to modern times. Almost, I think, the unreasoning, bestial purity was best. Oh, something is there, waiting for me. Perhaps someday the revelation will burst in upon me and I will see the other side of this monumental grotesque joke. And then I'll laugh. And then I'll know what life is.

Tonight I wanted to step outside for a few moments before going to bed; it was so snug and stale-aired in the house. I was in my pajamas, my freshly washed hair up on curlers. So I tried to open the front door. The lock snapped as I turned it; I tried the handle. The door wouldn't open. Annoyed, I turned the handle the other way. No response. I twisted the lock; there were only four possible combinations of handle and lock positions, and still the door stuck, white, blank, and enigmatic. I glanced up. Through the glass square, high in the door, I saw a block of sky, pierced by the sharp black points of the pines across the street. And there was the moon, almost full, luminous and yellow, behind the trees. I felt suddenly breathless, stifled. I was trapped, with the tantalizing little square of night above me, and the warm, feminine atmosphere of the house enveloping me in its thick, feathery smothering embrace.

This morning I am at low ebb. I did not sleep well last night, waking, tossing, and dreaming sordid, incoherent little dreams. I awoke, my head heavy, feeling as if I had just emerged from a swim in a pool of warm polluted water. My skin was greasy, my hair stiff, oily, and my hands as if I had touched something slimy and unclean. That thick August air does not help. I sit here lumpishly, an ache at the back of my neck. I feel that even if I washed myself all day in cold clear water, I could not rinse the sticky, untidy film away; nor could I rid my mouth of the furry unpleasant taste of unbrushed teeth.

Tonight, for a moment, all was at peace inside. I came out of the house-across-the-street a little before twelve, sick with unfulfilled longing, alone, self-reviling. And there, miraculously, was the August night. It had just rained, and the air was thick with warm damp and fog. The moon, full, pregnant with light, showed strangely from behind the small frequent clouds, poised like a picture puzzle that had been broken, with light in back, outlining each piece. There seemed to be no wind, but the leaves of the trees stirred, restless, and the water fell from them in great drops on the pavement, with a sound like that of people walking down the street. There was the peculiar smell of mold, dead leaves, decay, in the air. The two lights over the front steps were haloed with a hazy nimbus of mist, and strange insects fluttered up against the screen, fragile, wing-thin and blinded, dazed, numbed by the brilliance. Lightning, heat lightning, flicked off and on, as if some stagehand were toying with the light switch. Two crickets, deep in the cracks in the granite steps, sang a sweet, haunting-thin trill. And because it was my home, I loved them. The air flowed about me like thick molasses, and the shadows from the moon and streetlamp split like schizophrenic blue phantoms, grotesque and faintly repetitious.

Upstairs, in the bright, white, sterile cubicle of the bathroom, smelling of warm flesh and toothpaste, I bent over the washbowl in unthinking ritual, washing the proscribed areas, worshiping the glittering chromium, the light that clattered back and forth, brittle, blinding, from the faucets. Hot and cold, cleanliness coming in smooth scented green bars; hairs in thin, penciled lines, curving on the white enamel; the colored prescriptions, the hard, glassed-in jars, the bottles that can cure the symptoms of a cold or send you to sleep within an hour. And then to bed, in the same potentially fertile air, scented of lavender, lace curtains and the warm feline odor like musk, waiting to assimilate you . . . everywhere the pallid waiting. And you are the moving epitome of all this. Of you, by you, for you. God, is this all it is, the ricocheting down the corridor of laughter and tears? of self-worship and self-loathing? of glory and disgust?

FROM A LETTER TO EDDIE COHEN

Your letter came just now . . . the one about your walk in the city, about war. You don't know quite what it did to me. My mental fear, which can be at times forced into the background, reared up and caught me in the pit of my stomach; it became a physical nausea which wouldn't let me eat breakfast.

Let's face it: I'm scared, scared and frozen. First, I guess, I'm afraid for myself...the old primitive urge for survival. It's getting so I live every moment with terrible intensity. Last night, driving back from Boston, I lay back in the car and let the colored lights come at me, the music from the radio, the reflection of the guy driving. It all flowed over me with a screaming ache of pain...remember, remember, this is now, and now, and now. Live it, feel it, cling to it. I want to become acutely aware of all I've taken for granted. When you feel that this may be the good-bye, the last time, it hits you harder.

I've got to have something. I want to stop it all, the whole monumental grotesque joke, before it's too late. But writing poems and letters doesn't seem to do much good. The big men are all deaf; they don't want to hear the little squeaking as they walk across the street in cleated boots. Ed, I guess this all sounds a bit frantic. I guess I am. When you catch your mother, the childhood symbol of security and rightness, crying desolately in the kitchen; when you look at your tall, dreamy-eyed kid brother and think that all his potentialities in the line of science are going to be cut off before he gets a chance...it kind of gets you.

Here I sit [apparently baby-sitting] in the deep-cushioned armchair, the crickets rasping, buzzing, chirring outside. It's the library, my favorite room, with the floor a medieval mosaic of flat square stones. The color of old bookbindings...rust, copper, tawny orange, pepper-brown, maroon. And there are deep comfortable maroon leather chairs with the leather peeling off, revealing a marbled pattern of ridiculous pink. The books, all that you would fill your rainy days with, line the shelves; friendly, fingered volumes. So I sit here, smiling as I think in my fragmentary way: *Woman is but an engine of ecstasy, a mimic of the earth from the ends of her curled hair to her red-lacquered nails.* Then I think, remembering the family of beautiful children that lie asleep upstairs: *Isn't it better to give in to the pleasant cycles of reproduction, the easy, comforting presence of a man around the house?* I remember Liz, her face white, delicate as an ash on the wind; her red lips staining the cigarette; her full breasts under the taut black jersey. She said to me, "But think how happy you can make a man someday."

Yes, I'm thinking, and so far it's all right. But then I do a flip over and reach out in my mind to E. [Emile], seeing a baseball game, maybe, perhaps watching television, or roaring with careless laughter at some dirty joke with the boys, beer cans lying about green and shiny gold, and ashtrays. I spiral back to me, sitting here, swimming, drowning, sick with longing. I have too much conscience injected in me to break customs without disastrous effects; I can only lean enviously against the boundary and hate, hate, hate the boys who can dispel sexual hunger freely, without misgiving, and be whole, while I drag out from date to date in soggy desire, always unfulfilled. The whole thing sickens me.

Yes, I was infatuated with you [apparently Emile]; I am still. No one has ever heightened such a keen capacity of physical sensation in me. I cut you out because I couldn't stand being a passing fancy. . . . Before I give my body, I must give my thoughts, my mind, my dreams. And you weren't having any of those.

There is so much hurt in this game of searching for a mate, of testing, trying. And you realize suddenly that you forgot it was a game, and turn away in tears.

If I didn't think, I'd be much happier; if I didn't have any sex organs, I wouldn't waver on the brink of nervous emotion and tears all the time.

After a while I suppose I'll get used to the idea of marriage and children. If only it doesn't swallow up my desire to express myself in a smug, sensuous haze. Sure, marriage is self-expression, but if only my art, my writing, isn't just a mere sublimation of my sexual desires which will run dry once I get married. If only I can find him . . . the man who will be intelligent, yet physically magnetic and personable. If I can offer that combination, why shouldn't I expect it in a man?

How complex and intricate are the workings of the nervous system. The electric shrill of the phone sends a tingle of expectancy along the uterine walls; the sound of his voice, rough, brash and intimate across the wire tightens the intestinal tract. If they substituted the word "lust" for "love" in the popular songs it would come nearer the truth.

Eddie, I thought. How ironic. You are a dream; I hope I never meet you. But your bracelet is the symbol of my composure ... my division from the evening. I love you because you are me ... my writing, my desire to be many lives. I will be a little god in my small way. At home on my desk is the best story I've ever written. How can I tell Bob that my happiness streams from having wrenched a piece out of my life, a piece of hurt and beauty, and transformed it to typewritten words on paper? How can he know I am justifying my life, my keen emotion, my feeling, by turning it into print?

Tonight I am ugly. I have lost all faith in my ability to attract males, and in the female animal that is a rather pathetic malady. My social contact is at the lowest ebb. My one link with Saturday night life is gone, and I have no one left. No one at all. I don't care about anyone, and the feeling is quite obviously mutual. What is it that makes one attract others? Last year I had several boys who wanted me for various reasons. I was sure of my looks, sure of my magnetism, and my ego was satiated. Now, after my three blind dates—two ... flopped utterly and completely, the third has also deflated—I wonder how I ever thought I was desirable. But inside, I know. I used to have sparkle, self-assurance. I didn't turn green and serious and grave-eyed at first. Now I know what the girl meant in *Celia Amberley* when she said: "If he will kiss me, everything will be all right; I'll be pretty again." First I need some boy, any boy, to be captivated by my appearance—some boy like Emile. Then I need someone real, who will be right for me now, here, and soon. Until then I'm lost. I think I am mad at times.

In September of 1950 Plath entered her freshman year at Smith College with several scholarships. Entries from this period in the journal are not dated, and in any case so many cuts have been made in the text that the reader should not be encouraged to attempt to read these excerpts in a close narrative way, but rather thematically. While Plath was under extreme pressure to perform scholastically, in order to keep her scholarships and to maintain her own high academic standards, she felt an equal pressure to be accepted socially, especially with men, and a great passion for her own creative work—poems and stories.

At this point her mother was home in Wellesley, teaching, and sharing her home with Plath's maternal grandparents—Plath's father had died when she was eight. Her younger brother, Warren, was at Exeter, also on scholarship.

NORTHAMPTON

God, who am I? I sit in the library tonight, the lights glaring overhead, the fan whirring loudly. Girls, girls everywhere, reading books. Intent faces, flesh pink, white, yellow. And I sit here without identity: faceless. My head aches. There is history to read . . . centuries to comprehend before I sleep, millions of lives to assimilate before breakfast tomorrow. Yet I know that back at the house there is my room, full of my presence. There is my date this weekend: someone believes I am a human being, not a name merely. And these are the only indications that I am a whole person, not merely a knot of nerves, without identity. I'm lost. Huxley would have laughed. What a conditioning center this is! Hundreds of faces, bending over books, fans whirring, beating time along the edge of thought. It is a nightmare. There is no sun. There is only continual motion. If I rest, if I think inward, I go mad. There is so much, and I am torn in different directions, pulled thin, taut against horizons too distant for me to reach. To stop with the German tribes and rest awhile: But no! On, on, on. Through ages of empires, of decline and fall. Swift, ceaseless pace. Will I never rest in sunlight again—slow, languid, and golden with peace?

Now I know what loneliness is, I think. Momentary loneliness, anyway. It comes from a vague core of the self—like a disease of the blood, dispersed throughout the body so that one cannot locate the matrix, the spot of contagion. I am back in my room at Haven House after the Thanksgiving holidays. Homesick is the name they give to that sick feeling which dominates me now. I am alone in my room, between two worlds. Downstairs are the few girls who have come in—no freshmen, no one I really know. I could go down with letter paper as an excuse for my presence, but I won't yet—not yet. No, I won't try to escape myself by losing myself in artificial chatter: "Did you have a nice vacation?" "Oh, yes, and you?" I'll stay here and try to pin that loneliness down. I hardly can remember those four days of Thanksgiving—a blur of home, smaller than when I left, with the spots on the darkened yellow wallpaper more visible; my old room, now no longer really mine, with all my things gone; I can't deceive myself out of the bare stark realization that no matter how enthusiastic you are, no matter how sure that character is fate, nothing is real, past or future, when you are alone in your room with the clock ticking loudly into the false cheerful brilliance of the electric light. And if you have no past or future, which, after all, is all that the present is made of, why then you may as well dispose of the empty shell of present and commit suicide. But the cold reasoning mass of gray entrail in my cranium which parrots, "I think, therefore I am," whispers that there is always the turning, the upgrade, the new slant. And so I wait. What avail are good looks? To grab temporary security? What avail are brains? Merely to say "I have seen; I have comprehended"? Ah, yes, I hate myself for not being able to go downstairs naturally and seek comfort in numbers. I hate myself for having to sit here and be torn between I know not what within me. Here I am, a bundle of past recollections and future dreams, knotted up in a reasonably attractive bundle of flesh. I remember what this flesh has gone through; I dream of what it may go through. I record here the actions of optical nerves, of taste buds, of sensory perception. And, I think: I am but one more drop in the great sea of matter, defined, with the ability to realize my existence. Of the millions, I, too, was potentially everything at birth. I, too, was stunted, narrowed, warped, by my environment, my outcroppings of heredity. I, too, will find a set of beliefs, of standards to live by, yet the very satisfaction of finding them will be marred by the fact that I have reached the ultimate in shallow, two-dimensional living—a set of values. This loneliness will blur and diminish, no doubt, when tomorrow I plunge again into classes, into the necessity of studying for exams. But now that false purpose is lifted and I am spinning in a temporary vacuum. At home I rested and played; here, where I work, the routine is momentarily suspended and I am lost. There is no living being on earth at this moment except myself. I could walk down the halls, and empty rooms would yawn mockingly at me from every side. God, but life is loneliness, despite all the opiates, despite the shrill tinsel gaiety of "parties" with no purpose, despite the false grinning faces we all wear. And when at last you find someone to whom you feel you can pour out your soul, you stop in shock at the words you utter—they are so rusty, so ugly, so meaningless and feeble from being kept in the small cramped dark inside you so long. Yes, there is joy, fulfillment and companionship— but the loneliness of the soul in its appalling self-consciousness is horrible and overpowering.

The reason that I haven't been writing in this book for so long is partly that I haven't had one decent coherent thought to put down. My mind is, to use a disgustingly obvious simile, like a wastebasket full of wastepaper, bits of hair, and rotting apple cores. I am feeling depressed from being exposed to so many lives, so many of them exciting, new to my realm of experience. I pass by people, grazing them on the edges, and it bothers me. I've got to admire someone to really like them deeply— to value them as friends. It was that way with Ann*: I admired her wit, her riding, her vivacious imagination—all the things that made her the way she was. I could lean on her as she leaned on me. Together the two of us could face anything— only not quite anything, or she would be back. And so she is gone, and I am bereft for a while. But what do I know of sorrow? No one I love has ever died** or been tortured. I have

*A close friend during freshman year who left Smith but kept up her friendship with Sylvia
**Her father, Otto Plath, died when she was eight.

never wanted for food to eat, or a place to sleep. I have been gifted with five senses and an attractive exterior. So I can philosophize from my snug little cushioned seat. So I am going to one of the most outstanding colleges in America; I am living with two thousand of the most outstanding girls in the United States; what have I to complain about? Nothing much. The main way I can add to my self-respect is by saying that I'm on scholarship, and if I hadn't exercised my free will and studied through high school I never would be here. But when you come right down to it, how much of that *was* free will? How much was the capacity to think that I got from my parents, the home urge to study and do well academically, the necessity to find an alternative for the social world of boys and girls to which I was forbidden acceptance? And does not my desire to write come from a tendency toward introversion begun when I was small, brought up as I was in the fairy-tale world of Mary Poppins and Winnie-the-Pooh? Did not that set me apart from most of my schoolmates? [And] the fact that I got all A's and was "different" from the rough-and-tumble—*how* I am not quite sure, but "different" as the animal with the touch of human hands about him when he returns to the herd.

I am jealous of those who think more deeply, who write better, who draw better, who ski better, who look better, who love better, who live better than I. I am sitting at my desk looking out at a bright antiseptic January day, with an icy wind whipping the sky into a white-and-blue froth. I can see Hopkins House, and the hairy black trees; I can see a girl bicycling along the gray road. I can see the sunlight slanting diagonally across the desk, catching on the iridescent filaments of nylon in the stockings I hung over the curtain rod to dry. I think I am worthwhile just because I have optical nerves and can try to put down what they perceive. What a fool!

After being conditioned as a child to the lovely never-never land of magic, of fairy queens and virginal maidens, of little princes and their rosebushes, of poignant bears and Eeyore-ish donkeys, of life personalized, as the pagans loved it, of the magic wand, and the faultless illustrations—the beautiful dark-haired child (who was you) winging through the midnight sky on a star-path in her mother's box of reels—of Griselda in her feather cloak, walking barefoot with the Cuckoo in the lantern-lit world of nodding mandarins, of Delight in her flower garden with the slim-limbed flower sprites, of the Hobbit and the dwarves, gold-belted with blue and purple hoods, drinking ale and singing of dragons in the caverns of the valley—all this I knew, and felt, and believed. All this was my life when I was young. To go from this to the world of "grown-up" reality. To feel the tender skin of sensitive child-fingers thickening to feel the sex. . . . To feel the sex organs develop and call loud to the flesh; to become aware of school, exams (the very words as unlovely as the sound of chalk shrilling on the blackboard), bread and butter, marriage, sex, compatibility, war, economics, death, and self. What a pathetic blighting of the beauty and reality of childhood. Not to be sentimental, as I sound, but why the hell are we conditioned into the smooth strawberry-and-cream Mother-Goose-world, Alice-in-Wonderland fable, only to be broken on the wheel as we grow older and become aware of ourselves as individuals with a dull responsibility in life? · To learn snide and smutty meanings of words you once loved, like "fairy." To go to college fraternity parties where a boy buries his face in your neck or tries to rape you if he isn't satisfied with burying his fingers in the flesh of your breast. · To learn that there are a million girls who are beautiful and that each day more leave behind the awkward teenage stage, as you once did, and embark on the adventure of being loved and petted. · To be aware that you must compete somehow, and yet that wealth and beauty are not in your realm. · To learn that a boy will make a careless remark about "your side of town" as he drives you to a roadhouse in his father's latest chromium-plated convertible. · To learn that you might have been more of an artist than you are if you had been born into a family of wealthy intellectuals. · To learn that you can never learn anything valid for truth, only momentary, transitory sayings that apply to you in your moment, your locality, and your present state of mind. · To learn that love can never come true, because the people you admire, like Perry,* are unattainable since they want someone like P.K. · To learn that you only want them because you can't have them. · To yearn for an organism of the opposite sex to comprehend and heighten your

---

*The brother of Dick Norton, an important boyfriend. Sylvia was also very attracted to Perry.

thoughts and instincts, and to realize that most American males worship woman as a sex machine with rounded breasts and a convenient opening in the vagina, as a painted doll who shouldn't have a thought in her pretty head other than cooking a steak dinner and comforting him in bed after a hard 9–5 day at a routine business job.

There comes a time when you walk downstairs to pick up a letter you forgot, and the low confidential voices of the little group of girls in the living room suddenly ravels into an incoherent mumble and their eyes slide slimily through you, around you, away from you in a snaky effort not to meet the tentative half-fear quivering in your own eyes. And you remember a lot of nasty little tag ends of conversation directed at you and around you, meant for you, to strangle you on the invisible noose of insinuation. You know it was meant for you; so do they who stab you. But the game is for both of you to pretend you don't know, you don't really mean, you don't understand. Sometimes you can get a shot back in the same way, and you and your antagonist rival each other with brave smiles while the poison darts quiver, maliciously, in your mutual wounds. More often you are too sickened to fight back, because you know the fear and the inadequacy will crawl out in your words as they crackle falsely on the air. So you hear her say to you, "We'd rather flunk school and be sociable than stick in our rooms all the time," and very sweetly, "I never see you. You're always *studying* in your *room!*" And you keep your mouth shut. And oh, how you smile!

Linda is the sort of girl you don't remember when you meet her for the second time. She is rather homely, and nondescript as an art gum eraser. Her eyes are nervous and bright like neurotic goldfish. Her skin is muddy; maybe she has acne. Hair: straight, brown, oily. But she left some of her stories with you. And she can write. Better than you ever dreamed of writing. She tossed off conversation that breathed love and sex and fear and infatuation and yet was only a series of sharp, brief pistol-shot sentences. You took out your story—the one that won third prize in *Seventeen*. You felt sick as you reread the paragraphs of lyrical sentimentality that seemed so real and genuine a few months ago. You couldn't even say it was antiseptic and understated: it was hideously obvious. So you got rid of your astonishment that someone could write so much more dynamically than you. You stopped cherishing your aloneness and poetic differentness to your delicately flat little bosom. You said: She's too good to forget. How about making her a friend and competitor—you could learn a lot from her. So you'll try. So maybe she'll laugh in your face. So maybe she'll beat you hollow in the end. So anyhow, you'll try, and maybe, possibly, she can stand you.

Frustrated? Yes. Why? Because it is impossible for me to be God—or the universal woman-and-man—or anything much. I am what I feel and think and do. I want to express my being as fully as I can because I somewhere picked up the idea that I could justify my being alive that way. But if I am to express what I am, I must have a standard of life, a jumping-off place, a technique—to make arbitrary and temporary organization of my own personal and pathetic little chaos. I am just beginning to realize how false and provincial that standard, or jumping-off place, must be. That is what is so hard for me to face.

Perry said today that his mother said, "Girls look for infinite security; boys look for a mate. Both look for different things." I am at odds. I dislike being a girl, because as such I must come to realize that I cannot be a man. In other words, I must pour my energies through the direction and force of my mate. My only free act is choosing or refusing that mate. And yet, it is as I feared: I am becoming adjusted and accustomed to that idea. . . .

I am part man, and I notice women's breasts and thighs with the calculation of a man choosing a mistress . . . but that is the artist and the analytical attitude toward the female body . . . for I am more a woman; even as I long for full breasts and a beautiful body, so do I abhor the sensuousness which they bring. . . . I desire the things which will destroy me in the end. . . . I wonder if art divorced from normal and conventional living is as vital as art combined with living: in a word, would marriage sap my creative energy and annihilate my desire for written and pictorial expression, which increases with this depth of unsatisfied emotion . . . or would I [if I married] achieve a fuller expression in art as well as in the creation of children?... Am I strong enough to do both well?... That is the crux of the matter, and I hope to steel myself for the test... as frightened as I am....

I was [always] nauseated at the sight of bobby pins. I would not touch them. Once, on the day I was going home from the hospital after having my tonsils out, a woman in my ward asked me to carry some bobby pins to the lady in the next bed. Revolted, I held out a stiff unwilling hand, flinching as the cold clammy little pins touched my skin. They were cold and shiny, as with grease, and sickeningly suggestive of warmth and disgusting, intimate contact with dirty hair.

This entry marks the first appearance in the journal of the acid portraits of those closest to her which later became almost routine for Plath. She did in fact adore her grandmother.

For future reference:
To be incorporated into a sarcastic poem about a fat, greasy and imperfect grandmother:

Laugh as you lift your eyes to the heavens
And think of her fat pink soul
Blundering among the logical five-pointed stars.

I have the choice of being constantly active and happy or introspectively passive and sad. Or I can go mad by ricocheting in between.

Cats have nine lives, the saying goes. You have one; and somewhere along the thin, tenuous thread of your existence there is the black knot, the blood clot, the stopped heartbeat that spells the end of this particular individual which is spelled "I" and "you" and "Sylvia." So you wonder how to act, and how to be—and you wonder about values and attitudes. In the relativism and despair, in the waiting for the bombs to begin, for the blood (now spurting in Korea, in Germany, in Russia) to flow and trickle before your own eyes, you wonder with a quick sick fear how to cling to earth, to the seeds of grass and life. You wonder about your eighteen years, ricocheting between a stubborn determination that you've done well for your own capabilities and opportunities . . . that you're competing now with girls from all over America, and not just from the hometown, and a fear that you *haven't* done well enough. You wonder if you've got what it takes to keep building up obstacle courses for yourself, and to keep leaping through them, sprained ankle or not. Again the refrain, what *have* you for your eighteen years? And you know that whatever tangible things you *do* have, they cannot be held, but, too, will decompose and slip away through your coarse-skinned and death-rigid fingers. So you will rot in the ground, and so you say, what the hell? who cares? But *you* care, and somehow you don't want to live just one life, which could be typed, which could be tossed off in a thumbnail sketch: "She was the sort of girl . . ." And end in 25 words or less. You want to live as many lives as you can . . . you're a capitalist from way back . . . and because you're eighteen, because you're still vulnerable, because you still don't have faith in yourself, you talk a little fliply, a little too wisely, just to cover up so you won't be accused of sentimentality or emotionalism or feminine tactics. You cover up, so you can still laugh at yourself while there's time. And then you think of the flesh and blood people you know, and wonder guiltily where all this great little flood of confidence is getting you. (That's the pragmatic approach . . . *where* are you getting? *What* are you getting? Measure your precepts and their values by the tangible good you derive from their use.) Take the grandparents, now. What do you know about them? Sure, they were born in Austria, they say "cholly" for "jolly" and "ven" for "when." Grampy is white-haired, terribly even-tempered, terribly old, terribly endearing in his mute and blind admiration of everything you do. (You take a bitter and rather self-righteous pride in the fact that he's a steward at a country club.) Grammy is spry, with a big fat bosom and spindly arthritic legs. She cooks good sour-cream sauce and makes up her own recipes. She slurps her soup, and drops particles of food from her plate down the front of her dresses. She is getting hard of hearing, and her hair is just beginning to turn gray. There is your dead father who is somewhere in you, interwoven in the cellular system of your long body which sprouted from one of his sperm cells uniting with an egg cell in your mother's uterus.

You remember that you were his favorite when you were little, and you used to make up dances to do for him as he lay on the living room couch after supper. You wonder if the absence of an older man in the house has anything to do with your intense craving for male company and the delight in the restful low sound of a group of boys, talking and laughing. You wish you had been made to know botany, zoology and science when you were young. But with your father dead, you leaned abnormally to the "humanities" personality of your mother. And you were frightened when you heard yourself stop talking and felt the echo of her voice, as if she had spoken in you, as if you weren't quite you, but were growing and continuing in her wake, and as if her expressions were growing and emanating from your face. (Hereupon you ponder, and wonder if that's what happens to older people when they die contented . . . that they feel they have somehow transcended the wall of flesh which is crumbling fatally and forever around them and that their fire and protoplasm and pulse have leapt over bounds and will live on in offspring, continuing the chain of life. . . .) Then there is your brother—six feet four inches tall, lovable and intelligent. You fought with him when you were little, threw tin soldiers at his head, gouged his neck with a careless flick of your ice skate . . . and then last summer, as you worked on the farm, you grew to love him, confide in him, and know him as a person . . . and you remember the white look of fear about his mouth that day they had all planned to throw you in the washtub—and how he rallied to your defense. Yes, you can outline the people you've lived with these eighteen years in a few sentences. . . . Yet could you give an account of their lives, their hopes, their dreams? You could try, perhaps, but they would be much the same as yours . . . for you are all an inexplicable unity—this family group with its twisted tensions, unreasoning loves and solidarity and loyalty born and bred in blood. These people are the ones most basically responsible for what you are.

And the boys . . . Jimmy Beale, who drew you pictures of pretty girls in fifth grade, and roller-skated along the beach and planned to get married in a little white house with roses on a picket fence. (You remember, absurdly now, how his little sister was drowned on the beaches while walking on ice cakes, and how you didn't know just how to react to his white, drawn face when you saw him back at school. You wanted to say nice things and how sorry you were, and then you felt a sudden hardening and strange anger at him for his weakness, which intensified yours. So you stuck out your tongue at him and made a face. And you never played with him again.) There was tall gawky John Stenberg, who printed "Sylvia loves John" on his printing press and scattered little slips of paper all over the streets and in every desk at school. Mortified, yet secretly excited by such attention, you scorned his gift of a rabbit's foot and a date to the carnival. (Later years would have found you infinitely grateful for any of his attentions whatever.)

In the summer of 1951, before her sophomore year, Sylvia had a job baby-sitting for a family in Swampscott, Massachusetts, looking after their young children and helping out in the kitchen; her friend Marcia had a parallel job down the road. The experience was the source of her later poem "The Baby-sitters."

SWAMPSCOTT

Lying on my stomach on the flat warm rock, I let my arm hang over the side, and my hand caressed the rounded contours of the sun-hot stone, and felt the smooth undulations of it. Such a heat the rock had, such a rugged and comfortable warmth, that I felt it could be a human body. Burning through the material of my bathing suit, the great heat radiated through my body, and my breasts ached against the hard flat stone. A wind, salty and moist, blew damply in my hair; through a great glinting mass of it I could see the blue twinkle of the ocean. The sun seeped into every pore, satiating every querulous fiber of me into a great glowing golden peace. Stretching out on the rock, body taut, then relaxed, on the altar, I felt that I was being raped deliciously by the sun, filled full of heat from the impersonal and colossal god of nature. Warm and perverse was the body of my love under me, and the feeling of his carved flesh was like no other—not soft, not malleable, not wet with sweat, but dry, hard, smooth, clean and pure. High, bone-white, I had been washed by the sea, cleansed, baptised, purified, and dried clean and crisp by the sun. Like seaweed, brittle, sharp, strong-smelling—like stone, rounded, curved, oval, clean—like wind, pungent, salty—like all these was the body of my love. An orgiastic sacrifice on the altar of rock and sun, and I arose shining from the centuries of love, clean and satiated from the consuming fire of his casual and timeless desire.

And so it is that with my leaning toward allegories, similes and metaphors, I suddenly find a vehicle to express a few of the many disturbing thoughts which have been with me since yesterday . . . to describe the feeling I had toward an anonymous part of the Massachusetts coastline. Simple as this task may seem, I wanted to wait until I could do it even partial justice because it forms the core of my continually evolving philosophy of thought and action.

On a relatively unfrequented, stony beach there is a great rock which juts out over the sea. After a climb, an ascent from one jagged foothold to another, a natural shelf is reached where one person can stretch at length, and stare down into the tide rising and falling below, or beyond to the bay, where sails catch light, then shadow, then light, as they tack far out near the horizon. The sun has burned these rocks, and the great continuous ebb and flow of the tide has crumbled the boulders, battered them, worn them down to the smooth sun-scalded stones on the beach which rattle and shift underfoot as one walks over them. A serene sense of the slow inevitability of the gradual changes in the earth's crust comes over me. A consuming love, not of a god, but of the clean unbroken sense that the rocks which are nameless, the waves which are nameless, the ragged grass which is nameless, are all defined momentarily through the consciousness of the being who observes them. With the sun burning into rock, and flesh, and the wind ruffling grass and hair, there is an awareness that the blind immense unconscious impersonal and neutral forces will endure, and that the fragile, miraculously knit organism which interprets them, endows them with meaning, will move about for a little, then falter, fail, and decompose at last into the anonymous soil, voiceless, faceless, without identity.

From this experience I emerged whole and clean, bitten to

the bone by sun, washed pure by the icy sharpness of salt water, dried and bleached to the smooth tranquility that comes from dwelling among primal things.

From this experience also, a faith arises to carry back to a human world of small lusts and deceitful pettiness. A faith, naïve and childlike perhaps, born as it is from the infinite simplicity of nature. It is a feeling that no matter what the ideas or conduct of others, there is a unique rightness and beauty to life which can be shared in openness, in wind and sunlight, with a fellow human being who believes in the same basic principles.

Yet, when such implicit belief is placed in another person, it is indeed shattering to realize that a part of what to you was such a rich, intricate, whole conception of life has been tossed off carelessly, lightly—it is then that a stunned, inarticulate numbness paralyzes words, only to give way later to a deep hurt.* It is hard for me to say on paper what I believe would best be reserved for a lucid vocal discussion. But somehow I did want you to know a little of what your surprising and perhaps injudiciously confidential information did to me yesterday. A feeling that there was no right to condemn, but that still somehow there was a crumbling of faith and trust. A feeling that there was a way to rationalize, to condone, if only by relegating a fellow human from the unique to the usual.

So there it is. The rock and the sun are waiting on the next day off—and solace.

Now I am not sure about that letter I sent. Not sure at all. For was I not the one who acquiesced, mutely responsive and receptive? Was I not guilty of letting a boy be drawn to self-hatred? And yet does it not all come again to the fact that it is a man's world? For if a man chooses to be promiscuous, he may still esthetically turn up his nose at promiscuity. He may still demand a woman to be faithful to him, to save him from his own lust. But women have lust, too. Why should they be relegated to the position of custodian of emotions, watcher of the infants, feeder of soul, body and pride of man? Being born

---

*The reference here is unclear—most likely this was a draft of a letter to Dick Norton. In *The Bell Jar* Esther Greenwood has a similar horrified reaction to a confidence from her boyfriend.

a woman is my awful tragedy. From the moment I was conceived I was doomed to sprout breasts and ovaries rather than penis and scrotum; to have my whole circle of action, thought and feeling rigidly circumscribed by my inescapable femininity. Yes, my consuming desire to mingle with road crews, sailors and soldiers, barroom regulars—to be a part of a scene, anonymous, listening, recording—all is spoiled by the fact that I am a girl, a female always in danger of assault and battery. My consuming interest in men and their lives is often misconstrued as a desire to seduce them, or as an invitation to intimacy. Yes, God, I want to talk to everybody I can as deeply as I can. I want to be able to sleep in an open field, to travel west, to walk freely at night.

There comes a time when all your outlets are blocked, as with wax. You sit in your room, feeling the prickling ache in your body which constricts your throat, tightens dangerously in little tear pockets behind your eyes. One word, one gesture, and all that is pent up in you—festered resentments, gangrenous jealousies, superfluous desires unfulfilled—and that will burst out of you in angry impotent tears, in embarrassed sobbing and blubbering to no one in particular. No arms will enfold you, no voice will say, "There, there. Sleep and forget." No, in your new and horrible independence you feel the dangerous premonitory ache, arising from little sleep and taut strung nerves, and a feeling that the cards have been stacked high against you this once, and that they are still being heaped up. An outlet you need, and they are sealed. You live night and day in the dark cramped prison you have made for yourself. And so on this day, you feel you will burst, break, if you cannot let the great reservoir seething in you loose, surging through some leak in the dike. So you go downstairs and sit at the piano. All the children are out; the house is quiet. A sounding of sharp chords on the keyboard, and you begin to feel the relief of loosing some of the great weight on your shoulders.

Quick footsteps up cellar stairs. A sharp thin annoyed face around the banister. "Sylvia, will you please not play the piano in the afternoon during office hours. It bangs right through downstairs."

Paralyzed, struck numb, branded by his cold voice, you lie: "Sorry. I had no idea you could hear."

So that too is gone. And you grit your teeth, despising your-self for your tremulous sensitivity, and wondering how human beings can suffer their individualities to be mercilessly crushed under a machinelike dictatorship, be it of industry, state or organization, all their lives long. And here you agonize for a mere ten weeks of your life, when you have only four more weeks to go anyway.

Liberty, self-integral freedom, await around the corner of the calendar. All of life is not lost, merely an eighteenth sum-mer. And perhaps something good has been sprouting in the small numb darkness all this while.

The wind has blown a warm yellow moon up over the sea; a bulbous moon, which sprouts in the soiled indigo sky, and spills bright winking petals of light on the quivering black water.

I am at my best in illogical, sensuous description. Witness the bit above. The wind could not possibly blow a moon up over the sea. Unconsciously, without words, the moon has been identified in my mind with a balloon, yellow, light, and bobbing about on the wind.

The moon, according to my mood, is not slim, virginal, and silver, but fat, yellow, fleshy, and pregnant. Such is the distinction between April and August, my present physical state and my sometime-in-the-future physical state. Now the moon has undergone a rapid metamorphosis, made possible by the vague imprecise allusions in the first line, and become a tulip or crocus or aster bulb, whereupon comes the metaphor: the moon is "bulbous," which is an adjective meaning fat, but suggesting "bulb," since the visual image is a complex thing. The verb "sprouts" intensifies the first hint of a vegetable qual-ity about the moon. A tension, capable of infinite variations with every combination of words, is created by the phrase "soiled indigo sky." Instead of saying blatantly "in the soil of the night sky," the adjective "soiled" has a double focus: as a description of the smudged dark-blue sky and again as a phan-tom noun, "soil," which intensifies the metaphor of the moon being a bulb planted in the earth of the sky. Every word can be analyzed minutely—from the point of view of vowel and consonant shades, values, coolnesses, warmths, assonances and dissonances. Technically, I suppose the visual appearance and sound of words, taken alone, may be much like the mechanics of music ... or the color and texture in a painting. However, uneducated as I am in this field, I can only guess and experiment. But I do want to explain why I use words, each one chosen for a reason, perhaps not as yet the very best word for my purpose, but nevertheless, selected after much deliberation. For instance, the continuous motion of the waves makes the moonlight sparkle. To get a sense of fitful motion, the participial adjectives "winking" (to suggest bright staccato sparks) and "quivering" (to convey a more legato and tremulous movement) have been used. "Bright" and "black" are obvious contrasts of light and dark. My trouble? Not enough free thinking, fresh imagery. Too much subconscious clinging to clichés and downtrodden combinations. Not enough originality. Too much blind worship of modern poets and not enough analysis and practice.

My purpose, which I mentioned quite nebulously awhile back, is to draw certain attitudes, feelings and thoughts into a pseudoreality for the reader. ("Pseudo" of necessity.) Since my woman's world is perceived greatly through the emotions and the senses, I treat it that way in my writing and am often overweighted with heavy descriptive passages and a kaleidoscope of similes.

I am closest to Amy Lowell, in actuality, I think. I love the lyric clarity and purity of Elinor Wylie, the whimsical, lyrical, typographically eccentric verse of E. E. Cummings, and yearn toward T. S. Eliot, Archibald MacLeish, Conrad Aiken....

And when I read, God, when I read the taut, spare, lucid prose of Louis Untermeyer, and the distilled intensities of poet after poet, I feel stifled, weak, pallid, mealymouthed and utterly absurd. Some pale, hueless flicker of sensitivity is in me. God, must I lose it in cooking scrambled eggs for a man ... hearing about life at second hand, feeding my body and letting my powers of perception and subsequent articulation grow fat and lethargic with disuse?

Slight revision: "And the wind has blown a warm yellow moon up over the sea: a bulbous moon which sprouts in the soiled indigo sky and spills winking white petals of light upon quivering black plains of ocean water."

I wonder about all the roads not taken and am moved to quote Frost . . . but won't. It is sad to be able only to mouth other poets. I want someone to mouth me.

Why am I obsessed with the idea I can justify myself by getting manuscripts published? Is it an escape—an excuse for any social failure—so I can say, "No, I don't go out for many extracurricular activities, but I spend a lot of time writing." Or is it an excuse for wanting to be alone and meditate alone, not having to brave a group of women? (Women in numbers have always disturbed me.) Do I like to write? Why? About what? Will I give up and say, "Living and feeding a man's insatiable guts and begetting children occupies my whole life. Don't have time to write"? Or will I stick to the damn stuff and practice? Read and think and practice? I am worried about thinking. Mentally I have led a vegetable existence this summer.

September 1. Here follows my first sonnet, written during the hours of 9 to 1 A.M. on a Saturday night, when in pregnant delight I conceived my baby. Luxuriating in the feel and music of the words, I chose and rechose, singling out the color, the assonance and dissonance and musical effects I wished—lulling myself by supple *l*'s and bland long *a*'s and *o*'s. God, I am happy—it's the first thing I've written for a year that has tasted wholly good to my eyes, ears and intellect.

Sonnet: To Spring?

You deceive us with the crinkled green
of juvenile stars, and you beguile us with
a bland vanilla moon of maple cream:
Again you tame us *with* your April myth.
Last year you tricked us by the childish jingle
of your tinsel rains; again you try,
and find us credulous once more. A single
diabolic shower, and *we* cry

to see the honeyflavored morning tilt
clear light across the watergilded lawn.
Although another of our years is spilt
on avaricious *earth*, you lure us on:
Again we are deluded and infer
that somehow we are younger than we were.

NORTHAMPTON

September 1951. I see it all now. Or at least I begin to see. I see in the boy who, because of necessity (lack of other contacts), has become the only answer to a need, the germs of all I fear and would avoid. I see the equally blinding necessity of taking what is best for the time being, lest there be no such chance in the future.

Why am I so perturbed by what others rejoice in and take for granted? Why am I so obsessed; why do I so hate what I am being drawn into so inexorably? Why, instead of going to bed in the kindly, erotic dark, and smiling languidly to myself in the night, say "Someday I will be physically and mentally satiated, if I lead myself in the right path . . ." Why do I sit up later, until the physical fire grows cold, and lash my brains into cold calculating thought?

I do not love; I do not love anybody except myself. That is a rather shocking thing to admit. I have none of the selfless love of my mother. I have none of the plodding, practical love. . . . I am, to be blunt and concise, in love only with myself, my puny being with its small inadequate breasts and meager, thin talents. I am capable of affection for those who reflect my own world. How much of my solicitude for other human beings is real and honest, how much is a feigned lacquer painted on by society, I do not know. I am afraid to face myself. Tonight I am trying to do so. I heartily wish that there were some absolute knowledge, some person whom I could trust to evaluate me and tell me the truth.

My greatest trouble, arising from my basic and egoistic self-love, is jealousy. I am jealous of men — a dangerous and subtle envy which can corrode, I imagine, any relationship. It is an envy born of the desire to be active and doing, not passive and listening. I envy the man his physical freedom to lead a double life—his career, and his sexual and family life. I can pretend to forget my envy; no matter, it is there, insidious, malignant, latent.

My enemies are those who care about me most. First: my mother. Her pitiful wish is that I "be happy." Happy! That is indefinable as far as states of being go. Or perhaps you can run it off glibly, as Eddie did, and say it means reconciling the life you lead with the life you wish to lead (often, I think, meaning the reverse).

At any rate, I admit that I am not strong enough, or rich enough, or independent enough, to live up in actuality to my ideal standards. You ask me, what are those ideal standards? Good for you. The only escape (do I sound Freudian?) from the present setup as I see it is in the exercise of a phase of life inviolate and separate from that of my future mate, and from all males with whom I might live. I am not only jealous; I am vain and proud. I will not submit to having my life fingered by my husband, enclosed in the larger circle of his activity, and nourished vicariously by tales of his actual exploits. I must have a legitimate field of my own, apart from his, which he must respect.

So I am led to one or two choices! Can I write? Will I write if I practice enough? How much should I sacrifice to writing anyway, before I find out if I'm any good? Above all, CAN A SELFISH EGOCENTRIC JEALOUS AND UNIMAGINATIVE FEMALE WRITE A DAMN THING WORTHWHILE? Should I sublimate (my, how we—throw words around!) my selfishness in serving other people—through social or other such work? Would I then become more sensitive to other people and their problems? Would I be able to write honestly then of other beings besides a tall, introspective adolescent girl? I must be in contact with a wide variety of lives if I am not to become submerged in the routine of my own economic strata and class. I will *not* have my range of acquaintances circumscribed by my mate's profession. Yet I see that this will happen if I do not have an outlet . . . of some sort.

Looking at myself, in the past years, I have come to the conclusion that I *must* have a passionate physical relationship with someone—or combat the great sex urge in me by chastic means. I chose the former answer. I also admitted that I am obligated in a way to my family and to society (damn society anyway) to follow certain absurd and traditional customs—for my own security, they tell me. I must therefore confine the major part of my life to one human being of the opposite sex. . . . That is a necessity because:

(1) I choose the physical relationship of intercourse as an animal and releasing part of life.

(2) I cannot gratify myself promiscuously and retain the respect and support of society (which is my pet devil)—and because I am a woman: ergo: one root of envy for male freedom.

(3) Still being a woman, I must be clever and obtain as full a measure of security for those approaching ineligible and aging years wherein I will not have the chance to capture a new mate—in all probability. So, resolved: I shall proceed to obtain a mate through the customary procedure: namely, marriage.

That leaves innumerable problems. Since I have grown up enough to decide to marry, I now must be very careful. I have the aforementioned blots of self-love, jealousy and pride to battle with as intelligently as possible. (No, I *cannot* delude myself.)

The self-love I can hide or reweld by the biblical saw of "losing myself and finding myself." For instance, I could hold my nose, close my eyes, and jump blindly into the waters of some man's insides, submerging myself until his purpose becomes my purpose, his life, my life, and so on. One fine day I would float to the surface, quite drowned, and supremely happy with my newfound selfless self. Or I could devote myself to a Cause. (I think that is why there are so many women's clubs and organizations. They've got to feel emancipated and self-important somehow. God forbid that I become a Crusader. But I might surprise myself, and become a second Lucretia Mott or something equivalent.) Anyway, there are two tentative solutions for getting rid of selfishness—both involving a stoic casting-off of the thin tenuous little identity which I love and cherish so dearly—and being confident that, once on the other side, I shall never miss my own little ambitions for my conceited self, but shall be content in serving the ambitions of my mate, or of a society, or Cause. (Yet I will not, I cannot accept any of those solutions. Why? Stubborn selfish pride. I will not make what is inevitable easier for myself by the blinding ignorance-is-bliss "losing-and-finding" theory. Oh, no! I will go, eyes open, into my torture, and remain fully cognizant, unwinking, while they cut and stitch and lop off my cherished malignant organs.)

So much for self-love: I carry it with me like a dear cancerous relative—to be disposed of only when desperation sets in.

Now for jealousy. I can loop out of that one easily: by excelling in some field my mate cannot participate actively in, but can only stand back and admire. That's where writing comes in. It is as necessary for the survival of my haughty sanity as bread is to my flesh. I pay the penalty of the educated, emancipated woman: I am critical, particular, aristocratic in tastes: perhaps my desire to write could be simplified to a basic fear of nonadmiration and nonesteem. Suddenly, I wonder: am I afraid that the sensuous haze of marriage will kill the desire to write? Of course—in past pages I have repeated and repeated that fear. Now I am beginning to see why! I am afraid that the physical sensuousness of marriage will lull and soothe to inactive lethargy my desire to work outside the realm of my mate—might make me "lose myself in him," as I said before, and thereby lose the need to write as I would lose the need to escape. Very simple.

If all my writing (once, I think, an outlet for an unfulfilled sensitivity—a reaction against unpopularity) is this ephemeral, what a frightening thing it is!

Let's take pride, now. Pride is mixed in with self-love and jealousy. All are rooted in the same inarticulate center of me, I think. I feed myself on the food of pride. I cultivate physical appearance—pride. I long to excel—to specialize in one field, one section of a field, no matter how minute, as long as I can be an authority there. Pride, ambition—what mean, selfish words!

Now back again to the present—the mating problem. What is best? Choice is frightening. I do not know: this is what I want. I only can hazard guesses on those poor fellows I meet by saying "This is what I do *not* want." What profession would I choose, if I were a man? Is that a criterion? To choose the man I would be if I were a man? Pretty risky. Occupation? Teacher comes closest now—leisurely enough not to drive me to madness, intelligent of course—hell, *I don't know!* Why can't I try on different lives, like dresses, to see which fits best and is most becoming?

The fact remains, I have at best three years in which to meet eligible people. Few come as close as the one I now know.* I would be betting on dark horses, not on a sure thing. Yet I am disturbed rather terribly by this sure thing. I am obsessed that it is this, or nothing, and that if I don't take this, it will be nothing, but if I do take this, I will be squeezed into a pretty stiff pattern, the rigor of which I do not like. Why not? Ah, I will tell you some of the seeds which will fester in me, sprouting dangerously under foreseen conditions:

(1) He is drawn to attractive women—even if it is not to search for a mate: all through life I would be subject to a physical, hence animal jealousy of other attractive women—always afraid that a shorter girl, one with better breasts, better feet, better hair than I will be the subject of his lust, or love—and I would always be miserably aware that I had to live up to his expectations or else someone else would. A woman, confined to the home, doesn't have the opportunity to feed her ego on attractive men.

(2) He regards a wife as a physical possession, to be proud of, like "a new car." Great! He is vain, proud, too. Score fault number one! He wants other people to be conscious of his valuable possession. What? You say, "That is only normal"? Maybe it is only normal, but I resent the hint—of what? of material attitude. Okay, so I don't believe in spirit. I also don't believe in "owning" people—like a good whore or a pet canary.

(3) He wants, after he is dead, for a community to remember him—to admire him for a life he saved, a life he gave. No doubt that is why he wants to be a general practitioner in a small town—he could smugly and rightly consider himself the guardian of life and death and happiness of a large group of humans. (Perry would be a surgeon—so, I would have Dick

---

*Dick Norton in many ways represented a sort of fifties ideal: the serious, attractive boy-next-door who wanted to be a doctor and have a proper doctor's wife. He was very close to his mother—whose sweet pronouncements on the role of woman are immortalized in *The Bell Jar*—who was in turn a good friend of Sylvia's mother.

be a surgeon. I am like Perry. Dick is gregarious; he loves life collectively. Perry is isolated; he loves life in the singular, not the plural.) I would have him specialize. He is not being selfless when he wants to be a country doctor—he is being proud, full of desire for self-esteem and importance. He would of course need a wife (if only for physical and mental gratification, to cook meals and raise children—all purely pragmatic needs, save the mental one, which still is practical in that it involves pride again . . . and the satisfaction thereof) to fit into that environment. How good would I be at small-town living? I haven't proved popular at school. My friends are a select few. How could I ever expect to be the town-minded, extroverted country doctor's wife! God knows. I don't. He needs the good solid homemaking type—with a little less fire, a little more practical devotion to her lord. . . .

. . . The most saddening thing is to admit that I am not in love. I can only love (if that means self-denial—or does it mean self-fulfillment? Or both?) by giving up my love, of self and ambitions. Why, why, why, can't I combine ambition for myself and another? I think I could, if only I chose a mate with a career demanding less of a wife in the way of town and social responsibility. But God, who is to say? You God, whom I invoke without belief, only I can choose, and only I am responsible. (Oh, the grimness of atheism!) . . .

An attack of sinus nearly always plunged Plath into depression—or perhaps it was the other way round.

7:30 P.M. *Wednesday, October 17.* I don't know why I should be so hideously gloomy, but I have that miserable "nobody-loves-me" feeling. I've been up here in the infirmary for a day and a half now, and really my head feels much better, not so stuffed and all. But still I feel very shaky, especially when I get up, from all the pills they've given me, maybe. Tomorrow I get up for my first written, which I've stupidly put off studying for by reading old *New Yorker* magazines. Also I've got a luncheon date with somebody from *Mademoiselle*, who's meeting all the thousands of girls who want to enter the College Board Contest. I can't think of a thing to wear. All my clothes are brown, navy or velvet. No matching accessories. Hell, how I've piddled off money, penny by penny, for unmatching items. How can I expect to criticize the country's leading fashion mag when I can't even dress correctly myself? To top it off, I've just talked to Mother over the phone, and made her unhappy, Dick unhappy, me unhappy. Instead of whizzing off for a gala weekend Friday . . . I languish. Not even *really* sick up here, which I could bear. No. I *could* go home if I wanted to. But it would be a strain on my health and my academic work. As is, I'm shaky. I've two weeks back work to catch up on. It's the "best thing" as far as common sense is concerned to go to bed early Saturday night and to work all weekend. But heck, I keep thinking of me dancing with Dick in my black velvet, and meeting his fascinating friends . . . oh, well. Brace up. Build up your body and be ready to meet the next party, the next boy, the next weekend with renewed strength. As it is now, I'm too well to be really ill and pampered, too groggy to make being up worthwhile. Sinusitis plunges me in maniac depression. But at least the lower I go the sooner I'll reach bottom and start the upgrade again.

May, 1952. . . . I am not the girl I was a year ago. Thank time. No, I am now a sophomore at Smith College, and therein lies all the difference. All? By implication, yes: mentally I am active as before, more realistic perhaps. (Come now, what do you mean by "realistic"?) Well, I consider myself more aware of my limitations in a constructive way. I will still whip myself onward and upward (in this spinning world, who knows which is up?) toward Fulbrights, prizes, Europe, publication, males. Tangible, yes, after a fashion, as all weave into my physical experience — going, seeing, doing, thinking, feeling, desiring. With the eyes, the brain, the intestines, the vagina. From the inactive (collegiately), timid, introvertly tended individual of last year I have become altered. I have maintained my integrity by not being an office-seeker for the sake of publicity, yet I have directed my energies in channels which, although public, also perform the dual service of satisfying many of my creative aims and needs. For example, I was elected secretary of Honor Board this spring — sent roses, flowers. And what do I do? I work with a stimulating group of the faculty. Dean Randall, et al. I learn the inside story about academic infringements —

and get character material as well. Then, I am correspondent to the *Springfield Daily News* on Press Board—which not only nets me about $10 per month, but gives me the strange thrill of feeling typewriter keys clatter under my fingers, of seeing my write-ups appear in inches in the daily Northampton column, of knowing everything that is going on in this great organic machine of a college. Also, I am going to be on the *Smith Review* next year, and hope that I can whip it out of its tailspin of this year. All, all, involve time lovingly spent. And next year, next year I will honor in English—concentrating in creative writing. At last I will be in small classes, doing independent research, becoming intimately acquainted with my instructors! This summer—ambitiously working seven days a week at the Belmont Hotel, waitressing. Thousands of people apply, and of them—I am accepted! Also, whether I kill myself in the attempt or not, I will pass my physical science requirement on my own (never will I take it next year!). And previous to the summer, there will be days spent with my lovely mathematical Alison in New York.

All, all becomes profitable. Education is of the most satisfying and available nature. I am at Smith! Which two years ago was a doubtful dream—and that fortuitous change of dream to reality has led me to desire more, and to lash myself onward, onward. I dreamed of New York, I am going there. I dream of Europe—perhaps . . . perhaps.

Now there comes the physical part—and therein lies the problem. Victimized by sex is the human race. Animals, the fortunate lower beasts, go into heat. Then they are through with the thing, while we poor lustful humans, caged by mores, chained by circumstance, writhe and agonize with the appalling and demanding fire licking always at our loins.

I remember a cool river beach and a May night full of rain held in far clouds, moonly sparks saying on the water, and the close, dank, heavy wetness of green vegetation. The water was cold to my bare feet, and the mud oozed up between my toes. He ran then, on the sand, and I ran after him, my hair long and damp, blowing free across my mouth. I could feel the inevitable magnetic polar forces in us, and the tidal blood beat loud, loud, roaring in my ears, slowing and rhythmic. He paused then, I behind him, arms locked around the powerful ribs, fingers caressing him. To lie, with him, to lie with him, burning forgetful in the delicious animal fire. Locked first upright, thighs ground together, shuddering mouth to mouth, breast to breast, legs emmeshed, then lying full length, with the good heavy weight of body upon body, arching, undulating, blind, growing together, force fighting force: to kill? To drive into burning dark of oblivion? To lose identity? Not love, this, quite. But something else rather. *A refined hedonism*. Hedonism: because of the blind sucking mouthing fingering quest for physical gratification. Refined: because of the desire to stimulate another in return, not being quite only concerned for self alone, but mostly so. An easy end to arguments on the mouth: a warm meeting of mouths, tongues quivering, licking, tasting. An easy substitute for bad slashing with angry hating teeth and nails and voice: the curious musical tempo of hands lifting under breasts, caressing throat, shoulders, knees, thighs. And giving up to the corrosive black whirlpool of mutual necessary destruction. Once there is the first kiss, then the cycle becomes inevitable. Training, conditioning make a hunger burn in breasts and secrete fluid in vagina, driving blindly for destruction. What is it but destruction? Some mystic desire to beat to sensual annihilation—to snuff out one's identity on the identity of the other—a mingling and mangling of identities? A death of one? Or both? A devouring and subordination? No, no. A polarization rather—a balance of two integrities, charging, electrically, one with the other, yet with centers of coolness, like stars.

(D. H. Lawrence did have something after all.) And there it is: when asked what role I will plan to fill, I say, "What do you mean, *role*? I plan not to step into a part on marrying—but to go on living as an intelligent mature human being, growing and learning as I always have. No shift, no radical change in life habits." *Never* will there be a circle, signifying me and my operations, confined solely to home, other womenfolk, and community service, enclosed in the larger worldly circle of my mate, who brings home from his periphery of contact with the world the tales only of vicarious experience to me, like so: ⊙ No, rather, there will be two overlapping circles, with a certain strong riveted center of common ground, but *both* with separate arcs jutting out in the world. A balanced tension, adaptable to circumstances, in which there is an elasticity of pull, tension, yet firm unity. Two stars, polarized: ◯◯ like so. In moments of communication that is complete, almost, like so ⧬ almost fusing into one. But fusion is an undesirable impossibility—and quite nondurable. So there will be no illusion of that.

So [Dick] accuses me of "struggling for dominance"? Sorry, wrong number. Sure, I'm a little scared of being dominated. (Who isn't? Just the submissive, docile, milky type of individual and that is not he, not me.) But that doesn't mean I, ipso facto, want to *dominate*. No, it is not a black-and-white choice or alternative like: "Either I'm victorious on top or you are." It is only *balance* that I ask for. Not the *continual* subordination of one person's desires and interests to the continual advancement of another's! That would be too grossly unfair.

Let's get to the bottom of his question: *Why* is he so afraid of my being strong and assertive? Why has *he* found it necessary to be himself so aggressive and positive in planning and directing actions and events? Could it be because he has a "mother complex"? Just what is his relation toward his mother anyway? She has become a matriarch in the home—a sweet, subtle matriarch, to be sure, but nonetheless, a "Mom" (cf. Philip Wylie, *Generation of Vipers*). She has become ruler of finances, manager of the home, *"mother"* of her husband, who, even to my unschooled eye, has a striking amount of the characteristics of a small, childish, irresponsible *boy*—who can sulk, beg for service, attention, encouragement, and *get it*. (Handsome, somewhat vain, but still in the position very often of a schoolboy.) It is *she* who takes over the responsibility of facing reality. Not that this relationship, either, is so black-and-white, but that there *are* these elements in it, and they are important to illustrate my argument. Therefore, I accentuate them. She has, then, had a great influence over her sons. The one *I* am concerned with admits that he thinks he rebelled against the firm opinionated influence and made a tangible break by seducing a waitress, a Vassar girl, or what have you. Is there not a sort of duality, then, in him—a desire, born of childhood, to be "mothered," to be a child, suckling at the breast (a transfer of eroticism from mother to girl friend)—and yet to *escape* the subtle feminine snare and be free of the insidious feminine domination he has sensed in his home all these years: to assert his independent unattached virile vigor (and push his career to the utmost)? He does not seem to be particularly close to or admiring of his father. Is he subconsciously and consciously trying simultaneously to break out of a pattern that would imply following in his father's footsteps—and ricochet to the *opposite* end of the spectrum by imposing his own pattern on his wife? "I have my own career all marked out," he says somewhat defensively. It would seem so. It would seem he is building a protective wall around him to secure him from the matriarchal dominance which he is probably trying to escape from.

He would then be selfish—admitting also that he has never loved anybody. Why? Is he as afraid to give of himself, compromise, and sacrifice as I am? Quite possibly. He also, as I do to a certain extent, has a superiority complex . . . which often generates condescending and patronizing attitudes that I find extremely offensive. Also, in spite of the fact that he has tried with a vengeance to enter into my appreciation of art and my writing interests—to actually *do* and not just appreciate (is that a sign that he must *compete* and *master* me—symbolic, what?)—he recently stated that a poem "is so much inconsequential dust." With that attitude, how can he be so hypocritical as to pretend he likes poetry? Even *some* kinds of poetry? The fact remains that writing is a way of life to me: and writing not just from a pragmatic, money-earning point of view either. Granted, I consider publication a token of value and a confirmation of ability—but writing takes practice, continual practice. And if publication is not tangible immediately, if "success" is not forthcoming, would he force me into a defensive attitude about my passionate avocation? Would I be forced to give it up, cut it off? Undoubtedly, as the wife of such a medical man as he would like to be, I *would* have to. I do not believe, as he and his friends would seem to, that artistic creativity can best be indulged in masterful singleness rather than in marital cooperation. I think that a workable union should heighten the potentialities in *both* individuals. And so when he says, "I am afraid the demands of wifehood and motherhood would preoccupy you too much to allow you to do the painting and writing you want . . ." the fear, the expectancy is planted. And so I start thinking, maybe he's right. Maybe all those scared and playful stream-of-consciousness letters were just touching again and again at this recurring string of doubt and premonition. As it stands now, he alternately denies and accepts me, as I silently do him. There is sometimes a great destructive, annihilating surge of negative fear and hate and recoiling: "I *can't*, I won't." And then there are long talks, patient, questioning, the physical attraction, soothing again, pacifying, lulling. "I love you." "Don't say that. You don't really. Remember what we said about the word 'love.'" "I know, but I love this girl, here and now, I don't know who she is, but I love her." There is always coming again strongly the feeling as frantic in another way: really, what if I should deny this and *never meet anyone as satisfying or* (as I have been hoping) *better*? To use a favorite metaphor: It is as if both of us, wary of oysters so rich and potent and at once digestively dangerous as they are, should agree to each swallow an oyster (our prospective mate) tied to a string (our reserve about committing ourselves). Then, if either or both of us found the oyster disagreeing with our respective digestive systems, we could yank up the oyster before it was too late, and completely assimilated in all its destructive potent (with marriage). Sure, there might be a little nausea, a little regret, but the poisoning, corrosive, final, destructive, would not have had a chance to set in. And there we are: two scared, attractive, intelligent, dangerous, hedonistic, "clever" people.

So weighing danger, I find it carries the balance. (He probably will, too.) Therefore I say: "*Je ne l'espouserai jamais! JAMAIS, JAMAIS!*" And even there the doubts begin if you find no one else as complete, as satisfying. If you spend the rest of your life bitterly regretting your choice? A choice you *must* make. And soon. Which will have the courage to be first? If I met someone I could love, it would be so painless. But I doubt if I will be that lucky again. Could I change my attitude and subordinate *gladly* to his life? Thousands of women *would*! It would depend on fear-of-being-an-old-maid and sex-urge-being-strong-enough. They *aren't*, at nineteen (although the latter *is* pretty potent). So there I am—if I could only say with faith: somewhere there is a man I could love and *give* of myself to *with* trust and with*out* fear. If only. Then I wouldn't cling so desperately and strangely to this one beautiful, intelligent, sensual human companion as I do. Or he to me. But desiring human flesh, companionship— How we need that security! "How we need another soul to cling to. Another body to keep us warm! To rest and trust." I said so for Bob. I say it now again. How many men are left? How many more chances will I have? I don't know. But at nineteen I will take the risk and hope that I *will* have another chance or two!

In 1952, after her sophomore year at Smith, Plath had a summer job waiting tables at the Belmont Hotel on Cape Cod. She enjoyed herself tremendously socially but overdid it and became sick again, sick enough to go home and quit the job— a move she later regretted.

CAPE COD

The Mill Hill Club was big, commercialized, with a band, dance floor and a continuous round of aggressive entertainment, so we sat, side by side, in a leatherette booth by an open window with a view of pines and a slice of lemon-colored moon— listening to a birdlike man hammering hell out of a banjo, a great girl vocalist, and a splendid mimic. Singing, drinking, dancing, laughing (me in his arms, close, hot, banged into by people, crushed together, someone's heel prodding your calf, my elbow in a stranger's ribs...his face, strange too in the light, looking down, laughing, smiling into mine, lips seeking to kiss, laughter always, and knowing he liked the way I was, gay and tanned and glowing...), we passed the hours. Next day (foolishly, I thought) I made an afternoon date for tennis.

All that night, coughing, fevered, I couldn't sleep, but lay in the narrow bed, with the faint grit of sand I never could quite get off the sheets, and stared at the swatch of winking stars I could see over the roof of the boys' dorm. They shone, calm and mocking, through the thin filmy nylon stockings hung up in the window to dry. All the pros and cons and nasty, mealymouthed fears and dreads went swarming through my teeming, seething brain. The sickness I felt had reached a crisis; it was not turning back as I had hoped, but was, rather, advancing steadily. What to do? Whom to turn to? Where to go? What to tell Phil* today? And so the morning came, and with

---

*Phil McCurdy, a good friend from Plath's hometown

it the verbal birth of an idea that had been sprouting in my subconscious all along at the sight of Wellesley-dwelling Princetonian. Why not, why not—*go home with him and recuperate there*? In peace and quiet!

A trip to the doctor's Sunday morning in the Belmont truck with tall, skinny blond Jack Harris, whose skin is always pink and peeling, and witty, big Pat Mutrie, who can have you laughing just with a word, with a look. Bumping along, feeling hot and messy, over the country Cape roads, finally to come to the [doctor's] office. . . . The doctor hopped about, peering into my sinuses and down my throat, saying, "Well, dear, it may break your little heart, but I think you should go home for a few days to recuperate." Jubilant at his strategic and official confirmation of my plan, I drove back to the Belmont and threw all manner of clothes into my little black suitcase— bathing suit, dirty pajamas, tennis shorts, and even a date dress and pearls just in case I should get well fast enough . . . and Phil should chance to ask me out! . . .

"Er . . . Phil . . ." I began brightly, leaning on the windowsill and gazing in at him and the good-looking, lean blond boy beside him, both of them dressed in tennis shorts. "Ah . . . Phil, how would you like company on the way home?"

A queer look passes over his face, and the other boy (Rodger) starts laughing. "What happened?" Phil asks. "Did you get fired?"

"No. I just have got to go home to get some penicillin shots. Doctor's orders." That sounds official.

"Well, sure," he says.

"Can I get in now? I've got all my things." So I run up and get the absurd little black suitcase and, for some odd reason, my tennis racket. Fortunately for me it is starting to rain. No tennis, thank God.

I get in between the two boys and we drive off. Suddenly everything is very funny, very ridiculous. We are all laughing, and Rodger is looking over his glasses down his cute nose, pulling my hair, and being a hacker in general.

"We are going to pick up the Weasel," he says.

"The Weasel?" I ask. I look scared. He laughs. So we drive into a driveway by a big white house with a lot of pillars. "It's all pillars," I observe brightly. That, it seems, is the name of the place: The Pillars. It also seems this is where the millionaire lives. Art Kramer's* millionaire. (Weasel, it develops, is the millionaire's Princetonian chauffeur.)

So Art comes out, in a suit, smiling in his endearing simian fashion, and leaning against the car. It is a small world. Then Weasel comes out, blond, blue-eyed, and in shirt sleeves. Not bad, but with a definite aura of weaselishness about him. He comes bearing gifts: beer cans. Full, too. He jumps into the back seat and we are off.

This time there is a great deal of laughing, and Rodge is trying to explain to Weasel how "this girl is the coolest thing I've seen yet; she comes up waving this pitiful little piece of paper, some doctor saying she should go home, and she goes home like she needs a vacation or something!" We stop for ice, and drive to a beach where there is a parking lot by sand dunes, and a view of witchgrass, and the rain coming down hard on a dirty, sodden, gray-green sea.

The beer tastes good to my throat, cold and bitter, and the three boys and the beer and the queer freeness of the situation makes me feel like laughing forever. So I laugh, and my lipstick leaves a red stain like a bloody crescent moon on the top of the beer can. I am looking very healthy and flushed and bright-eyed, having both a good tan and a rather excellent fever.

We drop off the other two boys then and start the three-hour drive back to Wellesley through the pouring rain. It is comfortable, being with Phil, and there is a lot to talk about. The only trouble is that my voice is beginning to leave me. It must be the dampness or something, but the pitch is about an octave lower. So I decide philosophically to make the best of it and pretend I naturally have a very husky, sexy low voice. I've never had it so good.

We pick up Phil's dog, a spoiled big-eyed black cocker spaniel who sits with us in the front seat, looking very sad and very loving. Phil pats her, and so do I. Our hands meet, and he absently pats mine. I think all of a sudden maybe I could get very fond of this guy after all.

I get out of the car when it pulls up in front of the little white house I haven't seen for almost three weeks. I am suddenly very tired, very hungry. I say good-bye to Phil, who asks if I want to go out that night. "No, Phil, thanks." He

*Princeton student

doesn't understand. I am going to be very sick. "Tennis tomorrow?" No, again.

Mother and Warren look up, startled, as I walk in. "Hello," I croak gaily. "I'm home for a visit." Mother smiles and says, "Wait till I tell Grammy! She dreamed you were coming home last night!" (As Frost said, Home is where, when you go there, they have to take you in!)

WELLESLEY

July 11, Friday. A recuperation, tedious, with shots of penicillin, and now I have been breathing quite well for a week. The Belmont called up early one morning, and Mother answered. They wanted to know definitely when I'd be coming back so they could hire another girl in the interim. (Some devilish split part in my personality had been whispering to me all week subconsciously: "Why go back? You're tired, fagged out, and the work is getting rough—no days off, pay not especially good. Then, too, only a few people who really like you. Why not stay home for the summer—rest, get your science done, write, go out with Phil [Brawner, Princeton student], play tennis. You can *afford* to loaf. You *deserve* to, what with winning one of the two big prizes in *Mademoiselle*'s College Fiction Contest with 'Sunday at the Mintons',' so take a break for once. Sinusitis is such a beautiful excuse.") So the devil got into my vocal chords and I started prompting Mother— "Say you don't know when I'll be well. . . . That I'm still miserable. . . . That I loved it there, but maybe it would be more convenient to get someone else." So Mother said so, and they said they were sorry, as everybody liked me, but they would get someone else. We looked at each other in dubious triumph.

Twenty-four hours later I got a letter from Polly and from Pat M. (saying how they missed me), from Art Kramer (saying how seeing me that day gave him just enough courage to want to ask me out), and from the Editor-in-Chief of Alfred A. Knopf, Publishers (saying how he liked the advance proofs of my story "Sunday at the Mintons'," which is coming out in *Mlle*, and how he'd like to publish a novel [!] by me sometime in the future). That little packet was IT: all I needed to start me raring to live again. In that brief interval I cursed myself for stupidly getting out of the Belmont job—for losing Ray, Art, Polly, Gloria—and all the might-have-beens: the wonderful-people-I-might-have-met-but-didn't. And the beach four hours a day, and the swimming. And the tan and blond sun-bleached hair. I was glum, morose, thinking: why didn't I tell them I'd be back in two weeks: then I could have rested completely and had a little social vacation in the bargain. (Fool. Fool. Damn Fool.)

And then I began to understand the difference between death-or-sickness-in-life as versus life. When sick (both physically, as symptoms showed, and mentally, as I was trying to escape from something) I wanted to withdraw from all the painful reminders of vitality—to hide away alone in a peaceful stagnant pool, and not be like a crippled stick entangled near the bank of a jubilantly roaring river, torn at continually by the noisy current. So I went home, knowing that if I did so it would be hard to come back. The horrible exertion of forcing myself back into the current persisted all during the worst days of my depressing sinus infection—and the call came 24 hours too early. Then came the switch in attitude: out of all the rationalizing, all the intellectual balancing of pros and cons, it comes down to the fact that when you are alive and vital, competition and striving with and among *people* overbalances everything else. No matter how logically I had reasoned out about the Belmont being dangerous for my health, unremunerative in proportion to the work performed, impossible as far as science study was concerned—*still* the magnetic whirlpool of slender, lovely young devils called and called to me above all. Life was not to be sitting in hot amorphous leisure in my backyard idly writing or not-writing, as the spirit moved me. It was, instead, running madly, in a crowded schedule, in a squirrel cage of busy people. Working, living, dancing, dreaming, talking, kissing, singing, laughing, learning. The responsibility, the awful responsibility of managing (profitably) 12 hours a day for 10 weeks, is rather overwhelming when there is nothing, no one, to insert an exact routine into the large unfenced acres of time—which it is so easy to let drift by in soporific idling and luxurious relaxing. It is like lifting a bell jar off a securely clockworklike functioning community, and seeing all the little busy people stop, gasp, blow up, and float in the inrush (or rather outrush) of the rarified scheduled atmosphere—poor little frightened people, flailing impotent arms in the aimless air. That's what it feels like: getting shed of a routine. Even though one has rebelled terribly against it, even then, one feels uncomfortable when jounced out of the repetitive rut. And so with me. What to do? Where to turn? What ties, what roots? As I hang suspended in the strange thin air of back-home?

For the rest of the summer Plath took a mother's helper job with a Christian Scientist family, the Cantors, in Chatham, Massachusetts. The Cantors were very fond of her and tended to treat her as a daughter, though she also worked very hard.

CHATHAM

August 8, Friday—9:45 P.M. In bed, bathed, and the good rain coming down again—liquidly slopping down the shingled roof outside my window. All today it has come down, in its enclosing wetness, and at last I am in bed, propped up comfortably by pillows—listening to it spurting and drenching—and all the different timbres of tone—and syncopation. The rapping on the resonant gutters—hard, metallic. The rush of a stream down the drainpipe splattering flat on the earth, wearing away a small gully—the musical falling of itself, tinkling faintly on the tin garbage pails in a high-pitched tattoo. And it seems that always in August I am more aware of the rain. A year ago it came down on my porch and the lawn and the flat gray sea beyond at the Mayos—closing me in the great house in the day, talking to me alone in my room in the evening as I sat alone in bed writing, surveying my kingdom from my throne: the lone streetlight on the corner, hanging solitary in a nimbus of light, and beyond it the gray indistinguishable fog and the rain sound blending with the wash of the sea. It shut me in a rock cave with Dick on Marblehead Beach, drenching, soaking, and we threw rocks at a rusted tin can until it stopped coming down viciously and churning the sea to a flayed whiteness.

Two years ago August rain fell on me and Ilo, walking side by side, wordless, toward the barn. And it was raining when

I came out from the loft, crying, my mouth bruised where he had kissed me. Rain closed about the windows of the car Emile and I rode home in, and fell outside the kitchen where we stood, in the dark, with the smell of linoleum, and the water always falling on the leaves outside the screen.

Three years ago, the hot, sticky August rain fell big and wet as I sat listlessly on my porch at home, crying over the way summer would not come again—never the same. The first story in print came from that "never again" refrain beat out by the rain. August rain: the best of the summer gone, and the new fall not yet born. The odd uneven time.

August 9. . . . I left the children down with Joanie—and escaped in the beach wagon to Chatham town. Inching the shiny green machine through the rain-puddled narrow streets to the town parking lot, I felt an evil sense of victory and freedom. I was going to see Val Gendron* in the Bookmobile, and I did.

I walked in the back door of Lorania's Bookmobile, and my red slicker shed rivulets of water on the floor as I bent my head, scanning titles, while Val was talking to people up front. I sat on the floor then, looking at poetry books and the brightly covered, good clear-printed Modern Library editions. She was alone then, and remembered me.

So I asked her about a lot of things—how she got writing and where published, and where worked. She talked nicely to me—cynical, hard-bitten, with a sneer, and then a quick look, a smile, soft, fleetingly, that said she understood about how I was critical of my story, didn't like it now as much, and how it was best *writing* actually, the process, not the product. So she told me about the four page (1000 words) a day deal. No time limit—there's the catch. You don't have a time limit, it's the produce that counts. 365,000 words in a year is a hell of a lot of words. I start this fall. Four pages a day.

She is small, skinny, sallow, with black hair done up in back in a bun and braids under a visor khaki cap. A pointed face, glasses, and a dry, sarcastic drawl. Cats she has, in her shack, red-painted (she says) and no phone. Signs of loneliness?

---

*A professional writer

Of living too long with Val Gendron? Who to talk to? Who? I will find out. I will be no Val Gendron. But I will make a good part of Val Gendron part of me—someday. And the coffee grounds can be left out. For good. She has said I may visit her: a pilgrimage—to my First Author.

August 19—1 A.M. Face it kid, you've had a hell of a lot of good breaks. No Elizabeth Taylor, maybe. No child Hemingway, but God, you are growing up. In other words, you've come a long way from the ugly introvert you were only five years ago. Pats on the back in order? O.K., tan, tall, blondish, not half bad. And brains, "intuitiveness" in one direction at least. You get along with a great many different kinds of people. Under the same roof, close living, even. You have no real worries about snobbishness, pride, or a swelled head. You are willing to work. Hard, too. You have willpower and are getting to be practical about living—and also you are getting published. So you got a good right to write all you want. Four acceptances in three months—$500 *Mlle*, $25, $10 *Seventeen*, $3.50 *Christian Science Monitor* (from caviar to peanuts, I like it all the way).

After Val. God, the talk. First, her "shack," red half-house with white trim, and her slouching thin and grubby in the doorway grinning. Plaid shirt, paint-stained Levis. I walk in, feeling big and new and too clean. She is washing clothes in a basin. Dirty old clothes. Hot water gotten from kettle on stove.

I sit down in small kitchen. Wallpaper is brown background—colored Pennsylvania-Dutch-looking pattern. Dirty dishes on floor. Two cats: Prudence, a snooty black, sultry green-eyed Persian blood, and O'Hara. Ashtrays full of cigarettes. She smokes 2 cartons of Wings (cheap, nonadvertised) a week. Can't taste, no palate left.

So I look around. She likes to cook—stews and ragouts especially. Things with wine. There is a shelf of cookbooks over the refrigerator. Also a shelf of spices. She unscrews them and I smell each as she says, "Thyme, basil, marjoram..." and so on. There is also a preserving closet—jams, jellies, apple butter, beach plums. She picks and cans. Wild, sweet, tart, clear in glasses.

Outside is the garden. Neat grass lot reclaimed from pine woods. Flowers—some phlox, zinnias. Overgrown weeds in vegetables because of time Bookmobile job takes. There are strawberries, raspberries, peppers, beans, tomatoes, all in beds, squared off neat and clean-cut.

We take cake she has bought, a heap of green grapes, from the refrigerator. She grinds coffee, the smell is great, and we sit around waiting for the pot to boil. Meanwhile Prudence licks some frosting off the cake. Val cuts that part off, saves it for O'Hara. When the coffee is ready we climb the steep Cape Cod stairs to the workshop she has made herself.

It is all bookshelves over the walls, Williamsburg blue-gray, and cream yellow. A rug she is braiding is on the floor, and balls of wool rag in a basket. A studio couch, a typewriter. Piles of manuscripts around, in boxes, on her desk. We sit cross-legged on the floor, and start pouring ourselves cup after cup of coffee. I am a pig and have three hunks of cake. The four black kittens Prue is nursing come in and skitter around like black scritches of playful fluff. They are nosy, lean into my coffee cup, sneeze at the hot strong stuff and go skittering across the floor. One goes to sleep inside the edge of my skirt where it makes a comfortable fold on the floor.

I hear about agents—Ann Elmo. Something-and-Otis. I read "Miss Henderson's Marriage." I like pace, tempo. I think it is a shade dull, characters don't come across human—oh, indefinable quality. But construction has poise, balance. Enviable by me at this stage. Also look through files of correspondence between her and agents. She's got "Haitian Holiday" on her mind. Novelette about bastard girl, too. So many stories! So much published. . . .

Knows Rachel Carson. Woods Hole. She has hit a jackpot, still goes around like Val, old jalop, old clothes, got a hit here and doesn't know what to do with this thing, people telling her how to write, but she is working on something now . . . like good writer, enmeshed in present problem. Doesn't feed off leaf of laurel.

. . . A ride back at midnight, talk about Evita Peron. (Whore or courtesan, she put on a great little show. Val likes skyrockets. Pretty, cute.)

Writing work. Writer builds illusion for man-on-street: shroud of mystery—no one wants to think their emotions can be played with, roused, by literary learned craft and intention. No one wants to think: this guy can reach inside and yank my heart because he wants to keep his pot boiling. So when they ask where the writer gets his ideas: "I lie on my couch; God speaks to me. Inspiration." That satisfies.

Yelling above the jalop motor. Home, coffee-drunk. Exhilarated. (Can't stop thinking I am just beginning. In 10 years I will be 30 and not ancient and maybe good. Hope. Prospects. Work, though, and I love it. Delivering babies. Maybe even both kinds. Val grinning at me in the faint light, face in shadow, tough talk, but good to me. I will write her from Smith. I will work, maybe drive down wintertime and visit. Maybe take Dick even. God, she has been great to me. Tonight best yet. All the boys, all the longing, then this perfection. Perfect love, whole living.)

She had a cricket in the wall and it creaked and chirped. She said build a good life. I wonder. I like her, yet not as blindly as could be—I can be critical. But she has lived, sold, produced. And how much she has already begun to teach me.

Hell, you deserve more than being in *The Ladies' Home Journal*. If only I could get you in *The Atlantic*: "The Kid Colossus." I will aim at the highest, too. A plot. Like "Knife-like, Flower-like," only different. To prove what. To begin where, to end where—from what point of view. Oh, I will brood this year to find the form for the content.

Val said: visualize, emotionalize *afterwards*. Beginning writers work from the sense impressions, forget cold realistic organization. *First* get the cold objective plot scene set. Rigid. Then write the damn thing after lying on the couch and visualizing, whipping it to white heat, to life again, the life of the art, the form, no longer formless, without frame of reference.

September 20—Early toward young September 21. ("There are times," the young man told me softly, "when a man wishes a woman were a whore.") A vile dull evening. A horrible movie, both of us disgusted, staying in out of the rain, sleepy, critical. Driving in the roadster, jaunty, bored, through the Boston streets with the after-movie crowds thronging crosswalks, and the pink, green, blue, yellow neons all lighted blur in the streets, wet smooth puddled black. Bored, cross, all wrong. Why do I not wear heels . . . because I look like such a bobby-soxer in flat shoes? I am young, naïve, childish, sixteen emotionally. My reactions are too obvious, too excitable easily. I gush over trivia, embroidering problematically on mere cold factual phenomena. I build too much him on a pedestal breathless with admiration ("Oh, really, yes, yes, go on . . ."). And I freeze at a touch. Ah, I am also twice fishing for compliments, and I would deny it with vehemence but for the fact that I am caught— subconscious though my line may be, and he is, damn him, too right. All that is wrong, it appears, is "that we have not gotten drunk together." There is a wall. We have inhibitions. And I force him into acting with my absurd overflowing enthusiasms. They *are* absurd, and I *am* acting—because I feel peculiar. He is foreign, alien, yet the different cultural and moral backgrounds we draw upon do not *seem* to matter too badly. Perhaps I am on the defensive, who knows. Overreacting to the situation with a false burst of effusiveness. Because I want to conquer the cosmopolitan alien before I return to the rustic boy-next-door. (Feminine vanity?) *Is not my first desperate rush of enthusiasm* (remarked upon formerly by Dick) *a vestige of my old fear of people running away, leaving me, forcing me to be alone?* Is it not a device subconsciously calculated to interest, to hold, to retain my partner, be it male or female? (I remember when Nancy Colson walked me home from Scouts in Winthrop with another girl. They would always run away giggling together when I started to tell them a story. I did not understand. Bewildered, breathless, I would run after them. And then I learned that they had arranged to run away so they wouldn't have to listen to my lengthy, dull rambling.) I will cultivate restraint. I will stop being a loudmouthed puppy that falls all over people in a frantic effort to attract them. I want desperately to be liked. I have gone through a long period of awkward, self-conscious unpopularity. Although I could be called an extrovert now, there are still recurrent traces of my old inferiority complex. I put new people on a pedestal, worshiping them for their surprising kindness to me, for their benevolent notice. How many silver-plated statues have I erected, only to humanize them as I grew to know their vulnerable frailties?

* * *

Today was good. Mr. Crockett* for two and one half hours in the afternoon, and after long talking in his green pine garden over sherry I got the flash of insight, the after-college objective. It is a frightening and wonderful thing: a year of graduate study in England. Cambridge or Oxford. It is as yet a vague move: money being the one great problem. But I have two years to work toward it; there are scholarships, fellowships; I am young, husky, and eager to work.

Problems it resolves and arouses: I will go to Paris, to Austria, during vacations. England will be the jumping-off place. I will bicycle all over England on weekends. No summer hosteling with the dull drudging miles, weariness, and inability to enjoy the heights of life—but perhaps a stay in the city at a cheap inn, travel with a friend. Then back to England. I will write; stories, maybe even a novel. I think I will do graduate work in philosophy. I am going to do it.

Main fear, nagging: men. I am in love with two brothers,** embarrassingly so. I will leave. Unless I am lucky, both may give way to marrying while I am gone, so I will come back to a big void. On the other hand, I may fall in love, have an affair with someone over "there." I need a year to get perspective, to free myself before I decide to be "of human bondage." And the danger is that in this move toward new horizons and far directions I may lose what I have now, and not find anything except loneliness. I want to eat my cake abroad and come home and find it securely on the doorstep if I still choose to accept it for the rest of my life. I am gambling. The workings of my destiny will be revealing the years hence.

Today a dream was planted: a name: England. A desire: study abroad. A course of action directed toward this end.

Dinner at Nortons', warm, glowing aqua candles, bright sudden pink-petaled yellow-centered asters. Swordfish and sour cream broiled (with Perry pink-faced bending over testing the taste). Hollandaise and broccoli. Grape pie and ice cream, rich, warm. And port, sharp, sweet, startling, gulped with a sudden good sting behind the eyes and a relaxing into easy laughter. Good

---

*Mr. Crockett was Plath's high school English teacher, perhaps her first mentor.

**The Nortons

scalding black coffee. And Dick and I at home all evening, mutually warm, rich, seething with peace. "La Mer" often while dishes were done, and while sleepily relaxing by candlelight. The music, going on, disturbing, haunting, ineffably strange and deeply moving, with all the great blind surging of the sea, and the thin flashes of sound, of light, of insight.

Sitting in the gray room, all blurred around the edges, candlelight shafting in, warmly in arms of him, placid, content, drowsy, yet alert and awake, the greatness of the day and the import of the time broke in upon me with a flash of joy and fear. I was going away to England out of the warm secure circle to prove something. There would be the going away and the coming back, and whatever would greet me on returning, I would take stoically, accepting the responsibility of my own will, be it free or predetermined by my nature and circumstances.

Outside the window it was dark, and the light from the kitchen was on the undersides of the tree leaves. It was all stark and unmoving, black, edged with the light. The tree was tall and filled the dark bigness of the window square. I had never felt so happy in that particular way. I was escaping, going away; from what? I had a semisecret aim, and I would extend the cycle of sterility and creation. Gathering forces into a tight tense ball for the artistic leap. Into what? *The Atlantic*? A novel? Dreams, private dreams. But if I work? And always work to think, and know, and practice technique always?

This very serious depression, with its mention of suicide as the only way out, foreshadows the summer breakdown the next year that is the subject of The Bell Jar. *Very few people were aware of the situation, and even they were not allowed to see the depth of Plath's desperation. The high pitch of her typically fast bounce-back seems itself alarming in retrospect, but people close to Plath were used to her wide mood swings.*

NORTHAMPTON

November 3. God, if ever I have come close to wanting to commit suicide, it is now, with the groggy sleepless blood dragging through my veins, and the air thick and gray with rain and the damn little men across the street pounding on the roof with picks and axes and chisels, and the acrid hellish stench of tar. I fell into bed again this morning, begging for sleep, withdrawing into the dark, warm, fetid escape from action, from responsibility. No good. The mail bell rang and I jerked myself up to answer it. A letter from Dick. Sick with envy, I read it, thinking of him lying up there, rested, fed, taken care of, free to explore books and thoughts at any whim.* I thought of the myriad of physical duties I had to perform: write Prouty**; *Life* back to Cal; write-up Press Board; call Marcia. The list mounted obstacle after fiendish obstacle; they jarred, they leered, they fell apart in chaos, and the revulsion, the desire to end the pointless round of objects, of things, of actions, rose higher. To annihilate the world by annihilation of one's self is the deluded height of desperate egoism. The simple way out of all the little brick dead ends we scratch our nails against. Irony it is to see Dick raised, lifted to the pinnacles of irresponsibility to anything but care of his body—to feel his mind soaring, reaching, and mine caged, crying, impotent, self-reviling, and imposter. How to justify myself, my bold, brave humanitarian faith? My world falls apart, crumbles, "the centre cannot hold." There is no integrating force, only the naked fear, the urge of self-preservation.

I am afraid. I am not solid, but hollow. I feel behind my eyes a numb, paralyzed cavern, a pit of hell, a mimicking nothingness. I never thought. I never wrote, I never suffered. I want to kill myself, to escape from responsibility, to crawl back abjectly into the womb. I do not know who I am, where I am going—and I am the one who has to decide the answers to these hideous questions. I long for a noble escape from freedom—I am weak, tired, in revolt from the strong constructive humanitarian faith which presupposes a healthy, active intellect and will. There is nowhere to go—not home, where I would blubber and cry, a grotesque fool, into my mother's skirts—not to men, where I want more than ever now their

---

*Dick Norton was recovering from tuberculosis.
**Olive Higgins Prouty, the novelist, who sponsored Plath's scholarship

stern, final, paternal directive—not to church, which is liberal, free—no, I turn wearily to the totalitarian dictatorship where I am absolved of all personal responsibility and can sacrifice myself in a "splurge of altruism" on the altar of the Cause with a capital "C."

Now I sit here, crying almost, afraid, seeing the finger writing my hollow futility on the wall, damning me—God, where is the integrating force going to come from? My life up till now seems messy, inconclusive, disorganized: I arranged my courses wrong, played my strategy without unifying rules— got excited at my own potentialities, yet amputated some to serve others. I am drowning in negativism, self-hate, doubt, madness—and even I am not strong enough to deny the routine, the rote, to simplify. No, I go plodding on, afraid that the blank hell in back of my eyes will break through, spewing forth like a dark pestilence, afraid that the disease which eats away the pith of my body with merciless impersonality will break forth in obvious sores and warts, screaming "Traitor, sinner, imposter."

I can begin to see the compulsion for admitting original sin, for adoring Hitler, for taking opium. I have long wanted to read and explore the theories of philosophy, psychology, national, religious, and primitive consciousness, but it seems now too late for anything—I am a conglomerate garbage heap of loose ends—selfish, scared, contemplating devoting the rest of my life to a cause—going naked to send clothes to the needy, escaping to a convent, into hypochondria, into religious mysticism, into the waves—anywhere, anywhere, where the burden, the terrifying hellish weight of self-responsibility and ultimate self-judgment, is lifted. I can see ahead only into dark, sordid alleys, where the dregs, the sludge, the filth of my life lies, unglorified, unchanged—transfigured by nothing: no nobility, not even the illusion of a dream.

Reality is what I make it. That is what I have said I believed. Then I look at the hell I am wallowing in, nerves paralyzed, action nullified—fear, envy, hate: all the corrosive emotions of insecurity biting away at my sensitive guts. Time, experience: the colossal wave, sweeping tidal over me, drowning, drowning. How can I ever find that permanence, that continuity with past and future, that communication with other human beings that I crave? Can I ever honestly accept an artificial imposed solution? How can I justify, how can I rationalize the rest of my life away?

The most terrifying realization is that so many millions in the world would like to be in my place: I am not ugly, not an imbecile, not poor, not crippled—I am, in fact, living in the free, spoiled, pampered country of America and going for hardly any money at all to one of the best colleges. I have earned $1000 in the last three years by writing. Hundreds of dreaming ambitious girls would like to be in my place. They write me letters, asking if they may correspond with me. Five years ago, if I could have seen myself now: at Smith (instead of Wellesley) with seven acceptances from *Seventeen* and one from *Mlle*, with a few lovely clothes, and one intelligent, handsome boy— I would have said: that is all I could ever ask!

And there is the fallacy of existence: the idea that one would be happy forever and age with a given situation or series of accomplishments. Why did Virginia Woolf commit suicide? Or Sara Teasdale or the other brilliant women? Neurotic? Was their writing sublimation (oh, horrible word) of deep, basic desires? If only I knew. If only I knew how high I could set my goals, my requirements for my life! I am in the position of a blind girl playing with a slide rule of values. I am now at the nadir of my calculating powers.

The future? God—will it get worse and worse? Will I never travel, never integrate my life, never have purpose, meaning? Never have time—long stretches, to investigate ideas, philosophy—to articulate the vague seething desires in me? Will I be a secretary—a self-rationalizing, uninspired housewife, secretly jealous of my husband's ability to grow intellectually and professionally while I am impeded? Will I submerge my embarrassing desires and aspirations, refuse to face myself, and go either mad or become neurotic?

Whom can I talk to? Get advice from? No one. A psychiatrist is the god of our age. But they cost money. And I won't take advice, even if I want it. I'll kill myself. I am beyond help. No one here has time to probe, to aid me in understanding myself . . . so many others are worse off than I. How can I selfishly demand help, solace, guidance? No, it is my own mess, and even if now I have lost my sense of perspective, thereby my creative sense of humor, I will not let myself get sick, go mad, or retreat like a child into blubbering on someone else's shoulder. Masks are the order of the day—and the least I can do is cultivate the illusion that I am gay, serene, not hollow and afraid. Someday, god knows when, I will stop this absurd, self-pitying, idle, futile despair. I will begin to think again, and to act according to the way I think. Attitude is a pitifully relative and capricious quality to base a faith on. Like the proverbial sand, it slides, founders, sucks me down to hell.

At present, the last thing I can do is be objective, self-critical, diagnostic—but I *do* know that my philosophy is too subjective, relative and personal to be strong and creative in all circumstances. It is fine in fair weather, but it dissolves when the forty-day rains come. I must submerge it before a larger, transcending goal or craft; what that is I cannot now imagine.

Infirmary Blues

You push the button and the voice comes out of the wall
Hygienic and efficiently impersonal
"What can we do for you? What can we do?"
And you
Say to the waiting voice inside the wall:
"I don't think I want my supper meal.
My stomach feels queer and I don't want to eat at all."
There is a distant click and soon the soft-soled footsteps
    come down the hall;
And she hands you a glass of white medicine
That tastes like peppermint, cool-flavored and milk thin.
She says: "There will be toast and tea for you and
    junket by and by."
And you say all right and turn your face away because
    you are going to cry.
Outside the picture window the rain is pouring on the
    ground
And all the things you ever did or will do wrong are
    falling down without a sound
Out of the yesterday sky
To where all the little stilborn cretins of tomorrow
    lie.

November 14. All right, this is it. For the first time (since I heard about Dick) I have broken down and cried, and talked, and cried and talked again. I felt the mask crumple, the great poisonous store of corrosive ashes begin to spew out of my mouth. I have been needing, more than anything, to talk to somebody, to spill out all the tight, jealous, envious, apprehensive neurotic tensions in me: resentments at not being abroad, recriminations about missing the chance to get out of taking a routine science course; wish-dreams about the courses I could have taken instead—this year, last year, the year before; loneliness at having my two main outlets, Marcia and Dick, removed, distant, gone;* jealousy, falling apart of my creative attitude toward life, emptiness, intensified by the pathetic, weak, nasal, negative, critical, inarticulate, fumbling approach—grotesque almost—of one who shall be nameless.

All right, tonight, after good pizza, chianti, hot coffee, and laughter, I went upstairs to the green, white and red room which is light and vitality and Marcia. There, on the bed, she touched the soft spot, the one vulnerable spot in the hard, frozen, acrid little core in me, and I could cry. God, it was good to let go, let the tight mask fall off, and the bewildered, chaotic fragments pour out. It was the purge, the catharsis, I talked, and began to remember how I was before, how integrated, how positive, how rich—rooming with Marcia last year was one of the most vital experiences of my life. I shall never forget the passionate discussions, the clear articulate arguments; what ecstasy compared to the shrill, whining, stumbling of this one who lies, breasts full and drooping, eyes drooping, mouth drooping. God!

I lay and cried, and began to feel again, to admit I was human, vulnerable, sensitive. I began to remember how it had been before; how there was that germ of positive creativeness. Character is fate; and damn, I'd better work on my character. I had been withdrawing into a retreat of numbness: it is so much safer *not* to feel, *not* to let the world touch one. But my honest self revolted at this, hated me for doing this. Sick with conflict, destructive negative emotions, frozen into disintegration I was, refusing to articulate, to spew forth these emo-

---

*Marcia Brown, an important friend who was Sylvia's sophomore-year roommate, was now living elsewhere.

tions—they festered in me, growing big, distorted, like pus-bloated sores. Small problems, mentions of someone else's felicity, evidence of someone else's talents frightened me, making me react hollowly, fighting jealousy, envy, hate. Feeling myself fall apart, decay, rot, and the laurels wither and fall away, and my past sins and omissions strike me with full punishment and import. All this, all this foul, gangrenous sludge ate away at my insides. Silent, insidious.

Until tonight. Touching me, letting me be unproud and cry, she talked and listened, and the tightness relaxed that bound my ribs, that gripped my stomach. Escapist, cheater, I was, betraying a trust, a creative pledge to affirm life, hell and heaven, mud and marble.

It must be fatigue, lack of a sense of proportion, that makes me procrastinate and fear my science course. Damn, I *can* catch up and keep up in it. It may unduly emphasize details, I might be taking Soci or Shakespeare or German, but hell, it was my mistake, and I've got to cut being a spoiled child about it. No mother is around to absolve me of my burdens, so I retreat in a numb womb of purposeless business with no integration whatsoever.

I rode home at 11:30 tonight, forcing great gulps of frosty air into my lungs, looking at the stars, up behind the black bare trees, and gasping at Orion. How long, how long since I noticed stars; no longer, now, mere inane pinpricks on a smothering sky of cheap cloth—but symbols, islands of light, soft, mysterious, hard, cold—all things, as much as I made them.

And Dick is recriminating himself, readjusting, trying to grow, too. And not living in the luxurious erotic Garden of Eden I imagined, either.

And so I rehabilitate myself—staying up late this Friday night in spite of vowing to go to bed early, because it is more important to capture moments like this, keen shifts in mood, sudden veerings of direction—than to lose it in slumber. I had lost all perspective; I was wandering in a desperate purgatory (with a gray man in a gray boat on a gray river: an apathetic Charon dawdling upon a passionless, phlegmatic River Styx . . . and a petulant Christ child bawling on the train . . .). The orange sun was a flat pasted disc on a smoky, acrid sky. Hell was the Grand Central Subway on Sunday morning. And I was doomed to burn in ice, numb, cold, revolving in crystal, neutral, passive vacuums, void of sensation.

Tomorrow I will finish my science, start my creative writing story. It will be, I think, about a weak, tense, nervous girl becoming the victim of the self-centered love of a man who is the spoiled pet of his mother. There will be an analogy, a symbol, perhaps, of a moth being consumed in the fire. I don't know, something. I will start slowly, for there must be sleep, and work, and more sleep, to rebuild again the higher towers. Remember: "People still live in houses." The word, quite lovely, "terminal." And the thought of all the books I must read this summer: the idea of fate, character, destiny, free will.

You are twenty. You are not dead, although you were dead. The girl who died. And was resurrected. Children. Witches. Magic. Symbols. Remember the illogic of the fantasy. The strange tableau in the closet behind the bathroom: the feast, the beast, and the jelly bean. Recall, remember: please do not die again: let there be continuity at least—a core of consistency—even if your philosophy must be always a moving dynamic dialectic. The thesis is the easy time, the happy time. The antithesis threatens annihilation. The synthesis is the consummate problem.

How many futures—(how many different deaths I can die?) How am I a child? An adult? A woman? My fears, my loves, my lusts—vague, nebulous. And yet, think, think, think—and keep this of tonight, this holy, miraculous resuscitation of the creative integrating blind optimism which was dead, frozen, gone quite away.

To love, to be loved. By one; by humanity. I am afraid of love, of sacrifice on the altar. I am going to think, to grow, to sally forth, please please, unafraid. Tonight, biking home toward midnight, talking to myself, sense of trap, of time, rolled the stone of inertia away from the tomb.

Tomorrow I will curse the dawn, but there will be other, earlier nights, and the dawns will be no longer hell laid out in alarms and raw bells and sirens. Now a love, a faith, an affirmation is conceived in me like an embryo. The gestation may be a while in producing, but the fertilization has come to pass.

Good night. Oh Big Good Book.

* * *

Tuesday, November 18. You are crucified by your own limitations. Your blind choices cannot be changed; they are now irrevocable. You have had chances; you have not taken them, you are wallowing in original sin; your limitations. You cannot even decide to take a walk in the country: you are not sure whether it is an escape or a refreshing cure from cooping yourself in your room all day. You have lost all delight in life. Ahead is a large array of blind alleys. You are half-deliberately, half-desperately, cutting off your grip on creative life. You are becoming a neuter machine. You cannot love, even if you knew how to begin to love. Every thought is a devil, a hell—if you could do a lot of things over again, ah, how differently you would do them! You want to go home, back to the womb. You watch the world bang door after door in your face, numbly, bitterly. You have forgotten the secret you knew, once, ah, once, of being joyous, of laughing, of opening doors.

January 10, 1953. Look at that ugly dead mask here and do not forget it. It is a chalk mask with dead dry poison behind it, like the death angel. It is what I was this fall, and what I never want to be again. The pouting disconsolate mouth, the flat, bored, numb, expressionless eyes: symptoms of the foul decay within. Eddie wrote me after my last honest letter saying I had better go to get psychiatric treatment to root out the sources of my terrible problems. I smile, now, thinking: we all like to think we are important enough to need psychiatrists. But all I need is sleep, a constructive attitude, and a little good luck. So unbelievably much has happened since I last wrote in here:

Thanksgiving I met a man I could want to see again and again.* I spent three days with him up here at House Dance.

---

*The new man in her life was Myron Lotz, a Yale premed student who also played in the minor leagues. He seemed to have a lot of the qualities on Plath's prospective husband checklist. Despite its intense beginning, it was not a really serious romance, and later turned into a good friendship.

I got a sinus infection for a week. I saw Dick, went to Saranac with him, and broke my leg skiing. I decided again that I could never live with him ever.

Now midyears approach. I have exams to work for, papers to write. There is snow and ice and I have a broken leg to drag around for two hellish months.

Dick and I are doomed to *compete* always and never to co-operate. I can't explain the qualities in us that aggravate our passionate jealousies, but I feel he wants to prove his virile dominance (e.g. in his writings, women have no personalities but are merely sex machines on which he displays his prowess in sexual technique; he grew a mustache and said if he shaved it off because I wanted him to it would be a sign of weakness and submission). And, looking back on our relationship together, I see now clearly the pattern of my continual desperate striving to measure up to what I thought were his standards of athletic ability, etc. Always I panted after him on a bicycle. Another thing, with him, although he always led and set the pace for sexual play, I never felt that I was *feminine* (implying a certain physical fragility—so a boy could masterfully pick up his girl and carry her, for instance). Granted, I felt a seductive woman, but wearing flat heels always, feeling physically his equal in size disturbed me. If I am going to be a woman, fine. But I want to experience my femininity to the utmost. Seeing him after two months, I no longer felt the desire flame up in me. I didn't particularly want him to touch me. For one thing, since he can't kiss me at all, I have the feeling (purely mental) that his mouth is a source of poisonous tuberculosis germs, and, therefore, unclean. I am, therefore, physically aloof. Also, I don't feel any emotion toward him—no longer the passionate, nervous, tense, sex-motivated hunger that I know was reciprocal. I don't love him. I never did. I don't think I deluded myself, except during that lovely freshman spring when I made him into a golden god physically, morally, and mentally. Again I attribute my first attraction to a naïve idealism. And now, I feel a new eagerness at the potential getting-to-know this new man: a different, more sensible, rational, realistic eagerness which is not cynical, but rather creative. I think I am ready to accept him right away as a human, fallible being.

* * *

January 12. Again, I cannot help muse upon the imprisonment of the individual in the cell of her own limitations. Now that I am condemned to a consistently small radius of activity—mainly my room, I am aware more than ever of the fact that I *don't know* any of the girls in this house. Oh, I see them on the surface, gossip occasionally and (*act*) friendly, but still, I have known none of them really—nor what ideas motivate them, drive them. I am as distant from the girls in my class as I could be. The few whom I feel I'd like to be close with hardly speak to me from force of habit.

Once again I will be the cheerful, gay, friendly person that I am really inside, and then, perhaps by some miracle, I will feel closer to my housemates. I am obsessed by my cast as a concrete symbol of my limitations and separation from others. I would like to write a symbolic allegory about a person who would not assert her will and communicate with others, but who always believed she was unaccepted, apart. Desperately, in an effort to be part of a certain group, she breaks her leg skiing and has a morbid fear that her leg will not mend properly. When the cast is taken off, her leg has withered, and she shrivels up into dust, or something.

Anyhow, I shall chalk this first semester up as a nadir of every aspect of my life—scholastic, social, spiritual.

The nadir is passed. I know that now. By a miracle of incident and attitude I am happier and more ecstatic at this particular moment than all this year ever (except for the actual ecstasy in time of House Dance weekend). Again I am compelled to state how I believe that attitude is everything—how the blind, neutral dripping of the trees which I enjoyed intrinsically this early morning is now, suddenly, by mental magic, transmuted into something infinitely rich and ineffably strange, how the dismembered sound fragments integrate suddenly into a unity of music. And why all this sudden plunge upward of ecstasy? I was happier yesterday than ever before, so it is not as if one incident started me on the upgrade. But it certainly acted as a positive catalyst to accelerate the process. First let me tell you about the beginnings of my turning tide. Last time I talked to you, "lights were glimmering in faint perhapses." Now a few of the perhapses have come true. In every field of my endeavor, in every empty barren cubicle of myself, academic, social, artistic, interpersonal (and on and on into subdivision after subdivision), there is the upswing, the turning, the sprouting of creative life again. I have gone through my winter solstice, and the dying god of life and fertility is reborn. In fact, my personal seasonal life is two months ahead of the spring equinox this year!

So that is the incipient beginning part of it. I am glad I wrote some of the sick naked hell I went through down in here. Otherwise, from my present vantage point, I could hardly believe it!

I have taken to retreating to bed in the long afternoons, pulling down the blinds and filtering out the light, lying warm and soft and sexual under the resilient light quilt and dreaming of him [Myron Lotz] and talking to him. All right, I work well and hard most of the time; I am probably at my peak of sexual desire, and I should not wonder at my smoldering passion. So why not? Because, you fool, he doesn't realize how you are transmuting him in your mind into a strong, brilliant man who desires you mentally and physically. And being as he will continue quite unaware of his role in your mind, you *cannot* expect him to fulfill that role in life. You must not let yourself be disappointed. Remember, you consider "love" a most intricate and complex word; and among its manifold meanings is that of vulnerability arising from shared weaknesses. There is a time for everything; and you must beware your predilection for green apples. They may be sweet and tart and new and early, but it's about time you learned to wait for the season of harvest. Take it slow, please. He is to be no engine for your ecstasy. Not yet, anyway.

As for minute joys: I think this book ricochets between the feminine burbling I hate and the posed cynicism I would shun. One thing, I try to be honest. And what is revealed is often rather hideously unflattering. I want so obviously, so desperately to be loved, and to be capable of love. I am still so naïve; I know pretty much what I like and dislike; but please, don't ask me who I am. "A passionate, fragmentary girl," maybe?

As for minute joys: as I was saying: Do you realize the illicit sensuous delight I get from picking my nose? I always have, ever since I was a child. There are so many subtle variations of sensation. A delicate, pointed-nailed fifth finger can catch under dry scabs and flakes of mucous in the nostril and draw them out to be looked at, crumbled between fingers, and flicked to the floor in minute crusts. Or a heavier, determined forefinger can reach up and smear down-and-out the soft, resilient, elastic greenish-yellow smallish blobs of mucous, roll them round and jellylike between thumb and forefinger, and spread them on the under-surface of a desk or chair where they will harden into organic crusts. How many desks and chairs have I thus secretively befouled since childhood? Or sometimes there will be blood mingled with the mucous: in dry brown scabs, or bright sudden wet red on the finger that scraped too rudely the nasal membranes. God, what a sexual satisfaction! It is absorbing to look with new sudden eyes on the old worn habits: to see a sudden luxurious and pestilential "snot-green sea," and shiver with the shock of recognition.

Lying in bed per usual this morning, under the big, light, resilient feather puff, I started worrying about how I should have taken all different courses here. . . . God, I felt sick, or started to. Life is so only-once, so single-chancish! It all depends on your arranging and synchronizing it so that when opportunity knocks you're right there waiting with your hand on the doorknob. If I had known then what I do now (i.e., that I would like to go to graduate school), I never would have concentrated so on English and art. Koffka* was right: college is no time for the would-be scholar to specialize. Graduate school is the place for that. And now I don't *want* to take grad study in English: I can carry English on myself after the specializing I have done in Honors here. Honors is fine if you can't go to graduate school and want to experience a microcosm of it. But now I would like to go on in either philosophy or psychology! Writing on the side (she says ambitiously). But to write you have to live, don't you? Should I, then, get a job: in publishing company or factory or office? After all, I should be able to *observe* life intelligently and intuitively, an experience in living is something I'll *never* get in the idealized scholastic environment of graduate school where food and shelter are provided "gratis" if one is brilliant enough! As far as grad school goes, the most ideal sounds like Johns Hopkins,

---

*The Gestalt psychologist Kurt Koffka

where I could be taking elementary language and psych courses while doing intense work in English, or writing. I don't know of any other place where one could do that....I would no doubt be able to travel during vacations, and learn to be quite independent. Who knows? It is all so uncertain. The two main other places I would consider are Radcliffe (near home, Harvard, but the program is nowhere as flexible as Johns Hopkins) and Columbia (New York, New Haven, and free culture, *if* men are around to take you to plays). I have no desire to go west, even middle-west. For one thing, I might as well go "all the way" and head for England and Europe—or stay east, where education can't be beat. Really, I *do* want at least another year of education before I start living. Once I break the connection with school life it'll be hard getting back—on scholarship. . . .

I don't want to use higher education as an escape from responsibility, but I feel there is so much more awareness I should have before plunging onto the field of battle. This summer I must do gallons of reading in psych, philosophy—English: I have a colossal list of books. Why, oh, why, in all those camp and social summers, didn't I read more purposive lasting books instead of the young girl's novels? I suppose, though, that learning to get along with farmhands and Christian Scientists is at least, if not more, important than learning about Kant's categorical imperative. Still and all, I should like also in addition to be aware of the imperative!

Now that I talk this out with myself, the past doesn't look so deformed, nor the future so black. How much more hope I have now than my Mary Ventura (and how much less hope for freedom to wander than any casual glittering millionaire!). A philosophical attitude: a drinking and living of life to the lees: please don't let me stop thinking and start blindly frightenedly accepting! I want to taste and glory in each day, and never be afraid to experience pain; and never shut myself up in a numb core of nonfeeling, or stop questioning and criticizing life and take the easy way out. To learn and think: to think and live; to live and learn: this always, with new insight, new understanding, and new love.

11 A.M. Still going on, ignoring science, peering out the window for mail. This morning also in bed I started dragging the still,

stagnant, putridly and potently rich sea of my subconscious. I want to work at putting together the complex mosaic of my childhood: to practice capturing feelings and experiences from the nebulous seething of memory and yank them out into black-and-white on the typewriter. Like in my attempt: "The Two Gods of Alice Denway."

Remember Florence-across-the-street, who had orange Japanese lanterns in her garden that used to crumple in your fingers with a dry crinkling sound? Remember how you used to lock the bathroom door (they told you not to because it might stick, and then the firemen would have to come in the window and get you) and squat in fascinated discovery over the hand mirror on the floor and defecate? God, start remembering all the things; all the little things!

The lyric abstrusities of Auden ring mystically down the circular canals of my ear and it begins to look like snow. The good gray conservative obliterating snow. Smoothing (in one white lacy euphemism after another) out all the black bleak angular unangelic nauseous ugliness of the blasted sterile world: dry buds, shrunken stone houses, dead vertical moving people all all all go under the great white beguiling wave. And come out transformed. Lose yourself in a numb dumb snow-daubed lattice of crystal and come out pure with the white virginal veneer you never had. God, the allusive illusions of the song of the cold: If winter comes can spring be ... We're nearer to spring than we were in september, i heard a bird sing in the dark of december, january, febmar, aprimay, apricots, beneath the bough. And thou, there has always furthermore in addition inescapably and forever got to be a Thou. Otherwise there is no i because i am what other people interpret me as being and am nothing if there were no people. (Like the sound of the hack-neyed tree falling axed by old saws in the proverbial forest.)

Here Plath takes a cold look at her relationship with Myron Lotz.

Power: he offers that. I am strong, in spite of being childish and weak now and then. But I *am* strong, individual, thinking, for all that. I need a strong mate: I do not want to accidentally crush and subdue him like a steamroller as I would have Bob, certainly. I must find a strong potential powerful mate who can counter my vibrant dynamic self: sexual and intellectual, and while comradely, I must admire him: respect and admiration must equate with the object of my love (that is where the remnants of paternal, godlike qualities come in). I do not want to be primarily a mother: mine cannot be a pitying and forgiving-black-sheep love: so out with the young handsome puppy. *Mentally:* He has a photographic memory, to all practical purposes—scientific to the core—a good balance—yet he appreciates and understands the most idealistic poetry—and is uniquely sensitive to literary beauty. (I have decided I cannot marry a writer or an artist—after Gordon,* I see how dangerous the conflict of egos would be—especially if the wife got all the acceptances!) So here we have a scientist, appreciative of the creative arts: lovely. My writing could proceed well, if it proceeds at all, in such a noncompetitive and benevolent frame. Contrariwise, for him I would enjoy, I think, homemaking and pleasing his taste in food—while continuing to serve as a *life force*—physically and mentally stimulating and sustaining.

February 18. "Oh, I would like to get in a car and be driven off into the mountains to a cabin on a wind-howling hill and be raped in a huge lust like a cave woman, fighting, screaming, biting in a ferocious ecstasy of orgasm . . ." That sounds nice, doesn't it? Really delicate and feminine. . . . Do you think passionate people subconsciously consider a physical disability as an attack on sexual powers? I wonder at my morbid obsession with daydreams this past month.

February 20. Reading critical books about Yeats all day today, meals in bed, and the good corn-thickened soup and tuna salad, lush with mayonnaise and pink succulent laced shreds of meat, and sliced quarters of hard-boiled egg, slick rubbery white crescents cradling the brilliant yellow powdery yolk, cool long gulps of milk, the savory brown resilience of gingerbread— and tonight the warm glutinous cheese-curded macaroni, green

---

*Gordon Lameyer, a boyfriend who was also a poet

lima beans mealy and good on the tongue, and a sweet syrupy mash of peach slices. Somehow I am very thirsty, always, and the leg feels queer. Yesterday Dr. Chrisman cut it out of the cast and lifted the white plaster lid like a gravedigger opening a sealed coffin. The corpse of my leg lay there, horrible, dark with clotted curls of black hair, discolored yellow, wasted shapeless by a two-month interment. I felt very cold and exposed and vulnerable, and the X rays showed "it wasn't completely mended." Whirlpool bath at infirmary, and the skin flaking off raw and white and sore. Scraped at it with a razor at home gritting teeth at ugly thing: didn't want to claim it. Almost fell on stairs, stumbled on leg, felt sharp tingling pain. Not completely mended. Does that mean I don't walk on it for another month? Or do I bury the poor orphaned half-dead thing in another cast? Stepped on it today. Lightning didn't strike; didn't fall to floor. Queer: interim and rehabilitation is the worst, also indefiniteness. Classes missed, Myron called (voice and senses leave me when I talk to him suddenly on phone), car maybe not coming tomorrow, another falling of towers and toppling of masonry. I feel stuffy, as if there were not enough air to breathe—hot, and uneasy. Two months of no exercise have made me weak and phlegmatic mentally and physically. On the short walk from here to the libe I drink the cold pure night air and the clear unbelievably delicate crescent-moonlight with a greedy reverence. Days are bizarre collections of hothouse languidities, mystical and poignant sensuous quotations ("white thy fambles, red thy gan, and thy quarrons dainty is . . ." Dark, liquid loveliness of words half dimly understood). Wrote first villanelle today and yesterday; another angle on the passage of time: tried to juxtapose the eternal paradox of ephemeral mortal beauty and eternal passage of time—a few puns: "plot" (course as well as with cunning) and "schemes" (patterns as well as treachery). What I've been getting around to saying all this time is: want to quote from Yeats books something that struck me re Dryden's translation of Lucretius: "The tragedy of sexual intercourse is the perpetual virginity of the soul." "Sexual intercourse is an attempt to solve the eternal antinomy, doomed to failure because it takes place only on one side of the gulf." Swedenborg: "The sexual intercourse of angels is a conflagration of the whole being. . . ."

* * *

Sunday, March 1. Sunlight raying ethered through the white-net of the new formal bought splurgingly yesterday in a burst of ecstatic rightness. Silver high heels are the next purchase—symbolizing my emancipation from walking flat-footed on the ground. Silver-winged bodice of strapless floating-net gown. It is unbelievable that it could be so right! Comparing the junior prom of this year with the junior prom of two years ago is grossly unfair—the white naïve flat-footed puritanism of the innocent kiss then and the ecstasy of idealism (to topple half a year hence), and the rational exquisitely mature mental and physical heights of *this* promising event elude comparison. I want to be silverly beautiful for him: a sylvan goddess. Honestly, life for me is certainly a gyre, spiraling up, comprehending and including the past, profiting by it, yet transcending it! I am going to make it my job to see that I never get caught revolving in one final repetitive circle of stagnation. Anyhow, God knows when I've felt this blissful beaming euphoria, this ineluctable ecstasy! I can't stop effervescing: I have so many merry little pots bubbling away in the fire of my enthusiasm: Myron, future trips, modern poetry, Yeats, Sitwell, T. S. Eliot, W. H. Auden, villanelles, maybe *Mlle*, maybe *The New Yorker* or *The Atlantic* (poems sent out make blind hope spring eternal—even if rejections are immanent), spring: biking, breathing, sunning, tanning. All so lovely and potential.

April 27. Listen and shut up, oh, ye of little faith. On one certain evening in a certain year 1953 a certain complex of pitched tensions, physiological urges, and mental dragonflies combined to fill one mortal imperfect Eve with a fierce full rightness, force, and determination corresponding to the ecstasy experienced by the starving saint on the desert who feels the crackling cool drops of God on his tongue and sees the green angels sprouting up like dandelion greens, prolific and infinitely unexpected.

Factors: something *did* happen. Russell Lynes of *Harper's* bought 3 poems ("Doomsday," "Go Get the Goodly Squab" and "To Eva Descending the Stair") for $100. Signifying what? First real professional acceptance, God, and all the possibilities. To keep cracking open my mind and my vocabulary, breaking myself into larger more magnanimous orbits of understanding.

Things have been happening like a chain of firecrackers, but every brilliant explosive fact must have a legitimate cause and effect. Editor of *Smith Review* this morning: the one office on campus I coveted; back to balance about psychology; prospect of Harvard Summer School—holiday tables under the trees. New York and Ray [a friend from The Belmont Hotel job] (and neurology and brilliance) this weekend. New Haven and Mike [Lotz] (sun, beach, strong good love) the next.

Tonight, spring, plural, fertile, offering up clean green leaf whorls to a soft moon covered with fuzz-fractured clouds. And God, the listening to Auden read in [Elizabeth] Drew's front living room, and Vind questioning, darting scintillant wit. My Plato! pedestrian I! And Drew (exuberant exquisitely frail intelligent Elizabeth), saying: "Now that is really difficult."

Auden tossing his big head back with a twist of wide ugly grinning lips, his sandy hair, his coarse tweedy brown jacket, his burlap-textured voice and the crackling brilliant utterances—the naughty mischievous boy genius, and the inconsistent white hairless skin of his legs, and the short puffy stubbed fingers—and the carpet slippers—beer he drank, and smoked Lucky Strikes in a black holder, gesticulating with a white new cigarette in his hands, holding matches, talking in a gravelly incisive tone about how Caliban is the natural bestial projection, Ariel the creative imaginative, and all the intricate lyrical abstrusities of their love and cleavage, art and life, the mirror and the sea. God, god, the stature of the man. And next week, in trembling audacity, I approach him with a sheaf of the poems. Oh, god, if this is life, half-heard, glimpsed, smelled, with beer and cheese sandwiches and the god-eyed tall-minded ones, let me never go blind, or get shut off from the agony of learning, the horrible pain of trying to understand.

Tomorrow we'll start running again after the leering clockwork chameleon that looks like the prince or princess in the fairy tales, but turns into a warted toad or a pincered cockroach when touched by mortal hands. Where, where to find that quality I long for that will grow goodly and green for fifty years—is it mind? Then Ray has mind, with a weaker body: thin, with no height, and you think of flat shoes, all your life long feeling big and swollen, lying like mother earth on your back and being raped by a humming entranced insect and begetting thousands of little white eggs in a gravel pit, and you think of Florida and sun, constraints of his society, loud clothes, all shrinking, paling, before the mind, and he perhaps ficklely loving delicate butterfly-like women of the insect kind, but there was the expert moving of his hands and head and tongue and the surprised knowledge that honest love could ignore defects and discrepancies of matter in the presence of lightning-crackling mind. Once I thought I could live with him, too. God, how I ricochet between certainties and doubts. The doubts of past convictions only cast aspersions on present assurances and maliciously suggest that those, too, shall pass into the realm of the null and the void—and then tonight the sight of the poetic one, the wanting... what? to conquer? to talk? This first... after the "don't kill me when you make love to me..." echoing in my ears. All these boys I love pieces of, and 3 years ago that would have been fine, but now, there is not one I know well enough, surely enough, to say, if asked: "O.K., here is a certificate guaranteeing that a Smith Phi-Bete-to-be, (maybe) potential minor poetess and story writer, onetime dilettante artist, reasonably healthy and attractive, alive, thinking, tall, sensuous, powerful, colorful white woman, age 21, is handing you 50 years during which she will love your faults, honor your bestialities, obey your whimsies, ignore your mistresses, nurse your progeny, paper the walls of your house with flowers, and adore you as her dying mortal god, conceive babies and new recipes in labor and travail, and remain faithful to you until you both rot and the inevitable synesthesia of death sets in." I have to be terribly sure it (marriage) is neither a glamorous gamble nor an ephemeral escape. I know none of these three boys* well enough to give prognosis for a lifetime, even a vague general one. I would have to *live* with a personality over a period of frequent contact... The only boy I know really well is the one I know well enough that I can never marry nor love—oh, a love, a growing sharing would be so good, so uncomplex. And in these rapid most complex days of speed, mood, and psychology, it is relatively impossible to "know" anyone, as it is impossible to "know" oneself. Suddenly everyone else is very married and happy, and one is very alone, and

---

*Dick Norton, Gordon Lameyer, and Myron Lotz

bitter about eating a boiled tasteless egg by oneself every morning and painting on a red mouth to smile oh-so-sweetly at the world with.

One relies so on single symbols which supposedly presage large assumptions. He goes to ballets, ergo he must be sensitive and artistic. He quotes poetry, ergo he must be a kindred spirit. He reads Joyce, ergo he must be a genius.

Let's face it, I am in danger of wanting my personal absolute to be a demigod of a man, and as there aren't many around, I often unconsciously manufacture my own. And then, I retreat and revel in poetry and literature where the reward value is tangible and accepted. I really do not think deeply, really deeply. I want a romantic nonexistent hero.

May 14. Tonight after ushering at "Ring Around the Moon" I started back alone to the house. It had just stopped raining; and I got halfway up the steps, and thought of how I would not be alone when I came in, and I turned and walked away down the sodden walk, down an alley, with stands of water in the hollows of the faulted paving, and the air warm and sweet with dogwood and flowering smells, and the lights quaint and soft, and the wet streets reflecting them. It was good to walk faceless and talk to myself again, to ask where I was going, and who I was, and to realize that I had no idea, that all I could tell you was my name, and not my heritage; my daily schedule for the next week, and not the reason for it; my plans for the summer, and not the purpose I had whittled out for my life.

I am lucky: I am at Smith because I wanted it and worked for it. I am going to be a Guest Editor on *Mlle* in June because I wanted it and worked for it. I am being published in *Harper's* because I wanted it and worked for it. Luckily I could translate wish to reality by the work.

But now, although I am a pragmatic Machiavellian at heart, I find the 3 men in my life distant because I acted first and post-mortemed afterward. I did not think clearly: "I want this; I must do thus to obtain this. I will hence do thus. Ergo, I shall get what I want." Stupid girl, you will never win anyone through pity. You must create the right kind of dream, the sober adult kind of magic: illusion born from disillusion.

Is anyone anywhere happy? No, not unless they are living

in a dream or in an artifice that they or someone else has made. For a time I was lulled in the arms of a blind optimism with breasts full of champagne and nipples made of caviar. I thought she was true, and that the true was the beautiful. But the true is the ugly mixed up everywhere, like a peck of dirt scattered through your life. The true is that there is no security, no artifice to stop the unsavory changes, the rat race, the death unwish— the winged chariot, the horns and motors, the Devil in the clock. Love is a desperate artifice to take the place of those two original parents who turned out not to be omnisciently right gods, but a rather pedestrian pair of muddled suburbanites who, no matter how bumblingly they tried, never could quite understand how or why you grew up to your 21st birthday. Love is not this if you make it something creatively other. But most of you are not very good at making things. "Beauty is in the eye of the beholder." What a pat speech. Why do my beheld beauties vanish and deform themselves as soon as I look twice?

I want to love somebody because I want to be loved. In a rabbit fear I may hurl myself under the wheels of the car because the lights terrify me, and under the dark blind death of the wheels I will be safe. I am very tired, very banal, very confused. I do not know who I am tonight. I wanted to walk until I dropped and not complete the inevitable circle of coming home. I have lived in boxes above, below, and down the hall from girls who think hard, feel similarly, and long companionably, and I have not bothered to cultivate them because I did not want to, could not, sacrifice the time. People know who I am, and the harder I try to know who they are, the more I forget their names—I want to be alone, and yet there are times when the liquid eye and the cognizant grin of a small monkey would send me into a crying fit of brotherly love. I work and think alone. I live with people, and act. I love and cherish both. If I knew now what I wanted, I would know when I saw it who he was.

I want to write because I have the urge to excel in one medium of translation and expression of life. I can't be satisfied with the colossal job of merely living. Oh, no, I must order life in sonnets and sestinas and provide a verbal reflector for my 60-watt lighted head. Love is an illusion, but I would willingly fall for it if I could believe in it. Now everything seems either far and sad and cold, like a piece of shale at the bottom of a canyon—or warm and near and unthinking, like the pink dogwood. God, let me think clearly and brightly; let me live, love, and say it well in good sentences, let me someday see who I am and why I accept 4 years of food, shelter, and exams and papers without questioning more than I do. I am tired, banal, and now I am getting not only monosyllabic but also tautological. Tomorrow is another day toward death (which can never happen to me because I am I, which spells invulnerable). Over orange juice and coffee even the embryonic suicide brightens visibly.

Only the following entry has survived of the Guest Editor experience at Mademoiselle. *The succeeding entries are the only ones preceding Plath's suicide attempt on August 24, 1953.*

NEW YORK

June 19, 1953. All right, so the headlines blare the two of them [the Rosenbergs] are going to be killed at eleven o'clock tonight. So I am sick at the stomach. I remember the journalist's report, sickeningly factual, of the electrocution of a condemned man, of the unconcealed fascination on the faces of the onlookers, of the details, the shocking physical facts about the death, the scream, the smoke, the bare honest unemotional reporting that gripped the guts because of the things it didn't say.

The tall beautiful catlike girl who wore an original hat to work every day rose to one elbow from where she had been napping on the divan in the conference room, yawned, and said with beautiful bored nastiness: "I'm so glad they are going to die." She gazed vaguely and very smugly around the room, closed her enormous green eyes, and went back to sleep.

The phones are ringing as usual, and the people planning to leave for the country over the long weekend, and everybody is lackadaisical and rather glad and nobody very much thinks about how big a human life is, with all the nerves and sinews and reactions and responses that it took centuries and centuries to evolve.

They were going to kill people with those atomic secrets. It is good for them to die. So that we can have the priority of killing people with those atomic secrets which are so very jealously and specially and inhumanly ours.

There is no yelling, no horror, no great rebellion. That is the appalling thing. The execution will take place tonight; it is too bad that it could not be televised . . . so much more realistic and beneficial than the run-of-the-mill crime program. Two real people being executed. No matter. The largest emotional reaction over the United States will be a rather large, democratic, infinitely bored and casual and complacent yawn.

WELLESLEY

Letter to an Over-grown, Over-protected, Scared, Spoiled Baby:

This is the immediate time for a decision: whether or not to go to Harvard Summer School. It is not the time to lose the appetite, feel empty, jealous of everyone in the world because they have fortunately been born inside themselves and not inside you.

It is a time to balance finances, weighty problems, objectives and plans for the future, to decide on relative importances. I am not a wealthy girl; I have a very small amount of money with which to meet next year's college expenses. The outgo this last month, and the amount spent on clothes ate up just about all of my winnings and prizes. Originally, my biggest satisfaction was that I would not have to get a job this summer and could sit down and write and learn shorthand, a practical skill that I could not afford to go to school to take, and that Mother could teach me in my own backyard . . . that I could keep up along with typing and thus never be at wits' end for a job. When I apply for jobs after college, or after graduate school, I will want to know typing and shorthand . . . my bargaining power will be much better.

Then I decided I would go to Harvard Summer School for several reasons: I wanted to take Frank O'Connor's writing course because I thought that I might be able to sell some of the stories I wrote for it. I also decided to try elementary psychology so the way would be open to take psych courses later, if I wanted to. I could thus combine the practical and the creative. Now the O'Connor course is closed to me.* Yet I still want the chance to write on my own, even if the prospect scares me to death because it means thinking and working on my own. So I would not want to take the full program of study, and thereby lose the main chance to have a "go" at writing for the most auspicious time in years . . . and probably the only such long time in at least a year. This is the summer where I build up a backlog. O.K., so I'd have to give up my scholarship to summer school, which means paying the same price for one course, which I might not give a damn about in the long run, or might agonize over every time I thought of the money (about $250) going out for it. I would have literally not more than $100 to $200 left at the end of my senior year . . . a mere pittance.

If I went to summer school, I would be meeting new people, no doubt queer people and nice people; I would have the library, and the "activities" and Cambridge. It might be a very nice luxury. Yet, I would be seeing Sally, and Jane, and hearing about their fascinating jobs, and feeling, in spite of myself, guilty as hell: and sourly spending $250 is something that in reality I do not care to do. Either choice I make will have to be followed out with a scheduled program, a creative and very disciplined outlook, or I am not worth the paper this is written on.

If I live at home, I will be alone all summer, unless I seek out neighbors. I will be not earning money, and not really spending money. I will have to be cheerful and constructive, and schedule my day much harder than if at Harvard. I will learn about shopping and cooking, and try to make Mother's vacation happy and good. That in itself would be worthwhile. I will work two hours a day at shorthand, and brush up my typing. I will write for three or four hours Each Day, and read for the same amount of time from a reading list I draw up carefully, so I won't read hit or miss.

I do not want to think that I am staying home because of

---

*Her application was rejected, which was a great blow.

fear: jealousy of Marcia and Mike, of Sally and Jane in their casual productive job-home. I like to be busy, to work hard, and I would in contrast feel lazy and guilty, as I said. Which shows how weak I am in one way.

Face this realistically. I will have to give up my scholarship if I go to Harvard. . . . The decision is my own. I have to be creatively "existential." It is damn hard, because I keep wanting to crawl back into the womb. . . .

In the middle of the summer, I will begin reading Joyce, so that I'll have a bulk read in time to begin thinking about the writing of my theses chapters, right at the beginning of the fall. I Will Not Lie Fallow or Be Lazy. And at home, I will not have the little man in my head mocking: is this worth it, worth it, worth it, this course for $250, while your mother does all the work at home?

I must make choices clearly, honestly, without getting sick so I can't eat, which is in itself a defense mechanism that wants to revert to childhood tactics to get sympathy and avoid responsibility.

At home, I must not also begin dreaming up idealistic pictures of summer school, envy of Marcia, who after all has a job to justify her rich summer (and who last summer had a hell of a time).

And by the way, everything in life is writable about if you have the outgoing guts to do it, and the imagination to improvise. The worst enemy to creativity is self-doubt. And you are so obsessed by your coming necessity to be independent, to face the great huge man-eating world, that you are paralyzed: your whole body and spirit revolt against having to commit yourself to a particular role, to a particular life which Might Not bring out the Best you have in you. Living takes a very different set of responses and attitudes from this academic hedony . . . and you have to be able to make a real creative life for Yourself, before you can expect anyone Else to provide one ready-made for you. You big baby.

Hardest thing is to know where and how to Give of Yourself . . . and that's a problem to ponder this summer.

Can you earn money writing? You have, in the teenage group, but the competition in the slicks is phenomenal. . . . The Literary Market seems at once harder and more esthetically rewarding.

I AM NOT GOING TO HARVARD SUMMER SCHOOL.

I will learn shorthand, typing, and write and read and write and read, and talk to myself about attitudes, see the Aldriches and neighbors, and be nice and friendly and outgoing, and forget my damn ego-centered self in trying to learn and understand about what makes life rich and what is most important.

You are an inconsistent and very frightened hypocrite: you wanted *time* to think, to find out about yourself, your ability to write, and now that you have it: practically 3 months of godawful time, you are paralyzed, shocked, thrown into a nausea, a stasis. You are plunged so deep in your own very private little whirlpool of negativism that you can't do more than force yourself into a rote where the simplest actions become forbidding and enormous. Your mind is incapable of thinking. If you went to Harvard, all your time would be planned, diagrammed for you — practically the way it will be at Smith next year: and just now that kind of security seems desirable — it is just another way of absolving you of taking responsibility for your own actions and planning, really, although now the issue is so confused it is hard to think *which* choice would take the most guts: and which kind of guts. Marcia is working and taking a course — you are doing neither: the woman at the vocational office said you should know shorthand: you can now learn it — you won't have it this good again, baby. You could even take psych at B. U. — if you had the guts to commute . . . but why blind yourself by taking course after course: when if you are anybody, which you are no doubt not, you should *not* be bored, but should be able to think, accept, *affirm* — and not retreat into a masochistic mental hell where jealousy and fear make you want to stop eating. Don't *ignore* all the people you could know, shutting yourself up in a numb defensive vacuum; *please* yank yourself up and don't spend years gaping in horror at the one time in your life you'll have a chance to *prove* your own discipline. . . . Catch perspective, kid — learn shorthand; study French: THINK CONSTRUCTIVELY — and get some respect for yourself. You always said you could write a *Ladies' Home Journal* story if you tried hard. NOW is the time to analyze, to recreate *in your own mind* — not merely to shovel the hole full of other people and their words. Now is the time to conjure up words and ideas on your own. You are frozen mentally —

scared to get going, eager to crawl back to the womb. First think: here is your room—here is your life, your mind: don't panic. Begin writing, even if it is only rough and ununified. First, pick your market: *Ladies' Home Journal* or *Discovery*? *Seventeen* or *Mlle*? Then pick a topic. Then think. If you can't think outside yourself, you can't write.... Get a *plot*. Make it funny. Be big and glad for other people and make them happy. If you do nothing, make 2 people happy. Tomorrow...*Smith Quarterly* article—each night, map out the next day's plans. If Dick could write and create alone, so can you. Pray to yourself for the guts to make the summer *work*. One *sale*: that would help. Work for that.

A.M. Right now you are sick in your head.... You fool— you are afraid of being alone with your own mind. You just better learn to know yourself, to make sure decisions before it is too late. Three *months*, you think, scared to death. You want to call that man [evidently a psychiatrist]. You earned enough money to go. Why don't you go? Stop thinking selfishly of razors and self-wounds and going out and ending it all. Your room is not your prison. You are. And Smith cannot cure you; no one has the power to cure you but yourself. Be an introvert for three months—stop thinking of noise, names, dances— you could have bought it. The price of all this is high. Neurotic women. Fie. Get a job. Learn shorthand at night. NOTHING EVER REMAINS THE SAME.

July 14. All right, you have gone the limit—you tried today, after 2 hours only of sleep for the last two nights, to shut yourself off from responsibility altogether: you looked around and saw everybody either married or busy and happy and think- ing and being creative, and you felt scared, sick, lethargic, worst of all, not wanting to cope. You saw visions of yourself in a straightjacket, and a drain on the family, murdering your mother in actuality, killing the edifice of love and respect built up over the years in the hearts of other people. You began to do something that is against all you believe in. Impasse: male relations; jealousy and frantic fear; female relations: ditto. Loss of perspective, humor. Colossal desire to escape, retreat, not talk to *anybody*. Thesis panic—lack of other people to be with—recrimination for past wrong choices. Fear, big and ugly and sniveling. Fear of not succeeding intellectually and academically: the worst blow to security. Fear of failing to live up to the fast and furious prize-winning pace of these last years—and any kind of creative life. Perverse desire to retreat into *not caring*. I am incapable of loving or feeling now: self-induced.

Out of it, kid. You are making monumental obstacles of what should be taken for granted—living on a past reputation.

New York: pain, parties, work. And Gary and Ptomaine and José the cruel Peruvian and Carol vomiting outside the door all over the floor*—and interviews for TV shows, and competition, and beautiful models and Miss Abels** (capable, and heaven knows what else). And now this: shock. Utter nihilistic shock.

Read a story: Think. You can. You must, moreover, not continually run away while asleep—forget details—ignore problems—shut walls up between you and the world and all the gay bright girls—please, think—snap out of this. *Believe* in some beneficent force beyond your own limited self. God, god, god: Where are you? I want you, need you: the belief in you and love and mankind. You must not seek escape like this. You must think.

Journals have disappeared—if they existed—for the two years after Plath's breakdown in the summer of 1953. Her recovery included shock treatments and insulin therapy, but perhaps the most important element was her relationship with Dr. Ruth Beuscher,† an extraordinary therapist who played an important role in Plath's life, both at the time and for years afterward. Plath was discharged from the hospital in December 1953. When she returned to Smith in spring of 1954, she was blonder, bolder, and a famous figure on campus. In April of 1954 she met Richard Sassoon, a Yale man who was not her usual all-American type but rather continental, highly sophisticated, and related to the literary Sassoons. This relationship was a very important one for Plath. She continued to see Gor-

---

*These elements later appeared in *The Bell Jar*.
**Plath's editor at *Mademoiselle*, Cyrilly Abels
†Now the Reverend Ruth Tiffany Barnhouse, M.D.

don Lameyer off and on, and spent the summer of 1954 at Harvard Summer School studying German and living with friends from Smith. She had a highly successful senior year at Smith— winning prizes, selling poems, and finally being awarded a Fulbright to study at Newnham College, Cambridge. Mrs. Plath had surgery that summer (1955), and Sylvia decided not to work but to stay home and care for her mother. There was a new man as well, Peter Davison, who had been an editor in New York and was himself a poet; it was only a summer affair, but Davison later became a friend.

TWO

Cambridge
1955 – 1957

Smith College
1957 – 1958

Plath threw herself into Cambridge life with great enthusiasm, while still pining away for her old boyfriend, Richard Sassoon, who was in Paris. The great successes at Smith were not so easily duplicated at Cambridge, and she began to measure herself by new standards. The prospect of spending Christmas holidays in Paris with Sassoon kept her spirits up; meantime, she kept excerpts from her strange, impassioned letters to Sassoon as part of her journal.

EXCERPT FROM A LETTER TO RICHARD SASSOON IN PARIS NOVEMBER 22, 1955

words revolve in flame and keep the coliseum heart afire, reflecting orange sunken suns in the secret petals of ruined arches. yes, the glowing asbestos thorns and whistling flame flowers reflect the cells of the scarlet heart and the coliseum burns on, without a hero, on the brink of blackness. so words have power to open sesame and reveal liberal piles of golden metallic suns in the dark pit that wait to be melted and smelted in the fire of spring which springs to fuse lumps and clods into veins of radiance.

so sylvia burns yellow dahlias on her dark altar of the sun as the sun wanes to impotence and the world falls in winter. birds contract to frozen feathered buds on barren boughs and plants surrender to the omnipotent white frosts which hold all colors cruelly locked in hexagonal hearts of ice.

at midnight, when the moon makes blue lizard scales of roof shingles and simple folk are bedded deep in eiderdown, she opens the gable window with fingers frozen crisp and thin as carrots, and scatters crumbs of white bread which skip and dwindle down the roof to lie in angled gutters to feed the babes in the wood. so the hungry cosmic mother sees the world shrunk to embryo again and her children gathered sleeping back into the dark, huddling in bulbs and pods, pale and distant as the folded bean seed to her full milky love which freezes across the sky in a crucifix of stars.

so it costs ceres all that pain to go to gloomy dis and bargain for proserpine again. we wander and wait in november air gray as rat fur stiffened with frozen tears. endure, endure, and the syllables harden like stoic white sheets struck with rigor mortis on the clothesline of winter.

artificial fires burn here: leaping red in the heart of wine-glasses, smoldering gold in goblets of sherry, crackling crimson in the fairy-tale cheeks of a rugged jewish hercules hewn fresh from the himalayas and darjeeling to be sculpted with blazing finesse by a feminine pygmalion whom he gluts with mangoes and dmitri karamazov fingers blasting beethoven out of acres of piano and striking scarlatti to skeletal crystal.

fires pale askew to pink houses under the aqua backdrop sky of *bartholomew fair* where a certain whore slinks in a slip of jaundice-yellow and wheedles apples and hobbyhorses from lecherous cutpurses. water scalds and hisses in the tin guts of the kettle and ceres feeds the souls and stomachs of the many too many who love satanic earthenware tea sets, dishes heaped with barbed and quartered orange pineapple and cool green globes of grapes, and macaroon cakes that soften and cling to the hungry mouth.

when the face of god is gone and the sun pales behind wan veils of chill mist, she vomits at the gray neuter neutralities of limbo and seeks the red flames and smoking snakes that devour eternally the limbs of the damned. feeding on the furies of cassandra, she prophesies and hears the "falling glass and toppling masonry" of troy while hector pats her torn and tangled hair and murmurs: "there, there, mad sister."

god is on vacation with the pure transcendent sun and the searing heat that turns the flawed white body of our love to glass: look! how the riddle of the world is resolved in this menagerie of mated glass, how clean and sparkling the light blesses these pure serene ones! suddenly from the bed of mire they ascend to astonish the angels of heaven who keep the light of their love enshrined in ice.

see, see! how the mind and mated flesh can make man the envy of god, who masturbates in the infinite void his ego has made about him. but do not ask for these tomorrow. he is a jealous god and he has had them liquidated.

I have talked to various little dark men who keep giving me, at my request, booklets colored yellow and titled: sunshine holidays. . . .

do you realize that the name sassoon is the most beautiful name in the world. it has lots of seas of grass en masse and persian moon alone in rococo lagoon of woodwind tune where passes the ebony monsoon. . . .

I am proud again, and I will have the varying wealths of the world in my hands before I come to see you again. . . . I will have them, and they are being offered to me even now, on turkish tables and by dark alladins. I simply say, turning on my other flank, I do not want these jingling toys. I only want the moon that sounds in a name and the son of man that bears that name.

in the beginning was the word and the word was sassoon and it was a terrible word for it created eden and the golden age back to which fallen eva looks mingling her crystal tears with the yellow dahlias that sprout from the lips of her jaundiced adam.

be christ! she cries, and rise before my eyes while the blue marys bless us with singing. and when, she asks (for even eva is practical), will this resurrection occur?

EXCERPT FROM A LETTER TO RICHARD SASSOON DECEMBER 11

What concerns me among multitudes and multitudes of other sad questions which one had better try to lure aside with parfaits and sunshine, is that there is a certain great sorrow in me now, with as many facets as a fly's eye, and I must give birth to this monstrosity before I am light again. Otherwise I shall resemble a dancing elephant... I am tormented by the questions of the devils which weave my fibers with grave-frost and human dung, and have not the ability or genius to write a big letter to the world about this. When one makes of one's own heavens and hells a few hunks of neatly typewritten paper and editors are very polite and reject it, one is, in whimsy, inclined to identify editors with god's ministers. This is fatal.

Perhaps when we find ourselves wanting everything it is because we are dangerously near to wanting nothing. There are two opposing poles of wanting nothing: When one is so full and rich and has so many inner worlds that the outer world is not necessary for joy, because joy emanates from the inner core of one's being. When one is dead and rotten inside and there is nothing in the world.

I feel now as if I were building a very delicate intricate bridge quietly in the night, across the dark from one grave to another while the giant is sleeping. Help me build this O so exquisite bridge.

I want to live each day for itself like a string of colored beads, and not kill the present by cutting it up in cruel little snippets to fit some desperate architectural draft for a Taj Mahal in the future.

FRANCE

New Year's Eve, 1956. At last, the shriek of whistles, the yell of porters and the moment of intuitive silence. The train began to move. Off into the night, with the blackness of a strange land knifing past. In my mind, a map of France, irregularly squarish, with a minute Eiffel Tower marking Paris toward the north, and a line of railway tracks, like a zipper, speeding open to the south, to Marseille, to Nice and the Côte d'Azur, where perhaps in the realm of absolute fact the sun is shining and the sky is turquoise. Away from sodden mud and cutting winds of gray Cambridge, away from the freezing white frosts of a cold gray London, where the sun hung in the white mists like a bloody egg yolk. Away from the rain and wet feet of Paris, with colored lights wavering in the gutters running with water, and the Seine flowed gray and sluggish by the quais and Notre Dame lifted two towers to a lowering, thick, curded gray sky.

On the train: staring hypnotized at the blackness outside the window, feeling the incomparable rhythmic language of the wheels, clacking out nursery rhymes, summing up the moments of the mind like the chant of a broken record: saying over and over: god is dead, god is dead, going, going, going: and the pure bliss of this, the erotic rocking of the coach. France splits open like a ripe fig in the mind; we are raping the land, we are not stopping. The pretty blonde turns out the light and it is warm and dark in the compartment with the blinds into the narrow corridor pulled down, and the night landscape outside the window slowly slowly coming alive in a chiaroscuro of shadows and stars. For we are leaving the thick clouds and smoky ceiling, we are plunging through into clear moonlight, first edging the thinning clouds like curded cream, then breaking forth pure and clear, in a spinning blueness. Single lights and clusters in villages. Then the weird whiteness of roads, as if made of broken white shells, or trails of bread crumbs left by the babes in the woods. Stars, now, too, against the sky, turning in spirals, growing to look like Van Gogh stars, and the strange black trees, wind-blown, tortuous, twisted, idiosyncratic pen sketches against the sky: cypresses. And quarries, steep like a cubist painting in blocks, and slanting roof-lines and rectangular whitish shacks, bleached in the light, with geometric shadows. Then blackness again, and land lying flat under the clear moon.

Drowsing for a while, stretched out on my back on the narrow compartment seat, with the good weight of Sassoon, sleeping fitfully, on my breast. And underneath always the tireless language of the train wheels, rocking us gently, within a network of steel. Slowing, calming, into lights of Lyon, and rousing from a dizzy coma to jump down the steep train steps onto the platform where vendors are selling bottled drinks and sandwiches. We buy a bottle of red wine and two large soft rolls of white bread with ham inside. We are very hungry and rip into the large soft sandwiches with our teeth, drinking down the wine in a white paper cup, finishing the peanuts we brought in a little paper bag and the cellophane parcel of dried figs, and finally the three small tangerines which we peel, smelling the sharp fragrance as the porous skin tears open, spitting the slippery white seeds into a brown paper bag which we put under the seat with the empty wine bottle and the crisp little coats of the peanuts, scattered about whispering underfoot. Hours leap or delay on the luminous dial of Sassoon's watch. Between dozing and waking to stare out into the all-comprehensive blackness, France runs past. Secret, hidden, giving only the moon, rocky hills now, with clotted patches of whiteness, perhaps snow, probably not. Then, lifting my head sleepily once, suddenly the moon shining incredibly on water. Marseille. The Mediterranean. At last, unbelievable, the moon on that sea, that azure sea I dreamed about on maps in the sixth grade, surrounded by the pink, yellow, green and caramel countries—the pyramids and the Sphinx, the Holy Land, the classic white ruins of the Greeks, the bleeding bulls of Spain, and the stylized pairs of boys and girls in native costume, holding hands, splendid in embroidered silks.

The Mediterranean. Sleep again, and at last the pink *vin rosé* light of dawn along the back of the hills in a strange country. Red earth, orange tiled villas in yellow and peach and aqua, and the blast, the blue blast of the sea on the right. The Côte d'Azur. A new country, a new year: spiked with green explosions of palms, cacti sprouting vegetable octopuses with spiky tentacles, and the red sun rising like the eye of God out of a screaming blue sea.

EXCERPT FROM A LETTER TO RICHARD SASSOON JANUARY 15, 1956

the kind of radiance that suddenly comes over you when I look at you dressing or shaving or reading and you are suddenly more than the daily self we must live with and love, that fleeting celestial self which shines out with the whimsical timing of angels.

that confident surge of exuberance in which I wrote you has dwindled as waves do, to the knowledge that makes me cry, just this once: such a minute fraction of this life do we live: so much is sleep, tooth-brushing, waiting for mail, for metamorphosis, for those sudden moments of incandescence: unexpected, but once one knows them, one can live life in the light of their past and the hope of their future.

in my head I know it is too simple to wish for war, for open battle, but one cannot help but wish for those situations that make us heroic. living to the hilt of our total resources. our cosmic fights, when I think the end of the world is come, are so many broken shells around our growth.

sunday noon: very stingily blue whipped to white by wind from russian steppes. the mornings are god's time, and after breakfast for those five hours somehow everything is all right and most things are even possible. the afternoons however slip away faster and faster and night cheats by coming shortly after four. the dark time, the night time is worst now. sleep is like the grave, worm-eaten with dreams.

EXCERPT FROM A LETTER TO RICHARD SASSOON JANUARY 28

it would be easy to say I would fight for you, or steal or lie; I have a great deal of that desire to use myself to the hilt, and where for men, fighting is a cause, for women, fighting is for men. in a crisis, it is easy to say: I will arise and be with thee.

but what I would do...is the hardest thing for me, with my absurd streak of idealism and perfectionism: I do believe I would sit around with you and feed you and wait with you through all the necessary realms of tables and kingdoms of chairs and cabbage for those fantastic few moments when we are angels, and we are growing angels (which the angels in heaven never can be) and when we together make the world love itself and incandesce. I would sit around and read and write and brush my teeth, knowing in you there were the seeds of an angel, my kind of angel, with fire and swords and blazing power. why is it I find out so slowly what women are made for? it comes nudging and urging up in me like tulip bulbs in april.

February 19, Sunday night. To whom it may concern: Every now and then there comes a time when the neutral and impersonal forces of the world turn and come together in a thundercrack of judgment. There is no reason for the sudden terror, the feeling of condemnation, except that circumstances all mirror the inner doubt, the inner fear. Yesterday, walking quite peacefully over the Mill Lane Bridge, after leaving my bike to be repaired (feeling lost, pedestrian, impotent), smiling that smile which puts a benevolent lacquer on the shuddering fear of strangers' gazes, I was suddenly turned upon by little boys making snowballs on the dam. They began to throw them at me, openly, honestly, trying to hit. They missed every time, and with that wary judgment that comes with experience, I watched the dirty snowballs coming at me, behind and in front, and, sick with wonder, kept walking slowly, determinedly, ready to parry a good hit before it struck. But none struck, and with a tolerant smile that was a superior lie, I walked on.

Today my thesaurus, which I would rather live with on a desert isle than a bible, as I have so often boasted cleverly, lay open after I'd written the rough draft of a bad, sick poem, at 545: Deception; 546: Untruth; 547: Dupe; 548: Deceiver. The clever reviewer and writer who is an ally of the generous creative opposing forces, cries with deadly precision: "Fraud, fraud." Which has been cried solidly for six months during that dark year of hell.

...Yesterday night: coming in to the party.... Everybody has exactly the same smiling frightened face, with the look that says: "I'm important. If you only get to know me, you will see how important I am. Look into my eyes. Kiss me, and you will see how important I am."

I too want to be important. By being different. And these girls are all the same. Far off, I go to my coat with Win; he brings me my scarf as I wait on the stair, and Chris is being red-cheeked and dramatic and breathless and penitent. He wants to be scolded, and punished. That is too easy. That is what we all want.

I am rather high, and distant, and it is convenient to be led home across the snowfields. It is very cold, and all the way back I am thinking: Richard, you live in this moment. You live now. You are in my guts and I am acting because you are alive. And meanwhile you are probably sleeping exhausted and happy in the arms of some brilliant whore, or maybe even the Swiss girl who wants to marry you. I cry out to you. I want to write you, of my love, that absurd faith which keeps me chaste, so chaste, that all I have ever touched or said to others becomes only the rehearsal for you, and preserved only for this. These others now pass the time, and even so little a way over the boundary, to kisses, and touches, I cry mercy and back away, frozen. I am in black, dressed more and more often in black now. I lost one of my red gloves at a cocktail party. I only have black ones left, and they are cold and comfortless.

"Richard," I say, and tell Nat, and tell Win, and tell Chris, as I have told Mallory, and Iko, and Brian, and Martin, and David: There Is This Boy In France. And today I told John, who is an excellent listener and who is willing to sit and hear me say how I have once been happy, and once been the highest in me, and grown to the woman I am now, all because of this boy named Richard. And John says: "I could love you violently, if I let myself." But he has not let himself. Why? Because I haven't touched him, I haven't looked into his eyes with the image he wants to see there. And I could. But I am too tired, too noble, in a perverse way. It sickens me. I wouldn't want him, even as he became a victim. So I tell him casually that I won't let it happen, playfully, because it is a stillborn child. I have given birth to so many of these.

And then, bitterly, I say: do I love Richard? Or do I use him as an excuse for a noble, lonely, unloving posture, under the perverse label of faith? Using him so, would I want him on the scene, thin, nervous, little, moody, sickly? Or would I rather cherish the strong mind and soul and blazing potency alone, refined from the marring details of the real world? Coward.

And coming into the dining room unexpectedly at breakfast, the three bright ones turn with a queer look and go on talking the way they do when Mrs. Milne [the housemother] comes in, in apparent continuity, veiling the subject of their words: "So strange, just staring into the fire." And they have condemned you for being mad. Just like that. Because the fear is already there, and has been for so long. The fear that all the edges and shapes and colors of the real world that have been built up again so painfully with such a real love can dwindle in a moment of doubt, and "suddenly go out" the way the moon would in the Blake poem.

A morbid fear: that protests too much. To the doctor. I am going to the psychiatrist this week, just to meet him, to know he's there. And, ironically, I feel I need him. I need a father. I need a mother. I need some older, wiser being to cry to. I talk to God, but the sky is empty, and Orion walks by and doesn't speak. I feel like Lazarus: that story has such a fascination. Being dead, I rose up again, and even resort to the mere sensation value of being suicidal, of getting so close, of coming out of the grave with the scars and the marring mark on my cheek which (is it my imagination?) grows more prominent: paling like a death-spot in the red, windblown skin, browning darkly in photographs, against my grave winter-pallor. And I identify too closely with my reading, with my writing. I *am* Nina in *Strange Interlude*; I *do* want to have husband, lover, father and son, all at once. And I depend too desperately on getting my poems, my little glib poems, so neat, so small, accepted by *The New Yorker*. To revenge myself on the blond one [another American student Plath perceived as a rival], as if the mere paper dykes of print can keep out the creative flood which annihilates all envy, all mere niggling fearful jealousy. Be generous.

Yes. That is what Stephen Spender misses in Cambridge criticism. And what I miss in the miserly backbiting which jokes and picks at grotesqueries: what of ourselves: Jane, gesturing clumsily with knives, knocking over toasters and table silver, breaking Gordon's necklace with awkward clutching mirth, taking supper from Richard, sleep and a room and a key from me, and never caring, utterly casual. How symbolic can we get? Resentment eats, killing the food it eats. Can she resent? She is on the side of the big, conquering boys, the creative ones. We have the impetuous puppies. Could we find those others? We have our Chris, our Nat. But do we?

Generous. Yes, today, I forgave Chris. For deserting me, and hurting me a little, even as the two faceless girls he has known hurt me, only because, a woman, I fight all women for my men. My men. I am a woman, and there is no loyalty, even between mother and daughter. Both fight for the father, for the son, for the bed of mind and body. I also forgave John, for having a rotten tooth, and a lousy pallor, because he was human, and I felt "I need human kind." Even John, as he sat there, distanced by those wise words of ours, even he could be a father. And I cry so to be held by a man; some man, who is a father.

So, now I shall talk every night. To myself. To the moon. I shall walk, as I did tonight, jealous of my loneliness, in the blue-silver of the cold moon, shining brilliantly on the drifts of fresh-fallen snow, with the myriad sparkles. I talk to myself and look at the dark trees, blessedly neutral. So much easier than facing people, than having to look happy, invulnerable, clever. With masks down, I walk, talking to the moon, to the neutral impersonal force that does not hear, but merely accepts my being. And does not smite me down. I went to the bronze boy whom I love, partly because no one really cares for him, and brushed a clot of snow from his delicate smiling face. He stood there in the moonlight, dark, with snow etching his limbs in white, in the semicircle of the privet hedge, bearing his undulant dolphin, smiling still, balancing on one dimpled foot.

And he becomes the child in "When We Dead Awaken." And Richard will give me no child. And it is his child I could want. To bear, to have growing. The only one whom I could stand to have a child with. Yet. I have a fear, too, of bearing a deformed child, a cretin, growing dark and ugly in my belly, like that old corruption I always feared would break out from behind the bubbles of my eyes. I imagine Richard here, being with me, and my growing big with his child. I ask for less and less. I would face him, and say simply: I am sad that you are not strong, and do not swim and sail and ski, but you have a strong soul, and I will believe in you and make you invincible on this earth. Yes, I have that power. Most women do, to one degree or another. Yet the vampire is there, too. The old, primal hate. That desire to go round castrating the arrogant ones who become such children at the moment of passion.

How the circling steps in the spiral tower bring us back to where we were! I long for Mother, even for Gordon, though his weaknesses . . . sicken me. And he will be financially comfortable. And he is handsome and strong. He skis, swims, yet all the attributes of god could not console me for his weak mind and his physical weakness. God, I would almost have him just to prove he was weak, although my doubt would not let him have the chance to be strong. Unless I were very careful. I would like him to be strong, too. Only there is so little hope, it is so late.

The only perfect love I have is for my brother. Because I cannot love him physically, I shall always love him. And be jealous of his wife, too, a little. Strange, that having lived in such passion, such striking and tears, such fierce joy, I could turn so cold, so disgusted, at all the superfluous playings with others, those flash attractions that seem my doom, now, because each one brings me so much closer to Richard. And still I hope there will be some man in Europe whom I will meet and love and who will free me from this strong idol. Whom I accept even in the heart of his weakness, whom I can make strong, because he gives me a goal and mind to work with.

And now it grows late, late. And I have the old beginning-of-the-week panic, because I cannot read and think enough to meet my little academic obligations, and I have not written at all since the Vence story (which will be rejected with *The New Yorker* rejection of my poems, and even as I bravely say so, I hope I am lying, because my love for Richard is in the story, and my wit, a little bit, and I want to have it frozen in print, and not rejected: see, how dangerous, I again identify with rejections too much!). But how can I go on being quiet, without a soul to talk to wholly here who is not somehow drastically involved, or near enough to at least be glad that I am unhappy. I want to cry to Richard, to all my friends at home, to come and rescue me. From my insecurity, which I must fight through myself. Finishing the next year here, enjoying the pressure of reading, thinking, while at my back is always the mocking tick: A Life Is Passing. My Life.

So it is. And I waste my youth and days of radiance on barren ground. How I cried that night I wanted to go to bed, and there was no one, only my dreams of Christmas, and the last year with Richard, whom I have so loved. And I drank the last of the bad sherry, and cracked a few nuts, which were all sour and withered to nothing inside, and the material, inert world mocked me. Tomorrow what? Always patching masks, making excuses for having read a bare half of what I purposed. Yet a life is passing.

I long to permeate the matter of this world: to become anchored to life by laundry and lilacs, daily bread and fried eggs, and a man, the dark-eyed stranger, who eats my food and my body and my love and goes around the world all day and comes back to find solace with me at night. Who will give me a child, that will bring me again to be a member of that race which throws snowballs at me, sensing perhaps the rot at which they strike?

Well; Elly is coming this summer (and Mother and Mrs. Prouty) and Sue next fall. I love both girls,* and for once, with them can be wholly woman, and we can talk and talk. I am lucky. That is not long to wait. Yet now, how much do I give? Nothing. I am selfish, scared, crying too much to save myself for my phantom writing. But at any rate it is better than last term, when I was going mad night after night being a screaming whore in a yellow dress. A mad poet. How clever of Dick Gilling; but he is very intuitive. I had not the heart, not the flexible heart, not the guts. But I refused to go on, knowing I could not be big, refusing to be small. I retreated, to work. And it *has* been better: 15 plays a week instead of two. Number? Not only that, but a real feeling of mastery, of occasional insight. And that is what we wait for.

Will Richard ever need me again? Part of my bargain is that I will be silent until he does. Why is it that the man must so often take the lead? Women can do so much, but apart like this, I can do nothing, shut off from writing him as I am by a kind of honor and pride (I refuse to babble anymore about how

*Old friends from home

I love him) and I must wait until he needs me. If ever, in the next five years. And look, with love and faith, not turning sour and cold and bitter, to help others. That is salvation. To give of love inside. To keep love of life, no matter what, and give to others. Generously.

Again Plath found herself slipping into a very serious depression.

February 20, Monday. Dear Doctor: I am feeling very sick. I have a heart in my stomach which throbs and mocks. Suddenly the simple rituals of the day balk like a stubborn horse. It gets impossible to look people in the eye: corruption may break out again? Who knows. Small talk becomes desperate.

Hostility grows, too. That dangerous, deadly venom which comes from a sick heart. Sick mind, too. The image of identity we must daily fight to impress on the neutral, or hostile, world, collapses inward; we feel crushed. Standing in line in the hall, waiting for a lousy dinner of hard-boiled egg in cheese-cream sauce, mashed potatoes and sallow parsnips, we overheard one girl say to another: "Betsy is depressed today." It seems almost an incredible relief to know that there is someone outside one-self who is not happy all the time. We must be at low ebb when we are this far into the black: that everyone else, merely because they are "other," is invulnerable. That is a damn lie.

But I am foundering in relativity again. Unsure. And it is damn uncomfortable; with men (Richard gone, no one here to love), with writing (too nervous about rejections, too desperate and scared about bad poems; but do have ideas for stories; just try soon), with girls (house bristles with suspicion and frigidity; how much is paranoia transference? the damnable thing is that they can sense insecurity and meanness like animals smell blood), with academic life (have deserted French and feel tem-porarily very wicked and shirking, must atone; also, feel stupid in discussion; what the hell is tragedy? I am).

So there. With bike at repair shop, gulped down coffee-with-milk, bacon and cabbage mixed with potato, and toast, read two letters from Mother which cheered me quite a bit: she is so courageous, managing Grammy and the house, and building up a new life, hoping for Europe. I want to make happy days for her here. She also was encouraging about teaching. Once I started *doing* it I wouldn't feel so sick. That frozen inertia is my worst enemy; I get positively sick with doubt. I must break through limit after limit: learn to ski (with Gordon & Sue next year?) and perhaps teach at an army base this summer. It would do me a hell of a lot of good. If I went to Africa or Istanbul, I could do articles about the place on the side. Enough romance. Get to work.

Thank god *The Christian Science Monitor* bought the Cambridge article and drawing. They should write a letter, too, about my request to write more. *New Yorker* rejection of poems may smack me in the stomach any morning. God, it is pretty poor when a life depends on such ridiculous sitting ducks as those poems, ready for editors' grapeshot.

Tonight must *think* about O'Neill's plays; sometimes, in panic, mind goes blank, world whooshes away in void, and I feel I have to run, or walk on into the night for miles till I drop exhausted. Trying to escape? Or be alone enough to unriddle the secret of the sphinx? Men forget. Said Laughing Lazarus. And I forget the moments of radiance. I must get them down in print. Make them up in print. Be honest.

Anyway, after breakfast, leaped into clothes and started off at a dogtrot to Redpath* class at Grove Lodge through snow. Gray day, moment of joy as snow tangled with blowing hair and felt red-cheeked and healthy. Wished I'd started earlier so I could linger. Noticed rooks squatting black in snow-white fen, gray skies, black trees, mallard-green water. Impressed. Great crowd of cars and trucks at corner by Royal Hotel. Hurried to Grove Lodge, noticed gray pleasantness of stone; liked building. Went in, took off coat, and sat down among boys, none of whom spoke. Felt sick of staring industriously down at the desk like a female yogi. Blond boy rushes in to announce Redpath has flu. And we stayed up till two last night virtuously reading *Macbeth*. Which was fine. Went awestruck over old speeches: "tale of sound and fury," especially. So ironic: I pick up poetic identities of characters who commit suicide, adultery, or get murdered, and I believe completely in them for a while. What they say is True.

---

*Her Shakespeare professor

Well, then, a walk to town, staring as ever at the towers of King's Chapel, feeling happy at Market Hill, but all stores closed, except Sayle's, where I bought an identical pair of red gloves to make up for the one I lost. Can't be completely in mourning. Is it possible to love the neutral, objective world and be scared of people? Dangerous for long, but possible. I love people I don't know. I smiled at a woman coming back over the fen path, and she said, with ironic understanding, "Wonderful weather." I loved her. I didn't read madness or superficiality in the image reflected in her eyes. For once.

It is the strangers that are easiest to love at this hard time. Because they do not demand and watch, always watch. I am sick of Mallory, Iko, John, even Chris. There is nothing there for me. I am dead to them, even though I once flowered. That is the latent terror, a symptom: it is suddenly either all or nothing: either you break the surface shell into the whistling void or you don't. I want to get back to my more normal intermediate path where the *substance* of the world is permeated by my being: eating food, reading, writing, talking, shopping: so all is good in itself, and not just a hectic activity to cover up the fear that must face itself and duel itself to death, saying: A Life Is Passing!

The horror is the sudden folding up and away of the phenomenal world, leaving nothing. Just rags. Human rooks which say: Fraud. Thank God I get tired and can sleep; if that is so, all is possible. And I like to eat. And I like to walk and love the countryside here. Only these eternal questions keep knocking at the gate of my daily reality, whch I cling to like a mad lover, questions which bring the dark perilous world where all is the same, there are no distinctions, no discriminations, no space and no time: the whistling breath of eternity, not of god, but of the denying devil. So we will turn to a few thoughts on O'Neill, steel ourselves to meet accusations about French, a *New Yorker* rejection, and the hostility or, even worse, utter indifference, of the people we break bread with.

Wrote one Good Poem: "Winter Landscape with Rocks": it moves, and is athletic: a psychic landscape. Began another big one, more abstract, written from the bathtub: take care it doesn't get too general. Good night, sweet princess. You are still on your own; be stoic; don't panic; get through this hell to the generous sweet overflowing *giving* love of spring.

P.S. Winning or losing an argument, receiving an acceptance or rejection, is no proof of the validity or value of personal identity. One may be wrong, mistaken, a poor craftsman, or just ignorant—but this is no indication of the true worth of one's total human identity: past, present and future!

Crash! I am psychic, only not quite drastically enough. My baby "The Matisse Chapel," which I have been spending the imaginary money from and discussing with modest egoism, was rejected by *The New Yorker* this morning with not so much as a pencil scratch on the black-and-white doom of the printed rejection. I hid it under a pile of papers like a stillborn illegitimate baby. I shuddered at the bathos in it. Especially after I read Pete De Vries's recent scintillant "Afternoon of a Faun." There are ways and ways to have a love affair. Above all, one must not be serious about it.

Still, the accommodating mind imagines that the poems, sent a week before, must be undergoing detailed scrutiny. I shall no doubt get them back tomorrow. Maybe even with a note.

February 25, Saturday. So we are scrubbed, hair washed fresh, feeling gutted and shaky; a crisis is passed. We reassemble forces, marshal a stiff squadron of optimism, and trek. On and on. Earlier in the week I started thinking about how stupid I was to have to make all those final declarations to all those boys last term. This is ridiculous; it should not be. Not that I can't choose the people I want to spend my time with, but there must have been some reason for getting into a situation where there was nothing to do but be final and obvious.

Probably it was because I was too intense with one boy after another. That same horror came with them which comes when the paraphernalia of existence whooshes away and there is just light and dark, night and day, without all the little physical quirks and warts and knobby knuckles that make the fabric of existence: either they were all or nothing. No man is all, so, ipso facto, they were nothing. That should not be.

They were also very conspicuously not Richard; I eventually came to telling them this as if they had a fatal disease and I was oh, so sorry. Fool: be didactic, now: take boys named Iko and Hamish for what they are, which may be coffee or rum and *Troilus and Cressida* or a sandwich on the millrace. These small particular things are good in themselves. I do not have to do them with the Only Soul in the world in the Only Body that is mine, my true one. There is a certain need of practical Machiavellian living: a casualness that must be cultivated. I was too serious for Peter,* but that was mainly because he did not participate in the seriousness deeply enough to find out the gaiety beyond. Richard knows that joy, that tragic joy. And he is gone, and I should probably be glad. It would somehow be more embarrassing to have him want to marry me now. I would, I think, probably say no. Why? Because both of us are moving toward security and somehow, accepting him, he might be drowned, squashed, by the simple bourgeois life I come from with its ideals for big men, conventional men: he is some-one I could never live home with. Maybe someday he will want a home, but he is so damn far from it now. Our life would be so private: he would perhaps miss the blood background and social strata I don't come from; I would miss the healthy, physical bigness. How important is all this? I don't know: it changes, like looking in different ends of a telescope.

Anyway, I am tired, and it is Saturday afternoon and I have all the academic reading and papers to do which I should have done two days ago, but for my misery. A lousy sinus cold that blunted up all my senses, bunged up nose, couldn't smell, taste, see through rheumy eyes, or even hear, which was worse, almost. And atop of this, through the hellish sleepless night of feverish sniffling and tossing, the macabre cramps of my period (curse, yes) and the wet, mussy spurt of blood.

Dawn came, black and white graying into a frozen hell. I couldn't relax, nap, or anything. This was Friday, the worst, the very worst. Couldn't even read, full of drugs which battled and banged in my veins. Everywhere I heard bells, telephone not for me, doorbells with roses for all the other girls in the world. Utter despair. Ugly, red nose, no force. When I was psychically saddest, crash, the sky falls in and my body betrays.

Now, despite the twitch of a drying cold, I am cleansed, and once again, stoic, humorous. Made a few criticisms of action and had a chance to prove points this week. Ran through lists of men I knew here, and was appalled: granted, the ones

*Peter Davison

I'd told to take off were not worth seeing (well, it's true), but how few I knew were! And how few I knew. So, again, I decided, again, it is time to accept the party, the tea. And Derek asked me to a wine party Wednesday. I froze, like usual, but said probably and went. After the first scare (I always feel I turn into a gargoyle when too long alone, and that people will point) it was good. There was a fire, five guitar players, nice guys, pretty girls, one Norwegian blonde named Greta, who sang "On Top of Old Smoky" in Norwegian, and a divine hot wine and gin punch with lemon and nutmeg which was good to savor and relieved the tremors I'd been having prior to the breaking of the cold. Then, too, a boy named Hamish . . . asked me out next week, and, quite by chance, said he'd take me to the *St. Botolph's** party (tonight). . . .

So I am . . . not worth the really good boys; or is it me? If [my] poems were really good, there might be some chance; but, until I make something tight and riding over the limits of sweet sestinas and sonnets, away from the reflection of myself in Richard's eyes and the inevitable narrow bed, too small for a smashing act of love, until then, they can ignore me and make up pretty jokes. The only cure for jealousy that I can see is the continual, firm positive forging of an identity and set of personal values which I believe in; in other words, if I believe it is right to go to France, it is absurd to feel pangs because Someone Else has gone to Italy. There is no [reason to] compare.

The fear that my sensibility is dull, inferior, is probably justified; but I am not stupid, if I am ignorant in many ways. I will tighten up my program here, knowing as I do that it is important for me to do a small number of things well, rather than a wide number sketchily. That much of the perfectionist is still with me. In this daily game of choice and sacrifice, one needs a sure eye for the superfluous. It changes every day, too. Some days the moon is superfluous, some days, most emphatically not. . . .

The dialogue between my Writing and my Life is always in danger of becoming a slithering shifting of responsibility, of evasive rationalizing: in other words: I justified the mess I made

---

*A new literary magazine in Cambridge

of life by saying I'd give it order, form, beauty, writing about it; I justified my writing by saying it would be published, give me life (and prestige to life). Now, you have to begin somewhere, and it might as well be with life; a belief in me, with my limitations, and a strong punchy determination to fight to overcome [them] one by one: like languages, to learn French, ignore Italian (a sloppy knowledge of 3 languages is dilettantism) and revive German again, to build each solid. To build all solid.

February 25. Went to psychiatrist this morning and like him: attractive, calm and considered, with that pleasant feeling of age and experience in a reservoir; felt: Father, why not? Wanted to burst out in tears and say Father, Father, comfort me. I told him about my break-up and found myself complaining mainly about not knowing mature people here: that's it, too! There is not one person I know here whom I admire who is older than I! In a place like Cambridge, that is scandalous. It means that there are many fine people I have not met; probably many young dons and men are mature. I don't know (and, I always ask, would they want to know me?). But at Newnham there isn't one don I admire *personally*. The men are probably better, but there is no chance of getting them for supervisors, and they are too brilliant to indulge in that friendly commerce which Mr. [Al] Fisher, Mr. [Alfred] Kazin and Mr. [George] Gibian were so dear about.

Well, I shall look up Dr. Beuscher's friend, and plan to see the Carabuts at Easter. I can give them youth, enthusiasm and love to make up for the ignorances. Sometimes I feel so very stupid; yet, if I were, would I not be happy with some of the men I've met? Or is it because I'm stupid that I'm not; hardly. I long so for someone to blast over Richard; I deserve that, don't I, some sort of blazing love that I can live with. My God, I'd love to cook and make a house, and surge force into a man's dreams, and write, if he could talk and walk and work and passionately want to do his career. I can't bear to think of this potential for loving and giving going brown and sere in me. Yet the choice is so important, it frightens me a little. A lot. . . .

What I fear most, I think, is the death of the imagination.

When the sky outside is merely pink, and the rooftops merely black: that photographic mind which paradoxically tells the truth, but the worthless truth, about the world. It is that synthesizing spirit, that "shaping" force, which prolifically sprouts and makes up its own worlds with more inventiveness than God which I desire. If I sit still and don't do anything, the world goes on beating like a slack drum, without meaning. We must be moving, working, making dreams to run toward; the poverty of life without dreams is too horrible to imagine: it is that kind of madness which is worst: the kind with fancies and hallucinations would be a Bosch-ish relief.

I listen always for footsteps coming up the stairs and hate them if they are not for me. Why, why, can I not be an ascetic for a while, instead of always teetering on the edge of wanting complete solitude for work and reading, and, so much, so much, the gestures of hands and words of other human beings. Well, after this Racine paper, this Ronsard purgatory, this Sophocles, I shall write: letters and prose and poetry, toward the end of the week; I must be stoic till then.

February 26, Sunday. A small note after a large orgy. It is morning, gray, most sober, with cold white puritanical eyes, looking at me. Last night I got drunk, very very beautifully drunk, and now I am shot, after six hours of warm sleep like a baby, with Racine to read, and not even the energy to type; I am getting the dt's. Or something.

Hamish came in cab, and there was a tedious time standing slanted against the bar in Miller's with some ugly gat-toothed squat grinning guy named Meeson trying to be devastatingly clever and making intense devastating remarks about nothing. Hamish pale, pink and light blue eyes. I drank steadily the goblets with the red-gold Whiskey Macs, one after the other, and by the time we left an hour later, I felt that strong, silted-up force that makes one move through air like swimming, with brave ease. [At the party there was] the syncopated strut of a piano upstairs, and oh, it was very bohemian, with boys in turtleneck sweaters and girls being blue-eye-lidded or elegant in black. . . . Bert was looking shining and proud as if he had just delivered five babies, said something obvious about having drunk a lot, and began talking about how Luke was satanic after we had run through the poetry in *St. Botolph's* and yelled about it: [omission] . . . Luke, very very drunk, with a stupid . . . smile on his pale face, dark sideburns and rumpled hair, black-and-white checked baggy pants and a loose swinging jacket, was doing that slow crazy English jive with a green-clad girl, quite black-haired and -eyed and a good part pixie, and when they stopped dancing, Luke was chasing her around. Dan Huws being very pale, frightfully pale and freckled, and me at last saying my immortal line of introduction which has been with me ever since his clever precocious slanted review*: "Is this the better or worse half?" and he looking incredibly young to even think hard yet. . . .

By this time I had spilled one drink, partly into my mouth, partly over my hands and the floor, and the jazz was beginning to get under my skin, and I started dancing with Luke and knew I was very bad, having crossed the river and banged into the trees, yelling about the poems, and he only smiling with that far-off look. . . . He wrote those things, and he was slobbing around. Well, I was slobbing around, "blub, maundering," and I didn't even have the excuse of having written those things; I suppose if you can write sestinas which bam crash through lines and rules after having raped them to the purpose, then you can [omission] . . . smile like a . . . beelzebub.

Then the worst thing happened, that big, dark, hunky boy, the only one there huge enough for me, who had been hunching around over women, and whose name I had asked the minute I had come into the room, but no one told me, came over and was looking hard in my eyes and it was Ted Hughes. I started yelling again about his poems and quoting: "most dear unscratchable diamond" and he yelled back, colossal, in a voice that should have come from a Pole, "You like?" and asking me if I wanted brandy, and me yelling yes and backing into the next room past the smug shining bulb face of dear Bert, looking as if he had delivered at least nine or ten babies, and bang the door was shut and he was sloshing brandy into a glass and I was sloshing it at the place where my mouth was when I last knew about it.

We shouted as if in a high wind, about the review, and he saying Dan knew I was beautiful, he wouldn't have written it

---

*In which Huws had made gentle fun of a Plath piece

about a cripple, and my yelling protest in which the words "sleep with the editor" occurred with startling frequency. And then it came to the fact that I was all there, wasn't I, and I stamped and screamed yes, and he had obligations in the next room, and he was working in London, earning ten pounds a week so he could later earn twelve pounds a week, and I was stamping and he was stamping on the floor, and then he kissed me bang smash on the mouth [omission]. . . . And when he kissed my neck I bit him long and hard on the cheek, and when we came out of the room, blood was running down his face. [Omission.] And I screamed in myself, thinking: oh, to give myself crashing, fighting, to you. The one man since I've lived who could blast Richard.

And now I sit here, demure and tired in brown, slightly sick at heart. I shall go on. I shall write a detailed description of shock treatment, tight, blasting short descriptions with not one smudge of coy sentimentality, and when I get enough I shall send them to David Ross.* There will be no hurry, because I am too desperately vengeful now. But I will pile them up. I thought about the shock treatment description last night: the deadly sleep of her madness, and the breakfast not coming, the little details, the flashback to the shock treatment that went wrong: electrocution brought in, and the inevitable going down the subterranean hall, waking to a new world, with no name, being born again, and not of woman.

I shall never see him again, and the thorny limitations of the day crowd in like the spikes on the gates at Queens last night: I could never sleep with him anyway, with all his friends here and his close relation to them, laughing, talking, I should be the world's whore, as well as Roget's strumpet. I shall never see him, he will never look for me. He said my name, Sylvia, and banged a black grinning look into my eyes, and I would like to try just this once, my force against his. But he will never come, and the blond one, pure and smug and favored, looks, is it with projected pity and disgust? at this drunken amorphic slut.

But Hamish was very kind and would have fought for me. It gave him a kind of glory to take me away from them, those fiends, and I am worth fighting for, I had been nice, to him,

---

*Editor of *St. Botolph's Review*

he said. We walked out as the blond one was coming in, and Oswald said in his dry sarcasm something about "Tell us about the bone structures" and that was the last party at St. John's where I lost the red glove, as tonight I lost the red bandeau which I loved with all the redness in my heart. Somehow these sluttish nights make me have a violent nunlike passion to write and sequester myself. I shall sequester. I don't want to see anybody because they are not Ted Hughes and I never have been made a fool of by a man. They are phonies, Hamish said. [Omission.] Shall I write, and be different? Always, I grab it, the writing, hold it to me, defend, defend, against the flux, the sameness of faces. He said my name, Sylvia, in a blasting wind which shot off in the desert behind my eyes, behind his eyes, and his poems are clever and terrible and lovely.

Well, Hamish and I took an incredibly long time walking about the misty streets in the moonlight and all was blurred behind a theatrical scrim of fog, and vague boys in black gowns staggered and sang. We hid behind a car, and he said, the proctors are out after me, and I kept blithering on about having faith and being lucky, always, if you believe in something, because you can walk on water. Finally, after many strange streets which I did not know, being far-far away in a land of whiskey and merry down, saying "Ted" to the lampposts and chiding myself with "Hamish, Hamish," keeping saying it aloud to him, because he took me away safely. We came to the gates of Queens, and I wanted like a baby to lie down and rest, just peace, peace, I kept whispering. Five boys, five late babies came up, and surrounded me, gently saying, what are you doing here, are you all right, my you smell nice, that perfume, and may we kiss you, and I just stood there huddled to the iron fence, smiling like a lost lamb and saying dear, dear, babies, and then Hamish was among them, and they climbed over and crossed the wooden bridge that Newton once put together without bolts.

Hamish helped me up on the wall, and in my tight skirt, I tried to step over the spikes; they pierced my skirt, my hands, and I felt nothing, thinking from the great distance that I might at last lie on a bed of spikes and not feel it, like the yogi, like Celia Copplestone, crucified, near an anthill, at last, peace, and the nails went through my hands, and my legs were bare to the thigh, and I was over. The stigmata, I said, frozen, looking at those raw frigid hands that should have been bleeding. But they were not bleeding. I had gotten over in an act of sublime drunkenness and faith. And then we went to Hamish's room and lay on the floor by the fire and I was just so damn grateful [omission] . . . and he kind of liked me and when would I learn my lesson. When? When? So it was suddenly two thirty, and I couldn't imagine being illegal, but I was, and we managed by the light of two matches to get downstairs, and walked out, a dark lone figure against the pale white blur of snow in the dead quiet crescent court.

He beckoned, I came walking along the outer path, through the crust of snow, breaking, hearing the dry crunch and then crossing the snow field to him, waiting for the sudden flash of light, the: hey, there, you stop! and the crack of pistols. It was dead quiet, and the cold snow was in my shoes and I felt nothing. We went through the gap in the box hedge, and Hamish tested the ice on the river; he said the porter chopped it, but it was whole, and bore us, and we crossed, free, walking home. And I heard the clocks striking three in the deathly quiet of dreaming people, and climbed the stairs somehow and went somehow after hot milk to bed.

And now it is today, and I slept only six hours and am weary and waiting till next day and next to recover. I must write Racine paper, today, dinner with Mallory (can I live) and then Ronsard desperately tomorrow.

Perhaps at dinner they will be laughing at me. Well, they are hardly white, even though they are men. But I shall be sober, oh, for so long. Why won't I see him again? But I won't. I dream of banging and crashing in a high wind in London. But I want to know him sober; I want to write to him, with that kind of discipline and blaze. So I shall shut up and get some sleep tonight and tomorrow, and do so.

February 27, Monday. Briefly, most briefly. Slept late this morning, woke in dark at 11:30 feeling worthless and slack, yet stubborn. Determined to jettison all obligations for two days and recuperate. This fatigue sucks leeching at my veins. It takes more effort to write excuses than to drag around, but I confronted Miss B. after lunch, and dressed in slacks and favorite paisley velvet jersey to make me feel better, and wrote a full-page poem about the dark forces of lust: "Pursuit." It is not bad. It is dedicated to Ted Hughes.

Felt sloppy and lazy; awkward not to go out, for food, because of seeing people: there is such a difference from being able to trudge across the murky snowfields to eat and being able to translate French and write a paper. It is as if I were hypnotized. The concentrated spurts of work I've done make me feel I've been here for eons. Yet I've let French go completely, and must do penance. I have such a damned puritanical conscience that it flays me like briars when I feel I've done wrong or haven't demanded enough of myself: I feel I've cheated myself on languages: I haven't really *worked* at learning it, and I must be tutored in German next year, instead of Italian. I must do a little reading of French (one hour) every day after this week. And two hours of writing (only, when I do poems, it eats up the whole day in a slow lust which I can't resist).

New Year's rules: get only one supervision next term; enough time to write and read languages. Think up ideas for articles. My God, Cambridge is full of scientists, printing presses, theater groups, and all I need is guts to write about them. That's why reporting on assignments is good, because it gives an excuse to overcome the initial shyness. Perhaps I'll try out for Varsity next term. Also I must give a party or two: sherry, tea or even dinner for 4. We'll see. Anything to *give out*.

Mother wrote today with a good letter of maxims; skeptical as always at first, I read what struck home: "If you compare yourself with others, you may become vain or bitter—for always there will be greater and lesser persons than yourself. . . . Beyond a wholesome discipline, be gentle with yourself. You are a child of the universe no less than the trees and the stars; you have a right to be here." Those words spoke to my heart with peace, as if in comment, kindly, on my life, my days. That first touched on that ricocheting judgment I've made: despairing of the inferior, disintegrated men I know (who I can't consider for marriage) and blowing up the blond one and the figureheads all out of proportion. Envy and pride, and where's the golden mean, the man who can be mine, I his. When I start getting jealous of the five editors of *Mlle* for being married (with a pang—this might be me, that sweet word: success) or Philip Booth for writing poems for *The New Yorker* and having a wife and all that, it is time to build up some inner prowess; I am letting too much go vacant; I must build up a little series of sitting ducks, possible ambitions, to knock down, or I'll find *myself* sitting at the beginning of Easter vacation, addled as an egg, twiddling my thumbs. We get well first, then we work. Meanwhile, read Hopkins for solace.

Apparently this was a draft of a letter addressed to Richard Sassoon, but not mailed, as Plath explains on p. 117.

March 1, Thursday. It is somehow March and very late, and outside a warm large wind is blowing so that the trees and clouds are torn and the stars are scudding. I have been gliding on that wind since noon, and coming back tonight, with the gas fire wailing like the voice of a phoenix, and having read Verlaine and his lines cursing me, and having just come newly from Cocteau's films *La Belle et la Bête* and *Orphée*, can you see how I must stop writing letters to a dead man and put one on paper which you may tear or read or feel sorry for.

So it is. Stephen Spender was at sherry this afternoon, blue-eyed and white-haired and long since become a statue who says "India, it depresses me terribly" and tells of the beggars who will always be beggars throughout eternity. Young men are leaving ships full of flowers and poems, and souls — delicate as snowdrops — duck-belled [sic] white heads in my teacups.

I can hear the wounded, miraculous furry voice of the dear *bête* whispering so slow through the palace of floating curtains. And the Angel Heurtebise and Death melt through mirrors like water. Only in your eyes did the winds come from other planets, and it cuts me so, when you speak to me through every word of French, through every single word I look up bleeding in the dictionary.

I thought that your letter was all one could ask; you gave me your image, and I made it into stories and poems; I talked about it for a while to everyone and told them it was a bronze statue, a bronze boy with a dolphin, who balanced through the winter in our gardens with snow on his face, which I brushed off every night I visited him.

I made your image wear different masks, and I played with it nightly and in my dreams. I took your mask and put it on other faces which looked as if they might know you when I had been drinking. I performed acts of faith to show off: I climbed a tall spiked gate over a moat at the dead hour of three in the morning under the moon, and the men marveled, for the spikes went through my hands and I did not bleed.

Very simply, you were not wise to give me your image. You should know your woman, and be kind. You expect too much of me; you know I am not strong enough to live merely in that abstract Platonic realm out of time and flesh on the other side of all those mirrors.

I need you to do this one more thing for me. Break your image and wrench it from me. I need you to tell me in very definite concrete words that you are unavailable, that you do not want me to come to you in Paris in a few weeks or ask you to come to Italy with me or save me from death. I think I can live in this world as long as I must, and slowly learn how not to cry at night, if only you will do this one last thing for me. Please, just write me one very simple declarative sentence, the kind a woman can understand; kill your image and the hope and love I give it which keeps me frozen in the land of the bronze dead, for it gets harder and harder to free myself from that abstract tyrant named Richard who is so much more, being abstract, than he really is in this world. . . . For I must get back my soul from you; I am killing my flesh without it.

Tuesday afternoon, March 6, 1956. Break through the barriers; I am in great pain, and another shell of the so circumscribed understanding is shattered. All the neat tight desperate schedules are gone, and I got a letter from my Richard this afternoon which shot all to hell but my sudden looking in myself and finding what I feared and fought so hard not to find: I love that damn boy with all I've ever had in me and that's a hell of a lot. Worse, I can't stop; being human, even, it would take me a good two or three years to get to know anybody enough to like him enough to love him enough to marry him. So, I am in a nunnery, for all practical purposes. Worse, not in a nunnery, but surrounded by men who constantly remind me that they are not Richard; I hurt Mallory, and maybe a few others, in a fury of revulsion (and, looking at Mallory, however sorry I am for that ruthlessness of mine, I know it could be no other way now, so revolted am I).

I love him to hell and back and heaven and back, and have and do and will. Somehow, this letter killed finally all those niggling doubts: you're as tall as he; you weigh more than he; you're physically as strong & healthier; you're more athletic; your home and background and friends are too placid and conventional to accept or understand him and will color your view in time: all this: Basta!

So, out of this hurt and sickness, this mad wish to just spend everything I have to go to Paris and calmly, quietly confront him, feeling my will and my love can melt doors: out of this, I retype the letter I wrote in answer to his which he may never read, and will probably never answer, because he seems to want a break clean and scrupulous as the edge of a guillotine:

"Only listen to me this last once. For it will be the last, and there is a terrible strength to which I am giving birth, and it is your child as it is mine, and so your listening must christen it.

"The sun is flooding into my room as I write and I have spent the afternoon buying oranges and cheese and honey and being very happy after having for two weeks been very ill, because I can see every now and then how one must live in this world even if one's true full soul is not with one; I give of my intensity and passion in minute homeopathic spoonfuls to the world; to the cockney woman in the subway lavatory when I said: look I'm human and she looked in my eyes and believed me and I kissed her; and the crooked man who sells malt bread; and a little dark-haired boy running a dog which urinated on the bridge post over a pool of white swans: to all these, I can give my fantastic urges of love, in little parcels which will not hurt them or make them sick, for being too strong.

"I can do this, and must do this. I hoped in a night of terror that I was not bound to you with that irrevocable love, for ever. I fought and fought to free myself as from the weight of a name that could be a baby or could be a malignant tumor; I knew not. I only feared. But although I have gone crying (god, have I) and battering my head against spikes, desperately thinking that if I were dying, and called, you might come, I have found that which I most feared, out of my weakness. I have found that it is beyond your power ever ever to free me or give me back my soul; you could have a dozen mistresses and a dozen languages and a dozen countries, and I could kick and kick; I would still not be free.

"Being a woman, it is like being crucified to give up my dearest lares and penates, my 'household gods': which are all the small, warm gestures of knowing and loving you: writing you (I have felt smothered, writing a kind of diary to you, and not mailing it: it is getting ominously huge, and each time is a witness of a wrestling with my worst angel) and telling you my poems (which are all for you) and little publishings, and, most terrible of all, seeing you, even for the smallest time, when you are so near, and god knows when we shall be pardoned for being so scrupulous.

"This part of the woman in me, the concrete, present, immediate part, which needs the warmth of her man in bed and her man eating with her and her man thinking and communing with her soul: this part still cries to you: why, why will you not only see me and be with me while there is still this small time before those terrible years and infinite years; this woman, whom I have not recognized for 23 years, whom I have scorned and denied, comes to taunt me now, when I am weakest in my terrible discovery.

"For I am committed to you, out of my own choice (although I could not know when I let myself first grow toward you that it would hurt, hurt, hurt me so eternally), and I perhaps know now, in a way I never should have known, if you made life easy and told me I could live with you (on any terms in this world, only so it would be with you)—I know now how deeply, fearfully and totally I love you, beyond all compromise, beyond all the mental reservations I've had about you, even to this day.

"I am not simply telling you this because I want to be noble; I very much *didn't* want to be noble. That most intimate immediate woman (which makes me, ironically, so much yours) tormented me into delusion: that I could ever free myself from you. Really, how ridiculous it was: how should a mistress free me. When even you, and even what gods there are, cannot free me, tempting me with all kinds of men on all sides?

"I thought even, at the most desperate time, when I was so sick and could not sleep, but only lie and curse the flesh [of Gordon] whom I was going to marry two years ago in a splurge of contrived social conscience: we looked so well together! So he is coming to study in Germany, and I thought perhaps if I could keep him skiing and swimming I might live with him, if only he never wrote or let me argue with him (because I always win) or looked at a bed. This cowardice terrified me; for it was that. I could not admit then, as I do now, the essential tragic fact:

"I love you with all my heart and soul and body; in your weakness as in your strength; and for me to love a man even in his weakness is something I have never all my life been able to do before. And if you can take that weakness in me which wrote my last cringing, begging-dog letter and admit that it belongs to the same woman who wrote the first letter in her strength and faith, and love the whole woman, you will know how I love you.

"I was thinking, of the few times in my life I have felt I was all alive, tensed, using everything in me: mind and body, instead of giving away little crumbs, lest the audience be glutted with too much plum cake.

"Once, I was on the top of the ski slope, having to go down to a small figure below, and not knowing how to steer; I plunged; I flew, screaming with joy that my body braced and mastered this speed; and then a man stepped carelessly in my path and I broke my leg. Then there was the time ... when the horse galloped into the street-crossing and the stirrups came off leaving me hanging around his neck, jarred breathless, thinking in an ecstasy: is this the way the end will be? And then there are the many many times I have given myself to that fury and that death which is loving you, and I am, to my own knifing hurt, more faithful than is kind to my peace and my wholeness. I live in two worlds and as long as we are apart, I always shall.

"Now that this sudden articulate awareness of my most terrible eternal predicament has come to me, I must know that you understand this and *why* I had to write you then and now: if you do not ever want to write to me again, send me a blank, unsigned postcard, something, anything, to let me know that you did not tear my words and burn them before knowing that

I am both worse and better than you thought. I am human enough to want to be talking to the only other human who matters in this world.

"I suppose I was most appalled that you should bind me to you (so that neither of us has the power to break this, through all hate, venom, disgust and all the mistresses in the world) and that you could leave me this cut open, my heart utterly gone, without anesthetic or stitching; my vital blood was spilling on the barren table, and nothing could grow. Well, it still is spilling. And I wonder why you fear seeing me even in the time we have: for I have faith in you, and cannot believe (as I once wanted to) that it's merely for convenience, so I won't overlap with other women. Why must you be so much like Brand: so utterly intransigent?

"I could see it, if you thought your being with me would bind me to you more, or give me less freedom to find someone else, but knowing now, as I do and you must, that I am so far bled white that no mere abstinence of knives can cure me, why do you forbid our making the small, limited world we have? Why so tabu? I ask you to ask yourself this. And if you have the courage or understanding in you, to tell me.

"When I was weak, there was a reason; now I see none. I see not why I should not live in Paris with you and go to your classes and read French with you. I am not anymore perilous, outside myself. Why do you make our case (which is hell enough, and we have enough to test us in these coming cruel years) so utterly and absolutely rigid? I can take the even harder horror of letting myself melt into feeling again, and knowing it must freeze again, if only I can believe it is making a minute part of time and space better than it would have been by stubbornly staying always apart when we have so little time to be near.

"I ask you to turn these things in your heart and mind, for I see a sudden deep question now: why do you flee me, if you know I would *rather* make life rich under shadow of the sword? You said before that I wanted something of you you couldn't give. Well, so I do. But now I understand what must be (which I didn't then) and understand also that my faith and love for you cannot be blunted or blinded by drinking or hurling myself into other men's beds. I found this, and know this, and what do I have?

"Understanding. Love. Two worlds. I am simple enough to love the spring and think it foolish and terrible that you can deny it to us when it is the wonder of it that is uniquely ours. With that strange knowing that comes over me, like a clairvoyance, I know that I am sure of myself and my enormous and alarmingly timeless love for you; which will always be. But in a way, it is harder for me, for my body is bound to my faith and love, and I feel I cannot really ever live with another man; which means I must become (since I could not be a nun) a consecrated single woman. Now, if I were inclined to a career as a lawyer or journalist that would be all right. But I am not. I am inclined to babies and bed and brilliant friends and a magnificent stimulating home where geniuses drink gin in the kitchen after a delectable dinner and read their own novels and tell about why the stock market is the way it will be and discuss scientific mysticism (which, by the way, is intriguing: in all forms: several tremendous men in botany, chemistry, math and physics, etc., here are all mystics in various ways)—well, anyhow, this is what I was meant to make for a man, and to give him this colossal reservoir of faith and love for him to swim in daily, and to give him children; lots of them, in great pain and pride. And I hated you most, in my unreason, for making me woman, to want this, and making me your woman alone, and then making me face the very real and terribly immediate possibility that I would have to live my life chastely as a schoolteacher who sublimated by influencing other women's children. More than anything else in the world I want to bear you a son and I go about full with the darkness of my flame, like Phèdre, forbidden by what austere *pudeur*, what *fierté*?

"In a way, I suppose, I felt you were like Signor Rappaccini, who bred his only daughter to exist solely on perilous poisonous food and atmosphere exhaled by a poisonous exotic plant: she became fatally unable to live in the normal world, and a death-menace to those who wanted to approach her from this world. Well, that is what I became, for a while. I really cruelly wounded several people here, desperately, because I wanted to get back to that normal world and live and love in it. Well, I couldn't, and I hated them for showing me that. . . .

"I know if I were coming [to Paris] in a chaos, a turmoil of accusations, or even making it harder to leave you again (which it may well be, but it is possible to manage this)—I know then that you would have a right to forbid. But all I want is to see you, be with you, walk, talk, in a way which I imagine people past the age of love could do . . . I am not pretending I would not passionately want to be with you, but we have come into the time and understanding where we could be most kind and good to each other. Even if those eternal years are upon us, why do you now refuse to see me?

"I believe I can ask you this, and not have you feel that there is some disease of overscrupulosity that makes letters reveal weakness or carry contagion. As a woman who knows herself now, I ask you. And if you have courage, and look into yourself, you will answer. For I shall come, and respect your wish; but I shall also now ask why you so wish. Do not, O do not make an artificial stasis which is unbreakable; break and bend and grow again, as I have done only today."

So I have, too, and cannot stop the crying, those flooding cathartic tears that angle for life and hope even as my love is across that damn channel, telling me not to come. Why, why? . . .

I read his letter and walked the wet pine-dark path tonight, with the warm rain dripping and shiny on the black leaves in the humid blurred starlight, crying and crying with this terrible pain; it hurts, Father, it hurts, oh, Father I have never known; a father, even, they took from me.

It all sounds so simple and ridiculous: I found out today that I am deeply and for-god-knows-how-long in love with a boy who will not let me come to him out of a ferocious cold scrupulosity and not only will not let me come, when it is possible, but is going this spring away to where it will be for infinite years impossible. And he will not let me come.

And I think of that magnificent poem by James Joyce: "I hear an army charging upon the land . . ." and the final irrevocable lines in which, after that dynamic thunder of horses and whirling laughter and long green hair coming out of the sea, there is the simple series of words with all the anguish in the world:

My heart, have you no wisdom thus to despair?
My love, my love, my love, why have you left me alone?

If I were a man, I could write a novel about this; being a woman, why must I only cry and freeze, cry and freeze?

Let me be strong, strong with sleep and strong with intelligence and strong with bone and fiber; let me learn, through this desperation, to spread myself out: to know where and to whom to give: to Nat, to Gary, to Chris even, to Iko, to dear Gordon in his way: to give the small moments and the casual talk that very special infusion of devotion and love which make our epiphanies. Not to be bitter. Save me from that, that final wry sour lemon acid in the veins of single clever lonely women.

Let me not be desperate and throw away my honor for want of solace; let me not hide in drinking and lacerating myself on strange men; let me not be weak and tell others how bleeding I am internally; how day by day it drips and gathers, and congeals. I am still young. Even twenty-three and a half is not too late to live anew.... I honestly hope that in five years I can make a new life if he is not coming; I certainly cannot just go on blindly thinking of ways in which to fill enough years so that he will come; I want somehow to live with him always; to wake and have him greet me, and bear children to him; such heavenly pride to carry his child. My god. I can't bear bathos. Let there be none; get it out, and decide what to do, and do it.

Oh, someone, I run through names, thinking someone: hear me, take me to your heart, be warm and let me cry and cry and cry. And help me be strong: oh, Sue, oh, Mr. Fisher, oh, Dr. B., oh, Mother. My god. I shall probably write Elly. That will help objectify this....

I luxuriate in this; I have been so tight and rigid since two months. Two months alone. I luxuriate in suddenly letting go and crying my insides out. I am tired and have been very discouraged by having sinus for so long, and that helps: all the despair, coming at me when I am most weak. I will read Hopkins: and, when our lives crack, and the loveliest mirror cracks, is it not right to rest, to step aside and heal; why must I rush on, dragging myself to classes: I don't really need that "escape" work offers: I need rest: I have enough, thank god, that I want to do, to read, to think about. I must have a sherry party next term, or tea, and ask Chris and Gary and Nat and Keith (who seems so sweet) and a girl or two. The right people and right number are terribly important: so everyone will talk and communicate, and not be chaotic, or too narrow. . . .

Someday when I am stumbling up to cook eggs and feed milk to the baby and prepare dinner for my husband's friends, I shall pick up Bergson, or Kafka, or Joyce, and languish for the minds that are outleaping and outskipping mine.

But how so? Are these women, this Miss Burton, this old Miss Welsford (who is coming to the end of her vigor), better for their years reading and writing articles like "The Political Tragedies of Jonson and Chapman" or books like *The Fool* and fearing the bright brilliant young ones like Dr. Krook?* I would live a life of conflict, of balancing children, sonnets, love and dirty dishes; and banging banging an affirmation of life out on pianos and ski slopes and in bed in bed in bed.

Someday. Today I lived through supervision: it is something even to live through hours of obligation now, without screaming: gently, gently, stoic one. Today, by the way, Miss Burton checked us when we impulsively said suicide was an escape (on defensive?) and she said it was a brave thing—if one could only live corruptly and miserably in this world—to leave it. NB. So we thought. Once.

Also today, Mrs. Krook discussing redemptive power of love, which philosopher F. H. Bradley left out of his *Ethical Studies* (much to his weakening) and which we will hear about in D. H. Lawrence. Next week. And I got back my paper "Passion as Destiny in Racine" with the comment that passion is only *one* aspect and not the fatal holocaust I made it: also mixed my metaphors re flames and cancers and appetites. . . .

After Dr. Krook, had good lunch at Eagle with Gary [Haupt]. Was only woman in dark pub atmosphere of good solid food, beer, sane talk, all-male; and was I better for it! Gary is blond, blue-eyed, most Germanic in a gentle way: a fine, analytic, slow, deliberate way of thinking: has met all the best minds everywhere, it seems: Here, studies under [David] Daiches, Krook, maybe [C. S.] Lewis: has [met] all the finest minds: E. M. Forster: well, anyway, I felt better than at any of our

---

*Dorothea Krook, Plath's favorite professor, who was a very important positive influence and a role model. Plath frequently—and inexplicably—refers to her as Doris Krook in the journal.

previous run-ins because I communicated, while intensely, at least with more calm and felt I wasn't just talking hectically *at* him, the way I have before, feeling he scorned my mind as female and illogical and slightly absurd.

Gary and I went on about scientific mysticism, probability in foreknowledge in cards, hypnotism, levitation, Blake (whom he admires immensely): I've read Wallace Stevens, and he's just beginning. I find myself whittling sharper edges on my talk, thinking more before speaking: trying to prove points, not just flooding in gestures: learn more of this, it's good. Gary can help, too, because, while essentially tinged with a romantic streak (almost laughable, in a nice way, he seems so pedestrian, the curse of a particular analytic temperament somehow), he is scrupulously accurate and logical; I'm having coffee with him this Thursday, tea with him & Keith next week. I must read. Read Bergson.

I was struck, even in a tedious session in a dark cubicle in Newnham with Miss Barrett lisping sweetly to those immature girls performing an autopsy on *Les Fleurs du Mal*, that I could translate Baudelaire by sight, almost immediately, except for the obvious vocabulary words I didn't know: I felt the sensuous flow of the words and meanings, and plunged in them alone, longing to read him and live with him. Maybe someday French will actually be natural to me. . . .

All this to stop crying. Also had marvelous cathartic blowup with Jane on Sunday. After she had underlined five of my new books in pencil with notes; evidently she felt that since I'd already underlined them in black, nothing further could harm them; well, I was furious, feeling my children had been raped, or beaten, by an alien. . . .

But in the midst of this terrible sorrow, this sickness, this weariness, this fear, I spin still: there is still the blessing of the natural world and those simply loved ones and all to read and see.

Called another Fulbright from an ad. May drive to Paris with him (is he short, deformed, ugly, ancient, married? He has a Ph.D. from Columbia and sounded young and pragmatic). I feel I somehow must just walk to Richard's early one morning and stand there, strong and contained, and say: hello. Then I can just walk in Paris, and maybe find some people to look up, some plays to see, and then take the train to meet Gordon in Germany. Gordon will be dear and strong and heal me by his kindness, even if he knows nothing of all this aching. I refuse to be weak and tell anyone else.

We shall see. It would be a kind of final gesture to face him. (Oh, yes, I still think I have power: he may be sleeping with his mistress, leaving orders for me not to be admitted, or not there, or if there, worse, refuse to see me, I am not desperate now. And that is why I feel I can honestly go. I do love him and do not see why I can't be with him to enjoy life, knowing we must leave it. We shall see.)

Come, my coach. Good night, good night.

Thursday night, March 8.... I love Pembroke: ran across the cobbled court and up the circular stone staircase with the gothic-arched keyhole windows that make me feel I should be wearing Elizabethan silks, and Gary (Haupt) was ready with home-ground coffee and news to tell me, mainly re Keith and Mrs. Krook (who might have me, Gary sounded optimistic). We talked on and on about Yale and Smith and various personalities (the professors he knows are phenomenal) and also Sassoon: it gave me such a peculiar surge of illicit pleasure to casually say: oh yes, I knew him; tell me about him. And so Gary went on and gave me a very distant opinion of why they rejected Sassoon from the Manuscript club: he wasn't a group man; dissatisfied with Yale; giving up all to write; influence of family name, etc. I chuckled inside, and thought: oh, my god. How absurd. And I love him so!

... Ran to catch Krook... who went on to D. H. Lawrence & incredible fable: *The Man Who Died*. She read sections, felt chilled, as in last paragraph of "The Dead," as if angel had hauled me by the hair in a shiver of gooseflesh: about the temple of Isis bereaved, Isis in search. Lawrence died in Vence, where I had my mystic vision with Sassoon; I was the woman who died, and I came in touch through Sassoon that spring [with] that flaming of life, that resolute fury of existence. All seemed shudderingly relevant; I read in a good deal; I have lived much of this. It matters. Finished Lawrence before supper....

... Mrs. Lameyer writes that Grammy was taken back to hospital; can't eat. Is she dying of cancer, even as I write? That dark vile mystery; I love that woman, I can't believe she could go out of the world and me not there; I can't believe home could be without her. It sickens me; afar off, I think of her, and cry. Those presences, those people loved and gone into the dark; I rail and rage against the taking of my father, whom I have never known; even his mind, his heart, his face, as a boy of 17 I love terribly. I would have loved him; and he is gone. I feel somehow much too old, with all the older ones dead before I have known them, and only the young ones, the babies, under me. I am so close to the dark. My villanelle was to my father; and the best one. I lust for the knowing of him; I looked at Redpath at that wonderful coffee session at the Anchor, and practically ripped him up to beg him to be my father; to live with the rich, chastened, wise mind of an older man. I must beware, beware of marrying for that. Perhaps a young man with a brilliant father. I could wed both.

March 9, Friday.... Felt like singing while cleaning up room: wrote a letter about how I'm forging a soul amidst great birth pangs and about how I felt concerning Sassoon to Mother, included copies of two best poems: "Pursuit" and "Channel Crossing."

Also wrote her re new inspiration: application for Eugene Saxton fellowship for young writers. My whole emphasis has swung again, to a realization that if I enter this academic, critical world I'll spend all my time reading and reading, and that I need a healthy overturning of the applecart, almost a refusal to read beyond a point, and to read more of what influences my writing, rather than paralyzes it: contemporary work. I want to stress the living-writing life now; the academic-critical-teaching life can wait. If I write this term (having whittled my program to a bare minimum: moralists and French, perhaps German) and live in Spain a month with Elly, then return to write for a month, and take off again, I should amass enough, what with my various prizes; might make me able to write a novel (love and suicide being large part: also college environment, position of intelligent woman in world: think in chapters, stories, fight through to triumph) and poetry to keep me in discipline. I'd rather write a novel, and I could live in southern France (Vence? Grasse?) or Italy or Spain for a year and forge my soul and just read French and German and soak up art, all on my own. I've got to try that. Think of ways. All prizes: from *Seventeen*, to *Mademoiselle*, to recent poetry coups, will be invaluable; also, newspaper experience.

It's a dream. We will work toward it. It would also help getting a job in the States if I'd a novel published. Begin it this summer. Outline: intelligent woman, fight, triumph: toleration of conflict, etc. Make complex and rich and vivid. Use letters to Sassoon, etc. I'm getting excited. Make it tense & tough, and for god's sake, not sentimental.

. . . Heffer's: bought lots of books by Huxley: the most recent, *Heaven and Hell*: of antipodes in mind: reached under hypnosis or mescaline. . . . Back here now: *The New Yorker* rejected poems, with a "sorry, please try again" at least. All these days of hope, it's been coming back to me regular mail. But today, fortunately, I could write ten novels and vanquish the gods; outside, tennis balls ping, birds twirp and chirr, and I must read Marlowe and Tourneur to do my last paper for Burton. Cheers for spring; for life; for a growing soul.

Saturday morning, March 10. I cannot keep still; I am on the edge; the dream comes to taunt me in the morning sun. Last night's whiskey with Hamish, glass after glass tossed down, at least five or six, is still strutting latent havoc in my veins, ready to betray me; the caffeine from the coffee this morning tenses fiber too, and I am appalled: *Granta* with bad poem by girl with same initials, ironically enough; bitterness about clique: they publish friends, always friends; must write some short sketches for them and *Varsity* after this next week: potent, witty, punchy: something they can't reject without being immoral.

What I want to say is: HE is here; in Cambridge. Smiling bulb-faced Bert, all scrubbed and polished, met me in the street on the way to the College library: "Luke* and Ted threw stones at your window last night." A huge joy galloped through me; they remembered my name; it was the wrong window and I was out drinking with Hamish, but they exist in this world; I talked on a minute; Ted it seems is assigned to write a synopsis

---

*Lucas Myers, an American writer at Cambridge very close to Ted Hughes

of James Joyce's *Ulysses* (!!!) and so on. I murmured something about: tell them to drop by, or something, and cycled off.

Now, tense, rebellious, with spring sprouting outside my window and playing merry hell with my blood, I have to cram for paper on Webster & Tourneur: why oh why didn't I do it yesterday. I should have known; and today will be shot to hell because he is Here and he may not bother to come again, having dates with Puddefoots or something, and I wait here, quivering like polished barbwire. If only I weren't so tired and full of feathers from that whiskey, I'd be able to cope. If he did or didn't. Probably the blond one is lunching with him even now. Thank god Bert is hers. But He. Oh he.

Spent last session with Dr. Davy [psychiatrist] this morning articulating: I fear oppressive and crushing forces, if I do not plot and manage and manipulate my path, joining: academic, creative & writing, and emotional & living & loving: writing makes me a small god: I re-create the flux and smash of the world through the small ordered word patterns I make. I have powerful physical, intellectual and emotional forces which must have outlets, creative, or they turn to destruction and waste (e.g. drinking with Hamish, and making indiscriminate love).

Please let him come; let me have him for this British spring. Please, please. . . .

Please let him come, and give me the resilience & guts to make him respect me, be interested, and not to throw myself at him with loudness or hysterical yelling; calmly, gently, easy, baby, easy. He is probably strutting the backs [the gardens by the river in Cambridge] among crocuses now with seven Scandinavian mistresses. And I sit, spiderlike, waiting, here, home; Penelope weaving webs of Webster, turning spindles of Tourneur. Oh, he is here; my black marauder; oh hungry hungry. I am so hungry for a big smashing creative burgeoning burdened love: I am here; I wait; and he plays on the banks of the river Cam like a casual faun.

March 10. Postscript: Oh the fury, the fury. Why did I even know he was here. The panther wakes and stalks again, and every sound in the house is his tread on the stair; I wrote "Mad Girl's Love Song" once in a mad mood like this when Mike didn't come and didn't come, and every time I am dressed in black, white and red: violent, fierce colors. All the steps coming up and running past I made into his step and cursed the usurpers that took his place. . . .

Now I lay, burning, fevered with this disease, and the sun glared at me all at once, a lowering orange eye, blank and mocking; it set on time, I clocked it. And again the dark eats at me: the fear of being crushed in a huge dark machine, sucked dry by the grinding indifferent millstones of circumstance. He is at a party now, I know; with some girl. My face burns, and I am turning to ash, like the apples of Sodom and Gomorrah.

I lay and heard the steps on the stair and the knock at the door and I leapt up to welcome the fruit of my will. It was John, coming to ask me to the movies; I wanted to see that movie, but wouldn't let myself; it will be harder to stay here and watch the clock go from eight to ten, and read *The Duchess of Malfi*. How I hate him: how I hate Bert for feeding my fury which I had quelled by wrenching out that poem last week.

I writhed and angered and talked to John, bidding him good-bye and sending him off; imagine, he tried to persuade me to go through Copenhagen instead of Paris!

I remember the dreams I've had the last two nights: the first: trying out for a play and being in a huge gymnasium where the clowns and actors were practicing. Everywhere there was the heavy circumstance of menace: I ran, huge weights were dropping on my head; I crossed the slippery floor, and afar off, laughing hobos bowled large black balls at me to knock me down; it was a terrifying time of jeopardy: similar to those moments caught between traffic, lumbering trucks and buses and bicycles coming from all angles, when I can only stand fast and shut my eyes, or blunder into a tangle of traffic and hope for luck. Black balls, black weights, wheeled vehicles, and the slippery floor: all trying to crush me, moving in heavy blundering attempts, just missing.

Then I was in my black coat and beret: Isis bereaved, Isis in search, walking a dark barren street. Into a café, searching, searching, and in a chair, hiding his face behind a newspaper, sat the dark one, suave, grinning. I stood, appalled, and he uncurled, and came with me, dark and sweet. Another dark man with the face of a Slavic cretin, or a yellowed Spaniard, of some indeterminate race, accosted me and said in a thick, furry voice, "It is night." He thought I was a whore; I broke away, running after my Richard, who walked ahead, his back toward me.

Men's voices downstairs. I am sick, sick. With this desperate fury. God knows what will happen to me in Paris. Love turns, lust turns, into the death urge. My love is gone, gone, and I would be raped. "It is night."

March 11, Sunday morning. Another day of hell. He is on the prowl, all the fiends are come to torment me: and I alone am escaped to tell thee. All of the eyes, the multitudes of eyes that report his being here. This morning, a male tread, a knock at the door; it is He? It was: mere Chris, after all this 10 days of absence. Only, a Chris gifted with instruments of torture: having just seen Luke and Ted down the street this very morning; they will not come. Not in the gray sober light of morning. They will not come.

But last night they came, at two in the morning, Phillippa said. Throwing mud on her window, saying my name, the two mixed: mud and my name; my name is mud. She came to look for me, but I was sleeping. Dreaming of being home in Winthrop on a lovely new spring day, walking in pajamas down the streets of melting tar to the sea, the salt freshness, and squatting in the sea in a tangle of green weeds were clam-diggers with osier baskets, rising, one after the other, to look at me in my pajamas, and I hid in spring shame in the trellised arbors of the Days' home.

Mail came through the sewer, and I got only bills. Mail and rice came through the sewer, that bubbling green mucky sewer we played in by the sea, transmuting what corruption, what lime-gilded periwinkles, into what radiant magic. They laughed and said they trusted the mail and rice coming through the sewer.

And all this while, those boys in the dark were treating me like what whore, coming like the soldiers to Blanche DuBois and rolling in the gardens, drunk, and mixing her name with mud. Two reports today, to insert more needles in my skin. I must cram for my paper. Oh, god give me the guts to live through this week. Let me someday confront him, only confront him, to make him human, and not that black panther which struts on the forest fringes of hearsay. Such hell. They refuse to face me in the daylight. I am not worth that. I must be, when, if they ever come. They will not come. I don't want to eat, to go to tea today. I want to rave out in the streets and confront that big panther, to make the daylight whittle him to lifesize.

PARIS

March 26, Monday morning. Eh bien! Quelle vie! I am here in Paris in a room at the Hotel Béarn just ready to move upstairs to a sunny attic room for 30 francs less a night; the people in the hotel are delightful and the *croissants* are moist and light and butter generous, so I shall stay, and consider myself lucky: scavenged a bit this morning for another cheaper place but they were all full for Easter holidays: it is a glorious blue day with all the freshness of the country and I skipped down the early morning streets feeling miraculously that I really belonged. It will be a fine stay. I can get along in my French, too. Remember Hotel de Valence: old woman was charming and although they were full, they have rooms for 400 francs.

Arrived in Paris early Saturday evening exhausted [omission] . . . and thought at the end that the sweetly burbling Janet Drake with her big dark eyes and painted white pixie face would drive me absolutely mad. Emmet in his sailor costume and cuteness appealed much less than the former night when he had acted like a man and read aloud part of his book on James Larkin, Irish labor leader. I just wanted to get off alone and wash and go to bed. It was twilight when we found a room for me at this Hotel Béarn, and I felt absolutely deserted. Overcome by a disastrous impulse to run to Sassoon as formerly; I took myself in leash [omission] . . . and decided to walk out toward Richard's and search for food on the way. Going downstairs, a nice-looking man in the telephone booth grinned at me, and I grinned back; well, after I got out and started walking (having stupidly left my map of Paris in Emmet's car) I realized the guy was following me. He overtook me and smiled again and I came right out and said, *"J'ai oublié mon plan de Paris, ainsi je suis un peu perdue."* Well, that was all he needed; so we went back to the hotel and he got his map to loan me during my stay; eventually we ended up walking all along the Boulevard St. Germain and I had steak tartar and wine and meringue at a little *brasserie* with him. Two arty musicians came in to play while we ate, one with a violin and coronet of paper flowers; the other with a peculiar box that he ground like a coffee machine and tinny music came out. I decided to go to bed early and rest to be strong and see Sassoon in the morning. It was a big concession because I felt terribly alone.

The guy turned out to be, interestingly enough, the Paris correspondent for the newspaper *Paese Sera* in Rome: an Italian Communist journalist, no less! Hence the Olivetti which he loaned me for today. Well, in spite of the fact he spoke no English, we communicated magnificently, to my surprise; he is very cultured and we discussed communism in different countries (he is very idealistic and very much a humanist) and art: he admires Melville and Poe and T. S. Eliot, which he'd read in French: "J. Alfred Prufrock"! and I asked him about the French and Italian artists he wrote up for his paper. All most reassuring. Got courage from this and felt I could manage without Richard if necessary.

Sunday: I got up, still tired, and set out in the fresh morning air down the Rue du Bac past the Place des Invalides to Rue Duvivier, feeling chipper and quite *gaie*, preparing my opening speech.

I rang at No. 4 outside of which an old beggar woman was singing in a mournful monotone. The dark and suspicious concierge met me and blandly told me that Sassoon was not back nor would he be back probably until after Easter. I had been ready to bear a day or two alone, but this news shook me to the roots. I sat down in her living room and wrote an incoherent letter while the tears fell scalding and wet on the paper and her black poodle patted me with his paw and the radio blared: "Smile though your heart is breaking." I wrote and wrote, thinking that by some miracle he might walk in the door. But he had left no address, no messages, and my letters begging him to return in time were lying there blue and unread. I was really amazed at my situation; never before had a man gone off to leave me to cry after. . . .

Friday, March 30. A strange day passing through ecstasy unto certain sorrow and the raining of questions sad and lonely on the dark rooftops. Met Gary early & walked to Pont Royal, where I met Tony, feeling very chic in my white pleated skirt and aqua sweater & red shoes & red & white polka-dotted hair-scarf; *citronnade* at kiosque and he was gay and quite sweet; a little more subdued with his sister gone; we took the metro to Pigalle and got out in the hot sun by the honky-tonk square and began climbing the little narrow roads to the top of Mont-martre; the shops were dark stenchful holes and reeked of garlic and cheap tobacco. In the sun there was a magic of decay: scabbed pastel posters, leprous umber walls, flowers sprouting out of filth. Climbed Rue Vieuville & series of steeply angled steps to Place du Tertre, which was chock full of tourists and bad bad artists in various stances doing charcoal portraits or muddy paintings of the domes of Sacré-Coeur; Tony and I walked about and looked at paintings until a small man asked if he could cut my silhouette *"comme un cadeau,"* so I stood in the middle of the square in the middle of Montmartre and gazed at the brilliant restaurants in the middle of a gathering crowd which ohed and ahed and which was just what the little man wanted—to attract customers: so I got a free silhouette and by this time Tony was putting his arm around my waist when we walked and I could feel that bristling barbed wit mellowing: we stood in front of Sacré-Coeur in the sun watch-ing the tourist buses grunt up the hill, full of deadpan people sheltered by sunproof-windproof-bulletproof-glass domes; in-side the church it was cool and dark as a well with red patches of light from the windows: Tony described Chartres a bit and some rather gratifying sensitivity came out. Had exquisite lunch just off commercial square where they were serving mobs under the trees and playing violin-lilty tunes, where the man with picture frame and paper flowers around his head was yelling and doing stunts. We avoided all this in the shady grove of the peaceful Auberge du Coucou and had fine *salade de tomate*, delectable *veau* sautéed in mushrooms and buttery potatoes and bottle of iced white wine which sent us floating into the after-noon like birds, all airy and gay; Tony bought me a bunch of violets and was increasingly attentive and I mellowed to fond-ness.

I left all thought of the American Express in the pale gold aura of wine and felt most beautiful and slightly damned; Tony mentioned the Rue du Bac metro stop and I thought: well, so he comes back to the hotel; I felt that the day was like a shimmering shell of pearliness and must be treated lightly like a soap bubble, so floated to the hotel and Tony showed no signs of farewell; so up the steps to the room where it was cool and we washed and lay down; he had grown more beautiful and golden to me all afternoon and I was only wishful and happy for this time with him for he was growing more rare and gentle, so we lay together and it was good and kissed gently and it was good and his skin was smooth and taut and his body was lean and sweetly put together, so shirt by slip we undressed and embraced until we were quite naked and I began to want him; but when I went off to the bathroom for a few minutes he reflected and later froze when I came back and it was I think partly because he felt I was complex and he lived in England and did not want involvings, and I was sorry a little because I had come so close to having him there in the dusk and his body was so right and lovely and strong and golden and he dawned gentle and sweet: I imagine he used to be like this when he was young, or when he played the piano; Oxford I think has ruined him, with that snob brash conceit and consciousness of going with the Rothschild girl and the "toast of Oxford," Lady Tweedsmuir's daughter Ann. So he dressed and with the layers put on his decorum. . . .

And again I ask myself: why? I must be so careful, and am going back to Cambridge and that gossip. I shall not go to London to descend on Ted; he has not written; he can come to me, and call me Sylvia not Shirley. And I shall be chaste and subdued this term and mystify those gossipmongers by work and seriousness!

April 1. Program: to win friends and influence people.
•*Don't drink much*—(remember misfortunes w. Iko after St. John's party, Hamish—2 dates, *St. Botolph's* party and London night); stay sober.
•*Be chaste* and don't throw self at people (c.f. David Buck, Mallory, Iko, Hamish, Ted, Tony Gray)—in spite of rumor and M. Boddy,* let no one verify this term the flows of last.
•*Be friendly and more subdued*—if necessary, smog of "mys-

---

*Michael St. George Boddy, a close friend of Ted Hughes

tery woman," quiet, nice, slightly bewildered at colored scandals. Refuse ease of Sally Bowles act.

•*Work on inner life to enrich*—concentrate on work for Krook—writing (stories, poems, articles for *Monitor*—sketches)—*French daily*.

•*Don't blab too much*—listen more; sympathize and "understand" people.

•*Keep troubles to self*.

•Bear mean gossip and snubbing and pass beyond it—be nice and positive to all.

•*Don't criticize anybody* to anyone else—misquoting is like a telephone game.

•Don't date either Gary or Hamish—be nice but *not too enthusiastic* to Keith et al.

Be stoic when necessary and *write*—you have seen a lot, felt deeply, and your problems are universal enough to be made meaningful—WRITE.

Plath met Gordon Lameyer, her old boyfriend, in Paris and they traveled together to Germany and Italy. The trip was a disaster; they quarreled constantly.

Thursday, April 5. Outside all morning the rain came down on the gray rooftops and I lay quiet and warm wondering on the workings of this *machine infernale*, how much is chance and accident, how much a combination of that working on the will and the will working back to hack out its own happenings and how much is the will attracting all events like iron filings to a magnet which some days is strong, some days weak. How many times in my dreams have I met my dark marauder on the stairs, at a turning of the street, waiting on my bright yellow bed, knocking at the door, sitting only in his coat and hat with a small smile on a park bench; already he has split into many men; even while we hope, the blind is drawn down and the people turned to shadows acting in a private room beyond our view.... Last night, stopping to talk with Giovanni, who had been waiting late with the poem in Italian which he translated then to French about the mounds of wheat and ice breaking, I realized—with what clarity, what fullness—that I only want to go home now, to the home where I have hewn out my peace and my sanctuary: not America but my Whitstead [her house at Cambridge], my gable and my garden: there I can rest and grow fresh as morning milk and find again my faith and innocence, that innocence which is faith, belief in the rightnesses of these encounters with other men and other monuments where one must take wrong turnings if only to find new ways; faugh, such nobility, such moralizing: try the concrete, name names.

Somehow last night it came over me with terror and a kind of deadness and despair that I did not want to go to Germany or to Italy with that kind, bewildered and how lucky (ironic that, he comes to more and more fortune) boy beside me at the ballet*: the ballet of Phèdre, my Phèdre with her dark flame and that billowing cloak of scarlet which was blood offered and blood spilt: the blond and proud Hippolyte with his green-maned horses, the pink and white fay Aricie, the stylized Neptune with his pale face and trident, and all those blue-green waves: can I be good for a week? no acidity, or lemon looks for those laborious puns and endless family trees: oh my God, what is it what is it? Why does one not learn to love and live with the boring daily bread that is good for one, that is comfortable, convenient and available? Like *Brave New World*. Ha. So one can suffer or become Shakespeare? Ironically, I suffer and do not become Shakespeare — and it is my life which is passing, my life which is smutched and battered and running, each heartbeat; each clock-tick being a fatal subtraction from the total number I was allowed in the beginning: or, not being such a complete fatalist, from the variety of numbers I was allowed to work from: how fortunate that we are blind. And yet where is there to go? I would profit by a week alone, a week reading and writing: my God, at this moment I wonder if I could have gone to live with Ted, but that is London and no place to wash (oh, who cares) and the Boddy might paunchily properly lurch up the stairs at any moment. And I do not know Ted enough to know how he talks, how he talks: one night when I return? I shall send the postcard of Rousseau's *Snakecharmer* with a question. One night is not enough. I must think much; perhaps he will not answer and that will be simpler. But now I am a vagabond: I cannot wait for Richard longer,

*Gordon Lameyer

it has been two weeks, and he must have felt my strong will; London is Ted or too expensive.

So I leave early tomorrow morning with Gordon for Munich; can I make it good, without cursing myself for living off him? He wanted it this way, with me as a friend, and I must remember how the night before we met so accidentally and luckily in the American Express I was too sick of small dark sleazy men at my elbow to venture out for supper; and Giovanni came then with his consolation and banana and drawers of dates and warm milk to comfort; how kind he has been. I considered sleeping with him even, but yesterday was in a way glad Gordon came, because Giovanni and I are so tender and kind to each other now that it is good [omission]. . . . With Whitstead barred, life has now become a rather terrible smorgasbord of different capitals and men who go with them: London and Ted, Paris and the dark absence of Richard and comfort and conversation of Giovanni, and Rome and the journey with Gordon. And now having coldly discussed finances all morning with Gordon and with growing coldness having weighed in a frenzy of chill a sudden temptation to tell him I wasn't going and discussed these things also over ham and eggs and red wine in a little café around the corner, too much has been done already to break away: I do want to see Venice and Florence and Rome even if only in five short days, for I shall know where and how I wish to return. How it cries inside me now. . . . And I would rather be alone with my typewriter than with Gordon, and his stupid stammering French and inability to make himself understood here, his utter lack of rapport, of that intuitive sensing of mood disgusts me, yes, does. I feel the waiter in the bar smiling, charging too much and asking Gordon if he wants milk; I grinned sidewise at him for that one; with Gordon I am much more a worse kind of self; yet *quoi faire?*

Quoi faire? Is it some dread lack which makes my alternatives so deadly? Some feeble dependence on men which makes me throw myself on their protection and care and tenderness? Ah, but I have been alone in Paris for two weeks, and there are no girls here, so except for Gary (whom I scrupulously said good-bye to and even gave up Chartres, because it would have been a kind of sacrilege without Richard or alone, for Gary even with his avowed sensitivity is so plodding in his manner that it kills nightingales) and Tony, whom I scared with my need and volcanic will, I have gone about alone. (Giovanni was a discovery and mine and a kind of triumph: it has been fine with him, just warm and tender enough and all that good talk in French and his friends and the little *épicerie* where he took me after my tears for wonderful crush of human warmth and communion, and a soup plate of good stew and potatoes and cheese and red wine in the little crowded place.) . . . I have fought and conquered a desolate city. I think of [Richard] ever; is it because he is vanished that the dark image haunts me? Remember that time dancing in Nice—his slight undisciplined body: he can't swim, he is weak in a certain sense, he will never play baseball or teach math: that orange-juice-and-broiled-chicken solidity is utterly lacking and it is what Gary has and Gordon has (in the story "Dark Marauder" there will be a great contrast between the delicate snail-and-wine taste of Richard and the plain steak-and-potatoes-with-nothing-done-to-them taste of Gary). And so I have been alone here, really, and my room might be taken back by the vacationing student if I tried to stay, and Giovanni might become a little difficult; and Richard might never come, and it is cold and wet now.

Yes, all the auguries are for departure: the Paris air grows cold and I shiver always and my white lingerie slowly turns gray and there is no bathtub; all gathers and with cold edges and blunt corners urges me to go; the train and the view will be a kind of solace; if only I can be civil to Gordon: why not? There is all that mess and scorn between us, and no bitterness ever entirely vanishes between the rejector and the rejected. I paid my complete train fare through from Paris to Rome in francs today and got that over; the plane ticket is formidable, and I shall pay part of that in England if he needs it. I feel used enough to having men pay for my food, and even hotels, and feel that Gordon chose to do this for my company, with the understanding it was to be merely friendly company; so that I am not in debt, except I shall try to rise above this heavy despair with my Richard deserting me and going and 3 weeks being long enough for a very dangerous woman or a few which he has found, and my not being really angry only sorrowful with those great dark tear-brimming eyes of reproach which I know I could not stand to look at if the position were reversed; at the ballet last night I saw us entertaining in a large room hung with chandeliers and he chucked a pretty little blond pixie under the chin the way he did me that first time with an almost insulting appreciation and challenge; my God, if he would come today I would stay here with him. I see him now even, back in Paris, calmly reading my letters and thinking: poor hysterical wronged one, and living with his Swiss girl, or Spanish girl. Could he ever be faithful in the way I so desperately need? Ah, and could I ever be colossal enough to accept him if he weren't without becoming a martyr or worse, deliberately offering myself up to other men as a sacrifice in retaliation and desperation, a dive to destruction? Perhaps this is all in the cards, those cards with just so many kings and queens and just so many choices!

And now the alternatives revolve in a fatal dance and with the mailing of my postcards Mother will know I am going to Rome and Ted will know I want to see him if only for one night (oh, I just want to be with him: he is the only one who can walk high as Richard and for that I even submit to all the Boddy pig-eyes and sniveling gossip and talk and even Jane and the chosen ones knowing; for that I even let him call me Shirley, the wrong name, and know he does not know how much I could rip past here and be tender and wise, for now I am become too easy too soon and he will not bother to discover); shall I go to Yugoslavia with him? Or will I curse myself for deserting Elly and Spain? I miss a good woman; how could I dare think Elly was promiscuous in her attraction of the easy dark kind of men, when in fact I give more to the strong clean lovely kinds; Ted can break walls; I could telegraph him tonight, [ask] if I could come home to London and live there till Whitstead: the danger would be of his visitors, and he will perhaps have some, of his talk [omission] . . . I lust for him, and in my mind I am ripped to bits by the words he welds and wields. . . . Gordon: he just now is the safest way: I would conquer two other countries—and however much I want to linger in Italy, is it not better to see five days and come back hungry to stay longer, having foraged first under a man's protection, still off season, able to explore without pickups? Ah, yes. If Richard would come back now: I could devour pride and go to his place and ask the concierge if there was word: he might be there, hiding. He might be coming tomorrow; there might be a message (all of which I shall find out about too late). I could stay a few days and go back to England from here.

It is the historic moment; all gathers and bids me to be gone from Paris. I forgot how Gordon was another kind of Gary, only a little better. If I stayed in Paris: and so *in medias res* Giovanni walks in and hears all about these terrible sadistic urges to destruction and in the *medias res* of a very warm and tender time I hear footsteps and that is my fate and a gentle knock which should be if fate were kind, which should be only isn't, isn't and so my decision is sealed and the alternatives go revolving and snickering in their little whistling void with orange peels and blue Gauloise wrappers and it is decided and he says come on, come on and so we come on. [Omission.]

April 18. Now the forces are gathering still against me, and my dearest grandmother, who took care of me all my life while Mother worked, is dying very very slowly and bravely of cancer, and she has not even been able to have intravenous feeding for six weeks but is living on her body, which will be all sublimed away, and then only she may die. My mother is working, teaching, cooking, driving, shoveling snow from blizzards, growing thin in the terror of her slow sorrow. I had hoped to make her strong and healthy, and now she may be too weak herself after this slow death, like my father's slow long death, to come to me. And I am here, futile, cut off from the ritual of family love and neighborhood and from giving strength and love to my dear brave grandmother's dying whom I loved above thought. And my mother will go, and there is the terror of having no parents, no older seasoned beings, to advise and love me in this world.

[Addressed to Richard Sassoon] Something very terrifying too has happened to me, which started two months ago and which needed not to have happened, just as it needed not to have happened that you wrote that you did not want to see me in Paris and would not go to Italy with me. When I came back to London, there seemed only this one way of happening, and I am living now in a kind of present hell and god knows what ceremonies of life or love can patch the havoc wrought. I took care, such care, and even that was not enough, for my being deserted utterly. You said that you told me "brutally" that when you returned to Paris your vacation would be spent. Well, mine is spent too, brutally, and I am spent, giving with both hands, daily, and the blight and terror has been made in the choice and the superfluous unnecessary and howling void of your long absence. Your handwriting has gone so wild and racked not all the devils could burn a meaning out of it.

Sylvia and Ted Hughes were married on June 16, 1956. After the wedding they went off for a honeymoon summer in the little fishing village of Benidorm in Spain. Their brief stay with the widow Mangada resulted in a Plath story with that title, though most of the descriptive material written at the time has a strangely flat quality in retrospect.

BENIDORM

Our new house is magnificent. We keep marveling that we bought it for the summer at the same price Widow Mangada was charging for her noisy small room, bad dirty bathroom, ant-infested kitchen (all to be shared with "*les autres*," the piggy Spaniards) and terrace overlooking the sea (the honking staring gawking crowds on the boulevard, rather) which turned out to be the worst, not the best feature. Ted was driven to retreat to the beds in the dark inner room, while after 10 in the morning, I was more conscious of being stared at on the balcony than of the typewriter in front of me. Now there is utter peace No fussy actress rushes into my new kitchen to snatch the potatoes out of my hand and show me how to peel them her way, or peers under the lids of my frying pans on the petrol stove. We are left utterly tranquil. The first two days we were still recovering from our month of exterior business-rush living and the emotional turmoil of the week at the widow's; workmen hammered continually in the kitchen and bathroom, putting in the water motor for the shower, toilet and faucets. Finally yesterday, they finished, plastered up the holes, and we have clean sparkling water, cold, but wonderful, much better than the widow's ancient faulty plumbing and wiring.

Everything is going beautifully in this new place. I have a strong feeling that it is the source, and will be in the 10 weeks to come, of creative living and writing. Yesterday Ted read me three new fables he'd just written for his fine animal book about how all the animals became: the tortoise one was the funniest and dearest yet; the hyena, more serious, about a bitter perverted character, and the fox and the dog alive with plot and marvelous. . . . I have great hopes for this as a children's classic. Even as I write, Ted is working at the main table on the elephant and the cricket stories. Living with him is like being told a perpetual story: his mind is the biggest, most imaginative, I have ever met. I could live in its growing countries forever. I also feel a new direct pouring of energy into my own work, and shall break the jinx on my story writing this week, trying the bullfight story and perhaps one on the widow Mangada (funny?) along with chapters in my new novel that might do for articles for *Harper's*; also an article with sketches, on Benidorm for *The Christian Science Monitor*. Must learn Spanish and translate French too.

Never in my life have I had conditions so perfect: a magnificent handsome brilliant husband (gone are those frayed days of partial ego-satisfaction of conquering new slight men who fell easier and easier), a quiet large house with no interruptions, phone, or visitors: the sea at the bottom of the street, the hills at the top. Perfect mental and physical well-being. Each day we feel stronger and wider awake.

Yesterday, while we were marketing in the evening for wine and oil, a rain shower fell, and the lighting effects were startlingly beautiful: looking into the sun, which was shining, we saw through a silver sheet of rain a blinding shining street between dark pueblos; in the other direction, against dark clouds, the white pueblos shone arched over by the most perfect complete rainbow I've ever seen, one end rooted in the mountains, the other in the sea. We bought a loaf of bread at our new shop, and somehow elated by the rainbow, made our way through the fresh goat droppings to our white house with its bright border of pungent red geraniums.

July 23. Alone, deepening. Feeling the perceptions deepen with the tang of geranium and the full moon and the mellowing of hurt; the deep ingrowing of hurt, too far from the bitching fussing surface tempests. The hurt going in, clean as a razor, and the dark blood welling. Just the sick knowing that the wrongness was growing in the full moon. Listening, he scratches his chin, the small rasp of beard. He is not asleep. He must come out, or there is no going in.

Up the hilly street come the last donkey carts from the village, families going home up the mountain, slow, the donkey bells jangling. A couple of laughing girls. A skinny little boy with a lean dog on a leash. A French-speaking family. A mother with a fussing white-lace-frilled baby. Dark and quiet, completely still under the full moon. A cricket somewhere. Then there is his warmth, so loved, and strange, and the drawing in to the room where wrongness is growing. Wrongness grows in the skin and makes it hard to touch. Up, angry, in the darkness, for a sweater. No sleep, smothering. Sitting in nightgown and sweater in the dining room staring into the full moon, talking to the full moon, with wrongness growing and filling the house like a man-eating plant. The need to go out. It is very quiet. Perhaps he is asleep. Or dead. How to know how long there is before death. The fish may be poisoned, and the poison working. And two sit apart in wrongness.

What is wrong? he asks as the sweater is yanked out, wool slacks, and raincoat. I'm going out. Do you want to come? The aloneness would be too much; desperate and foolish on the lonely roads. Asking for a doom. He dresses in dungarees and shirt and black jacket. We go out leaving the light on in the house into the glare of the full moon. I strike out hillward toward the weird soft purple mountains, where the almond trees are black and twisted against the flooded whitened landscape, all clear in the blanched light of wrongness, not day, but some beige, off-color daguerrotype. Fast, faster, up past the railway station. Turning, the sea is far and silver in the light. We sit far apart, on stones and bristling dry grass. The light is cold, cruel and still. All could happen: the willful drowning, the murder, the killing words. The stones are rough and clear, and outlined mercilessly in the moonlight. Clouds cross over, the fields darken, and a neighboring dog yaps at the two strangers. Two silent strangers. Going back, there is the growing sickness, the separate sleep, and the sour waking. And all the time the wrongness is growing, creeping, choking the house, twining the tables and chairs and poisoning the knives and forks, clouding the drinking water with that lethal taint. Sun falls off-key on eyes asquint, and the world has grown crooked and sour as a lemon overnight.

Changed out of sweaty things to bathing suit; tomato, pepper, onion and eggs fried for lunch; deep, exhausting nap; rose, feeling blackjacked, to recover slowly over coffee. Went across the street to get some more milk for supper; past lovely vista, white fence with plants, into house; old house, weathered peasant said milk would be ready soon. Glimpse of blue sea through fig trees, with wide green scalloped leaves, thick with green fruit: we decided to wait. Ted finding ant track: half an hour spent playing god. Trail of black ants carrying straw grains or fly wings to hole; we lifted rock portal of house, threw confusion into clan: much bunching at break of new earth, retreats and fumblings. Saw two ants apparently stitched with cramp; almost transparent, beige, earth-colored spider running wildly around them, trussing them up with invisible web: ants struggling, slower; spider quick, running clockwise, counterclockwise; we tossed him another ant, bigger, which he looped in. Gave ants big dead fly, which they took with pincers, an ant to a leg, and stood, pulling. Saw still group of black ants; looked closer; all trussed to rock, twitching feebly and slowly, while black ant-spider guarded from rock, like robber baron. Big black silly beetle blundered over ants, like a rusty gentleman in pinstriped suit clambering up sand cliff.

Fish: sheened and wet in sun, colored and speckled and striated like rare glistening shells: small tight-fleshed fish with black streaks on shimmering pale blue sides; spined uglymouthed brown speckled fish; wicked black moray eel with triangular head, black nasty eyes and gorgeous yellow brocade back; red and pink shots of light from fins. Swimmer wading out of sea gripping squirming small octopus which twined and writhed long hanging legs; absurd bullet head; cracked octopus down on shore, legs piling and coiling, gift to fisherman.

After a brief trip to Paris and a long stay in Yorkshire with Ted's parents, the Hugheses returned to Cambridge, where they found a small, grimy apartment on Eltisley Avenue and set up housekeeping while Sylvia finished her studies at Cambridge.

WITHENS (YORKSHIRE)

Most people never get there*, but stop in town for tea, pink-frosted cakes, souvenirs and colored photographs of the place too far to walk to, visiting the Church of St. Michael and All Angels, the black stone rectory's rooms of memorabilia—wooden cradle, Charlotte's bridal crown of heirloom lace and honeysuckle, Emily's death couch, the small, luminous books and watercolors, the beaded napkin ring, the apostle cupboard. They touched this, wore that, wrote here in a house redolent with ghosts. There are two ways to the stone house, both tiresome.

One, the public route from the town along green pastureland over stone stiles to the voluble white cataract that drops its long rag of water over rocks warped round, green-slimed, across a wooden footbridge to terrain of goat-foot-flattened grasses where a carriage road ran a hundred years back in a time grand with the quick of their shaping tongues worn down to broken wall, old cellar hole, gate pillars leading from sheep turf to grouse country. The old carriage road's a sunk rut, the spring-clear well and gurgle under grass too green to believe. The hunk of matted gray hair and a long skull to mark a sheepfold, a track worn, losing itself, but not lost.

The other—across, the slow heave, hill on hill from any other direction over bog down to the middle of the world, green-slimed, boots squelchy—brown peat earth untouched except by grouse foot—blue white spines of gorse, the burnt-sugar bracken—all eternity, wildness, loneliness—peat-colored water. The house—small, lasting—pebbles on roof, name scrawls on rock—inhospitable two trees on the lee side of the hill where the long winds come, pierce the light in a stillness. The furious ghosts nowhere but in the heads of the visitors and

---

*The Brontë house

the yellow-eyed shag sheep. House of love lasts as long as love in human mind—

Anger jolts like heartburn in the throat

"ALL THE DEAD DEARS"

Mrs. Meehan-rich-flavored dialect story set in Yorkshire (*Wuthering Heights* background)—of present vivid influence of ghosts of those dead on woman who *almost* has second sight. Begin—"I saw an angel once"—"my sister Miriam"— tales of hanging, pneumonia death (implied murder), mad cousins, dead good one—war photo in hospital ward—dandy photo with straw Benjies and silver knobbed canes—"He's got his leg off. He was killed. He's dead and he's dead."

POEM

Wild hot fury—cold snow: thick white moor mist—lamps hanging. dim points. still: still: frozen leaves. bunched blackbird: rage—"one second more, the cat-hiss would come out." awareness of stifling, smothering fury—walk in white blank world—symbol of shutting off from normal clear vision— futile outburst. human limits versus grand marmoreal vast power of cold, snow, stars and blackness—vanished daisies: white in head, remembered from summer—she imposes them on dry barren broken stalks—vivid sense of opposition, polar crossing of season, climate—black stone fences—stark wild landscape—tawn cat, red coal fires, burning cheeks, cat under coal house—starlings at scraps of fat—frosted hedge—pose vast impersonal white world of nature against small violent spark of will.

NOVEL

Every person I see again. Everything comes full circle. Tony—pale, blond, shrunken—seen at railway station—whole floating Paris day returns—the circle of despair closes upon itself. The springtime of horror, drowning, where three men menaced and no choice was worth making, but one choice of all must be made. The German train shuttling to Munich—"You would have liked me if you knew me earlier." Take, seize, drink—amputate sight of links—be blind and steep in present. Darkened room. Pale lithe bodies. Yellow wallpaper—rose bouquets—refusal—rapid running away—petering into tea movie—knowledge someday the final thing will happen. I will see him from another life, nod in slightly lofty, slightly amused recognition from a world totally other, a world where the bedding of a young blond faun is utterly irrelevant, more, inconceivable, unwished.

Into the dark room, blind-windowed, car light goes gondoling along wall, slanting, curved bent in corner, then gone. Yet light comes steady sliced blue down chinks from streetlamp, layering square curtain lace shadow on flat wall like fragmented glass, coming moonly through cracked planes of water, splayed bright down desk side, fallen fault-angled on floor. Green bottle on sill involved in folded color shafts, blue cored and purpling, antique shelled, and dust on clear grape curve misted; intricate sea light; cylindrical complexity. Green subtle rose unpetaled, heart-light high mirror of distant farthering green suns that sink. Lingering yet between six-inch banded glass of window under blind, sudden the sun-sunk watered light westers apple green. Quilt feathered warm from soft geese down, full pouting cloud-molded lying under and around. Cloaked invisible, eccentric feathered, not noise, nor sound splices woven air nets, or startles straw lofts of needled hay. Sound seeks futile the safe needled hay, where lies, here lies the laughing one. Hidden in silk webbed hedges spidering unheard strands along the car wheels spinning. Switch-tailed squirreling mute tree leaves, alpine catalpa; singing wordless, owl-mouthed: prepare rabbit, and fear, fatidical ferret. Vulture gulped, hounded, doom-tongued crystal, moon condemned. Gone before the trumpet-toppling dawn. Dug down in soundless dung-daubed leaves. Never ferret, nor nervous rabbit down the dark gullet gone, recurs in fur-trimmed skin, not feathered sparrow speared on cruel prow of beak, unwatched, undone. Revert all to succulent marrow, alien bone, circling along the foreign blood. Unwound in the dark tide, lost perplexed in the labyrinthine dead end. Capering in the maples, demure cone pelting in the barbed fir, waddling among the nettles, and thrashing in the thistles. Yearly the dove feeds the sacred stone, grass-gagged, overgrown. Slumbering long within their plumdark sheathes of dumb flesh, blood stopped, they mind not mold soft mouths.

CAMBRIDGE

Monday afternoon, February 25. Hello, hello. It is about time I sat down and described some things: Cambridge, people, ideas. The years whirl by, & I am nowhere nearer articulating them than two years ago. I used to sit on my doorstep in Wellesley, & mourn my local stasis: If, I muttered to myself, I could Travel & meet Interesting People, oh, what I wouldn't write! How I would astound them all. Now, I have lived in Cambridge, London & Yorkshire [the Hughes family lived in Yorkshire]; Paris, Nice & Munich; Venice & Rome; Madrid, Alicante, Benidorm. Whiz. Where am I? A novel. To begin. Poems are moment's monuments. I am splitting the seams of my fancy terza rima. I need Plot: people growing: banging into each other & into circumstances: stewpot citizens: growing & hurting & loving & making the best of various bad jobs.

So this American girl comes to Cambridge to find herself. To be herself. She stays a year, goes through great depression in winter. Much nature and town description, loving detail. Cambridge emerges. So do Paris & Rome. All is subtly symbolic. She runs through several men—a femme fatale in her way: types: stolid Yale man critic Kraut-head Gary Haupt; little thin sickly exotic wealthy Richard; combine Gary & Gordon; Richard & Lou Healy [an old boyfriend]. Safe versus not safe. And of course: the big, blasting dangerous love. Also, double theme: combine Nancy Hunter [Smith roommate] & Jane: grave problem of identity. Peripheral boys: characters for amusement. . . .

Every day from now till exams: at least 2 to 3 solid pages describing a remembered incident with characters & conversation & descriptions. Forget about plot. Make it a vivid diary of reminiscence. Short chapters. By the time I go home there should be thus 300 pages. Revise over summer. Then either *Harper's* or *Atlantic* contest.

See each scene deep, love it like a complex faceted jewel. Get the light, shadow & vivid color. Set scene the night before. Sleep on it, write it in the morning.

But first: some quick notes on the present island. I am restless. Eager. Yet unproductive. Outside: a blue clear cold day that makes me want to be wandering through wooden stiles by the hawthorn hedges and squirrel tree to Granchester. But I biked to town today to shop: bank, P.O., where I mailed off two batches of Ted's poems, freshly typed, to *The Saturday Review of Literature*. Loaded my black patent-leather bag with sherry, cream cheese (for Grammy's apricot tart), thyme, basil, bay leaves (for Wendy's exotic stews—a facsimile of which now simmers on the stove), golden wafers (such an elegant name for Ritz crackers), apples and green pears.

I was getting worried about becoming too happily stodgily practical: instead of studying Locke, for instance, or writing— I go make an apple pie, or study *The Joy of Cooking*, reading it like a rare novel. Whoa, I said to myself. You will escape into domesticity & stifle yourself by falling headfirst into a bowl of cookie batter. And just now I pick up the blessed diary of Virginia Woolf which I bought with a battery of her novels Saturday with Ted. And she works off her depression over rejections from *Harper's* (no less!—and I can hardly believe that the Big Ones get rejected, too!) by cleaning out the kitchen. And cooks haddock & sausage. Bless her. I feel my life linked to her, somehow. I love her—from reading *Mrs. Dalloway* for Mr. Crockett—and I can still hear Elizabeth Drew's voice sending a shiver down my back in the huge Smith classroom, reading from *To the Lighthouse*. But her suicide, I felt I was reduplicating in that black summer of 1953. Only I couldn't drown. I suppose I'll always be overvulnerable, slightly paranoid. But I'm also so damn healthy & resilient. And apple-pie happy. Only I've got to write. I feel sick, this week, of having written nothing lately. The Novel got to be such a big idea, I got panicked.

But; I know & feel & have lived so much: and am so wise, yes, in living for my age: having blasted through conventional morality, and come to my own morality. Which is the commitment to body & mind: to faith in battering out a good life. No God, but the sun anyway. I want to be one of the Makaris: with Ted. Books & Babies & Beef stews.

The paraffin heater dear Dr. Krook loaned us gurgles down its lucent blue petrol and the glowing red wire dome warms the room. Afternoon sun reflects from the windows of the duplicate brick houses across the street. Birds whistle & chirr. Above the orange brick chimneys & chimney pots, white clouds drift and fray in a rare blue sky. God, it is Cambridge. Let me get it down in these next three months—the end of my 22 months in England. And I told myself, coming over, I must find myself: my man and my career: before coming home. Otherwise—I'll just never come home.

And now: both! As I never dreamed: a sudden recognition scene. Act of faith. And I am married to a poet. We came together in that church of the chimney sweeps with nothing but love & hope & our own selves: Ted in his old black corduroy jacket & me in mother's gift of a pink knit dress. Pink rose & black tie. An empty church in watery yellow-gray light of rainy London. Outside, the crowd of thick-ankled tweed-coated mothers & pale, jabbering children waiting for the bus to take them on a church outing to the Zoo.

And here I am: Mrs. Hughes. And wife of a published poet. Oh, I knew it would happen—but never thought so miraculously soon. Saturday, February 23rd, just almost an exact year from our first cataclysmic meeting at the *St. Botolph's* party, we woke late, grumpy & full of backwash tides of sleep, depressed over Ted's 3 rejections of poems from *The Nation* (after 3 acceptances in a row, a stupid letter from M. L. Rosenthal, rejecting them for the wrong reasons), *Partisan Review* (oh, so interesting, but we are simply cram-full with poems) & *Virginia Quarterly*. Ted is an excellent poet: full of blood & discipline, like Yeats. Only why won't these editors see it??? I muttered to myself. They accept bad flat poems, with no music, no color—only bad prose statements about bad subjects: unpleasant, nasty, uncommitted.

And then, while we were going about the domestic trivialities—Ted tying his tie in the living room, me heating milk for coffee, *The Telegraph* came.

Ted's book of poems—*The Hawk in the Rain*—has won the first *Harper's* publication contest under the 3 judges: W. H. Auden, Stephen Spender & Marianne Moore! Even as I write this, I am incredulous. The little scared people reject. The big unscared practicing poets accept. I knew there would be something like this to welcome us to New York! We will publish a bookshelf of books between us before we perish! And a batch of brilliant healthy children. I can hardly wait to see the letter of award (which has not yet come) & learn details of publication. To smell the print off the pages!

I am so glad Ted is first. All my pat theories against marrying a writer dissolve with Ted: his rejections more than double my sorrow & his acceptances rejoice me more than mine—it is as if he is the perfect male counterpart to my own self: each of us giving the other an extension of the life we believe in living: never becoming slaves to routine, secure jobs, money: but writing constantly, walking the world with every pore open, & living with love & faith. It sounds so paragon. But I honestly believe we are: apart, we rotted in luxury, adored & spoiled by lovers. Cruelly walking over them. Together, we are the most faithful, creative, healthy simple couple imaginable!

Scene for tomorrow: precise description of departure from Paris in spring with Gordon: farewell to Giovanni: doubts, horrid stifled depression; grim train ride; elegant meal; flavorless life; snow in Munich; frightening surgical hotel. Describe Paris room, breakfast [Omission.] Scorn & disgust of girl; forecast of failure of trip ahead. "You'll never marry, if you're like this." Taunts & undermines weak manhood, lack of purpose. Pivot point of decision.

Sweet dreams.

February 26, Tuesday. It is about 7:30. Have been awake since black 3:30, Ted sneezing & fighting off cold; frigid gray dawn. Mind incredibly quick. Placing poems. Visions of books: poems, novels. Are we destined to be as successful as I picture? Or is it a wish-dream? Got up as brash, nerve-raking alarm ground off at 6 to make bad eggnog. Grim argument over silly question, Ted maintaining it would be good to read a bad book deeply for 2 years in prison—one would learn by one's true experience it was wrong. Me saying it was better to have nothing to look at than a bad book: that only those with critical apparatus beforehand would be able to discern badness, & what good would it do them. He criticizing my Earthenware Head poem. Bad time for criticism. Me with no new poem to fight on yet. Oh, for vacation. Enough hacking. Begin.

Monday, March 4. I am stymied, stuck, at a stasis. Some paralysis of the head has got me frozen. Perhaps the vision of 3 papers to do in one week, and all English literature to read and reread in less than 3 months has stunned me idiotic. As if I can escape by going numb and daring to begin nothing. Everything seems held up, what is it?

Mail doesn't come. I haven't had an acceptance since October 1st. And I have piles of poems and stories out. Not to mention my book of poems. Even Ted's letter about winning the contest, with its award details, hasn't come, so even vicarious pleasure is shorn from me. Bills come. I write nothing. The novel, or rather, the 3-page-a-day stint, is atrocious. I can't get at it. I am writing with a blunt pencil tied on a mile-long stick, at something far off over the horizon line. Will I break through someday? At least if I get 300 pages written by the end of May, I'll have the creaking, gushing skeleton plot of the whole thing. Then I can write slowly, rewriting each chapter, carefully with a subtle structured style. If I can ever find a subtle structured style.

It's hopeless to "get life" if you don't keep notebooks. I am angry now because, except for snow, I forget what the trip from France to Munich was like. I keep being true-confessional. All interior "she felts" and appallingly awkward. *Again, I feel the gulf between my desire & ambition and my naked abilities.* But I will doggedly write my 3 pages a day, even if my supervisors scorn me. Only it would help my morale no end to feel it was a good novel. But it's not a novel now. Just straight blither. But the girl will have to get through a year of life in 3 months of mine. And then, two months this summer to rewrite, carefully, knowing what I'm trying to do. I might as well be glad of the plot. I really don't know much but that. And plot's hard for me, so good. . . .

I feel really uncreative. After talking with Mary Ellen Chase, I self-paralyze myself & wonder what I've got in my head. How to teach anyone anything? That would do me the most good, I think. The day by day teaching. Looked at in one gulp, it terrifies. As does the Novel. The Exams. But hour by hour, day by day, life becomes possible. But I am dry, dry and sterile. How is it it does not show? I feel [inferior to] Mary Ellen Chase, even, with dozens of 2nd rate novels, best sellers. I have not one. I must produce. But it is too usual to write about the lack of ideas for writing. Ted showed such brilliant insight when he said I needed at least a year in a place to settle—but to change every year or so to stimulate to new writing. That is so true.

If I can digest changes, in my novel. Not swell tumid with inarticulateness. As I am now. Or to gibbering—my old blue devil—black-white, black-white. I get quite appalled when I realize my whole being, in its refusing and refusing after my 3-year struggle to build it flexible and strong again, my whole being has grown and interwound so completely with Ted's that if anything were to happen to him, I do not see how I could live. I would either go mad, or kill myself. I cannot conceive of life without him. After twenty-five years of searching in the best places, there is just no one like him. Who fits. Who fits so perfectly and is so perfectly the male being complement to me. Oh, speak. I am so stupid. Really stupid. . . .

I could write a terrific novel. The tone is the problem. I'd like it to be serious, tragic, yet gay & rich & creative. I need a master, several masters. Lawrence, except in *Women in Love*, is too bare, too journalistic in his style. Henry James too elaborate, too calm & well-mannered. Joyce Cary I like. I have that fresh, brazen, colloquial voice. Or J. D. Salinger. But that needs an "I" speaker, which is so limiting. Or Jack Burden. I have time. I must tell myself I have time.

Only the weight of Irwin Shaw and Peter De Vries and all the witty, clever, serious, prolific ones oppresses me. I feel, were it not for Ted, I'd sell my soul. It is so ironic to think of nobly writing and writing on this novel, and sacrificing friends & leisure & turning out a bad bad novel. But I feel I could write a best seller. I'm sure of it in a kind of reverse way: I am sick with what I am writing—but am sure it can grow, be rewritten [in]to an artwork. In its small way. About the voyage of a girl through destruction, hatred and despair to seek and to find the meaning of the redemptive power of love. But the horror is that cheapness and slick love would be the result of the thing badly written. Well-written, sex could be noble & gut-shaking. Badly, it is true confession. And no amount of introspection can cure it.

I suppose I will get these papers done, & for a while get rid of this albatross of pressure & write well in vacation. I've done it before—the papers—& not died. But I must get back into the world of my creative mind: otherwise, in the world of pies & shin beef, I die. The great vampire cook extracts the nourishment & I grow fat on the corruption of matter, mere mindless matter. I must be lean & write & make worlds beside this to live in.

Monday, March 11, 1957. I have thought: a pox on my "She thought-she felt" banal novel. *Read* The Horse's Mouth: *that's it.* For now at least. Break into a limited, folksy, vivid style that limits the girl, defines her: humor, vivid, but serious: "at bottom really grave." Wife of Bath. Better read *Herself Surprised*. Make your own style, don't copy. But a richer "Laundromat Affair" style. And watch it be a best seller. Much easier to work at: style will define material. Most difficult part: style. Vivid direct descriptions. First person: perhaps I can get away with third.

I am wicked, sick: a week behind. But will do 5 pages a day until plodding I catch up. Use words as poet uses words. *That* is it! Gulley Jimson is an artist with words, too—or, rather Joyce Cary is. But I must be a word-artist. The heroine. Like Stephen Dedalus walking by the sea: ooo-ee-ooo-siss. Hissing their petticoats.

Now: a quick description: to be in the Cambridge-spring part of the book. Fish and chip shop on a rainy night:

Fish & Chips

Turned onto the Fen Causeway in black warm blowing mist. Orange lights reflecting in puddles, lurid orange suns, spinning orange cocoons out of the thick mist. Orange rain drops. An unnatural color. She gritted her teeth, patting her hair. Soggy, rain-wet. On the left, the sunken Sheep's Green, weltering in full brooks and standing ponds, shoved its poplars whoosh into the ragging mists. Those poplars. On clear nights, full of stars, leaning, pointing, big stars caught in the branches. Or angels. On those nights, stuck shining with angels. Remember Tinka Bell. Looked like a firefly glow till you got up close. Little lady then, shining dainty, with dragonfly wings.

Squinting, the black, slippery tree branches looked to circle the orange streetlamps. Spinning a net of branches, spiderwebbing orange.

"Why do the branches go round the lights?"

"The lights," he said, his pale orange profile cutting itself ahead into the black, "reflect on the branches going round, not the others."

She plunged her hand into his pocket. Orange light made patent-leather strips on his shiny leather coat. They crossed the bare highway by the Royal Hotel, the brick ugly and leprous orange. Across a little iron-railinged bridge by the Botannical Gardens.

"I hate orange lights. They make the town sick."

"Some council. Some one or two fat men sitting. Orange lights proposed. Easier to see in snowstorms, one or two snowstorms. And fogs. For the drivers. And we have to walk about in the foul orange mess. Like orange lepers."

No one was out in the rain. The streets shone, and blue-white lights shone on the narrow crisscross streets off the main highway with its globed orange pedestrian crossing lights ticking and blinking of their own accord by the black-and-white painted strip, bordered with metal studs.

Russell Street. Ahead, far up on the right. Light spilt out in a warm puddle. Two men climbed into the light, into the bright white doorway of the fish and chip shop.

"Do you have money?"

"No. I wish you'd take care of us."

"Take care!"

He stopped dead, the rain falling softly, wetly. He shoved his hand into his trouser pocket, his jacket pocket. He brought out a handful of coppers.

"Count it up."

"Sixpence, and thruppence. And three, four pennies. How much is one fish? And I was so wanting fish."

He hoisted up his coat, feeling into another pocket. And brought up another sixpence.

"All. Absolutely. Damn!" The gun barrel shone from inside his sweater. He hauled at it, fixing it steady.

"Careful." She drew his black wool scarf to hide it. "Do come in with me. It'll look suspicious if you stay outside."

"A hell of a lot more suspicious if I walk in with a gun sticking out of my coat. Why can't you get the stuff yourself?"

"I hate going in alone."

They stopped in front of the little door to the shop. Through the steamed glass, the white, square interior glittered, dazzling. They blinked, and he thrust open the glassed door.

Two boys in leather jackets lounged against the counter, staring openly. She pulled her black gown up on her shoulders. It was always slipping back, catching her arms behind like a straightjacket.

The pale thin man behind the counter lifted up a wire basket of hissing French fries. The pleasant woman beside him smiled, questioning. He was staring off to the side, seeing salmon jumping. Something. She nudged him. "Hey."

"One fish. Six pennyworth of chips."

"Plaice or cod?" the woman asked.

The girl smiled at her.

"Cod," the boy said.

"I just thought you might like plaice," the woman told the girl. She took a paper bag, half filled it with crisped brown chips and a fried slab of cod. "Give it back to me after you've put the vinegar on."

The girl picked up the cracked metal tin of salt and snowed it into the bag. Then, taking the cut-glass bottle of vinegar, she showered the fish, lifted the edge of it, and doused the potatoes. She handed the bag back to the woman, who wrapped it up in a sheaf of newspaper.

The boy counted out the change. They had twopence left.

" 'Night." They pushed out into the wet dark. Slowly, she unwound the newspaper, finding the mouth of the paper bag.

"Here." He reached in and broke off a steaming hunk of fish, tilting his head back, and dropping it into his mouth. She burnt her fingers, pulling off part of the fried skin, with the fish sticking succulent to her fingers. She licked them, as they strolled slowly down Russell Street.

"I'd rather eat fish and chips on a rainy night than anything," she said, offering him the bag again. "Take some chips too. They're all at the bottom." She cradled the bag against her, feeling the warmth. A warm center against the rain.

The chips were soaked with vinegar.

"Is that the monastery?"

They came to a long brick building on the left, with light spilling out from behind drawn blinds. "Yes," he said.

Radio music blared from behind the curtains. She stopped dead.

"The monks are meditating." He walked on ahead, his hands shoved into his pockets, to the street corner. But she froze the scene in her eye.

The glass lantern, the streetlight at the end of the street, against a brick wall, lit up the white background of the sign: "St. Elegius Street." Black letters. So neat. Always, I must remember this: the clear light in the square of iron ribs and glass. How fresh that sign shows.

A burst of laughter from the radio. And then deep, resonant chimes. "Hark to the chimes. Come bow your head . . ." Over the radio. That camp grace they always sang.

"Is it Big Ben?" she called, softly, to his turned back. "Yes."

She waited. The hour began to strike.

Bong. Bong. Bong. Would it finish? The rain fell lightly.

Bong. Bong. Someone, an old woman, pulled the curtain of the monastery and stared out.

Bong. The girl stood, ready to run.

Bong. The sound held her, hauling up a sight of the Thames walk below Haymarket. The black chains, the black walls, the lights hanging in transparent green tree leaves.

Bong. Bong.

"Nine o'clock," the boy said.

She came up to him, and pushed her hand back into his, in his pocket, digging her nails in between his fingers. They walked on, peering in cracks of window curtains into lighted rooms.

"Would you live in that house?"

"It's a garage." She stared up at the second-floor window of the little brick building. The curtains weren't drawn, and she glimpsed red hangings stark against white-painted walls. A boy, an Indian, with dark hair and a red sweater, moved into the window space and beyond. One wall was painted plum color.

"The young architect owns it."

"I'd like it. Snug. Watertight."

They came out onto the main road, into the orange mists.

"Let's walk back through the horse park," she said. "The orange grits my teeth. I feel positively sick at it."

"That way's a mud trough."

"We've got boots on."

They turned left, cutting across the highway, through the stile. Horses were grazing, dark shapes against the orange light, backs bent, manes flowing. Moving slowly over the wet grasses, ankle deep in low webs of orange fen fog.

Sudden sense of renewed creative gift: ability to "make of the moment something permanent"—air: threaded through with "Blue Room"—clatter of cups and dishes—Negresses in fruity tropical colors—tangerine, lime, watermelon pink—

Words begin: interior monologue re-creating scene, rearranging—speaking it—flower pellet unfolding in clear glass of the mind—bloom—into what? *Make Diary*—catch each pellet and let it unfold in the storage aquarium of rare blooms—keep the creating creative *core* and integrity (not selling [word missing] for more than it's worth) and no woman can have more—continuous social life kills or betrays inner world: to make it rare and strange.

Before Plath began her year of teaching at Smith, her mother arranged for the Hugheses to have a long holiday at Eastham, on Cape Cod.

EASTHAM, CAPE COD

July 15, 1957. The virginal page, white. The first: broken into and sent packing. All the dreams, the promises: wait till I can write again, and then the painful, botched rape of the first page. Nothing said. A warm-up. A directive. It is almost noon, and through the short spined green pines the sky is a luminous overhung gray. Some bastard's radio jazzes out of the trees: like the green-eyed stinging flies: God has to remind us this isn't heaven by a long shot. So he increases the radios and lethal flies.

Slowly, with great hurt, like giving birth to some endless and primeval baby, I lie and let the sensations spring up, look at themselves and record themselves in words: the blind moves in and out on the window with a slight breeze, pale yellow-brown, tawn, and the curtains move, cotton with yellow sunburst flowers and black twigs on a white ground. We have not yet got good coffee, but the fatigue is slowly sinking in us, after two days of heavy sleep, sogged with bad dreams: diabolically real: Haven House, the feet of Smith girls past the room, which becomes a prison, always giving out on a public corridor, no private exits. The leer: the slow subtly faithless smile, and the horror of the worst, the dream of the worst, come at last into its own. Waking is heaven, with its certainties. Why these dreams? These last exorcisings of the horrors and fears beginning when my father died and the bottom fell out. I am just now restored. I have been restored for over a year, and still the dreams aren't quite sure of it. They aren't for I'm not. And I suppose never will be. Except that we will be living a safe life, no gin parties, no drunk ego-panderings. If I write stories, poems, and the novel. All I need to do is work, break open the deep mines of experience and imagination, let the words come and speak it all, sounding themselves and tasting themselves.

Each of these magic seven weeks: writing: not the novel yet, until I'm warmed up. Now the stories. Fiction for *The*

Atlantic Monthly to be ready for Dan Aaron's* introduction to Sam Lawrence**: two stories at least: "The Eye Beam One": like Kafka, simply told, symbolic, yet very realistic. How one is always and irrevocably alone. The askew distortions of the private eye. Set in Cambridge. And another: perhaps a version of the waitress story: only I haven't got it here. Make it up. Naturalistic. Jewel prose. Make out little paragraphs of what happens to whom. Then think it clear. Write it. . . .

Slick stories: money-makers: very gay, lively with lots of family. Use Aldriches, baby-sitting experiences. Summer living in with family on beach: Cantors. Very fast pitch. Rewrite "Laundromat Affair." Also, diabolic sister story. How she comes in, jealous of younger brother's marriage, not like the old days. Funny rather giddy characters. Try also one very serious one: emotional: lady on shipboard? New York secretary: setting, *Queen Elizabeth*. Yes.

Novel: *Falcon Yard*: central image: *love, a falcon*, striking once and for all: blood sacrifice: falcon yard, central chapter of book: the irrefutable meeting and experience. *Emblem*: lord & lady riding smiling with falcon on wrist. Get impersonally into Judith, create other characters who act in their own right & not just as projections of her. . . .

CAPE COD

Wednesday, July 17. No skipping after today: a page diary to warm up. All joy for me: love, fame, life work, and, I assume, children, depends on the central need of my nature: to be articulate, to hammer out the great surges of experience jammed, dammed, crammed in me over the last five years, and before that, although before that it wasn't so desperate, for there was a slower flow of experience, digestible enough to be written out in short stories and poems, when I had a certain slickness that is enviable now, although that slickness would now never enclose and present the experience welling up in me full and rich as fruit on a blue and white pottery platter. Anyway, if I

---

*The critic Daniel Aaron, Smith faculty
**Seymour Lawrence, the publisher

am not writing, as I haven't been this last half year, my imagination stops, blocks up, chokes me, until all reading mocks me (others wrote it, I didn't), cooking and eating disgusts me (mere physical activity without any mind in it) and the only thing that sustains me, yet is not enjoyed fully, is the endless deep love I live in. . . . Without that, I would rush about, seeking solace, never finding it, and not keeping the steady quiet deadly determined center I have even now at the end of one of my greatest droughts: It Will Come. If I Work.

Poems are bad to begin with: elaborate ones especially: they freeze me too soon on too little. Better, little exercise poems in description that don't demand philosophic bear traps of logical development. Like small poems about the skate, the cow by moonlight, à la the Sow. Very physical in the sense that the worlds are bodied forth in my words, not stated in abstractions, or denotative wit on three clear levels. Small descriptions where the words have an aura of mystic power: of Naming the name of a quality: spindly, prickling, sleek, splayed, wan, luminous, bellied. Say them aloud always. Make them irrefutable.

Then: the magazine story: written seriously, but easily, because it is easier to manipulate strictly limited characters, almost caricatures, some of them, than the diary "I" of the novel, who must also become, in her way limited, but only so that she can grow to the vision I have now of life, which tomorrow will be a fuller vision, and tomorrow.

Yesterday was the first day of work: a bad day. Spent time on a very desperately elaborate psychological idea and wrote maybe one good image (the boy with the whole ocean bottled in his head) to a raft of brittle, stilted artificial stuff. Not touching on my deep self. This bad beginning depressed me inordinately. It made me not hungry nor want to cook, because of the bestialness of eating and cooking without keen thought and creation. The beach: too late, after a hot walk along a gravelly, sunny sidewalk on Route 6, the deathly pink, yellow and pistachio colored cars shooting by like killer instruments from the mechanical tempo of another planet. Broken glass, then the scrub pine shadowing Bracket Road, the whisk of bird and squirrel in underbrush, green berried shrubs, and the rough tar. A great blue span of Atlantic under the cliff at Nauset Light, and a swim in the warmish green seaweeded water, rising and falling with the tall waves at tide turn. Lay in sun far up beach, but the sun was cold, and the wind colder. The boom, boom of great guns throbbing in the throat, then the ride back, bad-tempered. Making mayonnaise, and it coming out well. Fine. Then, grubbing over supper, with the badly begun poem like an albatross round the neck of the day, nothing else. And the tables and chairs insulting the way they are when a human being tries to live their merely phenomenal life and miserably doesn't succeed. They go smug, I-told-you-so. Now it is near ten, and the morning yet untried, unbroken. The feeling one must get up earlier and earlier to get ahead of the day, which by one o'clock is determined. Last night: finished *The Waves*, which disturbed; almost angered by the endless sun, waves, birds, and the strange unevenness of description — a heavy, ungainly ugly sentence next to a fluent, pure running one. But then the hair-raising fineness of the last 50 pages: Bernard's summary, an essay on life, on the problem: the deadness of a being to whom nothing can happen, who no longer creates, creates, against the casting down. That moment of illumination, fusion, creation: We made this: against the whole falling apart, away, and the coming again to make and make in the face of the flux: making of the moment something of permanence. That is the lifework. I underlined & underlined: reread that. I shall go better than she. *No children until I have done it*. My health is making stories, poems, novels, of experience: that is why, or, rather, that is why it is good, that I have suffered & been to hell, although not to all the hells. I cannot live for life itself: but for the words which stay the flux. My life, I feel, will not be lived until there are books and stories which relive it perpetually in time. I forget too easily how it was, and shrink to the horror of the here and now, with no past and no future. *Writing breaks open the vaults of the dead and the skies behind which the prophesying angels hide*. The mind makes and makes, spinning its web.

Write down the passing thought, the passing observation. How Mrs. Spaulding, with her heavy-lidded blue eyes, her long braid of gray hair, wants her life written: so much happened. The San Francisco earthquake and fire, with her mother giving away the baked beans and bread to refugees, and she crying and wanting to keep the beans; hearing a sound like railway trains jamming into each other on a siding, seeing her doll cradle rock, grabbing the doll, her mother grabbing her into the bed. Her husband dropping dead. Her having an operation, coming out of the hospital to dry her hair at her friend's house, and have it set. Her second husband walks in the door, sees her long hair hanging: what a beautiful sight. The little child getting sick and missing him. His wife dying on the same day her husband did. All this: raw, material. To be useful. Also, images of life: like Woolf found. But she: too ephemeral, needing the earth. I will be stronger: I will write until I begin to speak my deep self, and then have children, and speak still deeper. The life of the creative mind first, then the creative body. For the latter is nothing to me without the first, and the first thrives on the rich earth roots of the latter. Every day, writing. No matter how bad. Something will come. I have been spoiled to think it will come too soon: without work & sweat. Well, now for 40 days I work & sweat. Write, read, sun & swim. Oh, to live like this. We will work. And he sets the sea of my life steady, flooding it with the deep rich color of his mind and his love and constant amaze at his perfect being: as if I had conjured, at last, a god from the slack tides, coming up with his spear shining, and the cockleshells and rare fish trailing in his wake, and he trailing the world: for my earth goddess, he the sun, the sea, the black complement power: yang to ying. The sky is clear blue, and the needles of the pine shine white and steely. The ground is orange-red with fallen pine needles, and the robins and chipmunks steal their color from this red earth.

July 18, 1957. A brief before-bed fling to say how lousy today was. After the night drive with Spauldings last evening, the gnats biting itches into the bone, the late greasy dishes, the Woolf sting in *Jacob's Room* put off because of it, a strange sleep. No more dreams of queen and king for a day with valets bringing in racks of white suits, jackets, etc., for Ted & ball gowns and tiaras for me. A semiplangent dream of children, sullen, cloudy, oppressed, squatting and being eel-catchers. Then a pleasant view of Ted's rosy mother holding a lovely droll baby, with two older children at her right side, me taking the cheeks of the baby & squeezing them into a comical dear O-face: her children or mine?

Very tired, contrasted with the crisp blue new morning, bowls of coffee made with milk and a morning of futile shilly-shallying over the mother's helper story, with the characters obstinate, not moving or speaking, and me with no definite idea of who they are: shall Sassy be a shy bookworm, dominated by mother, who comes out of her shell & gets a man? Or a tomboy terror, very athletic, who falls in love for the first time against her mother's directions, with a nice simple guy? God knows. About three stories are pulling me: mother dominates daughter, only nineteen years older, or twenty: girl 17, mother 37: mother flirts with girl's dates. Girl fights for freedom & integrity. *Sat Eve Post* story: suddenly possible as I think about it. Get tension of scenes with mother during Ira and Gordon crisis. Rebellion. Car keys. Psychiatrist. Details: Dr. B.: baby. Girl comes back to self, can be good daughter. Sees vision of mother's hardships. Yes yes. This is a good one. A subject. Dramatic. Serious. Enough of the hyphenated society names. Mental hospital background. Danger. Dynamite under high tension. Mother's character. At first menacing, later pathetic, moving. Seen from outside first, then inside. Girl comes back: grown bigger: ready to be bigger. Like mother, yet furious about it. Wants to be different. Bleaches hair. Policemen. Annoying her. Story in newspapers. After suicide attempt. Earthy Dr. B. Nowhere to go. Back to school. Then what? Something. Laborious charts. MOTHER-DAUGHTER. Troubles. Graphic. A real story. "Trouble-making Mother."

Okay. An idea. Just when you thought nothing had come. Or could. In six weeks you better be on a pile of written mss. Do it. Like Kazin said, this summary about what it is just isn't the story. It's playing about. But for me to break open an idea in summary is at this early stage a life-saving event. Not to scratch on the glossy surface of my head begging an idea to hatch, complete as a day-old chicken, on the blank page. Even the mother's helper story should do something. Fresh, brazen stubborn girl Sassy? Get to kernel of character: what motivates her to do what? Conflict: Stages. Mother wants Sassy to be a social success instead of what she is and to like right boy: chooses Chuck. Enter Lynn & Gary. Mother wants Lynn to help Sassy be social by setting example. Mother & Lynn vs. Sassy. Freshness, scene set for change. Sassy falls for Gary who falls for Lynn who is pinned & static. Lynn perceives this:

helps Sassy get Gary (on shipwreck) and Mother lose Chuck.
Shifts field. Own boyfriend comes back. Mother is shown the
light. How clear, how lovely. Now just write the damn thing....

July 20, 1957, Saturday. A new era has begun: it is not yet
seven thirty. I have my four hour morning ahead, whole as a
pie. And I am slowly, amazedly, beginning to delight again in
the workings of my own mind: which has been shut off like
an untidy corpse under the floorboards during the last half year
of exam cramming, slovenly Eltisley [Avenue, in Cambridge,]
living, tight budgeting, arranging of moving: us, great trunks,
hundreds of books and little thin delicate expensive pottery
cups. A space of paralysis. And now, aching, but surer and
surer, I feel the wells of experience and thought spurting up,
welling quietly, with little clear sounds of juiciness. How the
phrases come to me: I have begun the story about the Trouble-
Making Mother, and instead of scratching at a bare plastic
surface which resists my nails, I am sitting in the heart of it,
pouring it out, untidily, all right, but it comes, and the ordering
and shaping of it will come. And then the tale of the twenty-
four cakes will come....

We dream: and my dreams get better. Newnham last night,
clear, not low-skied, fetid, as in my old exam dreams. Neutral,
verging on pleasant: books on robins, queer birds, and exam
folio on natural design: pressed flowers: sheafs of pressed pink
and yellow trumpet flowers, wild and small. Podgy examiners,
Miss Cohen, Miss Morris. And waking, with my skin not yet
quite on, to Ted bringing cold orange juice to quench sleep-
thirst, and the bowls of coffee, green china-glass bowls.

In his dream we walked a meadow: a baby tiger, and a tiger
beyond a hedge. A tiger-man, with a great Chinesey yellow
face knocking at the door with a gun. Ted defending, bluffing
with an empty rifle: I could kill a tiger with snipe shot at this
distance. Magnificence. For the Novel.

Virginia Woolf helps. Her novels make mine possible: I
find myself describing: episodes: you don't have to follow your
Judith Greenwood to breakfast, lunch, dinner, or tell about her
train rides, unless the flash forwards her, reveals her. Make
her enigmatic: who is that blond girl: she is a bitch: she is the
white goddess. Make her a statement of the generation. Which

is you. Episodes: exterior: the white wedding cake halls of Newnham: concrete as no one has been concrete: the American innocence on the saturated spot of history. Worn walks, scooped stone steps: scooped by whom: famous names? Innocence beyond innocence, having passed intact through the disintegrating forces of lust, vanity, hate, ambition: plenitude, having passed through penury. No garden before the fall: but a garden handmade after it. B.W.: distressingly pedantic, bearish: would be a critic, trying to read "When I was young and easy under the apple boughs." Satirize him: shuffle, sinus, water blue eyes and faint whitish-yellow cast to skin: simple life: potato and steak. Heavy books by Yale professors inscribed: to B., in appreciation of his work in English . . . his affair with an older, ugly girl-artist who was past mistress of a loose, libertine poet and couldn't get over it. All for the novel. Beginning Monday: try for 7 or 8 pages a day.

> *The Girl in the Mirror*
> *Menagerie with a Red Fox*

July 25, Thursday. . . . Today: clear, flung, blue, pine-chills, orange needles underfoot. Writing weather, after three days of murking clouds, rain: silver tinselly rain, all theatrical and limpid big drops on Monday, then the deluge, cold, straight, and quite magnificent. We sat out on the dripping porch in chairs, rain pooling the green-plastic seat covers, smearing the screens with translucent panes of water, seeping into the dry fissured ground. Sunday was heaven: a mark in life, a clear line on a clean page: we were rested, writing free, tan, quite enchanted with our work, the sky, and our finding a sandbar, all smooth and shallow to bathe on between Nauset Light and Coast Guard Beach: we played: floating, my hands and feet bobbing like corks, my hair wet from my forehead, trailing to bait the fishes. A surge of glory and power. Then back to work. Writing and scrawling corrections, retyping, my story on the Trouble-Making Mother: close to my experience, slice out of a big pothering deep-dish pie. . . . I must say, I'm surprised at the story: it's more gripping, I think, than anything I've ever done. No more burble about Platinum Summers manipulated from behind my eye with a ten-foot pole. Real, dramatic crises.

A growth in the main character. Things and emblems of importance. I got depressed with the ending on Tuesday: four pages of anticlimactic question and answer between doctor and Sara, dry and chopped, logical as an adding machine: now, you've decided this, how do you feel about that. Bad as a rich involved poem with a bare flat two-line moral tacked on the end: this is the truth, kiddies, without any fancy stuff. Well, Tuesday night & yesterday morning I thought & found the answer: keep the audience guessing: fast, quick end, gathered up into the dramatic sheath of the story. I think I made it. Sent it off to *The Sat Eve Post*: start at the top. Try *McCall's, Ladies' Home Journal, Good Housekeeping, Woman's Day*, before getting blue. If they wrote little praises about my style in other stories, but wished for a more serious subject, why, this is my best styled story and has enough seriousness, identity problems, fury, love etc. to be a winner. If I got only one story accepted, I'd have a bulwark to lean my foot against between me and the last published one: my infancy, in 1952, five years ago. I would be helped by that: it would cast an aura of immediate potential over my present strugglings and catapult me out of the adolescent market into my own among all the money-earning brain-loaded adults. But, if not, I must work, and not whine. In five years after five years of steady work, I might have grounds to complain. Not now, after my first good story for five years, with hardly a word written in between.

The artist's life nourishes itself on the particular, the concrete: that came to me last night as I despaired about writing poems on the concept of the seven deadly sins and told myself to get rid of the killing idea: this must be a great work of philosophy. Start with the mat-green fungus in the pine woods yesterday: words about it, describing it, and a poem will come. Daily, simply, and then it won't lower in the distance, an untouchable object. Write about the cow, Mrs. Spaulding's heavy eyelids, the smell of vanilla flavoring in a brown bottle. That's where the magic mountains begin.

It is, O god, August 9th: a Friday, uncomfortably near the uprooting of roots, a clear blue-white morning about 9:30, and me coldly and gingerly writing about 14 lines on my long lumbering dialogue verse poem with two people arguing over a Ouija board. It is quite conversational sounding in spite of the elaborate 7-line pentameter stanzas rhyming ababcbc and is more ambitious than anything I've ever done, although I feel to be doing it like a patchwork quilt, without anything more than the general idea that it should come out a rectangular shape, but not seeing how the logical varicolored pieces should fit. At least it gets me out of that incredible sense of constriction which I have on trying to find subjects for small bad poems, and feeling always that they should be perfect, which gives me that slick shiny artificial look. So I will try to wean myself into doing daily poetic exercises with a hell-who-cares-if-they're-published feeling. That's my trouble. I see it very clear now: bridging the gap between a bright published adolescent which died at 20 and a potentially talented & mature adult which begins writing about 25. It is tempting to cling to the old lyric sentimental stuff: the prose shows how far I am behind: I haven't published a story for 5 years. The prose is not so easy to come into maturity as the poetry, which, by its smallness & my practice with form, can look complete. The main problem is breaking open rich, real subjects to myself & forgetting there is any audience but me & Ted.

I have never in my life, except that deadly summer of 1953, & fall, gone through such a black lethal two weeks. I couldn't write a word about it, although I did in my head. The horror, day by day more sure, of being pregnant. Remembering my growing casualness about contraception, as if it couldn't happen to me then: clang, clang, one door after another banged shut with the overhanging terror which, I know now, would end me, probably Ted, and our writing & our possible impregnable togetherness. The glittering and coming realities: my job at Smith, which I need more than anything to give me a sense of reality, of serving, specifically, from day to day, and meeting minds & working & practicing with them; our future, Ted with no job, me with no job, the avalanche of bills putting us into debt, and, worst of all, hating and hating the intruder when, four years from now, say, we could be the best parents possible. Also, the idea of 20 years of misery and a child being unloved, as it inadvertently, through our fault, killed our spiritual and psychic selves by freezing them into a stasis out of the necessity of sacrificing everything to earning money. Then we lived in, sickly, from day to day, counting the days over the longest time I'd gone: 35 days, 40 days, and then the crying sessions in the doctor's office, the blood test Sunday, in avalanches of rain & thunder, riding the streaming roads, up to our knees on our bikes in the dips filling inch by inch with rainwater, drenched to the skin, bent to break under the lightning. I pictured final judgment on a bridge: a thundercrack & last pyre of electricity. But nothing happened. Nothing, till Monday, when, after a busy, deceptive morning of shopping, I sat at the typewriter and the hot drench itself began, the red stain dreamed of and longed for during the white sterile ominous minutes of the six weeks. And the swearing to whatever gods or fates there be that I would never complain or bewail anything as long as the baby didn't come: the ultimate worst, aside from physical mutilations and sicknesses and deaths, or the loss of love.

And, punctually, I got the next worseness to cope with a day later: Yesterday, the rejection of my poetry book, after an almost malicious false alarm from Mother, and after half a year of hoping and yes, even counting on the damn thing. It was like receiving back the body of a cancerous lover whom you hoped dead, safely, at the morgue, in a wreath of flowers to commemorate the past.

August 9 (cont.) It Came Back. And with the misery of knowing half of the poems, published ones, weren't any longer, or in two years would definitely not be, passable in myself because of their bland ladylike archness or slightness. And I become linked to the damn book again, weeding it out like an overgrown garden: once the weeds were scenic, but not anymore. And if [Adrienne] Rich wasn't so dull, and Donald Hall so dull, and they putting in a hundred pages of dull published poems, I wouldn't feel so lousy. It would have backed me up at Smith in my work, given me that toehold on my adult work instead of making me go on from a five year gap, and only 16 poems published in the last year.

Worst: it gets me feeling so sorry for myself that I get concerned about Ted: Ted's success, which I must cope with this fall with my job, loving it, and him to have it, but feeling so wishfully that I could make both of us feel better by having it with him. I'd rather have it this way, if either of us was successful: that's why I could marry him, knowing he was a better poet than I and that I would never have to restrain my little gift, but could push it and work it to the utmost, and still feel him ahead. I must work for a state in myself which is stoic: the old state of working & waiting. I have had the most unfortunate hap: the bright glittery youth from 17 to 20 and then the breakup and the dead lull while I fight to make the experience of my early maturity available to my typewriter.

Yesterday: I faced another fact square on: I have not only been grossly spoiled: *I haven't worked at all*. Not one tenth hard enough. This I know now: it was outlined by our visit to the two young writers Mrs. Cantor sent over: they are both through with the first drafts of novels, 350 pages of typing: now that's, simply mechanically, a hell of a lot of typing not to mention writing & rewriting. They have had six months to our six weeks. So what. I haven't used six weeks. I haven't written a poem for six months until this long exercise in freer speech and extended subject, and haven't written a story since October except for one, "The Trouble-Making Mother," which is a slick story, but one I consider good, which was rejected without a word from *The Sat Eve Post*, and a flashy light one about a mother's helper which I consider artificial and not worth rewriting and which will, in a week, no doubt come back from *The Ladies' Home Journal* along with the little "Laundromat Affair." So what have I written: bad conscience about *Mademoiselle* and *Harper's* and *The Atlantic* plagues me: they'd print anything I wrote that was good enough. So all I have to do is work. Mavis Gallant wrote every night for ten years after work to get regular in *The New Yorker*, although she gave up everything. But, to salve my conscience, I must feel the pain of work a little more & have five stories pile up here, five or ten poems there, before I start even hoping to publish and then, not counting on it: write every story, not to publish, but to be a better writer—and ipso facto, closer to publishing. Also; don't panic. I'd rather not live in this gift luxury of the Cape, with the beach & the sun always calling, and me feeling guilty to stay in out of the sun...but more guilty to go out in the sun when I haven't worked at writing like a dog. That is what I need to end this horror: the horror of being talented and having no recent work I'm proud of, or even have to show. Next summer, better to sweat in Hamp [Northampton] & save money & work on novel so I'll be worth a year's grant to work on, say, a verse play. Now I've started this dialogue, I am interested in verse plays. TV: try that. But be honest. No more mother's helper stories with phony plots. It wasn't all phony, but slicked over, without the quirks, to move fast. And Ted will be proud of me, which is what I want. He doesn't care about the flashy success, but about me & my writing. Which will see me through.

Wednesday, August 21, 1957. A low, sultry day. The sky a luminous white glower of light. I am caught in the six days before this is over. Stops and starts. In love with Henry James: *Beast in the Jungle* robs me of fear of job because of love of story, always trying to present it in mind, as to a class. The first week will be the worst, but from Sept. 1st on, I'll outline my first four weeks & prepare them in detail & become familiar with the library again. So there. Once I get into the blissful concreteness of this job, my life will catapult into a new phase: that I know. Experience, various students, specific problems. The blessed edges and rounds of the real, the factual....

Yesterday: the weird spectacle of fiddler crabs in the mud off Rock Harbor Creek: a mud flat at low tide, surrounded by a margin of dried brittle marsh grass, stretching away into the yellow-green salt marsh. Mud, damp toward center, alive with the rustle and carapaced scuttle of green-black fiddler crabs, like an evil cross between spiders and lobsters and crickets, bearing one gigantic pale green claw and walking sideways. At our approaching footsteps, the crabs near the bank scuttled up it, into holes in the black mucky earth, and into the grass roots, and the crabs in the soggy black center of the dried pool dug themselves into the mud, under little mud lids until only claws jutted from the little cliff of the bank, and elbows and eyes looked out of the myriad holes among the roots of the dry grasses and the drying clustered mussel shells, like some crustaceous bulbs among the tussocks. An image: weird, of another world, with its own queer habits, of mud, lumped, underpeopled with quiet crabs....

When Plath returned to Smith as a member of the faculty, a returning golden girl, she was astounded by the coldness that greeted her. She also had enormous doubts about her own

abilities to teach as well as she had hoped to, and her schedule
frequently overwhelmed her physically.

August 28, 1957.—"The fullness thereof"

September 6. First morning up early. Clear day, light yellow-
ing, cold, among elm leaves. Last night: walk in odd primeval
greening park—dark twisted rocks, crunch of acorns underfoot, every sprig of fallen bough shaping itself to squirrels.
Now: coffee-vision, in spite of Ted using coffee percolator
wrong, making poisonous brew, milk boiling over, mislaying
percolator directions, waiting for desk (desk comes, all squat,
ugly; doesn't fit doorway; men take door down, still doesn't
fit; joy; it was so ugly; will bring up little desk from home with
vineleaves on it). Story: woman with poet husband who writes
about love, passion—she, after glow of vanity and joy, finds
out he isn't writing about her (as friends think) but about Dream
Woman Muse.

September 12. Last night: the horror of unknown physical pain,
accelerating—the swollen back gum, blistered, loose, bleeding; the ripped stomach muscle from hoisting furniture: like a
knife, turning, pivoting on a knife, that throbbed; then the
leftover beef stew, with the white blobs of salt pork, fat, greasy,
and the hot faint rushes of fever at the sight of bacon fat, melted
in the pan, and the pork sausages exuding and oozing their
own fat—the clenched fear: hernia, hemorrhage looming, and
the horror of ether, the razor slitting the stomach, and life
throbbing away, red flood by red flood—I lay, crouched, kneeling on the khaki quilt on the living room floor where there was
air, remembering Spain and the poisonous red Spanish sausage;
the Channel crossing and the tuna sandwich and wine and acrid
vomit in the nose, searing the throat, and me crawling under
the chairs; the Atlantic crossing and me kneeling on the floor
of the little cabin under the electric light and the vomit shooting
out across the room from the rich dinner, the lobster and pecans

and martinis—now, in the bathroom, kneeling on the floor, thinking of fat, of the salt pork and fatty marrow larding the thick soup, and retching, dryly: "Salt pork," I said, and then it came, the first dilute retch of stew, dissolved in water, then the clench, then the ejection. Ted held my head, my stomach, over the white bowl of the toilet. Then I washed my face, the fatty fumes cleared, I could sleep, exhausted, cool, till the sun of morning, pale and slanted through the venetian blinds, and the sound of leaves, falling—

Tuesday, October 1.

Letter to a demon:

Last night I felt the sensation I have been reading about to no avail in James: the sick, soul-annihilating flux of fear in my blood switching its current to defiant fight. I could not sleep, although tired, and lay feeling my nerves shaved to pain & the groaning inner voice: oh, you can't teach, can't do anything. Can't write, can't think. And I lay under the negative icy flood of denial, thinking that voice was all my own, a part of me, and it must somehow conquer me and leave me with my worst visions: having had the chance to battle it & win day by day, and having failed.

I cannot ignore this murderous self: it is there. I smell it and feel it, but I will not give it my name. I shall shame it. When it says: you shall not sleep, you cannot teach, I shall go on anyway, knocking its nose in. Its biggest weapon is and has been the image of myself as a perfect success: in writing, teaching and living. As soon as I sniff nonsuccess in the form of rejections, puzzled faces in class when I'm blurring a point, or a cold horror in personal relationships, I accuse myself of being a hypocrite, posing as better than I am, and being, at bottom, lousy.

I am middling good. And I can live being middling good. I do not have advanced degrees, I do not have books published, I do not have teaching experience. I have a job teaching. I cannot rightly ask myself to be a better teacher than any of those teaching around me with degrees, books published and experience. I can only, from day to day, fight to be a better teacher than I was the day before. If, at the end of a year of hard work, partial failure, partial dogged communication of a

Sylvia Plath with her mother and her brother, 1950

*Richard Sassoon during his
senior year at Yale*

LEFT: *At home, the summer of*
The Bell Jar, *1953*

BELOW: *The summer of 1954,
the year after her breakdown*

Senior year at Smith, 1955

At home in Cambridge, winter 1956-57

Plath and Hughes in Yorkshire, 1956

Spring 1959

Sylvia and Ted with their daughter, Frieda, 1960

Plath with Frieda, London, 1960

Plath in Devon with Frieda and Nicholas, March 1962

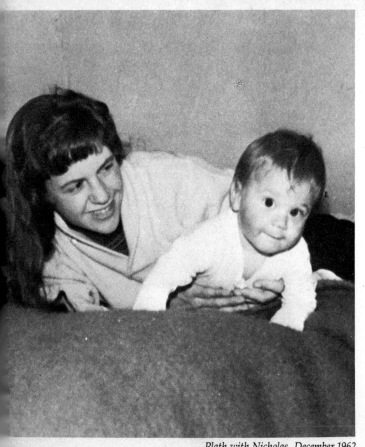

Plath with Nicholas, December 1962

poem or a story, I can say I am easier, more confident & a better teacher than I was the first day, I have done enough. I must face this image of myself as good for myself, and not freeze myself into a quivering jelly because I am not Mr. Fisher or Miss Dunn or any of the others.

I have a good self, that loves skies, hills, ideas, tasty meals, bright colors. My demon would murder this self by demanding that it be a paragon, and saying it should run away if it is anything less. I shall doggedly do my best and know it for that, no matter what other people say. I can learn to be a better teacher. But only by painful trial and error. Life is painful trial and error. I instinctively gave myself this job because I knew I needed the confidence it would give me as I needed food: it would be my first active facing of life & responsibility: something thousands of people face every day, with groans, maybe, or with dogged determination, or with joy. But they face it. I have this demon who wants me to run away screaming if I am going to be flawed, fallible. It wants me to think I'm so good I must be perfect. Or nothing. I am, on the contrary, something: a being who gets tired, has shyness to fight, has more trouble than most facing people easily. If I get through this year, kicking my demon down when it comes up, realizing I'll be tired after a day's work, and tired after correcting papers, and it's natural tiredness, not something to be ranted about in horror, I'll be able, piece by piece, to face the field of life, instead of running from it the minute it hurts.

The demon would humiliate me: throw me on my knees before the college president, my department chairman, everyone, crying: look at me, miserable, I can't do it. Talking about my fears to others feeds it. I shall show a calm front & fight it in the precincts of my own self, but never give it the social dignity of a public appearance, me running from it, and giving in to it. I'll work in my office roughly from 9 to 5 until I find myself doing better in class. In any case, I'll do something relaxing, different reading, etc., in the evenings. I'll keep myself intact, outside this job, this work. They can't ask more of me than my best, & only I know really where the limits on my best are. I have a choice: to flee from life and ruin myself forever because I can't be perfect right away, without pain & failure, and to face life on my own terms & "make the best of the job."

Each day I shall record a dogged step ahead or a marking time in place. The material of reading is something I love. I must learn, slowly, how to best present it, managing class discussion: I must reject the groveling image of the fearful beast in myself, which is an elaborate escape image, and face, force, days into line. I have an inner fight that won't be conquered by a motto or one night's resolution. My demon of negation will tempt me day by day, and I'll fight it, as something other than my essential self, which I am fighting to save: each day will have something to recommend it: whether the honest delight at watching the quick furred body of a squirrel, or sensing, deeply, the weather and color, or reading and thinking of something in a different light: a good explanation or 5 minutes in class to redeem a bad 45. Minute by minute to fight upward. Out from under that black cloud which would annihilate my whole being with its demand for perfection and measure, not of what I am, but of what I am not. I am what I am, and have written, lived and traveled: I have been worth what I have won, but must work to be worth more. I shall not be more by wishful thinking.

So: a stoic face. A position of irony, of double vision. My job is serious, important, but nothing is more important than my life and my life in its fullest realized potential: jealousy, envy, desperate wishes to be someone else, someone already successful at teaching, are naïve: Mr. Fisher, for all his student-love, has been left by his wife & children; Miss F., for all her experience and knowledge, is irrevocably dull. Every one of these people . . . has some flaw, some crack, and to be one of them would be to be flawed & cracked in another fashion. I'll shoulder my own crack, work on my James today, Hawthorne for next week & take life with gradual ease, dogged at first, but with more & more joy. My first victory was accepting this job, the second, coming up & plunging into it before my demon could say no, I wasn't good enough, the third, going to class after a night of no sleep & desperation, the fourth, facing my demon last night with Ted & spitting in its eye. I'll work hard on my planning, but work just as hard to build up a rich home life: to get writing again, to get my mind fertilized outside my job. . . .

No more knuckling under, groaning, moaning: one gets used to pain. This hurts. Not being perfect hurts. Having to bother about work in order to eat & have a house hurts. So what. It's about time. This is the month which ends a quarter of a century for me, lived under the shadow of fear: fear that I would fall short of some abstract perfection: I have often fought, fought & won, not perfection, but an acceptance of myself as having a right to live on my own human, fallible terms.

Attitude is everything. No whining or fainting will get me out of this job & I'd not like to think what would happen to my integral self if it did. I've accepted my first check: I've signed on, and no little girl tactics are going to get me off, nor should they.

To the library. Finish James book, memorize my topics, maybe the squirrel story. Have fun. If I have fun, the class will have fun.

Come home tonight: read Lawrence, or write, if possible. That will come too.

Vive le roi; le roi est mort, vive le roi.

Tuesday night, November 5. Brief note: to self. Time to take myself in hand. I have been staggering about lugubrious, black, bleak, sick. Now to build into myself, to give myself backbone, however much I fail. If I get through this year, no matter how badly, it will be the biggest victory I've ever done. All my spoiled little girl selves cry to escape before my bad teaching, ignorant somnolence is made drearily public among my old teachers and my new students. If I fainted, or paralyzed myself, or pleaded gibberingly to Mr. Hill that I couldn't carry on, I'd probably escape all right: but how to face myself, to live after that? To write or be intelligent as a woman? It would be a worse trauma than this, although escape looks very sweet & plausible. This way, I can build up a dull, angry resentment & feel I'm going through with it & will deserve my freedom in June, for sacrificing a year of my life. 7 more months.

First of all? Keep quiet with Ted about worries. With him around, I am disastrously tempted to complain, to share fears and miseries. Misery loves company. But my fears are only magnified when reflected by him. So Mr. Fisher called tonight & is coming to sit in on my class Friday. Instead of complaining to Ted, feeling my tension grow, echoed in him, I am keeping quiet about it. I will make my test of self-control this week being quiet about it till it's over. Ted's knowing can't help me in my responsibility. I've got to face it & prepare for it myself. My first day of Lawrence. Wednesday & Thursday to prepare for it. Keep rested. That's the main thing. Make up a couple of little lectures. Get class prepared.

The main thing is to get on top of this preparation. To figure how to start teaching them about style. For the first lesson, make up general lectures about form of papers, organization, read from papers. Don't get exasperated. A calm front: start at *home*. Even with Ted I must learn to be very calm & happy: to let him have his time & not be selfish & spoil it. Maturity begins here, however bad I am. I must prepare lectures, however poor.

January 4, 1958. New Year four days gone, along with res-olutions of a page a day, describing mood, fatigue, orange peel or color of bathtub water after a week's scrub. Penalty, and escape, both: four pages to catch up. Air lifts, clears. The black yellow-streaked smother of October, November, December, gone and clear New Year's air come—so cold it turns bare shins, ears and cheeks to a bone of ice-ache. Yet sun, lying now on the fresh white paint of the storeroom door, reflecting in the umber-ugly paint coating the floorboards, and shafting a slant on the mauve-rusty rosy lavender rug from the west gable window. *Changes:* what breaks windows to thin air, blue views, in a smother-box? A red twilly shirt for Christmas: Chinese red with black-line scrolls and oriental green ferns to wear every day against light blue walls. Ted's job chance at teaching just as long and just as much as we need. $1000 or $2000 clear savings for Europe. Vicarious joy at Ted's writing, which opens promise for me too: *New Yorker's* **3rd poem** ac-ceptance and a short story for *Jack and Jill.* 1958: the year I stop teaching and start writing. Ted's faith: don't expect: just write; listen to self, scribble. Fear about that: dumb silence. Yet: so what? It will take months to get my inner world peopled, and the people moving. How else to do it but plunge out of this safe scheduled time-clock wage-check world into my own voids. Distant planets spin: I dream too much of fame, pos-turings, a novel published, not people gesturing, speaking, growing and cracking into print. But with no job, no money worries, why, the black lid should lift. Look at life with humor: easy to say: things open up: know people: horizons extend. . . .

Night visions: the fire and coughing—zebra stripes of light laid on walls and angled ceilings from venetian blinds: *Falcon Yard*: rise above pure central line diary—lyric cry, no: but rich, humorous satire. Reconstruction. . . . Tables to bump into. Cameo—clear perspectives. Get back to perfect rhythms and words binging and bonging in themselves: green, thin, whine. . . .

The moment I stop, stop the itch of dreams and dream-lulling, squirrelish money-counting, paralysis sets in: paralysis of alternatives: to make up a scene? to describe a childhood incident by memory? I have no memory. Yes, there was a circle of lilac bushes outside Freeman's yellow house. Begin there: 10 years of childhood before the slick adolescent years, and then my diaries to work on: to reconstruct. Two poplar trees, green and orange striped awnings. I never learned to look at details. Recreate life lived: that is renewed life. The incident goes down, a grit in the eye of god, and is wept forth a hundred years and a day hence, a globed iridescent pearl world. Turn the glass globe and the snow falls slowly through ronds of quartz air. Metaphors crowd. Pellets of fact drop into the mind's glass of clear liquor and unfold petal by petal, red, blue, green, or pink and white—paper flowers creating an illusion of a world. Every world crowns its own kings, laurels its own gods. A Hans Andersen book cover opens its worlds: the Snow Queen, blue-white as ice, flies in a sleigh through her snow-thick air: our hearts are ice. Always: sludge, offal, shit against palaces of diamond. That man could dream god and heaven: how mud labors. We burn in our own fire. To voice that. And the horror: the strange bird who knows Longfellow, perches on a wire with a backdrop of English green-bushed landscapes. The white-bearded grandfather drowning in the sea-surge, the warm, slow, sticky rollers; the terror of paper crackling and expanding before the burnt-out black grate: whence these images, these dreams? Worlds—shut off by car-bustle, calendar-dictation. A world hung in a Christmas ornament, washed gilt, a world silvered and distended in the belly of my pewter teapot: open Alice's door, work and sweat to pry open gates and speak out words and worlds.

Each day an exercise, or a stream-of-consciousness ramble? Hates crackle and brandish against me: unsettling the image of brilliance. My face I know not. One day ugly as a frog the mirror blurts it back: thick-pored skin, coarse as a sieve, exuding soft spots of pus, points of dirt, hard kernels of impurity—a coarse grating. No milk-drawn silk. . . . Hair blued with oil-slick, nose crusted with hair and green or brown crusts. Eye-whites yellowed, corners crusted, ears a whorl of soft wax. We exude. Spotted bodies. Yet days in a dim or distant light we burn clear of our shackles and stand, burning and speaking like gods. The surface texture of life can be dead, was dead for me. My voice halted, my skin felt the pounds and pounds, pressure of other I's on every inch, wrinkled, puckered, sank in on itself. Now to grow out. To suck up and master the surface and heart of worlds and wrestle with making my own. To speak *morally*, for it is a moral. A moral of growth. Fern butting its head on concrete of here and now and ramming its way through. To get the faces, bodies, acts and names and make them live. To live as hard as we can, extending, and writing better. This summer: no job, or only very part-time job. German study and French reading. Reading own books: Berkeley, Freud, sociology. Most of all: myths and folktales and poetry and anthropology. History even. Knowing Boston. Boston diary: taste, touch, street names. Six o'clock rings, belling from the church where all the funerals come. Rooms. Every room a world. To be god: to be every life before we die: a dream to drive men mad. But to be one person, one woman—to live, suffer, bear children and learn other lives and make them into print worlds spinning like planets in the minds of other men.

. . . How everything shrinks on return—you can't go home again: Winthrop shrunk, dulled, wrinkled its dense hide: all those rainbow extensions of dreams lost luster, shells out of water, color blanching out. Is it that our minds colored the streets and children then and do so no longer? We must fight to return to that early mind—intellectually we play with fables that once had us sweating under sheets—the emotional, feeling drench of wonder goes—in our minds we must recreate it, even while we measure baking powder for a hurry-up cake and calculate next month's expenses. A god inbreathes himself in everything. Practice: *Be* a chair, a toothbrush, a jar of coffee from the inside out: *know* by feeling in.

* * *

Tuesday night, January 7. All day, or two days, you lay under the maple table and heard tears, phones ring, tea pouring from a pewter pot. Why not lie there until you rot or get thrown out with the rubbish, [the] book? A wreck on a shoal, time and tears vicissituding round about you, surging and sliding cool and blue-distant. Lie there, catching dust, pale rose and lavender scruff from the rug, blank-paged, and my voice quiet, choked in. Or to pass on air, blown with the other cries and complaints, to some limbo in the far nebulae. Anyhow: by dint of squandering some ink here, after counting your pages, you should see me through to the spring, to my so-called liberty— from what I seem to know, but for what I can only dream. Writing stories and poems is hardly so farfetched. But talking about it hypothetically is grim: a thing. Today, outside now, snow descends. This is where I came in. Dry taps on window. A greenish light from the lamps and flakes blowing oblique in the cone of light. An auspicious beginning for work tomorrow. After sun all week. And my lectures as usual, to prepare tomorrow morning—felt and feel mad, petulant, like a sick wasp—cough still and can't sleep till late at night, feel grogged and drugged till noon. Yet will I work and get through. One day at a time. After a brief bold encounter with Chas. Hill yesterday, blue and squinch-toothed, and his icy self, a call from Mr. Fisher and my stupid discussion this morning in the high white atticky study, all book-crammed, and his 7 volume novel in black thesis books with white lettering that I know must be so ghastly. The gossip. One gets sick trying to conjecture it. The eleven o'clock coffee break and the gossip. All the inferences: The Institution will regard you as irresponsible. Two-year conventions. Rot. I am in a cotton-wool wrap. All is lost on me—all double entendres. "I have divided loyalties," I say. "I am your friend," he says. "No one but me will tell you this. Oh, by the way, may I tell all this to Mr. Hill?" "I resigned twice," he said. "Once because of gossip that I was sleeping with students. President Nielson called up and found there were 10 in my class: 'Hell, Fisher, that's too much even for you!'" Now he is living deserted by his 3rd Smith wife for his selfishness. His vanity is as palpable as his neat white mustache. "It's all in your mind," he says, "about anxiety. I have it from various sources." If they deal in inference, hint, threat, double entendre, gossip, I'm sick of it. They mean vaguely well, somehow. But have no idea what is for my own good, only theirs. "What do you need to write?" Gibian asks over tea. Do I need to write anything? Or do I need time and blood? I need a full head, full of people. First know myself, deep, all I have gathered to me of otherness in time and place. Once Whitstead was real, my green-rugged room with the yellow walls and window opening onto Orion and the green garden and flowering trees, then the smoky Paris blue room like the inside of a delphinium with the thin nervous boy and figs and oranges and beggars in the streets banging their heads at 2 A.M., then the Nice balcony over the garage, the dust and grease and carrot peels of Rugby Street on my wedding night, Eltisley Avenue, with the gloomy hall, the weight of coats, the coal dust. Now this pink-rose-walled room. This too shall pass, laying eggs of better days. I have in me these seeds of life.

Sunday night, January 12. Fumings of humiliation, burned and reburned, heartburn, as if I could relive a scene again and over, respeak it, forge it to my own model, and hurl it out, grit into pearl. Grit into art. Blundering, booted, to the little coffee shop table, past muffled chairs, braced under draped coats. The intimate group of three, James leaving, black-haired, squinting, not speaking, air sizzling with unspoken remarks, "Do you really hate it here so much?" The pale British Joan, green-rimmed spectacles, green-painted fingernails, furred, with great dangling gold Aztec earrings, shaped like cubist angels, meaning remarks and meaning looks—Sally's great flat pale hands, like airborne white-bellied flounders, backs freckled, gesturing, stub-nails enameled with gilt paint. Superior. Condescending. Rude pink white-mustached Fisher: "Shame on you," grinning foolishly, pointing to red lipstick caked in a crescent on a coffee cup—"The mark of the beast." All the back references to common experience—"Is this yours?"—persian-lamb fezzed Monas holding up a pale tan pigskin pouch stamped in red and green and gold pattern. "No, I wish it were. Is it Susie's? Is it Judy's?" Parties. Dinners. Lady with fishy eyes. "It's all in your mind," Fisher says. "I have it from various sources." In polite society a lady doesn't punch or spit. So I turn to my work. Dismissed without a word from the exam committee, hearing Sally superciliously advising me not to tell my students questions, I am justifiably outraged. Spite. Meanness. What else. How I am exorcising them from my system. Like bile. See Aaron and get it out. See Marlies about exam and get it out. The girls stand by. Even the big, nasty, blank-faced [one] in her raccoon coat turned good, two and one-half hours of good talk Friday. Saturday exhausted, nerves frayed. Sleepless. Threw you, book, down, punched with fist. Kicked, punched. Violence seethed. Joy to murder someone, pure scapegoat. But pacified during necessity to work. Work redeems.

January 14, Tuesday. . . . Now I am uncaring, more and more, about Smith social life. I will lead my own: Sunday teas, dinners later for U. of M. teachers and my work. Even, I'll try if the prose isn't too bad. Poems are out: too depressing. If they're bad, they're bad. Prose is never quite hopeless. The poetry ms. came thumping back unprized from the $1000 contest. Who won? I'd like to know. The second defeat. Must watch where it goes the third time. But I got rid of my gloom and sulking sorrows by spending the day typing sheafs of Ted's new poems. I live in him until I live on my own. Starting June 1st. Will I have any ideas then? I've been living in a vaccuum for half a year, not writing for a year. Rust gags me. How I long again to be prolific. To whirl worlds in my head. Will I promise for 150 more days how I'll write, or take courage and start now? Something deep, plunging, is held back. Voice frozen. . . .

January 20, Monday. Wicked, my hand halted, each night at writing, I fell away into sleep, book unwritten in. Woke today at noon, coming drugged to the surface, after a lost weekend. All the deep rooted yawns. Plunged to the depths of my fatigue, and now: bushels of words. I skim the surface of my brain, writing. Prose now. Working over the kernel chapter of my novel, to crouch it and clench it together in a story. Friday night in Falcon Yard. A girl wedded to the statue of a dream, Cinderella in her ring of flames, mail-clad in her unassaultable ego, meets a man who with a kiss breaks her statue, makes man-sleepings weaker than kisses, and changes forever the rhythm of her ways. Get in minor characters, round them out.

Mrs. Guinea. Miss Minchell. Hamish. Monklike Derrick. American versus British. Can I do it? Over a year maybe I can. Style is the thing. "I love you" needs my own language. . . .

Free now, of a sudden, from classes, papers. Half the year over and spring to come, I turn, selfish, to my own writing. Reading a glut of *Sat Eve Post* stories till my eyes ached. These past days I realized the gap in my writing and theirs. My world is flat thin pasteboard, theirs full of babies, odd old dowagers, queer jobs and job lingo instead of set pieces ending in "I love you." To live, to gossip, to work worlds in words. I can do it. If I sweat enough. . . .

Jealous one I am, green-eyed, spite-seething. Read the six women poets in the *New Poets of England and America*. Dull, turgid. Except for May Swenson and Adrienne Rich, not one better or more-published than me. I have the quiet righteous malice of one with better poems than other women's reputations have been made by. Wait till June. June? I shall fall rust tongued long before then. Somehow, to write poems, I need all my time forever ahead of me—no meals to get, no books to prepare. I plot, calculate: twenty poems now my nucleus. Thirty more in a bigger, freer, tougher voice: work on rhythms mostly, for freedom, yet sung, delectability of speaking as in succulent chicken. No coyness, archaic cutie tricks. Break on them in a year with a book of forty or fifty—a poem every ten days. Prose sustains me. I can mess it, mush it, rewrite it, pick it up any time—rhythms are slacker, more variable, it doesn't die so soon. So I will try reworking summer stuff: the *Falcon Yard* chapter. Yet it is a novel chapter somehow: slack, uncritical. Too many characters in it. Must make some conflict. I am at least making more minor characters come alive. . . . Must avoid the exotico-romantico-glory-glory slop. Get in gem-bright details. What is my voice? Woolfish, alas, but tough. Please, tough, without any moral other than that growth is good. Faith *too* is good. I am too a puritan at heart. I see the back of the black head of a stranger dark against the light of the living room, band of white collar, black sweater, black trousers and shoes. He sighs, reads out of my vision, a floorboard creaks under his foot. This one I have chosen and am forever wedded to him.

Perhaps the remedy for suppressed talent is to become queer:

queer and isolate, yet somehow able to maintain one's queerness while feeding food and words to all the world's others. How long is it since bull sessions about ideas? Where are the violent argumentative friends? Of seventeen, of yesteryear? Now Marcia is set in her dogmatic complacency [omission] . . . netted in by supermarkets, libraries, and job routine. Entertaining? Probably. . . . She shells some resentment under her brisk breezy talk. I am too simple to call it envy: "Do all your students think you're just wonderful and traveled and a writer?" Acid baths. Given time . . . I'll attack her next year and get at her good innards. Innocence my mask. It always was, in her eyes, I the great dreamy unsophisticated and helpless thus unchallenging lout-girl. She, so pragmatic, now markets and cooks with no more savoir faire than I, I wife my husband, work my classes and "write." She remembers two things of me: I always chose books for the color and texture of their covers and I wore curlers and an old aqua bathrobe. To my roommate, with love. . . . I wonder if, shut in a room, I could write for a year. I panic: no experience! Yet what couldn't I dredge up from my mind? Hospitals and mad women. Shock treatment and insulin trances. Tonsils and teeth out. Petting, parking, a mismanaged loss of virginity and the accident ward, various abortive loves in New York, Paris, Nice. I make up forgotten details. Faces and violence. Bites and wry words. Try these.

January 22, Wednesday. Absolutely blind fuming sick. Anger, envy and humiliation. A green seethe of malice through the veins. To faculty meeting, rushing through a gray mizzle, past the Alumnae House, no place to park, around behind the college, bumping, rumping through sleety frozen ruts. Alone, going alone, among strangers. Month by month, colder shoulders. No eyes met mine. I picked up a cup of coffee in the crowded room among faces more strange than in September. Alone. Loneliness burned. Feeling like a naughty presumptuous student. Marlies in a white jumper and red dark patterned blouse. Sweet, deft: simply can't come. Wendell and I are doing a textbook. Haven't you heard? Eyes, dark, lifted to Wendell's round simper. A roomful of smoke and orange-seated black painted chairs. Sat beside a vaguely familiar woman in the very front, no one between me and the president. Foisted forward. Stared intently at gilt leaved trees, orange-gilt columns, a bronze frieze of stags, stags and an archer, bow bent. Intolerable, unintelligible bickering about plusses and minuses, graduate grades. On the back cloth a Greek with white-silver feet fluted to a maid, coyly kicking one white leg out of her Greek robe. Pink and orange and gilded maidens. And a story, a lousy sentimental novel chapter 30 pages long and utterly worthless at my back: on this I lavish my hours, this be my defense, my sign of genius against those people who know somehow miraculously how to be together, au courant, at one. Haven't you heard? Mr. Hill has twins. So life spins on outside my nets. I spotted Alison, ran for her after meeting—she turned, dark, a stranger. "Alison," Wendell took her over, "are you driving down?" She knew. He knew. I am deaf, dumb. Strode into slush, blind. Into snow and gray mizzle. All the faces of my student shining days turned the other way. Shall I give, unwitting, dinners? to invite them to entertain us? Ted sits opposite: make his problems mine. Shut up in public. Those bloody private wounds. Salvation in work. What if my work is lousy? I want to rush into print any old tripe. Words, words, to stop the deluge through the thumbhole in the dike. This be my secret place. All my life have I not been outside? Ranged against well-meaning foes? Desperate, intense: why do I find groups impossible? Do I even want them? Is it because I cannot match them, tongue-shy, brain-small, that I delude my dreams into grand novels and poems to astound? I must bridge the gap between adolescent glitter and mature glow. Oh, steady. Steady on. I have my one man. To help him I will.

Sunday night, January 26. A blank day of cooking and gusts of drowsiness. Mother gone on a broth of renewed communication: suddenly it comes over me—how much life is shuttered and buckled in the tongues of those we patronize and take for granted. "How did M's madness come on her?" we asked. The dining room stood dark, windowless, guarding its shadows, and the two uneven red candles, one tall, one short, stuck into the green bottles, wax-crusted, made a tawdry yellow light, as candles do, warring against the faintest gray daylight. M. became a religious fanatic and one morning, shortly before

Pearl Harbor, began to prophesy: she was Christ, she was Gandhi, she would not let her husband touch her. Mother listened to her, lying on her back, shut-eyed, with no food, no drink, talk, talk, talking for ten hours without a stop. A mental hospital for two years; [her husband]: "Stop chasing after butterflies and come home to take up your real responsibilities." Relapses, setbacks. He and his "perfect marriage"—never once did she contradict him or counter his wishes. She, her own heroine, living sainthoods, martyrdoms, novel sagas. Married to the wrong man, twenty-one years older than she. [Omission.]

Oh, spring vacation. Sometimes, secure, I wonder we don't stay here, Ted teaching (ho) at Amherst, or Holyoke (he has had inquiries from both) and me here. A joint income of $8 thousand. But even as I wake from the nice comfort, I see my own death, and his and ours smiling at us with candied smile: The Smiler. How a distant self must, vain and queenly, dream of being a great dramatic Dunn or Drew-type teacher, loved, wise, white-headed and wrinkled, a many-wrinkled wisdom.

I breathe among dry coughs and clotted noses. I must, on the morning coffee-surge of exultation and omnipotence, begin my novel this summer and sweat it out like a school year—rough draft done by Christmas. And poems. No reason why I shouldn't surpass at least the facile Isabella Gardner and even the lesbian and fanciful Elizabeth Bishop in America. If I sweat the summer out. . . .

I want one [a baby]. After this book-year, after next-Europe-year, a baby-year? Four years of marriage childless is enough for us? Yes, I think I shall have guts by then. The Merwins* want no children—to be free [omission]. . . . I will write like mad for 2 years—and be writing when Gerald and or Warren 2nd is born, what to call the girl? O dreamer. I waved, knocked, knocked on the cold window glass and waved to Ted moving out into view below, black-coated, black-haired, fawn-haunched and shouldered in the crisp-stamped falling snow. Fevered, how I love that one.

Jack and Jill rejection came. How I intuit ahead. No reason, but all my pink-potted dreams gone kaput. But with it a strange

---

*The poet W. S. Merwin and his wife, Dido

letter from *ARTnews* asking for a poem on art and speaking of an "honorarium" of $50–$75—a consolation prize? I shall submerge in Gauguin—the red-caped medicine man, the naked girl lying with the strange fox, Jacob wrestling with his angel on a red arena ringed by the starched white-winged caps of Breton peasant women. Oh, will this week end, to my one day, my Sunday, of rest? Will I somehow prepare my classes on Joyce, yet undone? I drive to the breaking point, but have tested and tried myself and only say: the end will come. A year to write in—to read Everything. Will it come and we do it? Answer me, book. Today: Matisse, exploding in pink cloths and vibrant rich pink shadows, pale peach pewter and smoky yellow lemons, violent orange tangerines and green limes, black-shadowed and the interiors: Oriental flowery—pale lavenders and yellow walls with a window giving out onto Riviera blue— a bright blue double-pear-shape of a violin case—streaks of light from the sun outside, pale fingers—the boy at the scrolled piano with the green metronome shape of the outdoor world. Color: a palm tree exploding outside a window in yellow and green and black jets, framed by rich black red-patterned draperies. A blue world of round blue trees, hatpins and a lamp. Enough. I shall sit and stare at Gauguin in the library, limit my field and try to rest, then write it. Don't count gold hens before eggshell congeals.

Secret sin: I envy, covet, lust—wander lost, red-heeled, red-gloved, black-flowing-coated, catching my image in shop windows, car windows, a stranger, sharper-visaged stranger than I knew. I have a feeling this year will seem a dream when done. I have some great nostalgia for my lost Smith-teacher self, perhaps because this job is now secure, bitable-size, and the new looming "threat of a new life" in a new (for me) city at the one trade which won't be cheated or "got-by" with patch-up jobs, waits, blank-paged: oh, speak. What then? What now? How much easier, how much smiling deadlier, to scrape and scrub a living off the lush trees of Joyce, of James. Morning, too, of Matisse odalisques, patterned fabrics, vibrant, blue-flowered tambourines, bare skin, breast-round, nipples-rosettes of red lace and the skirls and convoluted swirls of big palmy oaky leaves. . . .

. . . The new sense of power and maturity growing in me from coping with this job, and cooking and keeping house, puts me far from the nervous insecure miserable idiot I was last September. Four months has done this. I work. Ted works. We master our jobs and are, we feel, good teachers, natural teachers—this: the danger. The sense of elaborate exclusion, the unseeing gaze of Joan and calculated insolence and patronizing stance of Sally I shall be free from: I don't like it, yet I don't like them enough to court lost favor. When did the change come? With my bursting into tears in front of Marlies? Humiliations stomached like rotten fruit. I grow through them and beyond. My work must engross me these next four months— plays and poems, reading for [Newton] Arvin, working on a poem for *ARTnews*. Black-clad, I walk alone, and so what: caricature green-nailed Joan and pale freckle-spreckled Sally in stories. A new life of my own I shall make, from words, colors and feelings. The Merwins' high Boston apartment opens its wide-viewed windows like the deck of a ship.

Sunday, February 9. Night nearing nine. Outside: laughter of boys, the brooom-brooom of a car revving up. Today spent itself in a stupor, twilit, fortified by coffee and scalding tea: a series of cleansings—the icebox, the bedroom, the desk, the bathroom, slowly, slowly ordering—trying to keep the "filth of life at a distance"—washing hair, self, stockings and blouses, patching the ravages of a week, reading to catch up with my first week of Hawthorne stories—writing, for the first time, a long letter to Olwyn,* feeling colors, rhythms, words joining and moving in patterns that please my ear, my eye. Why am I free to write to her? My identity is shaping, forming itself— I feel stories sprout, reading the collection of *New Yorker* stories—yes, I shall, in the fullness of time, be among them— the poetesses, the authoresses. I must meantime, this June beginning, learn about planets and horoscopes to be in the proper starred house: I'll wish I had learned if I don't: tarot pack, too. Maybe I should stay alone, unparalyzed, and work myself into mystic and clairvoyant trances. To get to know Beacon Hill, Boston, and get its fabric into words. I can. Will. Now to do what I must, then to do what I want: this book too becomes a litany of dreams, of directives and imperatives. I

---

*Ted's sister

need not to be more with others, but to be more and more deeply, richly alone. Recreating worlds. . . . Now for a picture, enough of this blithering about calendar engagements: I am here: black velvet slacks stuck with lint, worn and threadbare slippers, dun-fuzzed with dark brown leopard spots on a pale tan ground, gilt bordered, then the polished blond-brown woodwork of the maple coffee table, the dull inner glow of white and silver highlights on the pewter sugar bowl with its domed lid and cupola peak, then the dented-red-skinned apples, mealy and synthetic tasting. Ted in the great red chair by the white bookcase of novels, his hair rumpled front, dark brown, but tighter than ever, and his face blue-greening along the jaw: Those faces he makes: owls, monsters: "The Man Who Made Faces": a symbolic story? Who are we, really? In his dark green sweater, white and green banded at the cuffs, bent over the pink tablet, black trousers, gray socks of pale thick wool, shoes black, cracked, shining in the light. He poises, pen in right hand, propping his chin, elbow on the tablet and the chartreuse-shaded light behind him. All about, in a three-quarter circle, papers, airmail letters, books, torn pink scraps of tissue, typed poems. I, chilled, feel his warmth [omission] . . . haul me over to be held and hugged: HUG his shirts instruct, at the inner neckband, coming back from the laundry starched and bound. Another story for *The New Yorker*: the evocation of my seventeenth summer, the spurt of blood of my period and the twins painting the house, the farm work and Ilo's kiss. A synthesis: the coming of age. A matter of moment: get M. E. Chase to tell me where to send *New Yorker* stories, to whom. I shall in a year do it.

I catch up: each night, now, I must capture one taste, one touch, one vision from the ruck of the day's garbage. How all this life would vanish, evaporate, if I didn't clutch at it, cling to it, while I still remember some twinge of glory. Books and lessons surround me: hours of work. Who am I? A freshman in college cramming history and feeling no identity, no rest? I shall ruminate like a cow: only that life and not before I am born: the windows jerk and sound in their frames. I shiver, chilled, the grave-chill against the simple heat of my flesh: how did I get to be this big, complete self, with the long-boned span of arm and leg? The scarred imperfect skin? I remember thick mal-shaped adolescence and the colors of my remembering return with a vivid outline: high school, junior high, elementary school, camps & the fern-huts with Betsy: hanging Johanna: I must recall, recall, out of the stuff is writing made, out of the recollected stuff of life.... "Get hold of a thing and shove your head into it," Ted says just now. I weary and will take hot milk to bed and read more Hawthorne. My lips are drying, chapped, and I bite them raw. I dreamed I had long stinging scratches down the fingers of my right hand, but looking down saw my hands white and whole and no red blood-scabbed lines at all.

Tuesday, February 10.... How clear and cleansed and happy I feel. Why? Last night's dinner cleared such air—Wendell an unexpected ally and miraculous gossip, so richly he held forth, and Paul and blond witchy dear Clarissa, her red mouth opening and curling like a petaled flower or a fleshly sea anemone, and Paul, gilded as always, but not quite so seedy, his blue eyes marred with red, his blond curls rough and Rossetti-like, cherubic, curling, his pale jacket and pale buff sweater setting off his gilt and gaudy head. Have I said I saw him running down the stairs of Seelye out into last week's falling snow with a bright absinthe-green suit on that made his eyes the clear unearthly and slightly unpleasant acid green of a churned winter ocean full of icecakes? We talked, and I must never again start drinking wine before my guests come—I slowed, but sickened late. Till midnight they stayed and Wendell favored us with department secrets...

Tuesday noon.... I had a vision in the dark art lecture room today of *the* title of my book of poems, commemorated above. It came to me suddenly with great clarity that *The Earthenware Head* was the right title, the only title. It is derived, organically, from the title and subject of my poem "The Lady and the Earthenware Head," and takes on for me the compelling mystic aura of a sacred object, a terrible and holy token of identity sucking unto itself magnetwise the farflung words which link and fuse to make up my own queer & grotesque world out of earth, clay, matter; the head shapes its poems and prophecies, as the earth-flesh wears in time, the head swells ponderous with gathered wisdoms. Also, I discover, with my crazy eye for anagrams, that the intials spell T-E-H, which is simply "to Edward Hughes," or Ted, which is of course my dedication. I dream, with this keen spirit-whetting air, of a creative spring. So I shall live and create, worthy of Dr. B. and Doris Krook and myself and Ted and my art. Which is word-making, world-making. This book title gives me such staying power (perhaps these very pages will see the overturn of my dream, or even its acceptance in the frame of the real world). At any rate, I see the earthenware head, rough, crude, powerful and radiant, of dusky orange-red terra-cotta color, flushed with vigor and its hair heavy, electric. Rough terra-cotta color, stamped with jagged black and white designs, signifying earth, and the words which shape it. Somehow this new title spells for me the release from the old crystal-brittle and sugar-faceted voice of "Circus in Three Rings" and "Two Lovers and a Beachcomber," those two elaborate metaphysical conceits for triple-ringed life— birth, love and deaths, and for love and philosophy, sense and spirit. Now pray god I live through this windy season and come into my own in June: three and a half months, how the year dwindles. To get through this week and thesis. I feel great works which may speak from me. Am I a dreamer only? I feel beginning cadences and rhythms of speech to set world-fabrics in motion. Let me keep my eye off publication and simply write stories that have to be written. We reject the Merwins' flat: [Omission.] No thanks. We will perhaps stay here in June and stick up for top floor, light and a view, quiet and preferably furnished. Notes. Of [Bill] Van Voris:* pale with a mouth like [a] snail spread for sliding—a man who always keeps the expression on his face for a moment too long. My poems thin to a bare spare twenty, even those with quaint archaic turns of speech. How far I feel from them, from poems. Oh, to get in voice again, this book a wailing wall. What thoughts, few as they are, revolve in my head? The Doulde: *The Earthenware Head* (jutting forth from the African masks and doll masks on Mrs. Van der Poel's screen, with their blank eyes rounded with phosphor circles, and then insect heads and diminutive pincer mouths)—how all photograph portraits do catch our souls— part of a past world, a window onto the air and furniture of our own sunken worlds, and so to the mirror—twin, Muse.

---

*Smith faculty

* * *

Thursday morning, February 20.... I want *all* my time, time for a year, the first year since I was four years old, to work and read *on my own*. And away from Smith. Away from my past, away from this glass-fronted, girl-studded and collegiate town. Anonymity. Boston. Here the only people to see are the twenty people on the faculty whom I just don't want to see another year. Will I write a word? Yes. By the time I write in here again this ghastly day will be over, I having walked out my dreamy drugged state and given three classes, botched and unsure. The next three weeks, however, I shall prepare violently and fully a week ahead if it's the last thing I do. Oh, resolves. The three red apples, yellow speckled, thumb-dinted brown, mock me. I myself am the vessel of tragic experience. I muse not enough on the mysteries of Oedipus—I, weary, resolving the best and bringing, out of my sloth, envy and weakness, my own ruins. What do the gods ask? I must dress, rise, and send my body out....

A day in a life—such gray grit, and I feel apart from myself, split, a shadow, and yet when I think of what I have taught and what I will teach, the titles have still a radiant glow and the excitement and not the dead weary plod of today. I have gotten back the life-vision, whatever that is, which enables people to live out their lives and not go mad. I am married to a man whom I miraculously love as much as life and I have an excellent job and profession (this one year), so the cocoon of childhood and adolescence is broken—I have two university degrees and now will turn to my own profession and devote a year to steady apprenticeship, and to the symbolic counterpart, our children. Sometimes I shiver in a preview of the pain and the terror of childbirth, but it will come and I live through it.

Saturday night, February 22.... A scattered dull day—the answer to: what is life? Do we always grind through the present, doomed to throw a gold haze of fond retrospect over the past (those images of myself, for example, that floating April day in Paris in the Place du Tertre, wine and veal in sunlight with Tony, when I was without doubt most miserable before the horrors of Venice and Rome and the bloom of my best Cambridge spring and the vision of love) or ahead to the unshaped future, spinning its dreams of novels and books of poems and Rome with Ted out of a lumpish mist. [Omission.]

Sunday night, February 23. This must be the 26th February 23rd I have lived through: over a quarter century of Februaries, and would I could cut a slice of recollection back through them all and trace the spiraling stair of my ascent adultward—or is it a descent? I feel I have lived enough to last my life in musings, tracings of crossings and recrossings with people, mad and sane, stupid and brilliant, beautiful and grotesque, infant and antique, cold and hot, pragmatic and dream-ridden, dead and alive. My house of days and masks is rich enough so that I might and must spend years fishing, hauling up the pearl-eyed, horny, scaled and sea-bearded monsters sunk long, long in the Sargasso of my imagination. I feel myself grip on my past as if it were my life: I shall make it my future business: every casual wooden monkey-carving, every pane of orange-and-purple nubbled glass on my grandmother's stair-landing window, every white hexagonal bathroom tile found by Warren and me on our way digging to China, becomes radiant, magnetic, sucking meaning to it and shining with strange significance: unriddle the riddle: why is every doll's shoelace a revelation? Every wishing-box dream an annunciation? Because these are the sunk relics of my lost selves that I must weave, wordwise, into future fabrics. Today, from coffee till teatime at six, I read in *Lady Chatterley's Lover*, drawn back again with the joy of a woman living with her own gamekeeper, and *Women in Love* and *Sons and Lovers*. Love, love: Why do I feel I would have known and loved Lawrence. How many women must feel this and be wrong! I opened *The Rainbow*, which I have never read, and was sucked into the concluding Ursula and Skrebensky episode and sank back, breath knocked out of me, as I read of their London hotel, their Paris trip, their riverside loving while Ursula studied at college. This is the stuff of my life—my life, different, but no less brilliant and splendid—and the flow of my story will take me beyond this in my way—arrogant? I felt mystically that if I read Woolf, read Lawrence (these two, why? their vision, so different, is so like mine) I can be itched and kindled to a great work: burgeoning, fat with the texture and substance of life: This my call, my work. This gives my being a name, a meaning—"to make of the moment something permanent": I, in my sphere, taking my place beside Dr. Beuscher and Doris Krook in theirs—neither psychologist, priestess nor philosopher—teacher but a blending of both rich vocations in my own worded world. A book dedicated to each of them. Fool. Dreamer. When my first novel is written and accepted (a year hence? longer?) I shall permit myself the luxury of writing above: "I am no liar." I worked on two pages of carefully worded criticism of the Lawrence thesis: feel I am right, but wonder as always: will they see? will they scornfully smile me into the wrong? No: I stated clearly my case and I feel there is a good case made. Cups of scalding tea: how it rests me. We walked out about seven into the pleasant mild-cold still night to the library: the campus snow-blue, lit from myriad windows, deserted. Cleared, cleansed, stung fresh-cheeked chill, we walked the creaking-cricking plank paths through the botanical gardens and while Ted delivered thesis and book I walked four times round the triangle flanked by Lawrence House, the Student's Building and the street running from Paradise Pond to College Hall, meeting no one, secretly gleeful and in control, summoning all my past green, gilded gray, sad, sodden and loveless, ecstatic, and in-love selves to be with me and rejoice. . . .

Monday night, February 24. Weary, work not done, week scarcely begun: such mortal falls, the edge of heat keeps up so short a time. Yet today gathered into itself (approximating as it does the second anniversary [25th to be exact] of our meeting at the *St. Botolph's* party and the anniversary of the acceptance of Ted's book via telegram as winner of the NYC Poetry Center contest) some symbolic good joint-fortune. *Mademoiselle*, under the persona of Cyrilly Abels, wrote to accept one poem from *each* of us for a total of $60. Ted's "Pennines in April" and my "November Graveyard"—spring and winter on the moors, birth and death, or, rather, reversing the order, death and resurrection. My first acceptance for about a year: I feel the swing into the freedom of June begin—shall doggedly send out remaining 5 or 6 poems until I find some home for the best: but this came, linking our literary fortunes in the best way: I must work to get a book of poems together by next February at least. Ted drove me through a warm wet gray despondent morning to Arvin's lecture—I am sure I know *The Scarlet Letter* by heart. Then: good introduction to Picasso—blue period (old guitarist, laundress, old man at table) and the magnificent rose-vermilion-period saltimbanques, pale, delicate, poised and lovely. Don't like the mad distortions of his forties with my deep self much—world of sprung cuckoo clocks—all machinery and blare and schizophrenic people parceled out in patches and lines like dead goods: macabre visual puns.... Arvin's exam comes up with, in effect, a week of correcting for me to do. I am unfairly angry because I thought the job would pay $300, where it pays $100, and my art poem, if I wrote it, would almost meet, with hours of pleasure squandered, the sum. Faculty meeting long, smoky, controversial—Bill Scott, myopic, pale fallen-chinned physics professor very like the Mad Hatter with his bitten slice of bread and butter. Sometimes I wonder, are they all dodos? Surprises: Stanley "fired"—one year appointment ending next year: he volatile, enthusiastic, "immature"; they secretly jealous of him spending over a year on a non-academic project—a novel. What, alas, and hoho, must they think of me? A complete traitor. I go to buttress myself from snow in boots and woolens. Pray for my safe return.

Friday night, February 28. Vinously blurred, letting lamb fat and blood congeal to pale grease on the scattered plates, wine sediment curd in the bottom of glasses. Today, for some reason blest, day done with, and the reward shining, of no extra preparation for tomorrow, and turning, wistful, toward writing—rereading the thin, thinning nucleus of my poetry book *The Earthenware Head* and feeling, proud, how steady are the few poems I am keeping on—a sure twenty, sixteen of them already published (except for the damn, damned dilatory *London Magazine*). Rereading my long excerpt "Friday Night in Falcon Yard," too lumbering, leisurely, too artificial, too much in it: yet: this I will revise...

Sunday night, March 2. Again, late: it will be twelve before I sleep. A strange, stopped day: Ted and I having morning coffee—black and bitter-edged, with the Bramwells in their uncomfortable second-floor flat, chairs turned wrong-side-to, records scattered, white marble fireplace angular and function-less. James is leaving for their home in France tomorrow. Ted met him in the library yesterday, a few seconds before I came into the periodical room from my last class of the week: I looked into the room through the glass door before I opened it, saw no black-coated Ted, pushed the door open, saw James's back in brown and white tweed coat, then Ted, dark, disheveled and with that queer electric invisible radiance he gives off as he did that first day I saw him over two years ago: to think, irony of ironies, that two years ago I was feverishly studying Webster & Tourneur for my supervisions (which very plays I am this week examining my students on) and furiously, des-perately, talking myself into a crazy belief that I would some-how manage to see Ted and imprint my mark ineffaceably on him before he left for Australia and murder his pale freckled mistress named Shirley. Let all rivals forever be called Shirley. How, now, sitting here in the calm cleared living room where we have our ordered teas, I feel I have wrested chaos and despair—and all the wasteful accident of life—into a rich and meaningful pattern—the light through this door, into the dark dim pink-walled dining alcove, shines to our bedroom and bright from his writing of poems in the swept spacious bedroom the chink of light through the crack in between the doorframe and door betrays him to me: and suddenly all, or most, of that long 35-page chapter which should be—the events at least—the core of my novel seems cheap and easily come-by—all that sensational jabber about winds and doors and walls banging away and back. But that was the *psychic* equivalent of the whole experience: how does Woolf do it? How does Lawrence do it? I come down to learn of those two: Lawrence because of the rich physical passion—fields of forces—and the real presence of leaves and earth and beasts and weathers, sap-rich, and Woolf because of that almost sexless, neurotic *luminous-ness*—the catching of objects: chairs, tables and the figures on a street corner, and the infusion of radiance: a shimmer of the plasm that *is* life. I cannot and must not copy either. God knows what tone I shall strike. Close to a prose-poem of balanced, cadenced words and meanings, of street corners and lights and people, but not merely romantic: not merely caricature, not merely a diary: *not* ostensibly autobiography: in one year I must so douse this experience in my mind, imbue it with dis-

tance, create cool shrewd views of it, so that it becomes re-
shapen. All this—digression: James, the subject: yesterday, a
broken man, his craggy sallow face, with its look of genial
corrugated black lines—hair, brows, wrinkles and dark grain
of shaven beard, his bright, mirthful black eyes—all seemed
broken, askew. [Omission.] "When are you leaving America?"
I felt impelled to ask first, meaning, of course, when in summer. "Monday," he said. He can't work here, can't write here.
He talked loudly, in an audible whisper, and I wanted to quiet
him, and get out of there, with the dilly girls listening over
their periodicals. A chink opened into his hell: what it must be
to decide him to leave, and how absurdly vindicated I felt,
remembering Joan's mean-toned "Why are you going? Don't
you *like* it here?" How can James leave her? This always puz-
zles me. I need Ted . . . as I need bread and wine. I like James:
one of the few men here whose life doesn't seem available,
processed in uniform, cellophane-wrapped blocks, like synthetic orange cheese: James has the authentic, cave aged, mold-
ripened smell of the real thing. [Omission.] Joan seems young
and thin for him. At coffee this morning he seemed restored,
jovial. We talked of bulls and bullfights, after the two movies—
on Goya and bullfighting—last night. I borrowed James's autobiography and finished it tonight: 250 pages, *The Unfinished
Man*—about his experiences as a conscientious objector during
the war: desultory beginning, here, there, Stockholm, Finland
and all told *about*, characters portrayed, not actually moving
and talking on their own, but talked about, half-emerged, like
a frieze of flushed marble. And women: he seems to run from
them—his wife queerly in the background, diminishing to
America, to divorce; his child evaporating. A "told-about" love
affair with a queer Finnish girl, death-oriented, who commits
suicide (was he to blame, partly? did it really happen?) and a
rather illuminating statement that he ("like most men") believes
that loving a woman eternally isn't incompatible with leaving
her: loving, leaving—a lovely consonance. I don't see it: and
my man doesn't. The quiet of midnight settles over Route 9.
Already it is tomorrow and the days I cross off with such vicious
glee—just as I toss with premature eagerness empty bottles of
wine and honey into the wastebasket to be neat and clear of
clogging half-full jars—are those of my youngness and my
promise. I believe, whether in madness or in half-truth, that if

I live for a year with the two years of my life and learning at Cambridge I can write and rewrite a good novel. Ten times this 35 page chapter and rewriting and rewriting. Goal set: June 1959: a novel and a book of poems. I cannot draw on James's drama: war, nations, parachute drops, hospitals in trenches— my woman's ammunition is chiefly psychic and aesthetic: love and lookings.

Monday night, March 3. . . . A chapter story from Luke's novel arrived, badly typed, no margins, scrawled corrections, and badly proofread. But the droll humor, the atmosphere of London and country which seeps indefinably in through the indirect statement: all this is delicate and fine. The incidents and intrigues are something I could never dream up—unless, I add, I worked at it. . . . Nothing so dull and obvious and central as love or sex or hate: but deft, oblique. As always, coming unexpectedly upon the good work of a friend or acquaintance, I itch to emulate, to sequester. Got a queer and most overpowering urge today to write, or typewrite, my whole novel on the pink, stiff, lovely-textured Smith memorandum pads of 100 sheets each: a fetish: somehow, seeing a hunk of that pink paper, different from all the endless reams of white bond, my task seems finite, special, rose-cast. Bought a rose bulb for the bedroom light today and have already robbed enough notebooks from the supply closet for one and a half drafts of a 350 page novel. Will I do it. . . .

Wednesday, March 5. . . . I found the two pained and torturous typewritten sheets I wrote in October and November when trying to keep myself from flying into black bits—how new, now, is my confidence: I can endure—endure through weaknesses, bad days, imperfections and fatigue: and do my work without running away or crying: mercy, I can no more. If, knocking on wood (where does that come from?), I can survive in health till spring vacation, all shall be well. . . . Money pours in: salary check mysteriously gone up (Arvin's work? for exams?). Our bank account from salaries mounts to $700, our poetry earnings since September shall soon touch $850 and auspiciously reach their set aim by June: we are going to try for poetry contests, jingle contests—trifling sums, but my gripping acquisitive sense thrives: I knew America would do this for us. Ted, yesterday, had two poems, "Of Cats" & "Relic," accepted enthusiastically by *Harper's*—not one rejection yet in the last three batches—pray that *The Yale Review* and *The London Magazine* will not be recalcitrant: strange what vicarious pleasure I get from Ted's acceptances: pure sheer joy: almost as if he were holding the field open, keeping a foot in the door to the golden world, and thus keeping a place for me. Aim: to have my art poems—one to three (Gauguin, Klee and Rousseau)—completed by the end of March. I shall spend time in "the art library" at last. I feel my mind, my imagination, nudging, sprouting, prying and peering. The old anonymous millionairess seen this morning coming from the ugly boxed orangy stucco house next door, hobbling on one crutch down her path to the gleaming black limousine breathing oh-so-gently at the curb, burdened, bent, she, under the weight and bulk of a glossy mink coat, bending to get into the back of the car, as the rotund, rosy white-haired chauffeur held the door open for her. A bent mink-laden lady. And the mind runs, curious, into the crack in the door behind her: where does she come from, who is she? What loves and sorrows are strung on her rosary of hours? Ask the gardener, ask the cook, ask the maid: all the rough, useful retainers who keep a clockwork ritual of grace in a graceless house, barren-roomed and desolate....

Saturday night, March 8. One of those nights when I wonder if I am alive, or have been ever. The noise of the cars on the pike is like a bad fever: Ted sickish, flagging in discontent: "I want to get clear of this life: trapped." I think: Will we be less trapped in Boston? I dislike apartments, suburbs. I want to walk directly out my front door onto earth and into air free from exhaust. And I: what am I but a glorified automaton hearing myself, through a vast space of weariness, speak from the shell speaking-trumpet that is my mouth the dead words about life, suffering, and deep knowledge and ritual sacrifice. What is it that teaching kills? The juice, the sap—the substance of revelation: by making even the insoluble questions and multiple possible answers take on the granite assured stance of dogma. It does not kill this quick of life in students who come, each year, fresh, quick, to be awakened and pass on—but it kills the quick in me by forcing to formula the great visions, the great collocations and cadences of words and meanings. The good teacher, the proper teacher, must be ever-living in faith and ever-renewed in creative energy to keep the sap packed in herself, himself, as well as the work. I do not have the energy, or will to use the energy I have, and it would take all, to keep this flame alive. I am living and teaching on rereadings, on notes of other people, sour as heartburn, between two un-achieved shapes: between the original teacher and the original writer: neither. And America wears me, wearies me. I am sick of the Cape, sick of Wellesley: all America seems one line of cars, moving, with people jammed in them, from one gas station to one diner and on. I must periodically refresh myself in this crass, crude, energetic, demanding and competitive new-country bath, but I am, in my deep soul, happiest on the moors— my deepest soul-scape, in the hills by the Spanish Mediterra-nean, in the old, history-crusted and still gracious, spacious cities: Paris, Rome.

. . . I can see chinks of light: of a new life. Will there be pain? The birth-giving pain is not yet known. Last night, weary, up the odd Gothic blind stairwell to Arvin's for drinks: Fisher and the Gibians: dull, desultory talk about aborigines and me going out on the incoming of politics. Arvin: bald head pink, eyes and mouth dry slits as on some carved rubicund mask: a Baskin woodcut: huge, mammothed in the hall: a bulbous streaked head, stained, scarred, owl-eyed—"tormented man," and a great, feathered, clawed fierce-eyed owl sitting in an intolerable eternal niche of air above the head. . . . I sense an acrid repulsion between the two men [Ted and Arvin]. I . . . see Arvin: dry, fingering his key ring compulsively in class, bright hard eyes red-rimmed, turned cruel, lecherous, hypnotic and holding me caught like the gnome Loerke held. Fisher, arms flapping, ridiculous, jumping up as if to urinate or be sick, only to leave, leaving his pipe, his drink half-finished. "He's done that all year," said the Gibians.

Monday night, March 10. Exhausted: is there ever a day oth-erwise. Alfred Kazin to dinner tonight: he: broken, somehow, embittered and unhappy: graying, his resonance diminished. Lovable still: and he and Ann, his wife, too a writer, another couple to speak to in this world. How babies complicate life: he paying also for a son. Ted is queerly sick still: how hopeless, helpless I feel with Ted pale, raggle-haired, miserable-visaged and there no clear malady, no clear remedy. He coughs, sweats, feels sick to his stomach. Pale and sweet and distant he looks. . . . I fall on the bed, drugged, with this queer sickish greeny-vinous fatigue. Drugged, gugged, stogged and sludged with weariness. My life is a discipline, a prison: I live for my own work, without which I am nothing. My writing. Nothing matters but Ted, Ted's writing and my writing. Wise, he is, and I, too, growing wiser. We will remold, melt and remold our plans to give us better writing space. My nails are splitting and chipping. A bad sign. I suppose I really haven't had a vacation all year: Thanksgiving a black-wept nightmare and Christmas the low blow of pneumonia and since then a struggle to keep health. Almost asleep in Newton's class: must be up early, to laundry and to steal more pink pads of paper tomorrow. Kazin: at home with us, talking of reviews, his life: a second wife, blonde, and he being proud of her, touchingly. What is a life wherein one dreams of Fisher, furtive, in pink and gaudy purple and green houses, and Dunn and racks and racks of dresses?

Tuesday afternoon, March 11. . . . A thin green-yellow wash of light underlying bare ground, bare trees, warmly luminous and promising. Oh how my own life shines, beckons, as if I were caught, revolving, on a wheel, locked in the steel-toothed jaws of my schedule. Well, since January I have been holding a dialogue with myself and girding myself to stand fast without running. Now I am at a saturation point: fed up. The thought of outlining three hours of Strindberg plays this week appalls me. While Strindberg should be most fun of all. I turn to these pages as toward a cool fluid drink of water—as being closest to my life—words must sound, sing, mean. I hear a tin cup chink on a fountain brim as I say "drink." I must grow ingrown, queer, simply from indwelling and playing true to my own gnomes and demons. . . . Today, overslept caught in some gross and oppressive nightmare involving maps and pale sandy deserts and people in cars—a sense of guilt, bad-faith, embarrassment and sallow sulphurous misery brooding over all, listened to the same Arvin lecture on *Mardi* I heard four years ago and a lecture on the pure abstractionist Mondrian: as warm as Platonic linoleum squares.

Thursday morning, March 13. . . . I sit, warm, drowsy and at the other side of the shakes, writing here, trying to build up a calm center. Yesterday was a horror—Ted said something about the moon and Saturn to explain the curse which strung me tight as a wire and twanged unmercifully. Too tired for the saving humor, downed, doused in my vital quick. . . . Quarrel with Ted over sewing on buttons on jackets (which I *must* do), wearing his gray suit, and such trivia, he getting up from sickness, me going down into it. Gulping a chicken wing and a mess of spinach and bacon, all, all, turning to poison. *Dream Play*—ambitious production—the daughter dancing descent through a scrim of clouds, her voice stiff and stagy . . . the irony of the play being that it is *all true* in my own life. We had just finished quarreling about buttons and haircuts (like their salads and such as a basis for divorce), and especially the repetition of schooling the officer goes through—teaching and learning forever that twice two is . . . what? And I, sitting too in the same seat I occupied three, four, five, six, seven years ago, teaching what I learned one, two, three, four years ago, with less vigor than I studied and learned—living among ghosts and familiar faces I pretend not to recognize. . . . All rolling over on itself, tasting of sourdough, tasting of heartburn. Now I must leap into my clothes and stride to class, early, to steal three pink books: yes, for my novel: have just read the sensationalist trash which is *Nightwood**—all perverts, all ranting, melodramatic: "The sex God forgot."—self-pity, like the stage whine of the *Dream Play*. Pity us: Oh, Oh, Oh: Mankind is pitiable. . . .

Friday afternoon, March 14. . . . Deep sleep last night and queer nightmares—fragmented rememberings at breakfast: of Newton Arvin: withered, mysterious, villainous, shrunken heads to piece together, clues to deceptions: heads lollipop size, withered, painted ruddy over the shrunk corruption of approaching death. Dark elevations of floors and stairs in unlit libraries.

---

*Djuna Barnes's classic novel

Pursuit, guilt. . . . I am yet in a dream, unproductive, weary. Got a notice from the Guggenheim people and the Houghton Mifflin awards—hopeless to concern myself about until I have written my two books by the end of next year. Ted getting a phone call this afternoon from blessed paternal white-haired Jack Sweeney asking Ted to read at Harvard on the Morris Gray readership on Friday April 11th for the princely sum of $100 and expenses! One hour of his own poems: to us this looks like professional glory. Greasy dishes pile up in the kitchen, the garbage can overflows with coffee grounds, rancid fat, rotting fruit rinds and vegetable scrapings: a world of stinks, blemishes, idle dreams, fatigue and sickness: to death. I feel like a dead person offered the fruits and riches and joys of the world only if she will get up and walk. Will my legs be sturdy? My trial period approaches. To bed now and resolutely to work tomorrow. Save, conserve: wisdom, knowledge, smells and insights for the page: to wrestle through slick shellacked facades to the real shapes and smells and meanings behind the masks.

In the past two days, Sunday and Monday, Ted and I have had, respectively, dinner and tea (and lecture) with two American "poets." Queerness of queernesses. Ben Hurley and Ralph Rogers. Sunday afternoon we drove across the wide flat ice-gray Connecticut River and into the snow-covered Holyoke range with its bristles of bare winter trees and up into the ugly black-smeared brick atrocities of Victorian Holyoke. Raoul lives in a faculty house facing out over white snowfields into the purpling and bristled hills. We shouldered into his tiny room with its cot and, surprisingly, real fireplace with a log burning red. Walls covered with odd and tawdry papers: the sheet of an old piece of music, a print in color of an ancient French unicorn tapestry, theater bills; two women teachers: a young, soft dark-haired girl in a cover-up dress of electric blue: Joyce someone, who teaches modern philosophy and lisps somewhat, slightly bucktoothed. And Miss Mount, a fat dowdy fixed lady, with gray hair that looked as if it needed dusting, an ugly, or, rather, nondescript suit and layers of speckled fat skin. She proceeded, over sherry and a nut or two from a glass jar which Raoul passed around, to relate the story of Dylan Thomas's visit to Holyoke in raucous, shrill tones which allowed of no interruptions: a woman who never listens, a horrible woman, shaped in hard round bullet shapes, squat, unsympathetic as a dry toad. Dirty decaying teeth, hands with that worn glisten of flesh unmarried old ladies have: a glitter of rhinestones somewhere, a pin, or chain. We talked of nothing: the Dylan Thomas story lasted till dinnertime and Joyce, bearing a platter of white cut bread covered with a gray-pink pâté specked with something black, led us down the ugly brown stairs to an uncomfortable private dining room, a too-varnished, too-polished mahogany table and skittery stiff-backed chairs. I drank quickly and never modestly demurred when Raoul came round with the red wine. An ugly fattish yellow dolt-faced girl with purplish acne waited on us. I sat on Raoul's left, facing the irrepressible Miss Mount, who evidently had taken an immediate dislike to me and whom I proceeded to ignore. "Ben's here," Joyce softly and joyously exclaimed. And my first impression was: he's a madman. He gave the impression of being too brightly colored blue and yellow, and ravaged by years of sandblasting. Goggle, electric-blue frog eyes, a pocked, vivid tan coarse-pored skin, short blondish hair, and a pale sleazy whitish-cream jacket that didn't hang right and gave him a cockeyed, humpbacked look. Heavy black leather ski-type boots, or perhaps, hiking boots, and, again, pants that hung as on bandy legs. He began to talk immediately in a rather high, grating voice: frank, fanatic and open. I spent the mealtime talking with him, raising my voice, too: everybody giggled, gulped wine (except Miss Mount) and raised their voices. I began to go pleasantly erotic, feeling my body compact and sinewy, feeling like seducing a hundred men. But immediately, I turn to Ted: all I have to do is think of that first night I saw him, and that's it. Hurley raved: politics, Ezra Pound: we agreed a man was all of a piece, couldn't really compartmentalize himself, airtight. Hurley (winner of at least two Guggenheims) raved against the giving of Guggenheims to old safe famous people and advocated their bestowal on poets who spent the money on women and drink and were politically radical. We all flowed upstairs again, Hurley having, in the course of the meal (thick slabs of roast beef, watery string beans, roast potato and some ghastly ice cream, vanilla rounds with a green shamrock of mint-flavored ice cream in the middle), put on greenish-hued sunglasses. Hurley promptly pulled down the blinds of the window, all except one long thin strip of window, and cut out the snow-blinding view: the left strip showed stark and delicately-colored, like a Japanese watercolor—lavender mountains, white plains of snow, and a stipple of bushes, grasses and trees perfect as lines of a calligraph. We drank black, bitter espresso coffee which Antoine made in a queer chromium-tubed pot, and then brandy. Antoine passed a glass jar of pink, green, yellow and lavender Easter-egg candies. We left then. Hurley shaking hands good-bye and miraculously leaving my hand full of a bunch of his pamphlets on poetry and politics, his "Americana."

Thursday morning, March 20. . . . I give myself a week—through next Wednesday: and give up the idea of the long contest. Have narrowed down poem subjects to Klee (five paintings and etchings) and Rousseau (two paintings) and will try, arbitrarily, one a day. Each subject appeals, deeply, to me. Must drop them in my mind and let them grow rich, encrusted. And *choose*: choose one today. I sit in a stupor—torn, torn: a pure whole week, and me so far from my deep self, from the demon within, that I sit giddy on a painted surface. Yesterday: sat in the art libe soaking and seeping in pictures. I think I will try to buy the Paul Klee book. Or at least, get it over the weekend. Reminders now, of the sea wrack of the past week: the most sickening, the most embarrassing of experiences: Monday— tea with Ralph Rogers at the Roches' and a horror of a lecture in the Browsing Room. Paul, with his professional dewy blue-eyed look and his commercially gilded and curled blond hair on his erect, dainty-bored aristocrat head looking as if it had been struck on a Greek coin that since had blurred and thinned from too much public barter and fingering. "One of the finest minor poets in America," Paul breathed over the phone. Rogers sickened Ted and me the minute he walked into Paul's living room with his slick nervous smile, his jittery huckster hand jingling money in his pants pocket. Clarissa, apparently recently recovered from a sulk of tears, slouched about in a baggy white sweatshirt and a blue and white full skirt, and baby-buttoned ballet shoes, like Miss Muffet in a private tantrum. And the lecture: I writhed, bristled. In that dark-wooded and antique room with its dim light and worn, deep, comfortable chairs and darkened Oriental rugs, with the hollow-coffined grandfather clock ticking its sepulchral ticks and the oil portrait of Mary Ellen Chase leaning forward, as if out of the gilt restraining frame, her white hair an aureole, a luminous nimbus. Rogers garbled his bible of crudities to the literary Mademoiselle Defarges of Smith, knitting his slick and commercial words into cable-stitched sweaters and multi-colored argyles. Intolerable: catchpenny phrases. "This is the point, do you get it, I'll just tie this up." Ralph Rogers, it develops, has a handly little storage closet (personal, private) called the "subconscious" or, more glibly, the "subliminal," where he tosses all his old dreams, his ideas and visions. Buzz, snip, handy little demons get to work, and presto! a few hours, days or months later he writes out a poem—zip-zip. What's it mean? I dunno— You tell me. He reads some of his own trash: a jeweled dog and a boy licking a sticky lollypop. What's it mean? A poem's gotta move—He gets boys in academy to write him interpretations of his own poems: "fabulous!" He tosses a sheaf of paper on the table, waves a poem about the animal, March, with its "pussy-willow eyes" in "the latest issue of *The Atlantic*." Brags: "I've just sold this to *Poetry London–New York*." The more interpretations a poem has, the better a poem it is. Why, anyone can write: He even wrote a poem in twenty minutes on stage for a show called "Creation While You Watch"—one guy improvised mood music, another painted while Ralph Rogers fished up a mood poem in his unconscious and wrote it on the blackboard—that's pressure-cooker poetry.

Friday afternoon, March 28. A whole week, and I haven't written here, nor picked up the book. For good reason. For the first time a lapse of writing here spells writing. I was taken by a frenzy a week ago Thursday, my first real day of vacation, and the frenzy has continued ever since: writing and writing: I wrote eight poems in the last eight days, long poems, lyrical poems, and thunderous poems: poems breaking open my real experience of life in the last five years: life which has been shut up, untouchable, in a rococo crystal cage, not to be touched. I feel these are the best poems I have ever done. Occasionally I lifted my head, ached, felt exhausted. Saturday I groaned, took pellets of Bufferin, stitched in the worst cramps and faintness for months, which no pills dulled, and wrote nothing: that night we went to a dull dinner at the Roches' with Dorothy Wrinch, who acted like a gray-haired idiot, goggling, going through her little-gray-haired-misunderstood-genius-scientist act. She obviously does not care for Ted: he is too honest and simple and strong and un-Oxford and untwittery for her. She obviously was miffed I said I'd call her for coffee and never did: but I won't either. I don't care a damn for her and won't waste poem-time on people I can't stand. One night, late, we walked out and saw the lurid orange glow of a fire down below the high school. I dragged Ted to it, hoping for houses in a holocaust, parents jumping out of the window with babies, but nothing such: a neighborhood burning a communal acreage of scrubby grass field, flames orange in darkness, friendly shouts across the flaming wasteland, silhouettes of men and children fixing a border with tufts of lit grasses, beating out a blaze with brooms as it jeopardized a fence. We walked round, and stood where a householder stood grimly and doggedly wetting his chrysanthemum stalks and letting the waters run into a little dyke or ditch, separating his patch of lawn from the crackling red-lit weed stalks. The fire was oddly satisfying. I longed for an incident, an accident. What unleashed desire there must be in one for general carnage. I walk around the streets, braced and ready and almost wishing to test my eye and fiber on tragedy—a child crushed by a car, a house on fire, someone thrown into a tree by a horse. Nothing happens: I walk the razor's edge of jeopardy. . . .

This work, teaching, has done me much good: I can tell from the way my poems spouted this last week: a broad wide voice thunders and sings of joy, sorrow and the deep visions of queer and terrible and exotic worlds. . . .

We want to buy art books. De Chirico. Paul Klee. I have written two poems on paintings by De Chirico which seize my imagination—"The Disquieting Muses" and "On the Decline of Oracles" (after his early painting, *The Enigma of the Oracle*) and two on paintings by Rousseau—a green and moony moodpiece, "Snakecharmer," and my last poem of the eight, as I've said, a sestina on Yadwigha, "The Dream."*

I shall copy here some quotations from a translated prose poem by De Chirico, or from his diaries, which have unique

---

*The painting, by the Douanier Rousseau

power to move me, one of which, the first, is the epigraph to my poem "On the Decline of Oracles":

1) "Inside a ruined temple the broken statue of a god spoke a mysterious language."
2) "Ferrara: The old ghetto where one could find candy and cookies in exceedingly strange and metaphysical shapes."
3) "Day is breaking. This is the hour of the enigma. This is also the hour of prehistory. The fancied song, the revelatory song of the last, morning dream of the prophet asleep at the foot of the sacred column, near the cold, white simulacrum of god."
4) "What shall I love unless it be The Enigma?"

And everywhere in Chirico city, the trapped train puffing its cloud in a labyrinth of heavy arches, vaults, arcades. The statue, recumbent, of Ariadne, deserted, asleep, in the center of empty, mysteriously shadowed squares. And the long shadows cast by unseen figures—human or of stone it is impossible to tell. Ted is right, infallibly, when he criticizes my poems and suggests, here, there, the right word—"marvelingly" instead of "admiringly," and so on. Arrogant, I think I have written lines which qualify me to be The Poetess of America (as Ted will be The Poet of England and her dominions). Who rivals? Well, in history Sappho, Elizabeth Barrett Browning, Christina Rossetti, Amy Lowell, Emily Dickinson, Edna St. Vincent Millay— all dead. Now: Edith Sitwell and Marianne Moore, the aging giantesses, and poetic godmother Phyllis McGinley is out— light verse: she's sold herself. Rather: May Swenson, Isabella Gardner, and most close, Adrienne Cecile Rich—who will soon be eclipsed by these eight poems: I am eager, chafing, sure of my gift, wanting only to train and teach it—I'll count the magazines and money I break open by these best eight poems from now on. We'll see. . . .

. . . Sore. Grumpy with Ted, who sometimes strikes my finicky nerves [omission]. . . . And I am much worse—petulant, procrastinating, chafing with ill will at the inevitable grind beginning again.

All yesterday afternoon and today I have been too ratty miserable to do anything but manicure hands in bed and sneeze, twitch and read the latest women's magazines—*McCall's* and *The Ladies' Home Journal*: irony upon irony: *McCall's*, the "magazine of togetherness," is running a series of articles on illegitimate babies and abortions, an article called "Why Men Desert Their Wives"; three stories and articles considered, seriously here, humorously there, suicide from boredom, despair, or embarrassment. The serial story, "Summer Place," by Sloan *(The Man in the Gray Flannel Suit)* Wilson, is about a miserable middle-aged woman named, significantly enough, Sylvia, who commits adultery with the man she should have married twenty years ago but didn't because she was foolish and didn't realize when he raped her at the age of sixteen that they were meant for each other—adultery, love affairs, childless women, incommunicative and sullen couples—"Can this Marriage be saved?" the psychologist asks of two selfish, stupid, incompatible people who were idiots to marry in the first place. It came over me with a slow wonder that all these articles and stories are based on the idea that passionate and spiritual love is the only thing on earth worth having and that it is next to impossible to find and even harder to keep, once caught. I turned to Ted, who is as close and warm and dear as can be, closer, warmer, dearer than I ever was to myself—who sees me sick, ugly, sallow, sneezy, and hugs me, holds me, cooks me a veal chop and brings bowls of iced pineapple, steaming coffee at breakfast, tea at teatime. I feel, miraculously, I have the impossible, the wonderful—I am perfectly at one with Ted, body and soul, as the ridiculous song says—our vocation is writing, our love is each other—and the world is ours to explore. How did I ever live in those barren, desperate days of dating, experimenting, hearing Mother warn me I was too critical, that I set my sights too high and would be an old maid. Well, perhaps I would have been if Ted hadn't been born. I am, at bottom, simple, credulous, feminine and loving to be mastered, cared for—but I will kill with my mind, my ice-eye, anyone who is weak, false, sickly in soul—and so I have done. Our needs—of solitude, quiet, long walks, good meat, all our days to write on—few friends, but fine ones who measure nothing by externals—all these agree and blend. May my demons and seraphs guard me on the right way and we live long toward white hair and creative wisdom and die in a flash of light in each other's arms. He uses me—uses all of me so

I am lit and glowing with love like a fire, and this is all I looked for all my life—to be able to give of my love, my spontaneous joy, unreservedly, with no holding back for fear of lies, misuse, betrayal. And so, in the lousy shut-in world of this cold, last night I put on my new white nylon nightgown with red roses, very small, embroidered on the collar, and filled Ted's slippers with a chocolate rabbit and ten tiny chocolate eggs, each wrapped in a different color of tinfoil—green spots on silver, gold mottling, streaked peacock blue. I believe he has eaten them all.... Today, as so many days this year, and so many days in my life, has been a horrid painful limbo. Wake after a sleep and queer nightmare—of seeing a new comet or satellite—round but conical, with the point behind it like a faceted diamond. I was up somewhere on a dark high place watching it pass overhead like a diamond moon, moving rapidly out of sight and then, suddenly, there were a series of short sharp jerks and I saw the planet halted in a series of still-shot framed exposures, which for some reason was a sight not granted to the human eye, and at once I was lifted up, my stomach and face toward earth, as if hung perpendicular in midair of a room with a pole through my middle and someone twirling me about on it. I looked down at Ted's khaki legs stretched out on a chair, and the bodies of other faceless people crowding and the room and my whole equilibrium went off, giddy. As I spun and they spun below I heard surgical, distant, stellar voices discussing me and my experimental predicament and planning what to do next. I spun, screaming, sick, and woke up to a knife-cutting sore throat, a headache which is now at its height, and a swollen, streaming nose. Tried to write a poem about a fool on April Fools' Day, but was too weak and drugged to lift a pen, so it didn't work. Feel very blue. Hate wasting a weekend like this. To hell. This makes me want a Spanish climate to breathe. Pored over Beardsley. Felt utterly *fin de siècle* and *fin de moi-même*.

... The one thing I have done more than I ever thought I would do is write those eight good poems over spring vacation, and my book swells to 30 poems and 48 typewritten double-spaced pages. I aim for 30 more poems by next December 31st, the year's end: A book then and hopefully, all the poems accepted for publication. What ratty stuff gets printed in these quarterlies....

. . . I am attaining, with my return of health and the stubborn breakthrough of spring, the first real deep-rooted peace and joy I have known since early childhood, when I dreamt complete Technicolor stories and fairy tales.

TODAY: is an anniversary. Two years ago, on Black Friday the 13th, I took a plane from Rome through the mist-shrouded sky of Europe, to London — renounced Gordon, Sassoon — my old life — and took up Ted, and my resurrection came about with that green and incredible Cambridge spring. How I must write it up in my novel and in various stories for *McCall's* and *The New Yorker* — I *can* do it: These eight spring-vacation poems have given me confidence that my mind and my talent have been growing underneath my griefs and agonies and drudgeries — as if my demons and angels guarded and increased whatever gifts I ignored, forgot and despaired of during the black year, which has turned out to be the most maturing and courage-making year yet — I could have dreamed up no test more difficult. . . .

. . . I can write for the women's slicks: More and more this comes over me — as *easily* as I wrote for *Seventeen,* while keeping my art intact: I shall call myself *Sylvan Hughes* — pleasantly woodsy, colorful — yet sexless and close to my own name: a perfectly euphonious magazine name.

Ted Hughes was invited to give a reading at Harvard, a grand occasion which also marked Plath's first meeting with an arch-rival whose work she respected enormously, Adrienne Rich.

The drive back: warm, sunny and a new start: hills an incredible vivid purple and snow capped in the blue distance, flooded groves with trees up to mid-trunk in mirroring wet blue; a dead rabbit, a dead black and white skunk with its four little feet crisped up; twenty-seven doughty bug-nosed Volkswagens — we are doing a spontaneous statistical survey of them. Now, hearing Ted type in the bedroom [omission] . . . and the pink scruff and scraps on the rug, I postpone Melville, yearn to write a poem with the resurge of spring and my health this one day which two years ago brought me my dreams, my love, my artist and my artist's life. . . . Now at last about Friday: we fought through a horizontal whirlwind of sleet which covered my whole part of the window as the windshield wiper wasn't working and made me furiously twittery since I saw only the vast looming shapes of approaching trucks through the semi-opaque lid of sleet and each shape seemed, coming, looming, a menace, a possible death. We pushed on, eating good steak sandwiches, drinking from the thermos of scalding coffee, and counting Volkswagens like snow-going beetles. After two and three-quarters hours of begging Ted to go ten-miles-an-hourless than fifty, we came to the narrowing and familiar woodroad, Weston Road. We drove beyond Elmwood [Road, Wellesley,] to the Fells Drugstore, where I stepped out into slush-dammed brown puddles of icewater ankle deep. Ran in and bought a dry shampoo to cure my greasy hair. Home to Elmwood and unloading of sacks, drank off last of brandy. To Brownlee's, then, where we bared arms for our second polio shots, secured a prescription for cocaine, then on through laggard traffic, to Cambridge and Jack Sweeney, waiting gracious, white-haired, lovable, in the quiet sanctum of the poetry room. We slogged in ice, mud and rivulets. Fell into a taxi and rode to Radcliffe's Longfellow Hall. Sepulchral. Deserted. I imagined no one would come. Followed a white-dressed attendant down echoing marble-speckled and polished halls to a lavatory where a thick-bodied Radcliffe girl was combing her hair. There was no gilded liquid soap [but rather] dirt-expunging borax. And the bracing odor of disinfectant. Back to the hall to shake hands with Harry Levin's* dark, vigorous small Russian wife: "Harry is onder ze wedder. I bring a good ear." We went in, after greeting Mrs. Cantor, Marty [Marcia Brown] and Mike, and Carol Pierson, and the room blurred before my eyes. Very big room, very sparsely peopled—listeners scattered. I followed Mrs. Levin and saw Mairé's** luminous pallor, gold hair done in a low chignon, and a quaint small hat of black and russet feathers like a bird-down cloche. Ted began (after a fine and precise introduction by Jack, mentioning the steel-factory night watchman work and the job as a rose gardener)

---

*Joyce scholar, Harvard faculty
**Jack Sweeney's wife; an authority on ancient Irish traditions

to read. I felt cold, felt the audience thin and cold. The poems, which I knew by heart, sent the inevitable chill of awe and wonder over me: the foolish tears jumped to my eyes. Mrs. Levin squirmed, reached for her pocketbook and scribbled something in pencil on a rattling envelope, asked me to repeat the title of "The Thought-Fox." Afar off, somewhere, a clock struck five. Ted spoke of outtennysoning Tennyson—the audience laughed, a pleasant muted burble. Laughed and warmed. I began to relax: new poems gave good surprise—"To Paint a Waterlily": clear, lyric—rich and yet craggy. He ended on "Acrobats"—a perfect metaphor, really, for himself as a poetic acrobat-genius and the desirous and in many cases envious audience. A burst of warm genuine applause. Jack went up and asked Ted to read another. He did "The Casualty." I knew, with the same clairvoyance I had two years ago envisioning this foothold, how in ten years Ted would have a packed Harvard Stadium audience to applaud and adore. The audience broke up and suddenly seemed all friends—Peter Davison, Mrs. Bragg (now Harry Levin's secretary), Gordon Lameyer (no doubt jealous as hell, but noble, in his way, to come— pulling out a leaflet about his big-money project—the Framingham Music Circus, which will make him rich and for which he has raised hundreds of thousands of dollars in backing). Phil McCurdy, chastened, boyish-faced, married to Marla with a baby girl and teaching biology in Brookline High, illustrating science textbooks for Scribner's, offering us a joint trip to Maine on a friend's yacht this summer, which I hope might come true. Mother—thin and somehow frail—and blue-eyed Mrs. Prouty: "Isn't Ted *wonder*ful." Philip Booth: a new meeting for the first time—he, handsome and strangely nice-guy innocent-looking. We exchanged compliments, spoke of his aunt and the aging Smith psychiatrist Dr. Booth. He hemmed at my asking if he'd teach at Wellesley next year and admitted, with some joy, to just having heard: he'd been granted a Guggenheim. But he and his wife and kids will be around next year. Hope to meet again. Adrienne Cecile Rich: little, round and stumpy, all vibrant short black hair, great sparking black eyes and a tulip-red umbrella: honest, frank, forthright and even opinionated. The crowd thinned, and the Sweeneys, Ted and I and Adrienne slogged through rain to a taxi, switched (Jack, Ted and I) to our sodden Plymouth, and soon were tiptoeing gingerly down the red-brick cobbles of Walnut Street's hilly decline to Jack's polished hall, all slippery black and white linoleum. His apartment reached in the thin gilt barred elevator. Adrienne and Mairé there—also the doe-eyed tan Al Conrad,* an economist at Harvard, whom I felt cold and awkward with at first. I in my old and trusted lavender tweed dress, pale, with bright turquoise and white weave and blue and silver beads. Two bourbons and water on ice. Found out that the two huge paintings leaping out of the left wall were original Picassos (c. 1924). The brown, cream and black composition on the right, with its sinister black mask—a Juan Gris. And, in the library, the springing blue-green oil of a rider on a horse *(The Singing Rider)* by old Jack Yeats, just dead—W.B.'s brother— "rather like Soutine—like Kokoschka"** (whom I would know not, were it not for Mrs. Van der Poel). I felt distant from everyone. Feverish in lavender tweed. We left then, in Al's great station wagon, for "supper at Felicia's." A blur of light, neons. We parked on Hanover Street—a Paris bistro street of shops and diners. Walked, heads down, down a narrow street, past the wonderful room of a bakeshop, a greased paper, like butter frosting, lidding one window, a bare interior, a heavy wooden trestle table covered with yellow-browned round cakes, large, middling, small, and two men in white aprons laying white frosting on a three-tiered square cake. Then a narrow doorway with "Felicia's" printed over it, a crowd of ladies— who would emphatically consider themselves "girls," probably a crew of telephone operators—one with a corsage: set old-maidy or borderline-tarty faces: "Betty Clarke?" "Betty Andrews?" They gathered galoshes and umbrellas at the top of the stair head and left. We sat, I with Jack on my left, Al on my right. Began with a bottle of fine dry Italian white wine shaped like a blue-glass urn. Antipasto shrimps hot in red sauce and Felicia herself like an honest actress, hawk nose, bright peach-pink sweater and lipstick and powder to match, reeled off the menu: "fettuccini, linguine." I talked to Al about... tuberculosis, deep, deeper, enjoying him. A long time, through chicken cacciatore with queer pieces of bone and white chunk

---

*Adrienne Rich's husband
**The Austrian painter Oskar Kokoschka

meat. Then switched to Jack, who asked me to make a recording in June, on Friday the 13th.

Thursday morning, April 17. Time, almost time, to rise, dress and go to meet my morning classes. Still, when I wake up (and the sun shines bright in our room shortly after six), I feel as if I were rising from a grave, gathering my moldly, worm-riddled limbs into a final effort. Yesterday was poor—felt shot—worked on a couple of Yeats poems for class preparation and read and read in him: The scalp crawled, the hair stood up. He is genuine: an antitype of Eliot, and I do enjoy Eliot. Yeats is lyrical and sharp, clear, rock-cut. I think the reason why my favorite poems of my own are "The Disquieting Muses" and "On the Decline of Oracles" is because they have that good lyrical tension: crammed speech and music at once: brain and beautiful body at once. More and more I realize how I must stop teaching and devote myself to writing: my deep self must seclude, sequester, to produce lyrics and poems of high pitch intensity—differing from the neat prosy gray-suited poems of Donald Hall, et al. I am unrecognized. *The New Yorker* has not replied to the ms. I sent off two and a half weeks ago. *ARTnews* has not answered the two poems I sent them: I run for mail and get mocked by a handful of dull space-consuming circulars addressed to "Professor Hughes" and advertising tedious books on the art of writing an intelligible sentence. I have the joyous feeling of leashed power—also the feeling that within a year or two I should be "recognized"—as I am not at all now, though I sit on poems richer than any [from] Adrienne Cecile Rich. I amuse myself, am all itch and eager fury for the end of my term. . . .

Tuesday morning, April 22. . . . Yesterday was wiped out by the cramps and drug-stitched stupor of my first day of the curse, as it is so aptly called. Do animals in heat bleed, feel pain? Or is it that sedentary bluestockinged ladies have come so far from the beast-state that they must pay by hurt, as the little mermaid had to pay when she traded her fish tail for a girl's white legs? . . . An absurd quarrel with Ted Sunday night as we were dressing to go to Wiggin's—he accusing me of throwing away his awful old cufflinks "as I had done away with his coat," and for that matter, his book on witches, since I never could stand the torture parts. None of this being true. He wouldn't say it was foolish; I, as stubborn, wouldn't forget. So I ran out, sickened. Couldn't drive anywhere. Came back. Ted had gone out. Sat in the park—all vast, dark, ominously full of silent Teds, or no Ted—night-crawler hunters came with flashlights. I called, wandered. Then saw his figure striding down Woodlawn under streetlamps and raced after, paralleling his course hidden by the row of pines edging the woods. He paused, stared, and if he weren't my husband I would have run from him as a killer. I stood behind the last fat fir tree and wagged the branches on each side till he came over. We raced to dress, to Wiggin's. . . .

Evening: A day of misery: *The New Yorker* rejection of all the poems (Oh, Howard Moss, or "They" liked "The Disquieting Muses" and the Rousseau sestina)—a burning sense of injustice, sobs, sorrow: desire to fight back, and no time time or energy to do so till June. No work done: none—all my papers to correct and three hours of preparation to do. Finished *What Maisie Knew*: Ironically Henry James's biography comforts me and I long to make known to him his posthumous reputation—he wrote in pain, gave all his life (which is more than I could think of doing—I have Ted, will have children—but few friends) and the critics insulted and mocked him, readers didn't read him. I am made crudely, for success. Does failure whet my blade? . . .

April 29. . . . When I am blue, as yesterday, I think about death, about having to die having lived awake to so little of the world—of the dreams of glory—lives of great authors, movie stars, psychiatrists. People who don't have to grub for money. Then I think of my gross fears at having a baby which I suppose center around that crucial episode at the Boston Lying-in [Hospital] so many years ago when that anonymous groaning woman, shaved and painted all colors, got cut, blood ran, water broke, and the baby came with bloody veins and urinated in the doctor's face. Every woman does it: so I cower and want, want and cower. I also think of how far I fall short from the ideal of Doris Krook—what a slipshod part-time scholar I am—no nun, no devotee. And how, on the other hand, very far I fall short from writing—how many thousands publish in *The New Yorker, The Sat Eve Post,* who work, study, get material, and

I, I dream and boast I could do it but don't and maybe can't. What else? Oh, the desire to write a novel and a book of poems before a baby. The desire also for money, which I am miserly about, not buying clothes, nor frills, although I could go wild doing so—starting [with] dresses and frivolously colored shoes to match. Amazing how money would simplify problems like ours. We wouldn't go wild at all, but write and travel and study all our lives—which I hope we do anyway. And have a house apart, by the side of no road, with country about and a study and walls of bookcases.

Wednesday, April 30. . . . Spent . . . hours typing up a florid, unbalanced and embarrassingly serious, obvious version of a central incident in my novel: This summer I will study under Henry James and George Eliot for social surface, decorum: this I think I need, not the absurd "I love you kid let's go to bed" which equates every Jack and Jill with every other, but a complex, rich, colored and subtle syntactical structure to contain, to chalice the thought and feeling of each second. . . .

Thursday, Mayday. . . . Woke as usual, feeling sick and half-dead, eyes stuck together, a taste of winding sheets on my tongue after a horrible dream involving, among other things, Warren being blown to death by a rocket. Ted, my saviour, emerging out of the *néant* with a tall mug of hot coffee which, sip by sip, rallied me to the day as he sat at the foot of the bed dressed for teaching. About to drive off—I blink every time I see him afresh. This is the man the unsatisfied ladies scan the stories in *The Ladies' Home Journal* for, the man women read romantic women's novels for: oh, he is unbelievable and the more so because he is my husband and I somehow love cooking for him (made a lemon layer cake last night) and being secretary, and all. And, riffling through all the other men in the world who bore me with their partialness, the only one. How to make it sound special? Other than sentimental, in my novel: a gross problem. Am giving exams today, so must go early to write on board—but to record, here, a conscious change of tone, of heart: suddenly realized I am no longer a teacher— oh, I have a month [and] a day to go, but just as I jitterily *became* a teacher a month before my first class, so my prophetic

Pans and Kevas [Ouija spirits] are free already, and their impatient tugs toward writing at every itch applied by reading Marianne Moore, Wallace Stevens, etc., disturb my equilibrium—suddenly I no longer *care*—let *The Waste Land* run how it may—I am already in another world—or between two worlds, one dead, the other dying to be born. We are treated as ghosts by permanent members of the faculty—as shadows already departed with no flesh and blood interest in their future. . . . I am ridiculously apathetic about my work—distant, bemused, feeling, as I said, a ghost of the world I am working in, casting no shadow. And living thus a living death, which I shall expatiate upon at length as we deal with T. S. Eliot this week and next. How I shall live until May 22nd I wonder. The Arvin exams till June 1st present no problem: it is the platform preaching that wearies.

Saturday, May 3. Read a bit of William Dunbar, a bit of *The White Goddess*,* and unearthed a whole series of subtle symbolic names for our children whose souls haunt me—that my hurt and my two legs could be the doorway for walking, talking human beings—it seems too strange and fearful. We thought: Gwyn, Alison, Vivien, Marian, Farrar, Gawain. All white goddesses and knights. . . . I pick up my ms. of poetry and leaf through it, unable to invent, to create—all my projected nostalgia for my students can't shake the conviction that teaching is a smiling public-service Vampire that drinks blood and brain without a thank you.

Monday, May 5th. . . . Wish I could . . . have gone to see Anouilh play—I am superstitious about separations from Ted, even for an hour. I think I must **live in his heat** and presence, for his smells and words—as if **all my senses f**ed involuntarily on him, and deprived for more than a few hours, I languish, wither, die to the world. . . . Put on my red silk stockings with red shoes—they feel amazing, or rather the color feels amazing—almost incandescent fire silk sheathing my legs. I can't stop looking—the stocking goes almost flesh-color, but gathers rose and glows at the edges of the leg as it cuts its shape on

---

*By Robert Graves; an important influence on Plath's work

air, concentrating the crimson on the rounding-away, shifting as I shift. Quite satisfactory. I shall wear my white pleated wool skirt and deep lovely median blue jersey with the square neck to hear Robert Lowell this afternoon: read some of his poems last night and had oddly a similar reaction (excitement, joy, admiration, curiosity to meet and praise) as when I first read Ted's poems in *St. Botolph's*: taste the phrases: tough, knotty, blazing with color and fury, most eminently sayable: "where braced pig-iron dragons grip/The blizzard to their rigor mortis." Oh, god, after coffee, even I feel my voice will come out strong and colored as that! Want today to write about our Sunday night with Leonard and Esther Baskin, whom, suddenly and well, we met. Sunday a grumpy day, stogged in the middle of exams with gray wet weather and chill. Took Ted over to Sylvan's after supper to read the poems turned in for the spring contests and money prizes. Paul Roche was there, his face that bright artificial orangy tan, his eyes marbly-blue and his hair like rather pampered and crimped wheat—I feel curious as to his machinations, his avowedly "voluminous" correspondence and ability to meet people. . . .

Sunday, May 11. Mother's Day, Mother calling late last night to thank us for pink camellia and pink roses. Queer mother— stiff about helping us come to Boston. Her conscious mind always split off, at war with her unconscious: her dreams of terrible insecurity, of losing the house—her guarded praise at our getting poems published, as if this were one more nail in the coffin of our resolve to drown as poets and refuse all "secure" teaching work. . . . Another title for my book: *Full Fathom Five*. It seem to me dozens of books must have this title, but I can't offhand remember any. It relates more richly to my life and imagery than anything else I've dreamed up: has the background of *The Tempest*, the association of the sea, which is a central metaphor for my childhood, my poems and the artist's subconscious, of the father image—relating to my own father, the buried male muse and god-creator risen to be my mate in Ted, to the sea-father Neptune—and the pearls and coral highly-wrought to art: pearls sea-changed from the ubiquitous grit of sorrow and dull routine. I am going on with *The Wings of the Dove* and ravenously devouring a thousand page anthology of magnificent folk and fairy tales of all nations, my mind again repeopling itself with magics and monsters— I cram them in. Oh, only left to myself, what a poet I will flay myself into. I shall begin by setting myself magic objects to write on: sea-bearded bodies—and begin thus, digging into the reaches of my deep submerged head, "and it's old and old it's sad and old it's sad and weary I go back to you, my cold father, my cold mad father, my cold mad feary father..."— so Joyce says, so the river flows to the paternal source of godhead.

Tuesday morning, May 13.... I can't shape into writing now: my superficial mind must keep itself up: nine months dwindle to nine weeks, which obligingly dwindle to the present nine days. Partly this, keeps me from writing (tried a bad dull poem Sunday about our landlady which was deadly, dogged and depressed me terribly: as soon as I produce a bad one—within these structures of time: knowing I can't try again, knowing I can't throw it away, prodigal, and start afresh the next hour— I hear my chittering ogres and afreets or whatever mocking me in just the same insinuating, patronizing tone of George Gibian or Mrs. Van der Poel: Why not write summers? What makes you think you can, or want to, or will write anyway? You have shown little, you may show less!). My two allies are: Ted, and time to myself to perfect the crude personal roughness, generality and superficiality of that 35 page description of *Falcon Yard* I sent to *New World Writing*. Henry James teaches me hourly—he is *too* fine for me—but then, I am so crude and loud that his lesson can only serve to make me less crude, not more fine—teaches me how life is circuitous, rich, sentences and acts laden with all the riches of meaning and implication. Well, I am half through *The Wings of the Dove*: Millie seems to me so damnably *good* ... so *noble*: she sees and sees and will not flinch or be *mean*, be small: like Maggie Verver she will not indulge "the vulgar heat of her wrong." With which, under which, I should explode. By being "simple," aren't they, by that very quality, being highly wrought? Oh, if my Dody might be complex: the trouble with amorality is that it sets up no tensions except the rather simple one of the unavailability of what is wanted: once this is provided, the tensions are swamped in a rather gross all-embracing flood. I must erect a real china shop, only not fake, for my splendid bulls. I read of Millie with her ominous as-yet-undefined illness. And I can scarcely lift a pen. I don't write here partly for that reason: the thought of penmanship exhausts me. I feel to have undulant fever, but my temperature is perfectly normal: I am too tired to read, too tired to write, too tired to prepare my last three lessons, which I should at least strain myself for. I wander in my bathrobe and wool socks about the cold, beautifully bare and clean apartment: how cleanliness rests my soul. I have an arduous apprenticeship to begin this summer. Writing a volume of poems, writing a novel is so *small* in one sense: in comparison to the quality and quantity of others. And nothing, maliciously, evilly, confirms my ambition. I have an ominously red, sore and swollen eyelid, a queer red spot on my lip—and this enervating fatigue like a secret and destructive fever—can I do my dreams justice? . . . There is a doggedness in me that resents even these last two weeks and longs for liberation, won't run about dithering up preparation. I spent all yesterday rushing about, shopping, scouring, making a runny but delicious custard-meringue-raspberry pie. Paul and Clarissa came, Clarissa five months pregnant, thickening under a black loose shirt, her hair bright girt, Paul, double, probably quite wicked (we learned he has an older brother and sister: a fact difficult to adjust to our strong impression of his singularity—heard how he lay naked in the rose garden at Clarissa's mansion in Saginaw, crocheted, while intently observing TV, a light blue wool cape for Pandora with PR embroidered on it in white angora and a bunny tail at the back). [Omission.] Ted and I are aware of a great dearth of invitations, of Tony Hecht* even, one might say, owing us a dinner—but the reaction, partly sour, is also a relieved one: I'm sick of dinners—their cost, what one pays, is only socially fixed, repaid, by one's having to spend more and more of oneself, and this I am through with. It comes home, strongly, how exterior relations impoverish if one is not heart-deep in one's own work. Bless Ted for being like me in this and demanding, with a sauce of good other people, our sequestering, our dedication. How the problems, and I knock wood as I write, of a handsome and gifted poet husband, then, fray to mist, because of Ted's being himself, and me, one

---

*The poet Anthony Hecht

hopes, my own self. The church bell on the Church of the Blessed Sacrament opposite is just bonging out its queer version of twelve noon. I am now dressed in my red Christmas shirt with its subtle pattern of paisley black, green and gray foliage, and my very subtle smoky green skirt, deep gray-green, like a military color. I feel better for dressing: that poem by Yeats comes to mind. The one about our restlessness: always longing for the next, the different season: our longing being the longing for the tomb. And so tonight I will long to get in bed and to sleep: Ted's witchy Aunt Alice illustrates this admirably when she stays in bed for no reason except that there's no reason to get up if one only has to go back to bed again. I made a great dinner last night: the lamb was tough, though. Mrs. Van der Poel came: black, tiny, elegant, her gray hair curled into spit, or kiss curls, her heels high, her fur opulent, a highly trained and soulless silver poodle with a taste for modern art: her relations seem to suggest linkage to primary colors, the garish Léger cityscapes where women are turbine engines. I never felt such an inimical presence as Mrs. Van der Poel's. She makes me feel large, soft, and agreeably doltish. She is sterile, absolutely barren. Her coming, I feel, was forced. She said, when she first refused, that she'd "love to come another time," which I took up as a dogged duty—to give her the chance for another time, and after three or four shiftings, which I should have interpreted as refusal, she came, sat, chittered. About art, artists, notably Baskin—nothing. Either one wasn't worth her wisdom, or she wasn't in the mood, or she doesn't *have* the best kind of wisdom: she can put everything into bright, neat words, and this is killing. One suspects her dry bright tidy little voice could find a lucid epithet for the worst chaos. One wonders about her vanished husband. Priscilla: the name does for her. One supposes she keeps the Van der Poel for its high tone. Ted and I both came away with the strong impression that she dislikes Leonard Baskin. Why? She possesses an admirable, huge Baskin, "Hanging Man," she invited him to give three lectures on sculpture for her classes; she is, however, a professor, a chairman of the department, and he a creative artist with an avowed scorn of offices-in-the-art-building, department meetings, and such. At any event, she exuded dislike. I can't, nor can Ted, spot the sentence, the clause, but it was evident. Just now, restless, unproductive, I was wandering about the bare clean apartment eating a piece of buttered toast and strawberry jam when, stopping wolfish by the bathroom venetian blind, as I always do, to eye the vista for the mailman, I heard a burst of prophetic whistling and the man himself exploded, as it were, into view with his light blue shirt and beaten leather shoulder pouch. I ran to get ready to go downstairs and felt him pause, so hurried to the living room gable window. And there, as suddenly sprung up, was Ted in his dark green corduroy jacket waylaying the man and demanding mail. From the window I could see it was nothing, nor was it—a handful of flannel: circulars, soap coupons, Sears sales, a letter from Mother of stale news she'd already relayed over the phone, a card from Oscar Williams* inviting us to a cocktail party in New York on the impossible last day of my classes. No news. I feel a nervous havoc in my veins—and am close to starving myself—Ted's influence here is marked. When he won't eat I all too easily find it a bother to prepare food for myself and so fail in nourishment and sleep. A dull and useless day, dream-dictated. . . .

May 14, Wednesday. Grim night. My eyelid's hot stinging itch has spread, in actuality, or by sympathetic imagining nerves, to all my body—scalp, leg, stomach: as if an itch, infectious, lit and burned, lit and burned. I feel like scratching my skin off. And a dull torpor shutting me in my own prison of high-strung depression. Is it because I feel a ghost? My influence waning with my classes, who have no exam, but one paper and then no need to work or listen. At the faculty meeting I marveled so much time had passed and I was in my same aloneness, only further in, as if a transparent lid enveloped me and shut up all others whose faces have no personal meaning for me—they are going on next year, I am gone already in spirit, if lingering in a locust-itchy-crawly body. I feel about to break out in leprousy: nervous: hearing stairs creak: dying of cowardice—ready for all the lights mysteriously to go out and the horror of a monster to take me: nightmares haunt me: Joan of Arc's face as she feels the fire and the world blurs out in a smoke, a pall of horror. I wait for Ted's return from Paul's

---

*The poetry anthologist

reading of *Oedipus*. I itch. I feel between two worlds, as Arnold writes—"one dead, the other powerless to be born": all seems thus futile—my teaching has lost its savor: I feel the students are gone and [I] have none of the satisfaction as a teacher of planning a better more vital course next year: that is done. Then, on the other hand, I have nothing but a handful of poems—so unsatisfactory, so limiting, when I study Eliot, Yeats, even Auden and Ransom—and the few written in spring vacation to link me umbilically to a new not-yet-born world of writing—only the five-year distant adolescent successes in writing: a gap. Will I fill it, go beyond? I am hamstrung: papers to come, senior exams and Arvin's. My eyes are killing me— what is wrong with them? No mail—only letter from Patsy which holds out New York—a vision of time—a bridge from a dead world to a newborn one.

About this time, and for months afterward, Plath began to feel an upsurge of rage, an emotion she rarely allowed herself. In the passage that follows it is a rage against her husband in which a small incident takes on enormous proportions, and is quickly transferred to some girls in a public park. As Plath notes eight months later (December 27), the real source is her father, though it would be several years before she could make the connection in any deep way. Feeling the rage was tremendously important to her work; as she noted on August 27, "Fury jams the gullet and spreads poison, but, as soon as I start to write, dissipates, flows out into the figure of the letters: writing as therapy?"

May 19, Monday. Only it isn't Monday at all, but now Thursday, the 22nd of May, and I through with my last classes and a hot bath and disabused of many ideals, visions and faiths. Irony: the mature stance which covers up the maudlin ladies' magazine blurt of tears. Disgust. Yes, that's more like it: revulsion at much in myself and more in Ted [omission]. . . . Irony: in almost two years [I've been] turned from a crazy perfectionist and promiscuous human-being-lover, to a misanthrope, and—at Tony's, at Paul's—a nasty, catty and malicious misanthrope. [Omission.] So I put the two of us in our separate, oh, infinitely superior world: we are so nice, naturally, too nice—"smilers." So we are now, in society, nasty and cruel and calculated—oh, not first off, but only when attacked. No more brave innocent blinkings—all tooth and nail. And just as I rose to a peak of nastiness for perhaps the first time in my life—I have never been catty professionally and publicly—I got the final insight: not only am I just as nasty as everybody else, but so is Ted. [Omission.] How it works: how irony is the spice of life. My novel will hardly end with love and marriage: it will be a story, like James's, of the workers and the worked, the exploiters and the exploited: of vanity and cruelty: with a *ronde*, a circle of lies and abuse in a beautiful world gone bad. The irony I record here for the novel, but also for *The Ladies' Home Journal*. I am no Maggie Verver, I feel the vulgar heat of my wrong enough to gag, to spit the venom I've swallowed: but I'll take my cue from Maggie, bless the girl. How the irony builds up—every time I made one of my foolish bland statements I felt a chill, a dark rubber-visaged frog-faced fate, ready to loom up at the fullness of the moment to confront me with some horror as yet unseen, unforeseen. And all this time it has been going on, on the far edges of my intuition. I confided my faith in Ted, and why is the wife the last to see her husband's ulcer? Because she has the most faith, the carefully and lovingly nurtured blind faith that turns unquestioning to follow the course of the sun, hearing no outside cries of thirst from the desert, no curses in the wasteland. [Omission.] Oh, I said in a bright clear voice: "I am the only woman on the faculty who has a husband."... Well, mine is [omission]... a twister. I look at Lowell's first book: Jean Stafford then.* Well, at least she writes for *The New Yorker*—a good career, a good living—or maybe she's in a madhouse even as I speak, she's been an alcoholic. Who knows who Ted's next book will be dedicated to? His navel. [Omission.] Well, start with the background to the facts— the misanthropy felt for all except Ted and myself, the faith in Ted and myself and distrust of all others. Add last night— Ted reading the part of Creon for Paul's translation of *Oedipus* and practically telling me not to come. I said all right, but rebelled. I am superstitious about not hearing Ted read. I raced

---

*Jean Stafford was Lowell's wife at the time he dedicated his first book to her. Ted Hughes's first book was dedicated to Plath.

through my second set of papers (and still have another to go)
and leapt up, as if drawn on a leash, and started running, down
the stairs, out into the warm, heavy lilac-scented May dark.
The new moon stared at me over the trees—its shadow of
wholeness clearly drawn. I ran, skimming, although deep in
long tension and exhaustion, as if I would fly, my heart a
hurting fisted lump in my chest. I ran on, not stopping, down
the bumpy, steep hill by Paradise Pond, saw a rabbit, fuzzed,
bown, in the bushes behind the Botany Building. I ran on up
to the lighted colonial front of Sage Hall, white columns glowing in the electric lights, not a person in sight, empty echoing
pavements. The hall was glaring: two people, a fat girl and
ugly man, were in the side booth running a tape of music for
the recording. I tiptoed in, slipped into a seat in back, and tried
to still the funny knocking of my heart and my rasping breath
[omission]. . . . The minute I came in [Ted] knew it, and I knew
he knew it, and his voice let the reading down. He was ashamed
of something. He gave the last line with the expression of a
limp dish towel and I felt this faint flare of disgust, of misgiving. There he stood, next to the corrupt, white snail-faced
Van Voris, whose voice luxuriated over the words: loins, in-
cest, bed, foul. I felt as if I had stepped barefoot into a pit of
sliming, crawling worms. I felt like hawking and spitting. Ted
knew whom he stood beside and whose words he read. He
shrank, slouched away from it. But he could have gotten out
of it before. Long before. Paul would love to have Philip
Wheelwright read Creon. Ted didn't come to meet me afterwards. I stood in front, went out behind and asked the janitor
where the readers were. He had to tell me. In a small lighted
room Bill Van Voris slumped in a loose boneless position, legs
stuck straight out, on a flowery-upholstered couch. Ted sat
with a mean wrong face over the piano, banging out a strident
one-finger tune, hunched, a tune I'd never heard before. [Omis-
sion.] Oh, yes, the preying ones, how I shall manage it. He
didn't speak. He wouldn't come away. I sat down. We went
then. . . . Anyway, it was a stale, rancid evening. . . . Which
more of in the course of this. So it was an accident. [Omission.]
So today is my last day. Or was. Armed with various poems
by Ransom, Cummings and Sitwell, I went to class, received
applause in the exact volume of my enjoyment of the class—
a spatter at 9, a thunderous burst at 11, and something in

between both extremes at 3. I had made a kind of ceremonial stab at asking Ted to drive down with me till I got through this afternoon, so I could see him and rejoice the very minute I got through my first class. So we went. I was teaching, among other things, "parting without sequel": how perfect—I moralized about the joy of revenge, the dangerous luxury of hate and malice, and how, even when malice and venom are "richly deserved," the indulgence of these emotions can, alas, be ruinous. Ah, Ransom. All boomerangs. Before class I had twenty minutes. Ted arranged to bring books into the library and meet me in the car: to be waiting there till my classes ended. I went alone into the coffee shop, which was almost deserted. A few girls. And the back of the head of Bill Van Voris. He did not see me come in, nor ask for coffee, although I was almost within his view. But the girl he was sitting with in the booth opposite him could see me. She had very fine black eyes, black hair, and a pale white skin, and was being very serious. I took my coffee up and did not attract Bill's attention, but sat down in the booth directly in back of him, facing the back of his head and his student. Ha, I thought, listening, or, rather, hearing. I sipped my coffee and thought of Jacky [Van Voris], whose skin is dough color with fine tight wrinkles, whose hair is mouse color, whose eyes are of indeterminate color behind tortoiseshell rimmed glasses. Who is not perhaps as cultivatedly "intellectual" as Bill's students. I noted Bill's back well: the tasteful thin-grain corduroy jacket, fitting his broad masculine shoulders, a light-cinnamon color, tweedy or tobacco color, his pale bull neck, the little springing crisp whorls of his dark very-close-cropped hair. He was talking in his way: silly, pretentious, oh, yes, fatuous. She stammered prettily, as I left my ears unshuttered: something about "The hero . . . the comic as distinct from the classic hero." "Comic?" Bill's voice cracked up, a whisper, or wheeze nuzzled somewhere in it. "You mean . . ." She faltered, dark eyes asking for help. "Satiric," Bill proposed, all sure wisdom. I felt a stir, a desire to tap his shoulder, lean over and tell him to come off it, comic heroes were fine, satire didn't hold a monopoly. But I shut up. Bill quickly swerved to Restoration drama. Sniffing, inhaling the daisies in his own field. "Morality. Of course, all that material for jokes, that wonderful opportunity for bawdy jokes. Men and men leaving their wives." The girl responded, geared for the supreme, the most intense understanding: "Oh, I know, I know." They were still talking when I left the coffee shop for my class. At which I almost talked myself hoarse. I could see Al Fisher, sitting in the same seat, and me opposite, that official sexual rapport. Al Fisher and his dynasties of students: students made mistresses. Students made wives. And now, his silly, fatuous vain smile. When Bill gets tenure—probably not much but play about till then—he will begin Smith mistresses. Or maybe Jacky will die: she has death, and great pain, written on her stretched mouth: grim gripped lips and eyes that measure, reserved, cold, the chances she takes and has to take and will take. These images piled up. I felt tempted to drop in at the library before class and share with Ted my amusing insight, my ringside seat at Van Voris and the Seductive Smith Girl: or William S. is bad agayne. But I went to class. When I came out, I ran to the parking lot, half-expecting to meet Ted on the way to the car, but more sure of finding him inside. I peered through a perspective of car windows but saw no dark head. Our car was empty and the emptiness struck me as odd, particularly on this day which we have counted toward for twenty-eight weeks. I did see Bill, after what was probably over an hour and a half, bidding a warm smiling good-bye to his student between the green lilac bushes framing the path from the coffee shop to the parking lot. He began coming toward me and I quickly turned my back on him and got into the car, which I drove up to the library, figuring Ted would be in the reading room, oblivious of time, immersed in *The New Yorker* article by Edmund Wilson. He was not there. I kept meeting leftover students of mine from my three o'clock class. I had an odd impulse to drive home, but I was not destined to [see] anything shocking in the apartment yet, although I have been prepared to be. As I came striding out of the cold shadow of the library, my bare arms chilled, I had one of those intuitive visions. I knew what I would see, what I would of necessity meet, and I have known for a very long time, although not sure of the place or date of the first confrontation. Ted was coming up the road from Paradise Pond, where girls take their boys to neck on weekends. He was walking with a broad, intense smile, eyes into the uplifted doe-eyes of a strange girl with brownish hair, a large lipsticked grin, and bare thick legs in khaki Bermuda shorts. I saw this in several sharp flashes, like blows. I could not tell the color of the girl's eyes, but Ted could, and his smile, though open and engaging as the girl's was, took on an ugliness in context. His stance next to Van Voris clicked into place, his smile became too white-hot, became fatuous, admiration-seeking. He was gesturing, just finishing an observation, an explanation. The girl's eyes souped up giddy applause. She saw me coming. Her eye started to guilt and she began to run, literally, without a good-bye, Ted making no effort to introduce her, as I'm sure Bill would have. She hasn't learned to be deceitful yet in her first look, but she'll learn fast. He thought her name was Sheila; once he thought my name was Shirley: oh, all the twists of the tongue; the smiles. Strange, but jealousy in me turned to disgust. The late comings home, my vision, while brushing my hair, of a black-horned, grinning wolf all came clear, fused, and I gagged at what I saw. I am no smiler anymore. But Ted is. His esthetic distance from his girls so betrayed by his leaning stance, leaning into the eyes of adoration—not old adoration, but new, fresh, unadulterated. Or, perhaps, adulterated. Van Voris looks white. Lily-handed. Why is it I so despise this brand of male vanity? Even Richard had it, small, sickly as he was at nineteen. Only he was rich, had family and so security: a lineage of men able to buy better wives than they deserved. As Joan said: Ego and Narcissus. *Vanitas, vanitatum.* I know what Dr. B. would tell me, and I feel I can now tell her. No, I won't jump out of a window or drive Warren's car into a tree, or fill the garage at home with carbon monoxide and save expense, or slit my wrists and lie in the bath. I am disabused of all faith and see too clearly. I can teach, and will write and write well. I can get in a year of that, perhaps, before other choices follow. Then there are the various—and few—people I love a little. And my dogged and inexplicable sense of dignity, integrity that must be kept. I have run too long on trust funds. I am bankrupt in that line.

Later, much later. Some time the next morning. The fake excuses, vague confusions about name and class. All fake. All false. And the guilty look of stunned awareness of the wrong presence. So I can't sleep. Partly out of shock myself at the cheapness of vanity. [Omission.] And the complete refusal to explain. What Kazin said that spring evening was true: that's why Ted jumped at him. Only Kazin was wrong in one particular: it wasn't Smith girls. No—the eager leaning open grin and my vision of Van Voris with this—of Fisher, later, yes. Dishonesty—a rift. All stupidity and frankness on my side: what a fool one is to sincerely love. Not to cheat. To two-time. It is awful to want to go away and to want to go nowhere. I made the most amusing, ironic and fatal step in trusting Ted was unlike other vain and obfuscating and self-indulgent men. I have served a purpose, spent money, Mother's money, which hurts most, to buy him clothes, to buy him a half year, eight months of writing, typed hundreds of times his poems. Well, so much have I done for modern British and American poetry. What I cannot forgive is dishonesty—and no matter what, or how hard, I would rather know the truth of which I today had such a clear and devastating vision from his mouth than hear foul evasions, blurrings and rattiness. I have a life to finish up here. But what about life without trust—the sense that love is a lie and all joyous sacrifice is ugly duty. I am so tired. My last day, and I cannot sleep for shaking at horror. He is shamed, shameful and shames me and my trust, which is no plea in a world of liars and cheats and broken or vanity-ridden men. Love has been an inexhaustible spring for my nourishment and now I gag. Wrong, wrong: the vulgar heat of it: the picture of fatuous attention, doe-eyed rollings of smiles, startled recognition, flight—all cannot be denied. Only clearly explained. I do not want to ask for what should be given before the heavy hammy American cheap slang "let's make up." The heavy too-jocular jocularity. [Omission.] For I smell it [corruption]. The house stinks of it. And my vision fills in the blurred latenesses with oh, yes, Frank Sousa. I know. I know worse for knowing all myself and he not telling me or understanding what it is to know. [Omission.] Why did I make his concerns my own and wish to see him at his best and finest? . . . He does not care. He is sulking as he began to after I came to the reading. His accepting that and keeping up to it showed how far down he has gone. He wants to go down, to leave me to hunt for him on my last moment of teaching, to celebrate the end of a year of teaching by learning what my intuition clears for me like a pool of clearing water after the mud settles. Oh, I see the frogs on the mud bed. And the corruption in warts on their slick and unctuous black hides. So what now.

* * *

June 11, Wednesday. A green cool rainy night: peace and concord, almost a month behind in this book, but much to tell—I have avoided writing here because of the rough and nightmarish entry I must take up from—but I take up and knit up the raveled ends. I had a sprained thumb, Ted bloody claw marks for a week, and I remember hurling a glass with all my force across a dark room; instead of shattering, the glass rebounded and remained intact: I got hit and saw stars—for the first time—blinding red and white stars exploding in the black void of snarls and bitings. Air cleared. We are intact. And nothing—no wishes for money, children, security, even total possession—nothing is worth jeopardizing what I have, which is so much the angels might well envy it. I corrected, sullenly, my eyes red with a stinging itchy rash, honors papers—simply putting in time in the garden of the faculty club—they could all be "summas" or "cums" for all I cared—under Miss Hornbeak's acid eye. And then Arvin's exams, which I finished, along with all my obligations at Smith, about 10 days ago, on Sunday, June 1st. We have half of June, then July and August clear to write, but the looming blackness of no Saxton for Ted. The irony is that his own editor at Harper is adviser to the trustees and his project, although most warmly approved, is ineligible because of the very qualification we thought would win for him—his Harper-published book. So I shall try for a Saxton for 10 months and Ted for a Guggenheim this next year—he trying to rank T. S. Eliot, W. H. Auden, Marianne Moore, etc., behind him. I don't want to live in the country this year, but in Boston, near people, lights, sights, shops, a river, Cambridge, theater, editors, publishers—where we won't need a car and will be well away from Smith. So we will gamble—on a possible Saxton for me and at least on Boston jobs if we aren't earning by writing, but that last only a death's door resort. We must keep round-trip ship fare for Europe intact, and our mystic $1,400 of poetry earnings. I am just getting used to peace: no people, no assignments, no students. Peace, at least after our visit home to apartment hunt this weekend, and me to make a recording at Harvard and to celebrate our 2nd wedding anniversary—how can I say this calmly? This was a central problem in my other book, and here it begins well into marriage. An incident today to start a train of remembering our wearying and also rejuvenating week in New

York which cleared out Smith cobwebs: we went at twilight to walk in the green park (I have just written a good syllabic poem, "Child's Park Stones," as juxtaposed to the ephemeral orange and fuchsia azaleas, and feel the park is my favorite place in America). The evening was dim, light gray with wet humid mist, swimming green. I took a pair of silver-plated scissors in my raincoat pocket with the intent to cut another rose—yellow, if possible—from the rose garden (by the stone lion's head fountain), just come into bloom—a rose to begin to unbud as the red, almost black-red rose now giving out prodigal scent in our living room. We walked round on the road to the stucco house and were about to descend to the rose garden when we heard a loud crackling sound as of the breaking of twigs. We thought it must be a man we'd seen in another part of the park coming through the thick rhododendron groves from the frog pond. The yellow roses were blowzy, blasted, no bud in view. I leaned to snip a pink bud, one petal uncurling, and three hulking girls came out of the rhododendron grove, oddly sheepish, hunched in light manila-colored raincoats. We stood regnant in our rose garden and stared them down. They shambled, in whispered conversation, to the formal garden of white peonies and red geraniums, stood at a loss under a white arbor. "I'll bet they're wanting to steal some flowers," Ted said. Then the girls evidently agreed to walk off. I saw an orange rosebud, odd, which I've never before seen, and bent to clip it, a bud of orange velvet, after the girls were out of sight. The gray sky lowered, thunder rumbled in the pines, and a warm soft rain began to fall grayly as if gently squeezed from a gray sponge. We started home through the rhododendron groves where the girls had come out. I saw, as we had half-envisioned, but yet saw with a shock, a newspaper loaded with scarlet rhododendron blossoms neatly tucked behind a bush. I began to get angry. We walked farther, and saw another newspaper crammed full of bright pink rhododendrons. I had a wild impulse, which I should have followed to satisfy my bloodlust, to take up all the rhododendron flowers and set them afloat in the frog pond like rootless lilies to spite the guilty pickers and preserve the flowers as long as they would be preserved in water for the public eye. I picked up bunches of the scarlet ones, but Ted, also angry, wouldn't have it. But as we passed the pond and had come out onto open grass, we both turned back, of one accord, to put the blossoms in the pond. As I must have sensed, the girls were back—we heard muffled laughter and the cracking of branches broken carelessly. We came up slowly with evil eyes. I felt bloodlust—sassy girls, three of them—"Oh, here's a big one," a girl ostentatiously said. "Why are you picking them?" Ted asked. "For a dance. We need them for a dance." They half-thought we would approve. "Don't you think you'd better stop?" Ted asked. "This is a public park." Then the little one got brassy and fairly sneered, "This isn't your park." "Nor yours," I retorted, wanting strangely to claw off her raincoat, smack her face, read the emblem of her school on her jersey and send her to jail. "You might as well pull the bush by its roots." She glared at me and I gave her a mad wild still stony glare that snuffed hers out. Showily she directed another girl to get the other rhododendrons. We followed them to the pond, where they stood, consulted, then doubled back on their tracks. We followed to the edge of the rhododendron grove in the rain, lightning flashed, almost clear red, and we saw them hurrying down to a waiting car and loading the rhododendrons into the open back trunk. We let them go. If we made them uncomfortable it is almost enough. But we were angry. And I wondered at my split morality. Here I had an orange and a pink rosebud in my pocket and a full red rose squandering its savors at home, and I felt like killing a girl stealing armfuls of rhododendrons for a dance: I guess I feel my one rose a week is aesthetic joy for me and Ted and sorrow or loss for no one—yellow roses are gone blowzy—why not conserve one bud through full bloom to blowzy death and replace it with another: to possess and love an immortal many-colored rose during rose season while leaving a gardenful—but these girls were ripping up whole bushes— that crudeness and wholesale selfishness disgusted and angered me. I have a violence in me that is hot as death-blood. I can kill myself or—I know it now—even kill another. I could kill a woman, or wound a man. I think I could. I gritted to control my hands, but had a flash of bloody stars in my head as I stared that sassy girl down, and a blood-longing to [rush] at her and tear her to bloody beating bits.

THREE

Boston
1958 – 1959

England
1960 – 1962

Friday, June 20. My motto here might well be "My spirits, as in a dream, are all bound up." I have been and am battling depression. It is as if my life were magically run by two electric currents: joyous positive and despairing negative—which ever is running at the moment dominates my life, floods it. I am now flooded with despair, almost hysteria, as if I were smothering. As if a great muscular owl were sitting on my chest, its talons clenching and constricting my heart. I knew this fresh life would be harder, much harder, than teaching—but I have weapons, and self-knowledge is the best of them. I was blackly hysterical last fall beginning my job: The outside demands exacted my blood, and I feared. Now, a totally different situation, yet the same in emotional content. I have fourteen months "completely free" for the first time in my life, reasonable financial security, and the magic and hourly company of a husband so magnificent . . . big, creative in a giant way, that I imagine I made him up—only he offers so much extra surprise that I know he is real and deep as an iceberg in its element. So I have all this, and my limbs are paralyzed: inside demands exact my blood, and I fear—because I have to *make up* my demands: the hardest responsibility in the world: there is no outer recalcitrant material to blame for snags and failures, only the bristling inner recalcitrance: sloth, fear, vanity, meekness. I know, even as I wrote last fall, that if I face and command this experience and *produce* a book of poems, stories, a novel, learn German and read Shakespeare and Aztec anthropology and *The Origin of Species*—as I faced and commanded the different demands of teaching—I shall never be afraid again of myself. And if I am not afraid of myself—of my own craven fears and wincings—I shall have little left in the world to be afraid of—of accident, disease, war, yes—but not of my standing up to it. This is, of course, a manner of whistling in the dark. I have even longed for that most fearsome first woman's ordeal: having a baby—to elude my demanding demons and have a constant excuse for lack of production in writing. I must first conquer my writing and experience, and then will deserve to conquer childbirth. Paralysis. Once the outer tensions are gone: I sit on a cold gray June day in welcome of the green gloom of leaves, I fall back and back into myself, dredging deep, longing to revisit my first hometown: Winthrop, not Wellesley. Jamaica Plain even: The names are become talismans. The church clock, or is it angelus? strikes twelve in its queer measured sequences of bells. I have let almost a month slip by—going to New York, to Wellesley and apartment hunting. Frittering. Being with people. I say it is people I need, yet what good have they done me? Perhaps, as I try a story, I shall discover. I lean on the window, forehead to the glass, waiting for the blue-uniformed mailman to walk out from the house, having left letters of acceptance. . . .

I go suspended in the void, the vacuum, the exhaust of the year's teaching machine, which speeds off clicking and purring. I must, again for the first time . . . and for the longest time, tightly and creatively structure my days—fill myself with reading and writing projects—keep a clean and well-run house, get rid of my slovenly sickness. We found this week an "ideal" apartment—ideal aesthetically if not in high price and kitchen crammed against one wall of the living room. But the view, oh, the view, yes, the view. Two tiny rooms for $115 a month, and yet light, quiet and a sixth floor Beacon Hill view to the river, with two bay windows, one each for Ted and me to write in. I await only Marianne Moore's letter before I can send off *my* application for a Saxton grant, which would just cover an economical ten months of our contracted year and relieve my puritan conscience completely about the rent. The rented Beacon Hill flat gives our summer free peace. I write here, because I am paralyzed everywhere else. Compulsive. As if in reaction to the dance, the tarantella of the teaching year, my mind shuts against knowledge, study: I fritter, gliddery—pick up this and that, wipe a dish, stir up some mayonnaise, jump at the imagined note of the mailman's whistle above the roar of traffic. I am disappointed with my poems: they pall. I have only a few over 25 and want a solid forty. I have distant subjects. I haven't opened my experience up. I keep discarding and discarding. My mind is barren of ideas and I must scavenge themes as a magpie must: scraps and oddments. I feel paltry, wanting in richness. Fearful, inadequate, desperate. As if my mind clicked into a "fix," which stood frozen and blinkered. And I must slowly set my lands in order: make my dream of self with poems, breast-sucking babies, a Wife-of-Bath calm, humor and resilience, come clear with time. I face no school-scheduled year, but the hardest year where all choosing is mine, all making and all delays, defaultings, shyings off and all tardy sloths.

June 25th, Wednesday. A starred day, probably the first in this whole book. I was going to write here yesterday but was in a teary, blue wits' end mood. Today I sat to type back letters and more of Ted's and my poems to send out. Seated at the typewriter, I saw the lovely light-blue shirt of the mailman going into the front walk of the millionairess next door, so I ran downstairs. One letter stuck up out of the mailbox, and I saw *The New Yorker* on the left corner in dark print. My eyes dazed over. I raced alternatives through my head: I had sent a stamped envelope with my last poems, so they must have lost it and returned the rejects in "one of their" own envelopes. Or it must be a letter for Ted about copyrights. I ripped the letter from the box. It felt shockingly hopefully thin. I tore it open right there on the steps, over mammoth marshmallow Mrs. Whalen sitting in the green yard with her two pale artificially cute little boys in their swimsuits jumping in and out of the rubber circular portable swimming pool and bouncing a gaudy striped ball. The black thick print of Howard Moss's letter banged into my brain. I saw "MUSSEL HUNTER AT ROCK HARBOR seems to me a marvelous poem and I'm happy to say we're taking it for The New Yorker. . . ."—at this realization of ten years of hopeful wishful waits (and subsequent rejections) I ran yipping upstairs to Ted and jumping about like a Mexican bean. It was only moments later, calming a little, that I finished the sentence ". . . as well as NOCTURNE, which we also think extremely fine." Two POEMS—not only that, two of my *longest*—91 and 45 lines respectively: They'll have to use front-spots for both and are buying them *in spite* of having [a] full load of summer poems and not for filler. This shot of joy conquers an old dragon and should see me through the next months of writing on the crest of a creative wave.

Thursday, June 26. . . . Looked up spiders and crabs and owls in the sticky deserted gloom of the college library: pleasant to feel ownership of it in sodden summer. Wrote a brief poem this morning—"Owl Over Main Street" in "syllabic" verse. Could be better. The beginning is a bit lyrical for the subject and the last verse might be expanded. I should leave poems to lie, to be rescrawled, and not be so eager to stick them in my book. I'd like a good fifteen to twenty poems more. That owl we heard on our midnight walk around town, the great feathered underside of the bird's body, its wide wings spread over the telephone wires—a ghoulish skrwack. Also: the black spider in Spain knotting ants around its rock. Visions of violence. The animal world seems to me more and more intriguing. Odd dreams: drank from a plastic cylindrical bottle with a red tip and realized in horror it was starch-poison I put in it—waited for my stomach to wrench and wither, ran to icebox remembering about antidotes, and swallowed a raw egg whole: Ted says it's a symbolic dream of conception. Also, last night—a musical comedy and a hundred Danny Kayes. Pulled a piece of skin off my lip and my lips began welling blood, lip-shape—my whole mouth a skinless welling of brilliant red blood.

Thursday, July 3. . . . I have been writing poems steadily and feel the blessed dawn of a desire to write prose beginning: bought a literary *Mlle* to whet my emulous urge—don't feel angry now: have my own time. I am rejecting more and more poems from my book, which is now titled after what I consider one of my best and curiously moving poems about my father-sea-god muse: *Full Fathom Five*. "The Earthenware Head" is out: once, in England, "my best poem": too fancy, glassy, patchy and rigid—it embarrasses me now—with its ten elaborate epithets for head in 5 verses. I suppose now my star piece is "Mussel Hunter at Rock Harbor": The author's proofs came from *The New Yorker* yesterday. Three long columns of them in the blessed *New Yorker* print which I've envisioned for so long. My next ambition is to get a story in *The New Yorker*—five, ten more years work. A horrid two-day noise of an electric saw cutting a tree down and up and the priests' angered and disturbed these days. The truck is gone and I hope for peace—the traffic is regular and soft enough to be minimal. I began German—two hours a day, on July 1st. Have started translating Grimm's fairy tales, making a vocab list, but must work now on the grammar lessons—have gotten all verb and noun-case forms, but am surprised enough I can get the sense of a story after two years of not touching it. My life is in my hands. I'm plowing through Penguin books on Aztecs, the personality of animals, man and the vertebrates. So much to read, but this year I will make out schedules, lists—that is a help. Ted has given me several poetry subjects and assignments which are highly exciting: I've already written a good short poem on the groundhog and on landowners and am eager for others.

Friday, July 4. Independence Day: how many people know from what they are free, by what they are imprisoned. Cool air, Canadian air, changed the atmosphere in the night and I woke to cool weather, cool enough for hot tea and sweatshirt. I woke to feed our baby bird. Yesterday, with this queer, suffocating hysteria on me—partly, I think, from not writing prose: stories, my novel—I walked out with Ted in the dense humid air. He stopped by a tree on the street. There on bare ground, on its back, scrawny wings at a desperate stretch, a baby bird, fallen from its nest, convulsed in what looked like a death-shudder. I was sick with its hurt, nauseous. Ted carried it home cradled in his hand, and it looked out with a bright dark eye. We put it in a small box of cardboard, stuffed with a dish towel and bits of soft paper to simulate a nest. The bird shook and shook. It seemed to be off balance, fell on its back. Every moment I expected the breath in its scrawny chest to stop. But no. We tried to feed it with bread soaked in milk on a toothpick, but it sneezed, didn't swallow. Then we went downtown and bought fresh ground steak, very like worm shapes, I thought. As we came up the stairs the bird squawked piteously and opened its yellow froggish beak wide as itself so its head wasn't visible behind the fork-tongued opening. Without thinking, I shoved a sizeable piece of meat down the bird's throat. The beak closed on my fingertip, the tongue seemed to suck my finger, and the mouth, empty, opened again. Now I feed the bird fearlessly with meat and bread and it eats often and well, sleeping in between two-hourly feedings and looking a bit more like a proper bird. However small, it is an extension of life, sensibility and identity. When I am ready for a baby it will be wonderful. But not until then. Wickedly didn't do German for the last two days, in a spell of perversity and paralysis.

Last night Ted and I did PAN [Ouija board] for the first time in America. We were rested, warm, happy in our work and the overturned brandy glass responded admirably, oddly often with charming humor. Even if our own hot subconscious pushes it (it says, when asked, that it is "like us"), we had more fun than a movie. There are so many questions to ask it. I wonder how much is our own intuition working, and how much queer accident, and how much "my father's spirit." PAN informed us my book of poems will be published by Knopf, not World (they are "liars" at World—a strange note: do I feel this?). Also: fifty poems for my book. We will have two sons before we have a girl and should name the boys Owen or Gawen, the girl Rosalie. Pan recited a poem of his own called "Moist," stated his favorite poem of Ted's is "Pike" ("I like fish") and of mine is "Mussel Hunter" ("Kolossus likes it"). Kolossus is Pan's "family god." He advises me to lose myself in reading when depressed (it's the "hot weather") and claims my novel will be about love, and I should start writing it in November. Among other penetrating observations Pan said I should write on the poem subject "Lorelei" because they are my "own kin." So today for fun I did so, remembering the plaintive German song Mother used to play and sing to us beginning "*Ich weiss nicht was soll es bedeuten*. . . ." The subject appealed to me doubly (or triply): the German legend of the Rhine sirens, the sea-childhood symbol, and the death-wish involved in the song's beauty. The poem devoured my day, but I feel it is a book poem and am pleased with it. *Must* agonizingly begin prose—an irony, this paralysis, while day by day I do poems—and also other reading—or I will be unable to speak human speech, lost as I am in my inner wordless Sargasso.

Monday, July 7. I am evidently going through a stage in beginning writing similar to my two months of hysteria in beginning teaching last fall. A sickness, frenzy of resentment at everything but myself at the bottom. I lie wakeful at night, wake exhausted with that sense of razor-shaved nerves. I must be my own doctor. I must cure this very destructive paralysis and ruinous brooding and daydreaming. If I want to write, this is hardly the way to behave—in horror of it, frozen by it. The ghost of the unborn novel is a Medusa-head. Witty or simply observant character notes come to me. But I have no idea how to begin. I shall, perhaps, just begin. I am somewhere in me sure I should write a good "book poem" a day—but that is nonsense—I go wild when I spend a day writing a bad twelve lines—as I did yesterday. My danger, partly, I think, is becoming too dependent on Ted. He is didactic, fanatic—this last I see most when we are with other people who can judge him in a more balanced way than I—such as Leonard Baskin, for example. It is as if I were sucked into a tempting but disastrous whirlpool. Between us there are no barriers—it is rather as if neither of us—or especially myself—had any skin, or one skin between us and we kept bumping into and abrading each other. I enjoy it when Ted is off for a bit. I can build up my own inner life, my own thoughts, without his continuous "What are you thinking? What are you going to do now?" which makes me promptly and recalcitrantly stop thinking and doing. We are amazingly compatible. But I must be myself—make myself and not let myself be made by him. He gives orders—mutually exclusive: read ballads an hour, read Shakespeare an hour, read history an hour, think an hour and then "You read nothing in an hour—bits, read things straight through." His fanaticism and complete lack of balance and moderation is illustrated by his stiff neck, got from his "exercises"—which evidently are strenuous enough to disable him.

. . . On the path we found a dead mole—the first I have ever seen—a tiny creature with bare flat feet, looking like a tiny man's, and pallid white pushy-looking hands—a delicate snout and its sausage-shaped body all covered with exquisite gray-blue velvety fur. We also found a dead red squirrel, perfect, its eye glazed in death, and stiff. I felt somehow non-existent—had a sudden joy in talking to a grease-stained husky garage mechanic boy. He seemed real. Unless the self has enormous centering power, it flies off in all directions through space without the bracing and regulating tensions of necessary work, other people and their lives. But I won't get my writing schedule from outside—it must come from within. I'll leave off poems for a bit—finish the books I'm now in the middle of (at least five!), do German (that I *can* do) and write a kitchen article (for *The Atlantic*'s "Accent on Living"?), a *Harper's* Cambridge student life article—a story, "The Return," and suddenly attack my novel from the middle. Oh, for a plot.

Wednesday, July 9. Freshly bathed, it being early for once and not too hot. We are recovering after a week of the bird. Last night we killed him. It was terrible. He wheezed, lay on one side like a stove-in ship in his shit streaks, tail feathers drabbled, rallying to open his mouth, convulsing. What was it? I held him in my hand, cradling his warm heartbeat and feeling sick to the pit of my stomach: Ted no better—I let him take the bird for a day and he was as sick as I. We hadn't slept for a week, listening for his scrabble in the box, waking at blue dawn and hearing him flutter his pinfeather wings against the cardboard sides. We couldn't see what was wrong with his leg—only that it had folded, useless, under his stomach. We walked out through the park—not wanting to go back to the house and the sick bird. We went to the tree where we'd found him and looked up to see if there was a nest—we'd been too upset to look when we picked him up a week ago. From a dark hole about ten feet up in the trunk a small brownish bird face looked, then vanished. A white shit shot out in a neat arc onto the sidewalk. So that was why our little bird had his habit of backing to the edge of his papers. I resented the hale, whole birds in the tree. We went home: the bird peeped feebly, rallied to peck at our fingers. Ted fixed our rubber bath hose to the gas jet on the stove and taped the other end into a cardboard box. I could not look and cried and cried. Suffering is tyrannous. I felt desperate to get the sickly little bird off our necks, miserable at his persistent pluck and sweet temper. I looked in. Ted had taken the bird out too soon and it lay in his hand on its back, opening and shutting its beak terribly and waving its upturned feet. Five minutes later he brought it to me, composed, perfect and beautiful in death. We walked in the dark bluing night to the park, lifted one of the druid stones, dug a hole in its crater, buried him and rolled the stone back. We left ferns and a green firefly on the grave, felt the stone roll of our hearts.

Prose writing has become a phobia to me: my mind shuts and I clench. I can't, or won't, come clear with a plot. Must put poetry aside and begin a story tomorrow. Today was useless, a wash of exhaustion after the bird. Always excuses. I wrote what I consider a "book poem" about my runaway ride in Cambridge on the horse Sam: a hard subject for me, horses alien to me, yet the daredevil change in Sam and my hanging on god knows how is a kind of revelation: it worked well. Hard as my little gored picador poem was hard. But now I can't write as I used to—generally, philosophically, with "Thoughts that found a mare of mermaid hair/tangling in the tide's green fall"—I have to write my "Lorelei"—to *present* the mermaids, invoke them. Make them real. I write my good poems too fast—they are on objects, not themes, thus concrete, limited. Good enough, but I must extend. . . .

Saturday, July 12. I feel a change in my life: of rhythm and expectancy, and now, at 11 in the morning, tired, very, yet steady after our great talk last night. A change has come: will it tell, a month from now, a year from now? It is, I think, not a false start. But a revision of an old, crippling delusion into a sturdy-shoed, slow-plodding common-sense program. Yesterday was the nadir. All day I had been sitting at an abstract poem about mirrors and identity which I hated, felt chilled, desperate, about my month's momentum (over 10 poems in

that time) run down, a rejection from *The Kenyon* sealing hope-
lessness. I began realizing poetry was an excuse and escape
from writing prose. I looked at my sentence notes for stories,
much like the notes jotted here on the opposite page: I picked
the most "promising" subject—the secretary returning on the
ship from Europe, her dreams tested and shattered. She was
not gorgeous, wealthy, but small, almost stodgy, with few good
features and a poor temperament. The slicks leaned over me:
demanding romance, romance—should she be gorgeous? Should
Mrs. Aldrich, so normal and plodding and good with her seven
children, have an affair with young, sweet Mr. Cruikshank
across the street? I ran through my experience for ready-made
"big" themes: there were none. . . . All paled, palled—a glassy
coverlid getting in the way of my touching it. Too undramatic.
Or was my outlook too undramatic? Where was life? It dissipated, vanished into thin air, and my life stood weighed and
found wanting because it had no ready-made novel plot, be-
casue I couldn't simply sit down at the typewriter and by sheer
genius and willpower begin a novel dense and fascinating today
and finish next month. Where, how, with what and for what
to begin? No incident in my life seemed ready to stand up for
even a 20-page story. I sat paralyzed, feeling no person in the
world to speak to. Cut off totally from humanity in a self-
induced vacuum. I felt sicker and sicker. I couldn't happily be
anything but a writer and I couldn't be a writer. I couldn't even
set down one sentence: I was paralyzed with fear, with deadly
hysteria. I sat in the hot kitchen unable to blame lack of time,
the sultry July weather, anything but myself. The white hard-
boiled eggs, the green head of lettuce, two suave pink veal
chops dared me to do anything with them, to make a meal out
of them, to alter their single, leaden identity into a digestible
meal. I had been living in an idle dream of *being a writer*.
And here stupid housewives and people with polio were getting
their stories into *The Sat Eve Post*. I went into Ted, utterly
shattered, and asked him to tackle the veal chops. And burst
into tears. Useless, good-for-nothing. We talked it out, analyzed it. I felt the lead tons of the world lift. I have been
spoiled, so spoiled by my early success with *Seventeen*, with
Harper's and *Mademoiselle*, I figured if I ever worked over a
story and it didn't sell, or wrote a piece for practice and couldn't

market it, something was wrong. I was gifted, talented—oh, all the editors said so—so why couldn't I expect big returns for every minute of writing? A cracking good story a week? I demanded a 20-page plot about a top-of-the-head subject that didn't engage me. Now, every day, I am writing 5 pages, about 1,500 words on a small vignette, a scene charged with emotion, conflict, and that is that: to make these small bits of life, which I discarded as trivial, not serious "plot material." I cannot correct faults in rhythm, in realization—in thin air. I spend 3 hours, and shall from now on, in writing, not letting a bad or slight subject engulf the day.

Thursday, July 17. After two days of no-schedule, disrupted by our seeing Baskins, Rodman* [omission]...I sit down on a clear cold sunny day with nothing to beef at except the slick sick feeling which won't leave. It comes and goes. I feel I could crack open mines of life—in my daily writing sketches, in my reading and planning: if only I could get rid of my absolutist panic. I have, continually, the sense that this time is invaluable, and the opposite sense that I am paralyzed to use it: or will use it wastefully and blindly. I have all the world's reading on my back, instead of a possible book a day. I must discipline myself to concentrate on certain authors, certain fields, lest I welter, knowing nothing and everything. Across the street there is the chink, chink of hammers on nails, the tap of hammers on wood. Men are on the scaffolding. I am neither a know-nothing nor a bohemian, but I find myself wishing, wishing, to have a corner of my own: something I can know about, write about *well*. All I have ever read thins and vanishes: I do not amass, remember. I shall this year work for steady small growth, nothing spectacular, and the ridding of this panic. The windows shake in their sockets from some unheard detonation. Ted says they are breaking the sound barrier. Somewhere I have a vision, not of thwarting, of meanness, but of fullness, of a maturer, riper placidity, a humor to bear nightmare, an ordering, reshaping faculty which steadies and fears not. A housewife—with children and writing and reading in the midst of business, but fully, with good friends who are makers in

---

*Selden Rodman, editor of a popular poetry anthology

some way. The more I do, the more I can do. I should choose first the few things I wish to learn: German, poets and poetry, novels and novelists, art and artists. French also. Are they making or breaking across the street there? All fears are figments: I make them up.

Marianne Moore sent a queerly ambiguous spiteful letter in answer to my poems and request that she be a reference for my Saxton. So spiteful it is hard to believe it: comments of absolutely no clear meaning or help, resonant only with great unpleasantness: "don't be so grisly," "I only brush away the flies" (this for my graveyard poem), "you are too unrelenting" (in "Mussel Hunter"), and certain pointed remarks about "typing being a bugbear," so she sends back the poems we sent. I cannot believe she got so tart and acidy simply because I sent her carbon copies ("clear," she remarks). This, I realize, must be my great and stupid error — sending carbons to the American lady of letters. Perhaps I thus queered my chance of a Saxton. . . .

Saturday, July 19. Paralysis still with me. It is as if my mind stopped and let the phenomena of nature — shiny green rose bugs and orange toadstools and screaking woodpeckers — roll over me like a juggernaut — as if I had to plunge to the bottom of nonexistence, of absolute fear, before I can rise again. My worst habit is my fear and my destructive rationalizing. Suddenly my life, which had always clearly defined immediate and long-range objectives — a Smith scholarship, a Smith degree, a won poetry or story contest, a Fulbright, a Europe trip, a lover, a husband — has or appears to have none. I dimly would like to write (or is it to *have* written?) a novel, short stories, a book of poems. And fearfully, dimly, would like to have a child: a bloodily breached twenty-year plan of purpose. Lines occur to me and stop dead: "The tiger lily's spotted throat." And then it is an echo of Eliot's "The tiger in the tiger pit," to the syllable and the consonance. I observe: "The mulberry berries redden under leaves." And stop. I think the worst thing is to exteriorize these jitterings and so will try to shut up and not blither to Ted. His sympathy is constant temptation. I am made to be busy, gay, doing crazy jobs and writing this

and that—stories and poems and nursing babies. How to catapult myself into this? When I stop moving, other lives and
single-track aims shoulder me into shadow. I am fixed, fixated
on neatness—I can't take things as they come, or *make* them
come as I choose. Will this pass like a sickness? I wish I could
get some womanly impartial advice on this. Defensively, I say
I know nothing: lids shut over my mind. And this is the old
way of lying: I can't be responsible, I know nothing. Grub-
white mulberries redden under leaves. Teaching was good for
me: it structured my mind and forced me to be articulate. If I
don't settle my trouble from within, no outside shower of fortune will make the grass grow. I feel under opiates, hashish—
heavy with paralysis—all objects slipping from numb fingers,
as in a bad dream. Even when I sit at my typewriter, I feel as
if what I wrote were written by an imbecile ten miles off. I
am on the bird now, and have been for two days: I have written
eighteen pages of confused repetitious observation: Miriam felt
this, Owen said that, the bird did this. I have not gotten to the
dramatic part where they kill and bury the bird, whose sickness
has come to dominate their lives. I am sure of the solidity of
the subject but not sure of the emotional line and crisis of my
story: yet it will be a story. Tomorrow morning I will finish it
and begin it over again, drawing structure out of it. I must be
ghastly to live with. Incompetence sickens me to scorn, disgusts
me, and I am a bungler, who has taken a bad turn in fortune—
rejected by an adult world, part of nothing—of neither an
external career of Ted's—his internal career when written out,
perhaps—nor a career of my own, nor, vicariously, the life of
friends, nor part of motherhood—I long for an external view
of myself and my room to confirm its reality. Vague aims—
to write—fail, stillborn. I sense a talent, sense a limited fixity
of view stifling me now. I would be supremely happy, I tell
myself, if I could only get "in the swing" of writing stories. I
have two ideas! bless them—enough for a summer!—a serious
bird story where the bird becomes a tormenting spirit and by
its small sick pulse darkens and twists two lives—and the story
I'll get all the factual background for when I visit Spaulding's
on the Cape: I want to learn *how* she built and designed those
cottages. Work and work on human interest of how she'll get
a house herself. Saving her pennies, antiques—Lester's ill-

nesses. Humbly, I can begin these things. Start in two realities that move me, probe their depths, angles, dwell on them. I want to know all kinds of people, to have the talent ready, practiced, ordered, to use them. To ask them the right questions. I forget. I must not forget, not panic, but walk about bold and curious and observant as a newspaper reporter, developing my way of articulation and ordering, losing nothing, not sitting under a snail shell.

Sunday, July 27. A gray day, cool, gentle. The strangling noose of worry, of hysteria, paralysis, is miraculously gone. Doggedly, I have waited it out, and doggedly, been rewarded. The prose does not prosper. I am rewriting an old story, a two-year-old story, "The Return," amazed at the lush, gaudy, giddy romantic rhetoric. I have written four or five quite good poems this past ten days, after a sterile hysterical ten days of nonproduction. The poems are, I think, deeper, more sober, somber (yet well colored) than any I've yet done. I've written two about Benidorm, which was closed to me as a poem subject till now. I think I am opening up new subjects and have, instead of a desperate high-keyed rhetoric, a plainer, realer poetry. I've about 29 poems for my book—a perpetual maximum it seems, but have discarded already half of those written in my hectic April vacation week, and several written since, my earliest being "Faunus," "Strumpet Song," which I wrote just after I met Ted. I have a peculiar and very enervating fever, and have had, these last days. I have been ridiculously exhausted every morning, as if waking out of a coma, a queer deathlike state, when Ted brings me juice—and that, late enough, about ten o'clock, after ten hours of sleep. What is it? I am in the prime of life, my best years ahead to work in, to write poems and have children, and I am exhausted, a dull, electric burning dessicating my skull, my bloodstream. Will I write here in perfect health from our little Boston apartment in a month and more? I hope so. I feel I am beginning solidly and calmly to face the work ahead, expecting a minimum of produce with a maximum of work, study and devotion. Read some of Hardy's poems with Ted at tea—a moving, highly kindred mind, Hardy's, especially "An Ancient to Ancients," and "Last Words to a Dumb Friend."

August 2, Saturday. I have a strong feeling of sickness, of which I am heartily sick. A life of doing nothing is death. Our life is ridiculously ingrown, sedentary. [Omission.]

Later: Sunday morning: It is as if I needed crises of some sort to exercise my fiber. I find all cool, clear and possible this morning. The great fault of America—this part of it—is its air of pressure: expectancy of conformity. It is hard for me to realize that Dot and Frank* probably don't like Ted simply because he "won't get a job, a steady career." I have actually married exactly the sort of man I most admire. I will shut up about the future for a year and face work and encourage Ted's work, in which I have the greatest of faith. I find myself horrified at voicing the American dream of a home and children—my visions of a home, of course, being an artist's estate, in a perfect privacy of wilderness acres, on the coast of Maine. I will no doubt be an impractical vagabond wife and mother, a manner of exile. I must work for an inner serenity and stability which will bear me through the roughest of weathers externally: a calm, sustaining, optimistic philosophy which does not depend on a lifelong street address within easy driving distance of an American supermarket. And what fun to see England with Ted, to live in Italy, the south of France. If I can work this year like mad and get *one* woman's story published, a book of poems finished, I will be pleased: also, review and read German and French. Ironically, I have my own dream, which is mine, and not the American dream. I want to write funny and tender women's stories. I **must be also** funny and tender and not a desperate woman, like Mother. Security is inside me and in Ted's warmth. [Omission.]

August 3, Sunday. Felt a sudden ridiculous desire this morning to investigate the Catholic Church—so much in it I would not

---

*Plath's aunt and uncle

be able to accept: I would need a Jesuit to argue me—I am yet young, strong—must seek adventure and not depend on a companion. As for children—I'll be happier to have worked a year on writing, had a holiday—before I begin with them: once I have a baby, I won't be able to go on writing unless I have a firm foundation for it. The apartment, small as it is, will encourage little housework and cooking. Peace, I must tell myself, so it becomes an instinctive sense; peace is interior, radiating outward. I must keep notebooks of people, places—to recall them. Now: a plane drones, cars whoosh by, a few birds are chirping, a car door bangs, Ted has just thrown down a paper, sighed, and his pen is scratching rapidly. I must learn to lead my own life with him, but not lean on him for every move. . . .

August 8, Friday. "He is the transparence of the place in which He is and in his poems we find peace."—Stevens

I am awestruck, excited, smiling inside creamy as a cat: The day has evaporated, quite gone, in a rapt contemplation of my poem "Mussel Hunter at Rock Harbor," which came out in the August 9 issue of the blessed glossy *New Yorker*—the title in that queer, wobbly, half-archaic type I've dreamed poem and story titles in for about eight years. Queerest of all, I dreamed the poem would come out last night! Luckily I told Ted my dream—about Howard Moss and some poet who'd "finally got into *The New Yorker*," even though he had a note in italics at the bottom of the poem saying it had been almost completely revised and edited by a woman named, I think, Anne Morrow (a sense of Moss changing my lowercase letters to capitals, adding commas and subtracting hyphens?)—in my dream, my poem was clipped, as on a dummy copy, on the left-hand side of a page between a left-hand column and a right-hand page of ads. I was amazed when Florence Sultan* called me and told me my poem was in. I went over, drank wine with her and admired the baby, Sonia, who has suddenly got to be a dark curly-haired blue-eyed image of Florence, sweet and solid. There the poem was in her copy, *the* first poem in the

---

*Wife of Stanley Sultan, Smith faculty

magazine, page 22, taking up *almost* a whole page on the left, except for about an inch and a half of a 3-column story at the bottom—plenty of shiny white *New Yorker* space around my two-column poem, about 45 lines in each column. Well, this week will soon be over. I have the naïve idea people all over the world will be reading and marveling at the poem! Of course, it inhibits my poetry in one way (what other work could achieve this grandeur!) and yet, deep in me, it encourages my prose immensely—that I, too, may work my stories up to the exquisite several-paged surface of the ones next to and following my poems seems less like a mad goal.

August 27, Wednesday. Fury jams the gullet and spreads poison, but, as soon as I start to write, dissipates, flows out into the figure of the letters: writing as therapy? A venomous blowup with landlady, Mrs. Whalen. Insane accusations on her part, tremulous retorts and disgust on mine: a shaming encounter: behind our back, while we were at the Cape, she took the living room rug to be cleaned (which I had told her we had a right to as floor covering, it being a "furnished apartment") and substituted a filthy summer straw mat whose spots and stains loomed to meet the eye. She also took all the curtains. Deceit, insult, fury: last night we discovered this—or, rather, this morning—as we drove back at night through mist and cold black woods—I had a panic fear in the dark middle of the wood: we saw two deer: Ted, one, I, that and another: white head and ears pricked up, eyes glowing green, transfixed by the car lights. After the long rainy trip to and from NYC in one day Monday to pick up Warren. This was the last exhaustion—woke hollow at noon after a bare seven hours sleep—coffee only, and then we got stupidly involved reading magazines in the library at Smith, which always sickens me: vitriol between critics, writers, politicians: an arsonist burned to black crisp depicted in *Life* in the space before death, his skin hanging and curling away like peeled black paint; cremation fires burning in the dead eyes of Anne Frank: horror on horror, injustice on cruelty—all accessible, various—how can the soul keep from flying to fragments—disintegrating, in one wild dispersal? We read, dibbled, for hours—on no food, fools we—

shopped—peaches, corn. Then, as I half-sensed it, Mrs. Whalen had to come up—bad conscience about rug and curtains? Fury, rather, about our leaving the house windows open—she plumped her fat white bulk on the stairs, breathed, ranted—we let her go on—"apartment in a mess, terrible shape"—we took her up: "what, exactly, was the mess?" She hemmed, hawed—greasy wall by kitchen sink, dirty venetian blind in bathroom—moved, obviously, by the desire to circuit accusations of spying: she'd "just seen this on running through"—we'd left the apartment in apple-pie order. "Have you looked under the bed?" I said. I felt exhausted, starved, too stupid and sick to be clever and neat—she had no right to criticize the place—which is equivalent to criticizing my housework—no damage to the house: I would have picked up, but after the rug episode feel like smearing filth over it: I am not cool either. . . . All fury, grist for the mill. I shall rest and, resting more and more, see it whole. I am in the middle of a book on demoniacal possession—cases extremely diverting—but also inspiring—*metaphors* for states of human experiences as well as the experience itself—as Aphrodite is the personification of lust and rending passion, so these visions of demons are the objective figures of angers, remorse, panic: *Possession: Demoniacal and Other:* Oesterreich. (p. 94)

> Four years ago C. was one day going home from her work when she met in the street the apparition of a woman which spoke to her. Suddenly something like a cold wind blew down her neck as she was speaking, and she at once became as if dumb. Later her voice returned, but very hoarse and shrill. . . . She then loses the sense of her individuality. [p. 106 *Possession by fox*:] Neither excommunication nor censing nor any other endeavor succeeded. The fox saying ironically that he was too clever to be taken in by such manoeuvres. Nevertheless he consented to come out freely from the starved body of the sick person if a plentiful feast was offered to him. "How was it to be arranged?" On a certain day at four o'clock there were to be placed in a temple sacred to foxes and situated twelve kilometres away two vessels of rice prepared in a particular way, of cheese, cooked with beans, together with a great quantity of roast mice and raw vegetables, all favorite dishes of magic foxes:

Then he would leave the body of the girl exactly at the prescribed time. [p. 116 *Of Achilles (Janet hypnotizes "devil"):*] Although the patient appeared possessed, his malady was not possession but the emotion of remorse. This was true of so many possessed persons, the devil being for them merely the incarnation of their regrets, remorse, terrors and vices.

To brood over this, to use and change it, not let it flow through like a sieve. . . .

August 28, Thursday. A chill clear morning. Yesterday's anger has clearer, finer edges now: I could have said more than better than I did, but in four days we will be off—all here will lose its emotional tension and become a flat memory only, to be ordered, embellished by the chameleon mind. Dreamed last night I was beginning my novel—"What is there to look to?" Dody Ventura said—a beginning conversation—then a sentence, a paragraph, inserted first of all for description to "place," to "set" the scene: a girl's search for her dead father—for an outside authority which must be developed, instead, from the inside.

Midnight: Still tired, but curiously elated, as if absolved from suffocation—projects bubble—Boston and our flat seems as fine, finer than Widow Mangada's Mediterranean hideout or our Paris Left Bank room. Suddenly I like people, can be nice, natural. . . . I think I am growing more casual—am I? Or is this a lull in a merry-go-round of panic blackouts. To take all for what it is and delight in the small pleasures—a good dog poem by Ted: a green afternoon with Esther Baskin and Tobias [their son] under the trees, apples fallen, rotting on the ground, reading her essay of the bat, Ted's proof of the pike poem—Tobias blond, pink, cherubic, smiling, crowing, crawling, taking the papers from my purse and scattering them about— an atmosphere of books, poems, wood engravings, statues. . . .

Animal possession in Central Africa (p. 145):

A number of murders . . . ultimately traced to an old man who had been in the habit of lurking in the long grass beside the path to the river, till some person passed by alone when

he would leap out and stab him, afterwards mutilating the
body. He admitted these crimes himself. He could not help
it [he said] as he had a strong feeling at times that he was
changed into a lion and was impelled as a lion to kill and
mutilate...this "were-lion" has been most usefully em-
ployed for years in perfect contentment keeping the roads
of Chirome in good repair.

September 2, Tuesday. . . . Liz Taylor is getting Eddie Fisher
away from Debbie Reynolds, who appears cherubic, round-
faced, wronged, in pin curls and house robe—Mike Todd barely
cold. How odd these events affect one so. Why? Analogies? I
would like to squander money on hair styling, clothes. Yet
know power is in work and thought. The rest is pleasant frill.
I love too much, too wholly, too simply for any cleverness.
Use imagination. Write and work to please. No criticism or
nagging. [Omission.] He is a genius. I his wife.

Sunday morning, September 14. Two weeks here have inexplicably withered away. Yesterday we both bogged in a black
depression—the late nights, listening sporadically to Beethoven piano sonatas—ruining our mornings, the afternoon sun
too bright and accusing for tired eyes, meals running all off-
schedule—and me with my old panic fear sitting firm on my
back—who am I? What shall I do? The difficult time between
twenty-five years of school routine and the fear of dilatory,
dilettante days. The city calls—experience and people call,
and must be shut out by a rule from within. Tomorrow, Monday, the schedule must begin—regular meals, shoppings, laun-
derings—writing prose and poems in the morning, studying
German and French in the afternoon, reading aloud an hour,
reading in the evenings. Drawing and walking excursions. . . . I
must be happy first in my own work and struggle to that end,
so my life does not hang on Ted's. The novel would be best
to begin this next month. My *New Yorker* poems were a minor
triumph. Who else in the world could I live with and love?
Nobody. I picked a hard way which has to be all self-mapped
out and must *not* nag [omission] . . . (anything Ted doesn't like:
this is nagging); he, of course, can nag me about light meals,
straight-necks, writing exercises, from his superior seat. The

famed and fatal jealousy of professionals—luckily he is ahead of me so far I never need fear the old superiority heel-grinding—in weak-neck impulse. Perhaps fame will make him insufferable. I will work for its not doing so. Must work and get out of paralysis—write and show him nothing: novel, stories and poems. A misty, furred, gray-sunny Sunday. Must lose paralysis and catapult into small efforts—life for its own sake. A nightmare sequence—jazz breaking through Beethoven, soap opera downstairs shattering profound vocational meditation. Do we, vampirelike, feed on each other? A wall, soundproof, must mount between us. Strangers in our study, lovers in bed. Rocks in the bed. Why?...If I write eleven more good poems I will have a book. Try a poem a day: send book to Keightley*—ten more during the year—a fifty poem book—while the crass Snodgrasses publish and gain fame. Ted fought for publication before his book, which was an open sesame—gathering prizes and fame. And so do I now fight—but have broken three doors open since June: *The New Yorker*, *Sewanee* and *The Nation*: one a month. I feel suddenly today the absence of fear—the sense of slow, plodding self-dedication. This book led me through a year of struggle and mastery. Perhaps the book I am about to begin will do something akin. Smile, write in secret, showing no one. Amass a great deal. Novel. Poems. Stories. Then send about. Let no book-wishing show—work. I must move myself first, before I move others—a woman famous among women.

Monday, September 15. Brag of bravado, and the fear is on. A panic absolute and obliterating: here all diaries end—the vines on the brick wall opposite end in a branch like a bent green snake. Names, words, are power. I am afraid. Of what? Life without having lived, chiefly. What matters? Wind wuthering in a screen. If I could funnel this into a novel, this fear, this horror—a frog sits on my belly. Stop and ask why you wash, why you dress, you go wild—it is as if love, pleasure, opportunity surrounded me, and I were blind. I talk hysterically—or feel I will explode: I am in a fix: how to get out of it? Some little daily external ritual—I am too ingrown—as if

---

*Philip Keightley, a friend who was an editor at World Publishing Company

I no longer knew how to talk to anyone but Ted—sat with my face to a wall, a mirror. . . . I am in a vicious circle—too much alone with no fresh exterior experiences except the walking around, about, staring at people who seem, simply because they are other, to be enviable—the responsibility of my future weighs, terrifies. Why should it? Why can't I be pragmatic, common? At the end of a teaching day, no matter the reversals, I had earned ten dollars—motive enough, in many minds. I need a vocation and to feel productive and I feel useless. Ignorant. To develop writing when I feel my soul is bitty, scatty, tawdry? Why aren't I conceited enough to enjoy what I can do and not feel fear? Lawrence bodies the world in his words. Hope, careers—writing is too much for me: I don't want a job until I am happy with writing—yet feel desperate to get a job—to fill myself up with some external reality—where people accept phone bills, mail-getting, babies, marriage, as part of the purpose to the universe. A purposeless woman with dreams of grandeur. My one want: to do work I enjoy—must keep clear of any confiding in Mother [omission]. . . .

Thursday, September 18. Much happier today—why? Life begins, minutely, to take care of itself—and odd impulse brings a flood of joy, life—queer nice slightly sinister people: at the tattooist's. Also, even though I got up "late," nineish, on the wet gray day and felt the usual morning sickness, "what shall I do today that is worthwhile?," I got right to work after coffee and wrote 5 pages analyzing P.D. [Peter Davison—this work has disappeared]—one or two well-turned sentences. Then I sat and read on my "Bird in the House" story, which was so lumbering and bad I felt I could improve it, worked meticulously on 5 pages and felt better by lunch. A fine mail, even though I got a snotty letter from Weeks* rejecting my "Snake-charmer" (although "bewitched by the sinuosity," etc., etc.), for Ted had a lovely check of $150 for "Dick Straightup," which makes, with the "Thought-Fox" prize, about $1,000 earned this September. Walked out to deposit check and I got more and more drawn to the tattooist shop—it was chill, about to rain, but Ted acquiesced. We found the place with the display

---

*Edward Weeks, at *The Atlantic Monthly*

window on Scollay Square and stood outside, I pointing to the panther head, the peacocks, the serpents on the wall. The tattooist, with a pale, odd little fellow inside, [was] looking at us. Then the tattooist came to the door in black cowboy boots, a soiled cotton shirt and tight black chino pants. "You can't see good enough from out there. Come on in." We went, gog-eyed, into the little shop, brightly lit, tawdry: I shall spend all next morning writing it up. I got the man talking—about butterfly tattoos, rose tattoos, rabbit-hunt tattoos—wax tattoos—he showed us pictures of Miss Stella—tattooed all over—brocade orientals. I watched him tattoo a cut on his hand, a black, red, green and brown eagle and "Japan" on a sailor's arm, "Ruth" on a schoolboy's arm—I almost fainted, had smelling salts. The pale, rather excellent little professorial man who was trying out new springs in the machine, hung round about. Rose tattoos, eagle tattoos spin in my head—we'll go back. Life begins to justify itself—bit by bit—slowly I'll build it.

Saturday, September 27. . . . We stayed in writing, consolidating our splayed selves. I diagnosed, and Ted diagnosed my disease as doldrums—and I feel better, as if I can now start to cope: like a soldier, demobbed, I am cut loose of over twenty steady years of schooling and let free into civilian life—as yet, newly, I hardly know what to do with myself. I start, like a racehorse at the bugle, or whatever, hearing about schools opening—I get weird impulses to rush to Harvard, to Yale, begging them to take me on for a Ph.D., a master's, anything—only to take my life out of my own clumsy hands. I am going to work, doggedly, all year, at my own pace, being a civilian, thinking, writing, more and more intensely, with more and more purpose, and not merely dreaming, ego-safe, about the magnificent writer I could be. I have worked hard today on my bird story—words come right, rhythms come right, here, there, and it is a beginning of a new life.

Plath took a job working with patients' records in a Boston mental hospital, which she immediately recognized as a tremendous resource for her work. The patient who felt she might give birth to animals, for instance, appears in "Dark House" from "Poem for a Birthday":

> Any day I may litter puppies
> Or mother a horse. My belly moves.

October 14, Tuesday. A moment snatched, two and a half weeks later, chicken and squash ready in the oven for Ted's return from the library, back achy, eyes bleary from new job. I went out to three agencies a week ago Monday, got the first job I was interviewed for Tuesday—more hours than I wanted, and low pay, but with compensations of fascinating work and no homework—typing records in the psychiatric clinic at Mass. General, answering phones, meeting and dispatching a staff of over twenty-five doctors and a continual flow of patients—it is exhausting, now I'm new to it, but gives my day and Ted's an objective structure. Got a rejection of poems I thought a "sure thing" at *The New Yorker* and haven't had time or energy to brood—or write! But I figure the job is good for me—all my desires to be analyzed myself, except for occasional brief returns of the panic-bird, are evaporating: paradoxically, my objective daily view of troubled patients through the records objectifies my own view of myself. I shall try to enter into this schedule a wedge of writing—to expand it. I feel my whole sense and understanding of people being deepened and enriched by this: as if I had my wish and opened up the souls of the people in Boston and read them deep. A woman today—fat, fearing death—dreaming of three things, her dead father, her dead friend (dead in childbirth, rheumatic fever), her own funeral—she, in the coffin, and also standing and weeping among the onlookers. Her son falling downstairs and fracturing his skull, drinking poison (DDT)—her mother in the house when it exploded, burning to death. *Fear*: the main god: fear of elevators, snakes, loneliness—a poem on the faces of fear. Relevant note from Defoe's *Journal of the Plague Year*:

> . . . it was the opinion of others that it [the plague] might be distinguished by the party's breathing upon a piece of glass, where, the breath condensing, there might living creatures be seen by a microscope of strange, monstrous and

frightful shapes, such as dragons, snakes, serpents and devils, horrible to behold.

"The chaemeras" of the sick mind also.

HOSPITAL NOTES

Twenty-five-year-old twice-married once-divorced mother of three. "I hate my children." Fear of dark. Sleeps fully dressed.

Job: poultry company. Eviscerator of chickens. Loves job, really loves chickens, can eat them raw. Loves macaroni. Eats 1 lb. dry weight at a time. Constantly asks mother for more food.

Laura R.: Floridly tinted orange hair. Hatcheck girl. Models in nude for photographer. Lesbian girl friend.

Dorothy S.: Nightmares: saw own head amputated but hanging on by skin.

Mary M.: dream: working at bedside of man resembling one of former patients who is middle-aged and has family and who was very friendly to her but not improperly so. In dream, while in bedroom, went to closet and looked into laundry bag and found five heads. Four were those of children she cannot identify. The fifth head was that of her mother as she appeared when patient was a child.

Engaged to a man with a glass eye. 4 years ago: neighbor's dog in backyard barked at night and not only noise, but population in town was increasing. Owing to efforts of her husband there are no longer any dogs in her town . . . unable to see insomnia as a result of tensions in herself and continues to blame it on dogs in the neighborhood. (I do feel I have a schizophrenic patient between my hands.)

Spero P.: 34 years old. White, single elementary school principal. Fears asphyxia and death. Inability to maintain intense relationship with a girl when marriage is considered. Intensely absorbed in hatred of mother. Curses her as a vain, inhuman, vicious, strict, stubborn, foul old woman who administered inhuman beatings upon him when young. Fear of own impotence. States he can excel at anything and can prove it to anyone. Can annihilate anyone in argument.

Edward C.: Episodic attacks in which he doesn't feel himself. During attacks feels sense of unreality. When he watches TV he feels he is the one who is creating everything. Once a hurricane came and when the hurricane was over he felt it was he who had created the hurricane and all the damage that was done.

Barbara H.: Felt something moving in her stomach. Might turn to animal or be pregnant, and have puppies. Turn into mule or horse. Thought she was growing hair on face. 35, married, white.

Everything has to be perfect with Philomena T.: While making a cake found she'd left out one ingredient. Went crazy, pulling hair, banging fist, smashing hands against the wall.

Lillian J.: 68-year-old woman. Fascinating obsessional thought she's pregnant. Boyfriend (52) for last 30 years. Won't marry him. Sex play. Husband (first) died after 6 years marriage of TB. 11 room rooming house.

Edson F.: Large plot going on. Raped in his sleep—"They put me to stud." Produces a number of documents to indicate his existence. Birth certificate. Poll tax papers and naturalization papers.

John M.: Machinist. Newton Ball Bearing Co. Engineer, New England City Ice Co. Exterminator. Nightmare: grain of sand rested on chest, would increase in size to that of a house: sensation of smothering, being crushed.

Frank S.: "I feel guilty over my 'social malevolences.'" Dates onset of illness from reading of *The Rebel* by Camus. Feels he has significantly hurt emotionally vulnerable people by threatening and disdainful looks. In Germany felt desire to hurt or punish German people. Did this by threatening looks at passersby. During this time felt personality more magnetic and powerful than that of most people.

Readers of Letters Home, *Plath's letters to her mother, know that theirs was an extremely close and involved relationship. As Aurelia Plath notes, Sylvia often fused her life with her mother's. They had a symbiotic, deeply supportive union of great complexity in which it may not always have been easy to feel a separate person, an individual self. After Sylvia's marriage, there was a similar dependency on her husband—*

"it's rather as if neither of us, or especially myself, had any skin, or one skin between us." The constant struggle she had as an artist—to pass beyond the demons of fear and emptiness, to feel an authentic self, to reach her own power—required breaking out of the symbiosis, rejecting the amnesiac feeling of dissociated rage and thereby shattering the bell jar. The staggering guilt she felt over previous attempts in this direction was magically dissipated by Dr. Ruth Beuscher, her old therapist, whom she began seeing again in Boston at this time, unbeknownst to both her husband and her mother. "It makes me feel good as hell to express my hostility for my mother, frees me from the Panic Bird on my heart and my typewriter (why?)" The effect of this therapy was extraordinary—it gave rise to her first major work several months later: "Poem for a Birthday."

Much of the material in these pages relating to Sylvia Plath's therapy is of course very painful to me, and coming to the decision to approve its release has been difficult. I have no doubt that many readers will accept whatever negative thoughts she reveals here as the whole and absolute truth, despite their cancellation on other, more positive pages. In any case, the importance of this material to Sylvia Plath's work is certain, and in the interest of furthering understanding of her emotional situation, I have given my consent to the release of this material.

Aurelia Plath

Friday, December 12th. If I am going to pay money for her time & brain as if I were going to a supervision in life & emotions & what to do with both, I am going to work like hell, question, probe sludge & crap & allow myself to get the most out of it.

Ever since Wednesday I have been feeling like a "new person." Like a shot of brandy went home, a sniff of cocaine, hit me where I live and I am alive and so-there. Better than shock treatment: "I give you permission to hate your mother."

. . . So I feel terrific. In a smarmy matriarchy of togetherness it is hard to get a sanction to hate one's mother especially a sanction one believes in. I believe in R.B. because she is a clever woman who knows her business & I admire her. She is for me "a permissive mother figure." I can tell her anything, and she won't turn a hair or scold or withhold her listening, which is a pleasant substitute for love.

But although it makes me feel good as hell to express my hostility for my mother, frees me from the Panic Bird on my heart and my typewriter (why?), I can't go through life calling Dr. Beuscher up from Paris, London, the wilds of Maine long-distance. [Omission.] Life was hell. She [Sylvia's mother] had to work. Work, and be a mother, too, a man and a woman in one sweet ulcerous ball. She pinched. Scraped. Wore the same old coat. But the children had new school clothes and shoes that fit. Piano lessons, viola lessons, French horn lessons. They went to Scouts. They went to summer camp and learned to sail. One of them went to private school on scholarship and got good marks. In all honesty and with her whole unhappy heart she worked to give those two innocent little children the world of joy she'd never had. She'd had a lousy world. But they went to college, the best in the nation, on scholarship and work and part of her money, and didn't have to study nasty business subjects. One day they would marry for love love love and have plenty of money and everything would be honey sweet. They wouldn't even have to support her in her old age.

The little white house on the corner with a family full of women. So many women, the house stank of them. The grandfather lived and worked at the country club, but the grandmother stayed home and cooked like a grandmother should. The father dead and rotten in the grave he barely paid for, and the mother working for bread like no poor woman should have to and being a good mother on top of it. The brother away at private school and the sister going to public school because there there were men (but nobody liked her until she was sweet sixteen) and she wanted to: she always did what she wanted to. A stink of women: Lysol, cologne, rose water and glycerine, cocoa butter on the nipples so they won't crack, lipstick red on all three mouths.

Me, I never knew the love of a father, the love of a steady blood-related man after the age of eight. . . . the only man who'd love me steady through life: she came in one morning with tears . . . in her eyes and told me he was gone for good. I hate her for that.

[Omission.] He was an ogre. But I miss him. He was old, but she married an old man to be my father. It was her fault. [Omission.]

I hated men because they didn't stay around and love me like a father: I could prick holes in them & show they were no father-material. I made them propose and then showed them they hadn't a chance. I hated men because they didn't have to suffer like a woman did. They could die or go to Spain. They could have fun while a woman had birth pangs. They could gamble while a woman skimped on the butter on the bread. Men, nasty lousy men. They took all they could get and then had temper tantrums or died or went to Spain like Mrs. So-and-so's husband with his lusty lips.

Get a nice little, safe little, sweet little loving little imitation man who'll give you babies and bread and a secure roof and a green lawn and money money money every month. Compromise. A smart girl can't have everything she wants. Take second best. Take anything nice you think you can manage and sweetly master. Don't let him get mad or die or go to Paris with his sexy secretary. Be sure he's nice nice nice. [Omission.]

So what does [Mother] know about love? Nothing. You should have it. You should get it. It's nice. But what is it?

Well, somebody makes you feel Secure. House, money, babies: all the old anchors. A Steady Job. Insurance against acts of god, madmen, burglars, murderers, cancer. Her mother died of cancer. Her daughter tried to kill herself [omission]. . . . She didn't have enough insurance. Something Went Wrong. How could the fates punish her so if she was so very noble and good?

It was her daughter's fault partly. She had a dream: her daughter was all gaudy-dressed about to go out and be a chorus girl, a prostitute too, probably. [Omission.] The husband, brought alive in dream to relive the curse of his old angers, slammed out of the house in rage that the daughter was going to be a chorus girl. The poor Mother runs along the sand beach, her feet sinking in the sand of life, her money bag open and the money and coins falling into the sand, turning to sand. The father had driven, in a fury, to spite her, off the road bridge and was floating dead, face down and bloated, in the slosh of ocean water by the pillars of the country club. Everybody was looking down from the pier at them. Everyone knew everything.

She gave her daughter books by noble women called *The Case for Chastity*. She told her any man who was worth his salt cared for a woman to be a virgin if she were to be his wife, no matter how many crops of wild oats he'd sown on his own.

What did her daughter do? She . . . hugged them and kissed them. Turned down the nicest boys whom *she* would have married like a shot & got older and still didn't marry anybody. She was too sharp and smart-tongued for any nice man to stand. Oh, she was a cross to bear.

Now this is what I feel my mother felt. I feel her apprehension, her anger. . . . I feel . . . only the Idea of Love, and that she thinks she loves me like she should do. She'd do anything for me, wouldn't she?

I have done practically everything she said I couldn't do and be happy at the same time and here I am, almost happy.

Except when I feel guilty, feel I shouldn't be happy, because I'm [not] doing what all the mother figures* in my life would have me do. I hate them then. I get very sad about not doing what everybody and all my white-haired old mothers want in their old age. [Omission.]

I felt cheated: I wasn't loved, but all the signs said I was loved: the world said I was loved: the powers-that-were said I was loved. My mother had sacrificed her life for me. A sacrifice I didn't want. . . . I made her sign a promise she'd never marry. When [I was nine.] Too bad she didn't break it. . . .

She is worried about me and the man I married. How awful we are, to make her worry. We had good jobs and were earning between us about six thousand a year. My god. And we deliberately and with full possession of our senses threw these jobs (and no doubt our careers as teachers) over to live without lifting a finger. Writing. What would we do: next year, twenty years from now: when the babies came? We got reoffered the jobs (lucky the colleges weren't perfectly furious with us and

---

*The horrified reaction of Mary Ellen Chase—who had done so much for Plath both at Smith and in her Fulbright years—to Sylvia's decisions to marry and to abandon the academic world weighed very heavily on her. Chase regarded these acts as betrayals.

banging the doors shut) and turned them down again! We were crazy one way or another. What would the aunts and uncles say? What would the neighbors say? [Omission.]

The Man: R.B. says: "Would you have the guts to admit you'd made a wrong choice?" In a husband. I would. But nothing in me gets scared or worried at this question. I feel good with my husband: I like his warmth and his bigness and his being-there and his making and his jokes and stories and what he reads and how he likes fishing and walks and pigs and foxes and little animals and is honest and not vain or fame-crazy and how he shows his gladness for what I cook him and joy for when I make something, a poem or a cake, and how he is troubled when I am unhappy and wants to do anything so I can fight out my soul-battles and grow up with courage and a philosophical ease. . . . What is only pieces, doled out here and there to this boy and that boy, that made me like pieces of them, is all jammed together in my husband. So I don't want to look around anymore: I don't need to look around for anything. [Omission.]

So he has all I could ask for. I could have had money and men with steady jobs. But they were dull, or sick, or vain, or spoiled. They made me gag in the long run. What I wanted was inside a person that made you perfectly happy with them if you were naked on the Sahara: they were strong and loving in soul and body. Simple and tough.

So I knew what I wanted when I saw it. I needed, after thirteen long years of having no man who could take all my love and give me a steady flow of love in return, a man who would make a perfect circuit of love and all else with me. I found one. I didn't have to compromise and accept a sweet balding insurance salesman or an impotent teacher or a dumb conceited doctor [omission]. . . . I did what I felt the one thing and married the man I felt [was] the only man I could love, and want to see, do what he wanted in this world, and want to cook for and bear children for and write with. [Omission.] And I was, to all appearances, happy with him, Mother thought.

[Omission.] How can I be happy when I did something so dangerous as to follow my own heart and mind regardless of her experienced advice and Mary Ellen Chase's disapproval and the pragmatic American world's cold eye: but what does he do for a living? He lives, people. That's what he does.

Very few people do this anymore. It's too risky. First of all, it's a hell of a responsibility to be yourself. It's much easier to be somebody else or nobody at all. Or to give your soul to god like St. Therese and say: the one thing I fear is doing my own will. Do it for me, God.

There are problems and questions which rise to the surface out of this.

Mother: What to do with your hate for . . . all mother figures? What to do when you feel guilty for not doing what they say, because, after all, they have gone out of their way to help you? . . .

. . . R.B. won't tell me what to do: she'll help me find out and learn what is in myself and what I (not she) can best do with it. [Omission.]

Writing: My chain of fear-logic goes like this: I want to write stories and poems and a novel and be Ted's wife and a mother to our babies. I want Ted to write as he wants and live where he wants and be my husband and a father to our babies.

We can't now and maybe never will earn a living by our writing, which is the one profession we want. What will we do for money without sacrificing our energy and time to it and hurting our work? Then, worst:

What if our work isn't good enough? We get rejections. Isn't this the world's telling us we shouldn't bother to be writers? How can we *know* if we work hard now and develop ourselves we will be more than mediocre? Isn't this the world's revenge on us for sticking our neck out? We can never know until we've worked, written. We have no guarantee we'll get a Writer's Degree. Weren't the mothers and businessmen right after all? Shouldn't we have avoided these disquieting questions and taken steady jobs and secured a good future for the kiddies?

Not unless we want to be bitter all our lives. Not unless we want to feel wistfully: What a writer I *might* have been, if only. If only I'd had the guts to try and work and shoulder the insecurity all that trial and work implied.

Writing is a religious act: it is an ordering, a reforming, a relearning and reloving of people and the world as they are and as they might be. A shaping which does not pass away like a day of typing or a day of teaching. The writing lasts: it goes about on its own in the world. People read it: react to it as to a person, a philosophy, a religion, a flower: they like it, or do not. It helps them, or it does not. It feels to intensify living: you give more, probe, ask, look, learn, and shape this: you get more: monsters, answers, color and form, knowledge. You do it for itself first. If it brings in money, how nice. You do not do it first for money. Money isn't why you sit down at the typewriter. Not that you don't want it. It is only too lovely when a profession pays for your bread and butter. With writing, it is maybe, maybe-not. How to live with such insecurity? With what is worst, the occasional lack or loss of faith in the writing itself? How to live with these things?

The worst thing, worse than all of them, would be to live with not writing. So how to live with the lesser devils and keep them lesser?

Miscellanea: "Does Ted want you to get better?" Yes. He does. He wants me to see Dr. B. and is excited about my upswing in emotion and joy. He wants me to fight my devils with the best weapons I can muster and to win.

R.B. says: *There is a difference between dissatisfaction with yourself and anger, depression.* You can be dissatisfied and do something about it: if you don't know German, you can learn it. If you haven't worked at writing, you can work at it. If you are angry at someone else, and repress it, you get depressed. *Who am I angry at?* Myself. No, not yourself. Who is it? It is [omission] . . . all the mothers I have known who have wanted me to be what I have not felt like really being from my heart and at the society which seems to want us to be what we do not want to be from our hearts: I am angry at these people and images.

I do not seem to be able to live up to them. Because I don't want to.

What do they seem to want? Concern with a steady job that earns money, cars, good schools, TV, iceboxes and dishwashers and security First. With us these things are nice enough, but they come second. Yet we are scared. We do need money to eat and have a place to live and children, and writing may never and doesn't now give us enough. Society sticks its so-there tongue out at us.

Why don't we teach, like most writers? It seems teaching takes all our time and energy. We didn't do a thing teaching last year. Satisfaction with passive explication of the great works. Kills and drys one out. Makes everything seem explainable.

Main Questions:
  [Omission.]
  What to do for money & where to live: practical.
  What to do with fear of writing: why fear? Fear of not being a success? Fear of world casually saying we're wrong in rejections?
  Ideas of maleness: conservation of creative power (sex & writing).
  Why do I freeze in fear my mind & writing: say, look: no head, what can you expect of a girl with no head?
  Why don't I write a novel? [*I have! August 22, 1961: The Bell Jar.*]*
  Images of society: the Writer and Poet is excusable only if he is Successful. Makes Money.
  Why do I feel I should have a Ph.D., that I am aimless, brainless without one, when I know what is inside is the only credential necessary for my identity?
  NB: I do not hit often: once or twice.
  How to express anger creatively?
  Fear of losing male totem: what roots?
  R.B.: You have always been afraid of premature choices cutting off other choices. [Omission.]

Saturday morning, December 13. So learn about life. Cut yourself a big slice with the silver server, a big slice of pie. Learn how the leaves grow on the trees. Open your eyes. The thin new moon is on its back over the Green Cities' Service cloverleaf and the lit brick hills of Watertown, God's luminous

---

*A later handwritten note

fingernail, a shut angel's eyelid. Learn how the moon goes down in the night frost before Christmas. Open your nostrils. Smell snow. Let life happen.

Never felt guilty for bedding with one, losing virginity and going to the Emergency Ward in a spurt spurt of blood, playing with this one and that. Why? Why? I didn't have an idea, I had feelings. I had feelings and found out what I wanted and found the one only I wanted and knew it not with my head but with the heat of rightness, salt-sharp and sure as mice in cheese.

Graphic story: the deflowering. What it is like? Welcome of pain, experience. Phone call. Pay bill.

Seen on walk down Atlantic Avenue: a black hearse rounding the corner by the coffeehouse in a cinder-block garage under a corrugated tin roof. Velvet curtains like at the opera, and patent-leather black as Lothario's dancing shoe. Among the ten-ton trucks by the railroad station, this suave funeral parlor sedan, greased and groomed. Why, whereto? We walked, and the trucks rattled by, grazing our flanks. Across the street the hearse had stopped, drawn up back to the open door of the railway express shed. Men in black coats and derbies were sliding a redwood coffin off the rollers into the shed. Heavy, heavy. We stopped, stared, fingers freezing in our gloves, our breath spelling Indian puffs on the gray still deathly air. One black-coated man wore the permanent expression of grief stony on his face, an out-of-work actor perpetually reliving the role where he bursts in and tells that the brave army is cut to bits, that little Eyolf is gone after the rat wife and nothing but his crutch is left on the water to cross his wet bed. Gray hair, a long vein-mottled face, hollow eye sockets and fixed Greek-tragedy eyes and a mouth-mask of absolute misery: but static, frozen. He helps a red-faced, round-cheeked cherry-nosed man, whose face would break into smiles if his black coat and round topped black hat didn't keep him solemn as the job requires in the eyes of the watching public. We watched. The reddened rich-wood coffin slid into a packing crate of pale wood on a suitcase and trunk trolley. The packing crate had copper fluted handles on either side. A square wood lid fitted over the gap the coffin entered and tightened snugly with copper wing nuts like shiny butterflies. The round-faced man climbed on top of the packing crate and laboriously penciled some directives on the top: Christmas mail to somebody out West. Fragile: Perishable Goods: Handle with Care: Headside Up: Keep in a Cool, Dry Place. Whose body? Somebody bumped off? Some husband, father, lover, whore? *The last Dickensians*. The last caricaturers of grief, whose faces never alter from the one grimace. They sell their fixed selves like a commodity of great value to the legions of the bereaved, whisper, console, condole: "At a time like this, nothing but the best." . . .

A gay incursion: looking out the window for the mailman: can see, over the second cup of coffee, his brass buttons and round blue hat and blue-clad paunch. Can see his bulging brown leather mail satchel, scratched and blotched by the variable Boston weathers. Ran down in the elevator. A thin airmail letter after a fall of rejection for Saxton fellowship, *Harper's* rejection, *Encounter* rejection, *Atlantic* rejection, and book rejection from the World Publishing Company. An acceptance of three poems with a charming warm admiring letter from John Lehmann.* "Lorelei," "The Disquieting Muses," "The Snakecharmer": all my romantic lyricals. I knew his taste. How nice, how fine. That crack of courage. That foothold. And the sense to know I must change, be careless, deep in my writing. . . .

I may have a baby someday: I feel quite smiley about it. Where has the old scare gone? I still feel a deep awe of the pain. Will I live to tell of it?

Work. Work. Hysterical teary-bright call from mother. . . . My heart aches, dull, frozen [omission]. . . . Why should I the naughty one be happy? I am. She begged us to "come and live in her house for a while if we wanted a change." She wants to make the most of us, after all she feels, fears, we may go away at any minute.

Tuesday morning, December 16. Nine thirtyish: have rewritten and rewritten "Johnny Panic and the Bible of Dreams" and am going to start sending it out now. I think I can bear up under rejections: hope only that I get letters of commentary. I want it to go about. It's so queer and quite slangy that I think it may have a chance somewhere. Will send it out 10 times before I get sorry: by then, I should have two or three more stories. . . .

---

*Editor of *The London Magazine*

Have been happier this week than for six months. It is as if R.B., saying "I give you permission to hate your mother," also said, "I give you permission to be happy." Why the connection? Is it dangerous to be happy? [Omission.] I am enjoying myself with a great lessening of worry: the dregs of dissatisfaction with myself: not writing enough, not working hard, not reading hard, studying German—are things I can do if I want & will do. It is the hate, the paralyzing fear, that gets in my way and stops me. Once that is worked clear of, I will flow. My life may at last get into my writing. As it did in the Johnny Panic story.

Got an old *New World Writing*, Frank O'Connor's stories, and three Ionesco plays yesterday on our walk out. O'Connor's stories an inspiration of technique; "sure things." I feel it is as important to read what is being written now, good things (Herb Gold is good), to get out of my old-fashioned classroom idiom: She felt, she said. Prim, prim. Read "Amedee" and laughed aloud. The growing corpse: the mushrooms: met with by all the petty-bourgeous platitudes usually used up on trivia. The accepting [of] the horrific and ridiculous as if it were the daily newspaper delivery. Is it to say that platitudes take the edge off our real horrors so that we are all blinded to them, our corpses and poisonous mushrooms?

Truman Capote this weekend: a baby-boy, must be in his middle thirties. Big head, as of a prematurely delivered baby, an embryo, big white forehead, little drawstring mouth, shock of blond hair, mincy skippy fairy body in black jacket, velvet or corduroy, couldn't tell from where we sat. . . . Men hated the homosexual part of him with more than usual fury. Something else: jealousy at his success? If he weren't successful there would be nothing to anger at. I was very amused, very moved, only Holiday [sic] Golightly left me more chilly than when I read her. . . .

Wednesday A.M., *December 17.* A *Ladies' Home Journal* story, "The Button Quarrel"? Ask Dr. B. about psychological need to fight, express hostility between husband & wife. A story of an "advanced" couple, no children, woman with career, above sewing on buttons, cooking. The husband thinks he agrees, fight over sewing on buttons. Not really fight about that. Fight about his deep-rooted conventional ideas of womanhood, like all the rest of the men, wants them pregnant and in the kitchen. Wants to shame her in public; told from point of view of wise elderly matron? advice? ah, what is it.

Angry at R.B. for changing appointment to tomorrow. Shall I tell her? Makes me feel: she does it because I am not paying money. She does it and is symbolically withholding herself, breaking a "promise," like Mother not loving me, breaking her "promise" of being a loving mother each time I speak to her or talk to her. That she shifts me about because she knows I'll agree nicely & take it, and that it implies I can be conveniently manipulated. A sense of my insecurity with her accentuated by floating, changeable hours and places. The question: is she trying to do this, or aware of how I might feel about it, or simply practically arranging appointments?

A tirade with Ted over Jane Truslow,* "You know her," "How can I be expected to know which one?" and buttons, his telling Marcia and Mike that I: hide shirts, rip up torn socks, never sew on buttons. His motive: I thought that would make you do it. So he thought by shaming me, he could manipulate me. My reaction: a greater stubbornness than ever, just as his reaction is when I try to manipulate him into doing something, ergo, changing seats at Truman Capote. It would have been better looking-at-Capote to change seats, it would be better wearing-shirts-and-coats for Ted for me to sew on his buttons: what makes, or made, both acts impossible was the sense that the other was putting more in his decision than the act itself: it was a victory one over the other, not an issue of theater seats and buttons. I face this. I feel to know it. But he doesn't. Just as he tells me, when he wants to manipulate me one way (e.g., to stop "nagging," which means talking about anything he doesn't like), that I am like my mother, which is sure to get an emotional reaction, even if it's not true. [Omission.] His surest triumph and easy way to get me to do what he wants is to tell me I'm just-like-my-mother whenever I do or don't do something he wants. Realizing this is half the battle against it. Will he admit it to himself? I'm just as bad. Dirty hands, dirty hands. [Omission.]

---

*Smith student who married Peter Davison

* * *

Friday morning, December 26, 1958. About to see Dr. B. A cold after-Christmas morning. A good Christmas. Because, Ted says, I was merry. I played, teased, welcomed Mother. I may hate her, but that's not all. I . . . love her too. After all, as the story goes, she's my mother. "She can't encroach unless you're encroachable on." So my hate and fear derive from my own insecurity. Which is? And how to combat it?

Fear of making early choices which close off alternatives. Not afraid of marrying Ted, because he is flexible, won't shut me in. Problem: we both want to write, have a year. Then what? Not odd jobs. A steady money-earning profession: psychology?

How to develop my independence? Not tell him everything. Hard, seeing him all the time, not leading outer life.

Fear: access after seeing people at Harvard: feeling I've put myself out of the running. Why can't I throw myself into writing? Because I am afraid of failure before I begin.

Old need of giving Mother accomplishments, getting reward of love.

I do fight with Ted: two acrid fights. The real reasons: we both worry about money: we have enough till next September 1st. Then what? How to keep concerns about money and profession from destroying the year we have?

Neither of us wants a job connected with English: not magazine, publishing, newspaper or teaching: not now, teaching.

Problem of Ted and America. He doesn't see how to use it yet. I feel his depression. Don't want to force or manipulate him into anything he doesn't want. Yet he worries too, only is not articulate about it.

Don't know where we want to live. What profession we will work into. How much to count on writing. Poetry unlucrative. Maybe children's books.

Ted: steady, kind, loving, warm, intelligent, creative. But we are both too ingrown: prefer books too often to people. Anti-security compulsion. . . .

If I can build myself and my work I will be a contribution to our pair, not a dependent and weak half.

Hate of mother, jealousy of brother: only when I am dubious of the way of life to substitute into the place of the life they seem to favor. They will accept it, but we must be sure of our way. We are not; I am not. Discouragement about work. Haven't really worked at writing. Fear of aimless intellectual frittering. Need for a profession dealing with people on a level not superficial.

Jealousy over men: why jealous of Ted? Mother can't take him. Other women can. I must not be selfless: develop a sense of self. A solidness that can't be attacked.

Saturday, December 27, 1958. Yesterday had a session with R.B., quite long, and very deep. I dug up things which hurt and made me cry. Why do I cry with her and only with her? I am experiencing a grief reaction for [the loss of] Mother's love. [Omission.] What, then, do I expect in the way of love? Do I feel what I expect when I see R.B.? Is that why I cry? Because even her professional kindness strikes me as more to what I want than what I feel in Mother? I have lost a father and his love early; feel angry at her because of this and feel she feels I killed him (her dream about me being a chorus girl and his driving off and drowning himself). I dreamed often of losing her, and these childhood nightmares stand out: I dreamed the other night of running after Ted through a huge hospital, knowing he was with another woman, going into mad wards and looking for him everywhere: what makes you think it was Ted? It had his face but it was my father, my mother.

I identify him with my father at certain times, and these times take on great importance: e.g., that one fight at the end of the school year when I found him not-there on the special day and with another woman. I had a furious access of rage. He knew how I love him and felt, and yet wasn't there. Isn't this an image of what I feel my father did to me? I think it may be. The reason I haven't discussed it with Ted is that the situation hasn't come up again and it is not a characteristic of his: if it were, I would feel wronged in my trust on him. It was an incident only that drew forth echoes, not the complete withdrawal of my father, who deserted me forever. Ask: why didn't I talk about it afterwards? Is this a plausible interpretation? If it had come up since, it would be recollected by the stir-up of similar incidents and fears. Ted, insofar as he is a male presence, is a substitute for my father: but in no other way. Images of his faithlessness with women echo my fear of my father's relation with my mother and Lady Death.

How fascinating all this is. Why can't I master it and manipulate it and lose my superficiality, which is a careful protective gloss against it?

Read Freud's *Mourning and Melancholia* this morning after Ted left for the library. An almost exact description of my feelings and reasons for suicide: a transferred murderous impulse from my mother onto myself: the "vampire" metaphor Freud uses, "draining the ego": that is exactly the feeling I have getting in the way of my writing: Mother's clutch. I mask my self-abasement (a transferred hate of her) and weave it with my own real dissatisfactions in myself until it becomes very difficult to distinguish what is really bogus criticism from what is really a changeable liability. How can I get rid of this depression: by refusing to believe she has any power over me, like the old witches for whom one sets out plates of milk and honey. This is not easily done. How is it done? Talking and becoming aware of what is what and studying it is a help.

Dr. B.: You are trying to do two mutually incompatible things this year. 1) spite your mother. 2) write. To spite your mother, you don't write because you feel you have to give the stories to her, or that she will appropriate them. (As I was afraid of having her around to appropriate my baby, because I didn't want it to be hers.) So I can't write. And I hate her because my not writing plays into her hands and argues that she is right, I was foolish not to teach, or do something secure, when what I have renounced security for is nonexistent. My rejection-fear is bound up with the fear that this will mean my rejection by her, for not succeeding: perhaps that is why they are so terrible. The saving thing is, Ted doesn't care about the rejections except insofar as they bother me. So my work is to have fun in my work and to FEEL THAT MY WORKS ARE MINE. She may use them, put them about her room when published, but I did them and she has nothing to do with them.

It is not that I myself do not want to succeed. I do. But I do not need success with the desperation I have felt for it: that is an infusion of fear that successlessness means no approval from Mother: and approval, with Mother, has been equated for me with love, however true that is.

[Omission.] WHAT DO I EXPECT BY "LOVE" FROM HER? WHAT

IS IT I DON'T GET THAT MAKES ME CRY? I think I have always felt she uses me as an extension of herself; that when I commit suicide, or try to, it is a "shame" to her, an accusation: which it was, of course. An accusation that her love was defective. Feeling, too, of competing with Warren: the looming image of Harvard is equated with him. How, by the way, does Mother understand my committing suicide? As a result of my not writing, no doubt. I felt I couldn't write because she would appropriate it. Is that all? I felt if I didn't write nobody would accept me as a human being. Writing, then, was a substitute for myself: if you don't love me, love my writing and love me for my writing. It is also much more: a way of ordering and reordering the chaos of experience.

When I am cured of my witch-belief, I will be able to tell her of writing without a flinch and still feel it mine. She is . . . Not a witch. [Omission.]

Is our desire to investigate psychology a desire to get Dr. B.'s power and handle it ourselves? It is an exciting and helpful power. "You are never the same afterwards: it is a Pandora's box: nothing is simple anymore."

MY WRITING IS MY WRITING IS MY WRITING. Whatever elements there were in it of getting her approval I must no longer use it for that. I must not expect her love for it. [Omission.] I must change, not she. Why is telling her of a success so unsatisfying: because one success is never enough: when you love, you have an indefinite lease of it. When you approve, you only approve single acts. Thus approval has a short dateline. The question is: so much for that, good, but now, what is the next thing?

WHAT DO I FEEL GUILTY ABOUT? Having a man, being happy. . . . [Omission.]

One reason I could keep up such a satisfactory letter-relationship with her while in England was we could both verbalize our desired image of ourselves in relation to each other: interest and sincere love, and never feel the emotional currents at war with these verbally expressed feelings. I feel her disapproval. But I feel it countries away too. [Omission.] I wish . . . I could be sure of what I am: so I could know that what feelings I have, even though some resemble hers, are really my own. Now I find it hard to distinguish between the semblance and the reality. [Omission.]

One reason all people at Harvard are a reproach to me and make me jealous: because I identify them with Warren? How to stop this.

PROBLEM: The same act may be good or not good depending on its emotional content. Such as coitus. Such as giving presents. Such as choosing a job.

WHAT IS THE MATURE THING TO DO WITH [HOSTILITY] FOR MOTHER? Does the need to express it recede with a mature awareness? [Omission.] Does all hate pass off . . . ?

Ted & I are introverts and need a kind of external stimulus such as a job to get us into deep contact with people: even in superficial contact such as smalltalk which is pleasurable. . . . Writing as a profession turns us inward: we don't do reportage, criticism, freelance research. Poetry is the most ingrown and intense of the creative arts. Not much money in it, and that windfalls. Teaching is another distortion: it selects an abstract subject, a subject "about reality, spiritual and physical," organizes it into courses, simplifies the deluge of literature by time divisions and subject divisions and style divisions. Makes organized a small bit of it all and repeats that for twenty years. Psychology, I imagine, supplies more reality situations: the people you deal with are bothered with a variety of things, people and ideas, not just the symbolism of James Joyce. They have different jobs; different things are good for them. They do not take the Exam of Life together in the same room: each is different. There is no common grade scale. They have common problems but none is exactly the same. This requires an extension of other-awareness. Whatever Ted does, I would like to submit myself to it. It would require a long discipleship. However, I don't want to enter it until I have convinced myself I am writing and writing for my own pleasure and to express insights to others also, and learning techniques.

Ted and I talked about jobs yesterday: He is as pathological as I am in his own way: compulsive against society so he envisions "getting a job" as a kind of prison term. Yet says now his job at Cambridge was a rich experience which he then took as death. I would be pleased if he found something that he liked. What is so terrible about earning a regular wage? He admits it feels good. He is afraid of the Image: so many have regular jobs and are dead, why wouldn't it kill him? If he has his writing established in this year, I don't think it would kill him. But he doesn't want the sort of job, no more do I, that I/he could walk into without much preparation; a job to do with writing.

We agreed on a Friday afternoon blow-up: all problems and not only that, but praise: counting week's good things. Projecting constructive things for the next week. . . . We read over an hour of *King Lear* over tea. I read four Ionesco plays: *The Bald Soprano, Jack, The Lesson, The Chairs*: terrifying and funny: playing on our own old conventions and banalities and making them carried to the last extreme to show, by the discrepancy between real and real-to-the-last-thrust, how funny we are and how far gone. "We eat well because we live in a suburb of London and our name is Smith." A family crisis: a boy won't submit and say he adores hashed brown potatoes: the smallness of the object contrasted with the totality of emotion involved on all sides: a ridicule, a terror. Now all I need to do is start writing without thinking it's for Mother to get affection from her! How can I do this: where is my purity of motive? Ted won't need to get out of the house when I'm sure I'm not using his writing to get approval too and sure I'm myself and not him.

Reason I want R.B. to talk first? Desire not to have responsibility of analysis rest on me? I want to ask questions & will: it is my work and my advantage to work on it. Immense peace today after talk with her, deep grief expression: when will that last end?

Sunday, December 28. Before nine. Oatmeal eater, and two cups of coffee. Had my coffee vision in bed. Began clearly to remember Dick Norton. A possible theme: virgin girl brought up in idealism expects virginity from boy her family raves about as pure. He is going to be a doctor, a pillar of society; he is already swinging toward conventionalism. Takes her through lectures on sickle-cell anemia, moon-faced babies in jars, cadavers, baby born. She doesn't flinch. What she flinches at is his affair with a waitress. She hates him for it. Jealous. Sees no reason for being a virgin herself. What's the point in being a virgin? Argument with him: humor. She won't marry him. What are her motives? He is a hypocrite. "Well, should I go around telling folks?" Kiss the earth and beg pardon. No, that wouldn't be enough. The modern woman: demands as much experience as the modern man. . . .

Went to library yesterday afternoon with Ted. Looked up requirements for a Ph.D. in psychology. It would take about six years. A prodigious prospect. Two years for prerequisites, languages for M.A. Four years for the rest, it might be three. The work of applying, figuring out programs, etc., and not to mention money, a formidable thing. Awesome to confront a program of study which is so monumental: all human experience. Still, it was good to face what it would mean. I wonder if the statistics would overwhelm me.

Turn, with a kind of relief, to the business of learning a craft. I am reading Frank O'Connor's stories not just with the first innocence, letting it come at me, but with a kind of growing awareness of what he is doing technically. I will imitate until I can feel I'm using what he can teach. His stories are so clearly "constructed": not a whit unused: a narrative flow. That is what I most need and most miss. I write a sort of imagey, static prose: like the tattoo story: I understand for the first time why he didn't accept me for his course with my Minton story: I should have sent "The Perfect Setup" or the sorority story. They had plot, people changing, learning something. My trouble with Johanna Bean is that I have about three themes, none clear.

I am still dallying a good two hours too much before working: sewing on The Button, making a bed, watering a plant. Still sick of waking and will be till the story is more interesting than my own self-musings.

Ted read my signature on the letter to his parents as "woe" instead of "love." He was right, it looked surprising: the left hand knows not what the right writes. It would make me quite happy if he would find some steady something he *liked* to do. Dick Norton's mother was not so wrong about a man supplying direction and a woman the warm emotional power of faith and love. I feel we are as yet directionless (not inside, so much as in a peopled community way—we belong nowhere because we have not given of ourselves to any place wholeheartedly, not committed ourselves).

Ted labored all yesterday afternoon and evening making a wolf-mask out of Agatha's old, falling-apart sealskin. It is remarkably fuzzy and wolfish. About the party tonight: the sense of not wanting to go: the Unknown, everybody buying fabulous costumes and toys to go with them. I haven't even got a red hood or a basket, which is all I need, but can't see spending even a couple of $$/

Am reading Saint Thérèse's autobiography: a terror of the contradiction of "relic and pomp admiration" and the pure soul. Where, where is Jesus? Maybe only the nuns and monks come near, but even they have this horrid self-satisfied greed for misfortune which in its own way is [as] perverse as greed for happiness in this world: such as T.'s "precious blessing" of her father's cerebral paralysis and madness: a welcome cross to bear!

The only way to stop envying others is to have a self of joy. All creation is jammed in the selfish soul.

I think I am pregnant: I wonder when and if I will feel it.

Saturday, January 3, 1959. As usual after an hour with Dr. B., digging, felt I'd been watching or participating in a Greek play: a cleansing and an exhaustion. I wish I could keep the revelations, such as they are, fresh in mind. Relieved she suggested $5 for an hour. Enough, considerable for me. Yet not outrageous, so it is punishment. Felt brief panic at the thought she would not take me on or try to refer me to someone else.

All my life I have been "stood up" emotionally by the people I loved most: Daddy dying and leaving me, Mother somehow not there. So I endow the smallest incidents of lateness, for example, in other people I love, with an emotional content of coldness, indication that I am not important to them. Realizing this, I wasn't angry or bothered she was late. The terror of my last day of teaching last May, when this happened, especially with the face of that girl. If it happened more often, I would find it a character fault, but it doesn't seem to have happened.

Twister: I don't care if T. gives me presents as proof of *my* affection. What comes to mind? Hugging. I have never found anybody who could stand to accept the daily demonstrative love I feel in me, and give back as good as I gave. She [Dr. B.] said well: so you wouldn't be left on a limb with your love hanging out. Afraid of having love all unaccepted, left over. Shame at this.

At McLean* I had an inner life going on all the time but wouldn't admit it. If I had known this, I would have praised the Lord. I needed permission to admit I lived. Why?

Why, after the "amazingly short" three or so shock treatments, did I rocket uphill? Why did I feel I needed to be punished, to punish myself. Why do I feel now I should be guilty, unhappy: and feel guilty if I am not? Why do I feel immediately happy after talking to Dr. B.? Able to enjoy every little thing: shopped for meat, a victory for me, and got what I wanted: veal, chicken, hamburg. My need to punish myself might, horribly, go to the length of deliberately and to spite my face disappointing T. in this way or that. That would be my worst punishment. That and not writing. Knowing this is the first guard against it.

What do I expect or want from Mother? Hugging, mother's milk? But that is impossible to all of us now. Why should I want it still? What can I do with this want? How can I transfer it to something I can have?

A great, stark, bloody play acting itself out over and over again behind the sunny facade of our daily rituals, birth, marriage, death, behind parents and schools and beds and tables of food: the dark, cruel, murderous shades, the demon-animals, the Hungers.

Attitude to things: like a mother, I don't want anyone to say anything against T., not that he is lazy or shiftless: I know he works, and hard, but it doesn't show to the observer, for whom writing is sitting home, drinking coffee and piddling about. A play.

ASK ABOUT MOTHER-LOVE: Why these feelings? Why guilt: as **if sex, even** legally indulged in, **should be** "paid for" by pain? I would probably interpret pain as a judgment: birth-pain, even a deformed child. Magical fear Mother will become a child, my child: an old hag child.

Wednesday, January 7, 1959. The abstract kills, the concrete saves (try inverting this thesis tomorrow). How an Idea of What

---

*Where Plath was hospitalized after her suicide attempt

Should Be or What One Should Be Doing can drive an eating, excreting two-legged beast to misery. How dusting, washing daily dishes, talking to people who are not mad and [who] dust and wash and feel life is as it should be helps. . . .

Don't wake up in the morning because I want to go back to the womb. From now on: see if this is possible: set alarm for 7:30 and get up then, tired or not. Rip through breakfast and housecleaning (bed and dishes, mopping or whatever) by 8:30. Ted got coffee and oatmeal today: he doesn't like to do it, but does it. I am a fool to let him. Alarm-setting gets over the bother of waking at ragged odd hours around nine.

Be writing before 9, that takes the curse off it. It is now almost 11. I have washed two sweaters, the bathroom floor, mopped, done a day's dishes, made the bed, folded the laundry and stared in horror at my face: it is a face old before its time.

Nose podgy as a leaking sausage: big pores full of pus and dirt, red blotches, the peculiar brown mole on my under-chin which I would like to have excised. Memory of that girl's face in the med school movie, with a little black beauty wart: this wart is malignant: she will be dead in a week. Hair untrained, merely brown and childishly put up: don't know what else to do with it. No bone structure. Body needs a wash, skin the worst: it is this climate: chapping cold, desiccating hot: I need to be tan, all-over brown, and then my skin clears and I am all right. I need to have written a novel, a book of poems, a *Ladies' Home Journal* or *New Yorker* story, and I will be poreless and radiant. My wart will be nonmalignant.

Reading *The Horse's Mouth*: hard to get into. I see why it didn't sell much here: too rich a surface, all knots and spurtings of philosophy, but only as emanation from the bumpy colored surface of life, not imposed on it. Plot not spare and obvious, but a spate of anecdotes. Podgy old Sara eternal as Eve, Alison, Wife of Bath. This old battered hide: needs a brain and a creative verve to make it livable in, a heater in the ratty house.

Read Ainu tales: primitive: all at penis-fetish, anus-fetish, mouth-fetish stage. Marvelous untouched humor, primal: bang, bang you're dead. Stories of alter ego: same thing done by two people, only one is rich by it, other poor and dead: difference, attitude of mind only. NB.

The first thing is the early rising. Also, telling Ted nothing.

DOING. Finished, almost, story of Shadow: no Joanna Bean in it at all. Despair: have ideas: lack of know-how. Also, lack of ideas. How many girls go to sleep on marrying after college: see them twenty-five years later with their dew-eyes turned ice, same look, no growing except in outside accretions, like the shell of a barnacle. Beware.

Thursday, January 8. A poor day again. The old sickness on me and a morning dissipated in phone calls and calculatings with the money down $1,000. A deep wish to leap to Columbia and get a Ph.D. and make money by working. I don't know if I'm the sort to stay home all day and write. I think my head will get soft if I have no outer walls to measure it against. Or that I will stop speaking the human language.

Very bad dreams lately. One just after my period last week of losing my month-old baby: a transparent meaning. The baby, formed just like a baby, only small as a hand, died in my stomach and fell forward: I looked down at my bare belly and saw the round bump of its head in my right side, bulging out like a burst appendix. It was delivered with little pain, dead. Then I saw two babies, a big nine-month one, and a little one-month one with a blind white-piggish face nuzzling against it: a transfer image, no doubt, from Rosalind's cat and kittens a few days before: the little baby was a funny shape, like a kitten with white skin instead of fur. But my baby was dead. I think a baby would make me forget myself in a good way. Yet I must find myself....

Is it a defense, not working: then I can't be criticized for what I do. Why am I passive? Why don't I go out and work? I am inherently lazy. Teaching looks a blessed relief after this burden. Anyway, we don't get out and meet people. Ted stays in and brings in little but books. I am going sloppy. I will wash hair and shower tonight. How to bring my life together in a strong way? Not to wander and squander. So little I know of the world.

Nothing to measure myself against: no community to be part of. Ted refuses any church. Still, why can't I go alone? Find out and go alone. Other people are a salvation. It is up to me.

Last night's horror: Stephen Fassett* in it, stiff and sad. Walking by gravestones, dragging them away with a rope: a corridor, with dead corpses being wheeled down it, half decayed, their faces all mottled and falling away, yet clothed in coats, hats, and so on. We got pushed into the stream, and horror, the dead were moving. A dead corpse, all grinning and filth being propelled along standing by another man almost as bad, then a lump of flesh, stunted, round, with black cloves, or nails stuck in all over it, and only one long apish swinging arm, reaching out for alms. I woke screaming: the horror of the deformed and dead, alive as we are, and I among them, in the filth and swarming corruption of the flesh. I feel, am mad as any writer must in one way be: why not make it real? I am too close to the bourgeois society of suburbia: too close to people I know: I must sever myself from them, or be part of their world: this half-and-half compromise is intolerable. If only Ted wanted to do something. Saw a career he'd enjoy.... I feel the weight on me. The old misery of money seeping away. A cold corpse between me and any work at all. I need a flow of life on the outside, a child, a job, a community I know from preacher to baker. Not this drift of fairy tales.

Saturday, January 10. Cried yesterday morning: as if it were an hour for keening: why is crying so pleasurable? I feel clean, absolutely purged after it. As if I had a grief to get over with, some deep sorrow. I cried about other mothers coming to take care of their daughters for a while, with babies. Talked of how I could let Mother have her limited pleasure if I were "grown-up" enough not to feel jeopardized by her manipulating me. I sidestepped this problem ingeniously: talked of M. E. Chase, lesbians (what does a woman see in another woman what she doesn't see in a man: tenderness?). I am also afraid of M.E.C.: you must hate her, fear her: you think all old women are magical witches.

The crux is my desire to be manipulated. Whence does it come, how can I triumph over it? Why is my flow of inner

---

*He had a recording studio on Beacon Hill and recorded poetry for the Lamont Library at Harvard.

life so blocked? How can I free it? How can I find myself &
be sure of my identity?

Next time: start by asking if my stubborn shut-mouth at the
beginning is an attempt to force R.B. to talk first, take the
running of the hour out of my hands: she won't talk first, makes
me. And I eventually do.

How can I stop fearing other people? How can I know who
I am? How to let my native sense of meaning flow and connect
with people and the world? Why this sense of horror, coming
over me? Fear? If Ted had a positive program, joy in his work —
a work that would serve as a connection with people, a place,
it would help: while uncommitted, I am faced with dozens of
possibilities, places, ways: fear of death by premature choice,
cutting off of alternatives. How to say: I choose this, & not
fear the consequences.

Rejection of my Johnny Panic story without a note from
The Yale Review: all my little dreams of publishing it there
vanished: so writing is still used as a proof of my identity.
Bitterness at achievement of others.

Glimmer last night of pleasure, which slipped away: Agatha's top floor room, the gray snow-light of evening coming,
the tea, the enclosed feeling of peace, old carpets, old sofa,
old smoothed chairs: don't share sorrow with Ted of rejection:
he worries about me, I make up problems. Talk of poetry, cats,
Ted reading Smart's poem on cats. Martini at Marty's, seeing
her print blouse and slacks she is sewing, a real honest wish
to make something like that myself. Yet a rebellion at the time
on it. Interest in making clothes for children. Why can't I read
Yeats, Hopkins, if I love them. Why do I punish myself by
not looking at them? I think I will get a Ph.D. in English &
teach poetry.

Talked also with R.B. of Victorian women who fear men:
men treat women as brainless chattels: have seen so many
romances end in this sort of thing, waste of a woman, they
don't believe marriage can work without woman becoming
maid, servant, nurse and losing brain. Ulcers: desire for dependency & feeling it is wrong to be dependent: you reject
food (mother's milk), dependency, and yet get dependency by
being sick: it's the ulcer to blame, not you.

Where is joy? Joy in frogs, not in Idea of people looking

at my frog poem. Why must I punish myself, or save myself, by pretending I am stupid and can't feel? (The damn electrician sounds to be sawing the house in.) Would pregnancy bring a kind of peace? I would, she says, probably have a depression after my first baby if I didn't get rid of it now....

Promiscuity: my ingenious, evasive self-deceiving explanation: I had to give out affection in small doses so it would be accepted, not all to one person, who couldn't take it. Very queer. The fact that belies this is that I found no pleasure in anything except my relation with R., [Richard Sassoon] and that was a monogamous affair for me while it lasted. So I was trying to be like a man: able to take or leave sex, with this one and that. I got even. But really wasn't meant for it. What about exhibitionism? The whore, a male-type woman? For all comers?

She [Dr. B.] praises me, and I feel hungry for it: I castigate myself so completely. What a mess I am.

To see what to expect from Mother, etc., accept it and know how to deal with it. This presupposes an independence and sense of identity in myself, which I have not got. This is the main issue....

I have hated men because I felt them physically necessary: hated them because they would degrade me, by their attitude: women shouldn't think, shouldn't be unfaithful (but their husbands may be), must stay home, cook, wash. Many men need a woman to be like this. Only the weak ones don't, so many strong women marry a weak one, to have children, and their own way at once. If I could once see how to write a story, a novel, to get something of my feeling over, I would not despair. If writing is not an outlet, what is?...

Felt a joy yesterday, soon clouded.

Postscript: Am reading the Book of Job: great peace derived therefrom. Shall read the Bible: symbolic meaning, even though the belief in a moral God-structured universe not there. Live As If it were? A great device.

Will not tell Ted of rejection: will not make gloom concrete: that is an indulgence. He gets bothered because I am bothered and then I feel bad for his being bothered and so on. Will just quietly send it out again Monday....

* * *

Wednesday, January 20, 1959. Peculiar peace this morning: all is gray and dripping wet. We have a new cat whose needs and miaows are become a part of consciousness. I tried shutting it in the bedroom, but it cried and cried. It loves human warmth, cries to get in bed with us. A little stary tiger now curled drowsy blue-eyed on the couch. Playful, adventurous, named Sappho. . . .

A moment with Elizabeth Hardwick and Robert Lowell: she charming and high-strung, mimicking their subnormal Irish house girl, whom they have at last let go, he kissing her tenderly before leaving, calling her he would be late, and all the winsome fondnesses of a devoted husband. He with his stories about Dylan Thomas, the two bald men in Iowa, Thomas putting his hands on each head: I can tell the two of you apart because one wears glasses, and one's a good fellow and the other's a dry turd. Lowell's half-whisper and sliding glance. Peter Brooks, his tall wrinkled soft kind charming face, falling here and there, nerves: his iceblue-eyed pouty blond ballerina wife, Gerta K., saying to her [evidently, Hardwick], "Next to me I hear you're the biggest bitch in Cambridge." Lowell: "You should tell her: you're boasting."

Finished a poem this weekend, "Point Shirley, Revisited," on my grandmother. Oddly powerful and moving to me in spite of the rigid formal structure. Evocative. Not so one-dimensional. Spent a really pleasant afternoon, rainy, in the library looking up goatsuckers for a poem for Esther's* night creatures book. Much more than on frogs, and much more congenial a subject. I have eight lines of a sonnet on the bird, very alliterative and colored. The problem this morning is the sestet.

I feel oddly happy. To enjoy the present as if I had never lived and would tomorrow be dead, instead of "Jam tomorrow, jam yesterday, never jam today." The secret of peace: a devout worship of the moment. Ironically: with most people this is what comes naturally. . . .

. . . I make up problems, all unnecessary. I do not reverence the present time. Tomorrow: Ask R.B. why I need to have a problem. Why she was late. What am I hiding about "other people" to protect myself? Why am I so jealous of others? I

---

*Esther Baskin

am me, and the rain is lovely on these chimneys. . . .

We decided to live in England. I really want this. Ted will be his best there. I shall demand an icebox and a good dentist, but love it. Hopefully a big sonorous place in the country in easy distance of London, where I may work. I would so much like to. I will read novels by Lessing and Murdoch, also Bianca Van Orden. Sometimes life seems so meanderingly pleasant. And then I castigate myself for laziness. For not working for a Ph.D. or on a third book like A.C.R.* or having four children and a profession, or this, or that. All ridiculous. In worry I do nothing.

Joy: show joy & enjoy: then others will be joyful. Bitterness the one sin. That and the ever-prevalent sloth.

Tuesday, January 27. . . . A month of the New year evaporated. Read Wilbur and Rich this morning. Wilbur a bland turning of pleasaunces, a fresh speaking and picturing with incalculable grace and all sweet, pure, clear, fabulous, the maestro with the imperceptible marcel. Robert Lowell after this is like good strong shocking brandy after a too lucidly sweet dinner wine, dessert wine.

I speak with Dr. B. of being little, as if I were a homunculus. I made an appointment to cut and permanent my hair yesterday and canceled it. Unable to impose my will and wish on a professional hairdresser. . . . I'm not working, only studying to change my ways of writing poems. A disgust for my work. My poems begin on one track, in one dimension, and never surprise or shock or even much please. The world is all left out. World's criticism had a point: too much dreams, shadowy underworlds.

To ask Dr. B. what I can do to sift out grown self from contracted baby feelings, jolting jealousies. Learn German, Italian. Joy. How much and how many in this life want merely "a good deal." A self-interested shuffling of the cards in the right, plush-enough combination. I am worried about being lazy if happy, worried about being self-deluding if working on anything. So little myself all other identities threaten me. Dreamer forever. Robert Lowell and his wife and the Fassetts

---

*Adrienne Cecile Rich, the poet

are coming to dinner this week. I am wondering what to serve them all in one dish. Lemon meringue pie. Will read Hardwick's stories at the library. I want their success without their spirit or work. . . .

Wednesday, January 28. A clear blue day, a close-clipped furze of white snow crisping all the cockeyed angles of roof and chimney below, and the river white. Sun behind the building to the left, striking a gold-dollar glow from a domed tower I don't know the name of. If I can only write a page, half a page, here every day and keep myself counting blessings and working slowly to come into a better life.

Oddly happy yesterday, in spite of a bad morning, when I think I did nothing but work on a silly poem about a bull-ocean which evades all direct statement of anything under the pretense of symbolic allegory. Read A. C. Rich today, finished her book of poems in half an hour: they stimulate me: they are easy, yet professional, full of infelicities and numb gesturings at something, but instinct with "philosophy," what I need. Sudden desire to do a series of Cambridge and Benidorm poems. Am I crude to say "*The New Yorker* sort"? That means something.

Amazingly happy afternoon with Shirley yesterday. Took subway out. Smoky day, smoke white against snow-filled sky, smoke gray-black against pale twilight sky coming back. Brought my bundle of woolens and began to make the braided rug: immense pleasure cutting the good thick stuggs, wrestling with the material and getting a braid begun. Talked easily about babies, fertility, amazingly frank and pleasant. Have always wanted to "make something" by hand, where other women sew and knit and embroider, and this I feel is my thing. John sat in high chair, Shirley fed and bathed and bedded him, very easily. He was loving to me, hugging me and rubbing his forehead against mine. Felt part of young womanhood. How odd, men don't interest me at all now, only women and women-talk. It is as if Ted were my representative in the world of men. Must read some sociology, Spock on babies. All questions answered.

Can I do the poems? By a kind of contagion?

Came home & happily made a quick hamburg supper. Lowells coming tomorrow and all the cleaning and planning for that I put off till tonight. Must get my hair cut next week. Symbolic: get over instinct to be dowdy lip-biting little girl. Get bathrobe and slippers and nightgown & work on femininity. . . .

The cat is biting more now, but after mackerel this morning most endearingly climbed up my shoulder and nuzzled. Must try poems. DO NOT SHOW ANY TO TED. I sometimes feel a paralysis come over me: his opinion is so important to me. Didn't show him the bull one: a small victory. Also, be growing into a habit of happiness. That will work also. A check, $10 from *The Nation* for "Frog Autumn." Welcome. Am happy about living in England: to go to Europe at the drop of a channel-crossing ticket: I really want that. How odd: I would have been amazed five, ten years ago at the thought of this. And delighted. Must use R.B. to the hilt.

Friday, February 13, 1959. First time I've had the heart to write in here for weeks. A lousy green depressing cold. Cried with the old stone-deep gloom with R.B. yesterday. She said I don't work as well [when I feel] so bad: I think I'm going to get well and then I feel I can't; need to be punished. Get a job, in Cambridge, somewhere in a 10 day limit. I dream of bookstores, Design Research. That would be something. . . .

We are fools. The alarm on, we shower and rise. Five hours from seven to twelve is all we need for writing. She says: you won't write. This is so, not that I can't, although I say I can't.

Have been reading Faulkner. At last. *Sanctuary* and beginning the collected stories and excerpts. Will go on a jag. Absolutely flawless descriptive style: and much description: dogs, their smells, fuckings and terrors. Scenes. Whorehouse interiors. Colors, humor and above all a fast plot: rape with corn cobs, sexual deviation, humans shot and burned alive, he gets it in. And where are my small incidents, the blood poured from the shoes?

Thursday, February 19. The North Wind doth blow. Gray and snowflakes blowing suddenly like bits of white paper. Ann Hopkins white-and-black spotted fixed female cat trying to get settled in smaller and smaller boxes, finally managing, and hiding its head in foetal position for a cat, I imagine. Then crawling up under her red bedspread and lying under it in the middle of the bed, an inert red lump. Queer: born with flying-squirrel flaps and too many thumbs which bunch out from its feet.

A misery. Wrote a Granchester poem of pure description. I must get philosophy in. Until I do I shall lag behind A.C.R. A fury of frustration, some inhibition keeping me from writing what I really feel. I began a poem, "Suicide Off Egg Rock," but set up such a strict verse form that all power was lost: my nose so close I couldn't see what I was doing. An anesthetizing of feeling. Keeping me from work on a novel. To forget myself for the work, instead of nudging the work to be my reason for being and my self.

Dinners and parties all this week, which I am glad to forgo from now on. Heard Wilbur read: oddly, I was bored to death. I enjoy his poems more when I read them myself: his voice is dull, playing a joke on the poem with the audience, his clever poems on the Mind Cave-Bat and Lamarck merely ingenious. Eighteenth-century manners. Stanley Kunitz, in his best three or four poems much much finer. Stanley getting $15,000 from the Ford Foundation for two years of writing what he wants where he wants. We hearing nothing from the Guggenheim. I, sitting here as if brainless wanting both a baby and a career but god knows what if it isn't writing. What inner decision, what inner murder or prison break must I commit if I want to speak from my true deep voice in writing (which I somehow boggle at spelling) and not feel this jam-up of feeling behind a glass-dam fancy-facade of numb dumb wordage. Somewhat cheered by *The Spectator* printing my two small poems. I think success would be heartening now. But, most heartening, the feeling [as if] I were breaking out of my glass caul. What am I afraid of? Growing old and dying without being Somebody? It is good for me to be away from the natural stellar position at Smith. I look queerly forward to living in England: hope I can work for some weekly in London, publish in the women's magazines, maybe. England seems so small and digestible from here. . . .

Wednesday, February 25. The anniversary of our meeting, third. Last night a miserable dowie dowie fight over nothing, our usual gloom. I am ready to blame it all on myself. The day is an accusation. Pure and clear and ready to be the day of creation, snow white on all the rooftops and the sun on it and the sky a high clear blue bell jar.

Lousy dreams. Forget last night's. Gary Haupt was in it, refusing to speak and passing by with a stiff accusing and sallow face as if he smelt something bad. The other night it was men in costume, bright cummerbunds, knickers and white blouses, having a penalty given them, and not carried out, and suddenly forty years later they were lined up, I saw them small in the distance, and a man with his back to me and a great sword in his hand went down the line hacking off their legs at the knees, whereupon the men fell down like ninepins with their leg stumps and lower legs scattered. I believe they were supposed to dig their own graves on their leg stumps. This is too much. The world is so big so big so big. I need to feel a meaning and productiveness in my life.

Got somewhere last week with Dr. B., I think. The resurrection of the awful Woodrow Wilson interview at Harvard. What I fear worst is failure, and this is stopping me from trying to write because then I don't have to blame failure on my writing: it is a last ditch defense, not quite the last—the last is when the words dissolve and the letters crawl away. Knowing this, how can I go to work? Transfer this knowledge to my inmost demons?

Ted's thinking idea good. I listed five subjects and got no farther than Egg Rock. Wrote a ghastly poem in strict varying line lengths with no feeling in it although the scene was fraught with emotion. Then did it over, much better: got something of what I wanted. Pulled. To the neat easy A.C.R.-ish* lyricism, to the graphic description of the world. My main thing now is to start with real things: real emotions, and leave out the baby gods, the old men of the sea, the thin people, the knights, the moon-mothers, the mad maudlins, the Lorelei, the hermits, and get into me, Ted, friends, mother and brother and father and family. The real world. Real situations, behind which the great gods play the drama of blood, lust and death.

Lowell's class yesterday a great disappointment: I said a few mealymouthed things, a few B.U. students yattered noth-

---

*Adrienne Cecile Rich

ings I wouldn't let my Smith freshmen say without challenge. Lowell good in his mildly feminine ineffectual fashion. Felt a regression. The main thing is hearing the other students' poems & his reaction to mine. I need an outsider: feel like the recluse who comes out into the world with a life-saving gospel to find everybody has learned a new language in the meantime and can't understand a word he's saying.

When I write my first *Ladies' Home Journal* story I will have made a step forward. I don't have to be a bourgeois mother to do it either. The reason I don't write them is that it is safer from rejection not to—then I haven't the opportunity to be in jeopardy. . . .

Oh, to break out into prose.

Saturday, February 28. . . . Nightmare before going to R.B. this week: train broke down in subway in a fire of blue sparks, got on wrong track, driving in old car with Ted, drove into deep snowdrift and the car fell apart, struggled to a telephone after 11, her maid answered, and I felt she was home, either knowing this would happen and thus not coming out, or pretending she wasn't home. Bought blue shoes on the way back from seeing her. Relived with all the emotion the episode at the hospital in Carlisle.* Murderous emotions in a child can't be dealt with through reason, in an adult they can.

Read Faulkner yesterday, after Tolstoi's superb *Death of Ivan Ilyitch*, a sustained full-pitch rendering of the beast-man's fear and horror of dying. Is Ivan's knowledge, in a flash, at the last, that his life has been all wrong, a steady downgrade in just those points he thought it most a success, redemptive in any sense? He dies in peace, or at least, in a sudden recession of fear, in an access of light. But was the pain intended to bring this about? I think not. Suffering is because it is, the voice answers. . . .

Monday, March 9. After a lugubrious session with R.B., much freed. Good weather, good bits of news. If I don't stop crying she'll have me tied up. Got idea on the trolley for a poem

---

*A reference to her devastating shock treatments at Valley Head Hospital, described in *The Bell Jar*

because of my ravaged face: called "The Ravaged Face." A line came, too. Wrote it down and then the five lines of a sestet. Wrote the first eight lines after coming back from a fine afternoon in Winthrop yesterday. I rather like it—it has the forthrightness of "Suicide Off Egg Rock." Also finished a *New Yorker*ish but romantic iambic pentameter imitation of Roethke's Yeats poems. Rather weak, not, I think, book material, but I'll send it to *The New Yorker* and see what they think.

A clear blue day in Winthrop. Went to my father's grave, a very depressing sight. Three graveyards separated by streets, all made within the last fifty years or so, ugly crude block stones, headstones together, as if the dead were sleeping head to head in a poorhouse. In the third yard, on a flat grassy area looking across a sallow barren stretch to rows of wooden tenements, I found the flat stone, "Otto E. Plath: 1885–1940," right beside the path, where it would be walked over. Felt cheated. My temptation to dig him up. To prove he existed and really was dead. How far gone would he be? No trees, no peace, his headstone jammed up against the body on the other side. Left shortly. It is good to have the place in mind. . . .

My desire for a career apart from writing. Writing impossible as my one thing, it is so dried up, so often. I would like to study comparative literature. The discipline of a Ph.D. attracts me in my foolhardiness, or of reporting for weeklies, or of reviewing. I must use my brain in the world, not just at home on private things.

Great cramps, stirrings. It is still just period time, but I have even waves of nausea. Am I pregnant? That would queer my jobs for a while, I guess. If only I could come to the novel, or at least the *Ladies' Home Journal* stories. Maybe some good pregnant poems, if I know I really am.

Friday, March 20. Yesterday a nadir of sorts. Woke up to cat's early mewling around six. Cramps. Pregnant I thought. Not, such luck. After a long 40 day period of hope, the old blood cramps and spilt fertility. I had lulled myself into a fattening calm and this was a blow. . . . I'd like four in a row. Then dopey, and the cramps all day. I am getting nowhere with Dr. B. I feel I deliberately put myself into a self-pitying helpless

state. Next week. What good does talking about my father do?
It may be a minor catharsis that lasts a day or two, but I don't
get insight talking to myself. What insight am I trying to get
to free what? If my emotional twists are at the bottom of misery,
how can I get to know what they are and what to do with them?
She can't make me write, or if I do write, write well. She can
give me more directives or insight in what I am doing and for
what general ends I am doing it. I regress terribly there. I may
have all the answers to my questions in myself, but I need
some catalyst to get them into my consciousness. . . .

I cry at everything. Simply to spite myself and embarrass
myself. Finished two poems, a long one, "Electra on Azalea
Path," and "Metaphors for a Pregnant Woman," ironic, nine
lines, nine syllables in each. They are never perfect, but I think
have goodnesses. Criticism of 4 of my poems in Lowell's class:
criticism of rhetoric. He sets me up with Anne Sexton,* an
honor, I suppose. Well, about time. She has very good things,
and they get better, though there is a lot of loose stuff.

A desire to get my hair cut attractively instead of this mousy
ponytail. Will no doubt go out and get a pageboy cut as of
old. Is it money keeps me back? Must get fixed up. . . .

Refusal to write. I just don't. Except for these few poems,
which have been coming thicker and better. I see the right state
of mind like a never never land ahead of me. That casual, gay
verve. Alas alas. I maunch on chagrins. . . .

Got at some deep things with R.B.: facing dark and terrible
things: those dreams of deformity and death. If I really think
I killed and castrated my father may all my dreams of deformed
and tortured people be my guilty visions of him or fears of
punishment for me? And how to lay them? To stop them operating through the rest of my life?

I have a vision of the poems I would write, but do not.
When will they come? . . .

Thursday, April 23. As with April, spring manifests itself in
joyous news. I am tired, having got up and out of Ted's work-
room by 7, after two weeks of pre- and post-Guggenheim
lethargy. We are transfigured. After a near-miss, a query and

---

*Anne Sexton was in Lowell's poetry class with Plath

paltering over the budget and the place of travel, we got it, and rounded off to the furthest thousand, $5,000, which seems incredibly princely to us. After an invitation to Yaddo* for two months in September and October, which we at first interpreted as a consolation prize. Guggenheim day: Friday, April 10.

Also, yesterday, my second acceptance from *The New Yorker*: a pleasant two: the "Water Color of Grantchester Meadows," which I wrote bucolically "for" them, and "Man in Black," the only "love" poem in my book, and the "book poem" which I wrote only a little over a month ago on one of my fruitful visits to Winthrop. Must do justice to my father's grave. Have rejected the Electra poem from my book. Too forced and rhetorical. A leaf from Anne Sexton's book would do here. She has none of my clenches, and an ease of phrase, and an honesty. I have my 40 unattackable poems. I think. And a joy about them of sorts. Although I would love more potent ones. All the Smith ones are miserable death wishes. The ones here, however gray ("Companionable Ills," "Owl"), have a verve and life-joy. . . .

The "dead black" in my poem ["Man in Black"] may be a transference from the visit to my father's grave.

Worked and worked with R.B.: the skip of a week gave me courage and momentum: stayed awake the whole night before thinking over what I have come through and to. Concentrated on my suicide: a knot in which much is caught. . . . How to overcome my naïveté in writing? Read others and think hard. Never step outside my own voice, such as I know it.

I think: a *Wuthering Heights* article for red-shoe money. Correct the word in my *Monitor* poem. Start a poem for *The Bed Book*.** A story on the hospital. About the affair of Starbuck & Sexton.† A double story, "August Lighthill and the Other Woman." . . . Here is horror. And all the details. Get life in spurts in stories, then the novel will come. A way. By the time I get to Yaddo, three good publishable stories and *The Bed Book* done!

---

*The artists' colony in Saratoga Springs, New York
**The Bed Book*, a children's book, was published long after Plath's death.
†Anne Sexton and George Starbuck

* * *

Saturday, April 25. Clear day, dragged up as usual early, but exhausted, too much so to write, so worked on polishing up essay on Withens [Yorkshire] only to be stopped in title from final typing by not knowing spelling Withens or Withins. . . .

Sunday, May 3, 1959. . . . Retyped pages, a messy job, on the volume of poems I should be turning in to Houghton Mifflin this week. But A.S.* is there ahead of me, with her lover G.S.** writing *New Yorker* odes to her and both of them together: felt our triple-martini afternoons at the Ritz breaking up. That memorable afternoon at G.'s monastic and miserly room on Pinckney: "You shouldn't have left us": where is responsibility to lie? I left, yet felt like a brown-winged moth around a rather meager candle flame, drawn. That is over. As [W. D.] Snodgrass would say.

I wrote a book yesterday. Maybe I'll write a postscript on top of this in the next month and say I've sold it. Yes, after half a year of procrastinating, bad feeling and paralysis, I got to it yesterday morning, having lines in my head here and there, and Wide-Awake Will and Stay-Uppity Sue very real, and bang. I chose ten beds out of the long list of too fancy and ingenious and abstract a list of beds, and once I'd begun I was away and didn't stop till I typed out and mailed it (8 double-spaced pages only!) to the Atlantic Press. *The Bed Book*, by Sylvia Plath. Funny how doing it freed me. It was a bat, a bad-conscience bat brooding in my head. If I didn't do it I would do nothing. A ready-made good idea and an editor writing to say she couldn't get the idea out of her head. So I did it. I feel if *The Atlantic* is stupid enough to reject it someone else will snap it up, and better so, if they will also take my poems. . . . Suddenly it frees me — and Ted, too. I can go to the magazine rack this morning and get a *NY Times*, a *New Yorker*, a *Writer's Mag* and not feel drowned or sick. Me, I will make my place, a queer, rather smallish place, but room and view enough to be happy in. . . .

* * *

*Anne Sexton
**George Starbuck

Wednesday, May 13, 1959.... Bothered about R.B.: I seem to want to cover everything up, like a cat its little crappings with sand, perhaps before leaving for California?

Well, I must bring up those pressure points: suicide, deflowering, T.'s sister, and present writing; lack of rooted social life, yet not minding it; lack of children. Today. Also concern about mind getting lazy. Learning languages.

My *Bull of Bendylaw* book of poems is much better arranged. Also, at this rate, with "Arts in Society" accepting "Sculptor," "The Goring" (which I was beginning to think unsalable) and "Aftermath," I have only 13 poems to publish before all 45 are in print, and these poems should not be too hard to sell....

Monday, May 18.... Changed title of poetry book in an inspiration to *The Devil of the Stairs*, which I hope has never been used before. *The Bull of Bendylaw*, which was catching, had an obscure point, the idea of energy breaking through ceremonial forms, but this title encompasses my book & "Explains" the poems of despair, which is as deceitful as hope is. Hope this goes through.

Dreamed last night of being a matron with seven daughters, like dolls, whom I was to dress in party dresses, all graded rose-colors, yet I found blue and purple dresses among the yellow and pink. Great confusion. Have they their gloves, their pocket money in their pocketbooks?...

Wednesday, May 20. All I need now is to hear that G.S. or M.K.* has won the Yale and get a rejection of my children's book. A.S. has her book accepted at Houghton Mifflin and this afternoon will be drinking champagne. Also an essay accepted by *PJHH*, the copycat. But who's to criticize a more successful copycat. Not to mention a poetry reading at McLean. And G.S. at supper last night smug as a cream-fed cat, very pleased indeed, for A.S. is in a sense his answer to me. And now my essay, on Withens, will come back from *PJHH*, and my green-eyed fury prevents me from working. Or will drive me into hibernation & more work. Tell T. nothing. He gen-

---

*Maxine Kumin

eralized about the article on water voles he hadn't read, ex-patiating from *PJHH*'s note: Oh, all your stuff, the trouble with it is it's too general. So I won't bother showing him the story on Sweetie Pie I've done, keep the viper out of the household & send it out on my own. My first accepted story would give me intense joy: but even without it, I shall plod on and on, free as I am at present and for a year of the need to work, free as yet of children. Fight last night, he not bothering to perceive how intolerable it is to me to work (ho, have I worked? very little) and feel everything stagnating on my desk, and I lying awake and tense, the air fearfully wet and hot, the sheets damp and heavy. Got up finally and read all of Philip Roth's *Goodbye Columbus*, which except for the first novella I found excellent, rich, and always fascinating, entertaining. Even laughed. Got to bed at 3. Bad sleep. Woke to the same hostile silences. He did make coffee. Banged about. I showered and felt better and in this sweet nauseous thick air am waiting to get mail, rejec-tions, to go to Dr. B. (am very ashamed to tell her of immediate jealousies—the result of my extraprofessional fondness for her, which has inhibited me) and then the Sultans will disarrange the day, and the Booths for dinner. He should be some comfort, he is nice, if almost pathetically serious and earnest.

What to do with anger, ask her. One thing to say: Yes, I want the world's praise, money & love, and am furious with anyone, especially with anyone I know or who has had a similar experience, getting ahead of me. Well, what to do when this surges up and over & over? Last night I knew that Mother didn't matter—she is all for me, but I have dissipated her image and she becomes all editors and publishers and critics and the World, and I want acceptance there, and to feel my work good and well-taken. Which ironically freezes me at my work, corrupts my nunnish labor of work-for-itself-as-its-own-reward. Hit this today.

Learn from Roth. Study, study. Go inward. There it is pure. Or may be, one day.

Shower, keep clean, enjoy colors and animals. People, if possible. How I love the Baskins. The only people I feel are a miracle of humanity and integrity, with no smarm. I MUST WRITE ABOUT THE THINGS OF THE WORLD WITH NO GLAZING. I know enough about love, hate, catastrophe to do so.

Reading V. Woolf's *The Years*. With rain, she can unite a

family, here in London, there in the country, in Oxford. But too disparate. By skipping five, eleven years, and from person to person, suddenly a little girl is in her fifties with gray hair, and so we learn time passes, all moves. But the descriptions, the observations, the feelings caught and let slip.

Dreamt one dream I remember, as apposite and ironical to this morning's mail. Read J. D. Salinger's long *Seymour: An Introduction* last night and today, put off at first by the rant at the beginning about Kafka, Kierkegaard, etc., but increasingly enchanted. Dreamed, oh, how amusedly, that I picked up a *New Yorker*, opened to about the third story (not in the *back*, this was important, but with a whole front page, on the right, to itself) and read "This Earth—That House, That Hospital" in the deeply endearing *New Yorker*–heading type, rather like painstakingly inked hand-lettering. Felt a heart palpitation (my sleep becomes such a reasonable facsimile of my waking life) and thought "That's my title, or a corruption of it." And of course, it is: an alteration of "This Earth Our Hospital" and either a very good or an abominable variation of it. Read on: my own prose: only it was the Sweetie Pie story, the backyard tale, with the would-be Salinger child in it. Dr. B. congratulating me. Mother turning away, saying: "I don't know, I just can't seem to feel anything about it at all." Which shows, I think, that Dr. B. has become my mother. Felt radiant, a *New Yorker* glow lighting my face. Precisely analagous to that young British society girl Susan who, after being deflowered in a canoe house, asks her handsome young deflowerer: Don't I look *Dif*ferent? Oh, I looked different. A pale, affluent nimbus emanating from my generally podgy and dough-colored face.

This morning woke to get a letter in the mail from the estimable Dudley Fitts,* which I numbly translated to be a kind refusal of *The Bull of Bendylaw*, saying I missed "by a whisper," was the alternate, but my lack of technical finish (!) was what deterred him, my roughness, indecision, my drift in all but four or five poems. When my main flaw is a machinelike syllabic death-blow. A real sense of Bad Luck. Will I ever be liked for anything other than the wrong reasons? My book is as finished as it will ever be. And after the *Hudson* acceptance, I have great hopes that all 46 poems will be accepted within a

---

*Editor of The Yale Series of Younger Poets

few months. So what. I have no champions. They will find a lack of this, or that, or something or other. How few of my superiors do I respect the opinions of anyhow? Lowell a case in point. How few, if any, will see what I am working at, overcoming? How ironic, that all my work to overcome my easy poeticisms merely convinces them that I am rough, antipoetic, unpoetic. My God. . . .

. . . Reading in bed. Warm comforts. Began *The Lonely Crowd* this morning, an antidote to V. Woolf's tiresome *The Years*, finished last night. She flits, she throws out her gossamer net. Rose, at age 9, sneaks to the store in the evening alone. Then she is fat, gray-haired, 59, snatching at remarks, lights, colors. Surely this is not Life, not even real life: there is not even the ladies magazine entrance into sustained loves, jealousies, boredoms. The recreation is that of the most superficial observer at a party of dull old women who have never spilt blood. That is what one misses in Woolf. Her potatoes and sausage. What is her love, her childless life, like, that she misses it, except in Mrs. Ramsey, Clarissa Dalloway? Surely if it is valid there, she should not keep losing it to lighting effects followed over the general geographic area of England, which are fine, painstaking, but in the last ditch, school-essay things. Out of this fragmentary welter the best works rise. Of course life is fragmentary, deaf people not hearing the point, lovers laughing at each other over nonsense, but she shows no deeper currents under the badinage.

What to discuss with Dr. B.? Work, desire for work of meaning. To learn German. To write, be a Renaissance woman.

Sunday, May 31. A heavenly, clear, cool Sunday, a clean calendar for the week ahead, and a magnificent sense of space, creative power and virtue. Virtue. I wonder if it will be rewarded. I have written six stories this year, and the three best of them in the last two weeks! (Order: "Johnny Panic and the Bible of Dreams," "The Fifteen Dollar Eagle," "The Shadow," "Sweetie Pie and the Gutter Men," "Above the Oxbow," and "This Earth Our Hospital"). Very good titles. I have a list of even better. Ideas flock where one plants a single seed.

I feel that this month I have conquered my Panic Bird. I am a calm, happy and serene writer. With a pleasant sense of learning and being better with every story, and at the same time the spurred tension that comes from knowing they fall short, in this way or that, from what I see ahead, ten stories, twenty stories from now.

I have done, this year, what I said I would: overcome my fear of facing a blank page day after day, acknowledging myself, in my deepest emotions, a writer, come what may: rejections or curtailed budgets. My best story is "This Earth Our Hospital.". . . Full of humor, highly colored characters, good, rhythmic conversation. An amazing advance from "Johnny Panic," set in the same place, but told all as an essay, with only one or two other characters.

I think of a book, or a book of stories: *This Earth Our Hospital*. That is what I would call it, pray nobody beats me to it. I weep with joy.

Last night I sent off my application from here for a TV writing grant. Oddly enough, it would cause such complications in our plan that I half don't want it, yet it would mean an income, combined, of $10,000 the year. I have an amazingly interesting biography, am young, promising. Why won't they give me one of the five? Money, money. I like CBS, too. They are more inventive than most stations. Another test, like *Mlle*'s June month—only more dangerous: would I pass, keep myself intact? Interesting.

Sent off "Above the Oxbow," which I wrote up from an "exercise" I did last July and which moved me very much, and "This Earth Our Hospital" to *The Atlantic*, a very good contrast. If they don't take the latter story they're crazy. It would be a Best American Short Story.

Amusingly, and significantly, these two stories at *The Atlantic* free me from an overemphasis on the two at *The New Yorker*, which I feel now will probably be rejected. I will have two more and better stories out by the time I hear from *The Atlantic*, and slowly pile them up. I feel to have come, for the first time in my life, to a breakthrough into that placid, creative Wife of Bath humored Sea I only saw in glimpses from a very narrow, reef-crammed strait. The house is clean, polished. My assignments are off, and I have a list of others to begin:

The System & I: a humorous essay about 3 or 4 run-ins with socialized medicine.

The Little Mining Town in Colorado: about a young girl's

plunge into the hothouse world of soap opera while she is bedded with rheumatic fever: relation with her parents and her very strong nurse figure (this suggested by Steve Fassett's account of his nurse, who really didn't want him to get well; he was her life for 15 years and in such a sybaritic, no, no, such a symbiotic relationship pattern found it intolerable when he opposed his will to hers). Point at which soap opera and real worlds fuse, and then separate. . . .

Supper at Frances Minturn Howard's on Mount Vernon Street. The sense of old, subtle elegance. Red plush sofas, tarnished, yet glinting silver tea paper on the walls. Oil miniatures of cousins, Julia Ward Howe background. A supper, light and delectable, of ham, succulent with fat and cloves and crust, asparagus, and a thread-thin noodle cooked in chicken broth and browned with cheese and bread crumbs. Vanilla ice cream, fresh strawberries and finger-size jelly rolls for dessert.

Her garden: a cool white-painted well. Spanish wrought-iron flowerpot holders. A brick flower bed built up all around. Tall, Dutch tulips, just past their prime. Ivy, a fountain with a dolphin. A frog in the shrubbery. Solomon's seal. Bleeding hearts. And the brick walls whitewashed to the height of a room, giving a light, Spanish patio effect. Dutchman's-pipe, or some such vine, forming a lattice of green leaves over the brick wall at the back. A great tree, what is it, those mosquito trees, tree of heaven, plunging up to the light between the buildings. Rum and lemon juice, and the cool elegant plopping of the water. . . .

Jain monks in India; seeable only in 3-month rainy season as they have a vow to move on every night otherwise. Elaborate metaphorical pleas for money and scholarships at Harvard from Poona, Agra, etc. Indian fairy tales, bad translations of the great poets. . . .

I feel in a rug-braiding mood today. Very sleepy, as after a good lovemaking, after all that writing this week. My poems are so far in the background now. It is a very healthy antidote, this prose, to the poems' intense limitations. . . .

A happier sense of life, not hectic, but very slow and sure, than I have ever had. That sea, calm, with sun bland on it. Containing and receiving all the reefy, narrow straits in its great reservoir of peace.

* * *

Saturday, June 13. ... Stayed up till about 3 this morning, feeling again the top of my head would come off, it was so full, so full of knowledge. Found out yesterday, George Starbuck won the Yale. He is sure this proves him the Best. Calling up, "Oh, didn't I tell you?" I had inured myself to a better book than mine, but this seemed a rank travesty. ...

For Dr. B.: It is not *when* I have a baby, but *that* I have one, and more, which is of supreme importance to me. I have always been extremely fond of the definition of Death which says it is: Inaccessability to Experience, a Jamesian view, but so good. And for a woman to be deprived of the Great Experience her body is formed to partake of, to nourish, is a great and wasting Death. After all, a man need physically do no more than have the usual intercourse to become a father. A woman has 9 months of becoming something other than herself, of separating from this otherness, of feeding it and being a source of milk and honey to it. To be deprived of this is a death indeed. And to consummate love by bearing the child of the loved one is far profounder than any orgasm or intellectual rapport. ...

... Read Jean Stafford, so much more human than Elizabeth Hardwick. Hardwick's characters utterly unlikable in any way. A sense of the superior position of writer and reader—even the baby, as Agatha* shrewdly observed, although it only appears for a paragraph, is a nasty louse, unredeemed. Stafford full of color, warmth, humor, even her witches and child-thiefs are human, humorous, part of the world, not small flat cutouts with sticky eyelashes. ...

MENTAL HOSPITAL STORIES: Lazarus theme. Come back from the dead. Kicking off thermometers. Violent ward. LAZARUS MY LOVE.

I feel insufferable impatience. This week my *Bed Book* should be either accepted or rejected by the Atlantic Press. I have sent my revision to Emilie McLeod. After the grim news Starbuck got the Yale, to which I am now resigned, if disappointed in Fitts's judgment, and that Maxine [Kumin] also got a letter from Henry Holt (and how many other women also?) I feel very dubious about wanting to be published by Holt: a pride, a sense that I wouldn't want it unless they put me up

*Stephen Fassett's wife

for the Lamont. If only Knopf accepted my book I'd say hell to the Lamont. Knopf, or Harcourt, Brace or Macmillan (maybe) or Viking. If only [M. L.] Rosenthal would write me about Macmillan. But my book, grim as it is, needs a prize to sell it.

NOW: the story about George, Anne and the children. An insufferable woman (myself of course) gets involved in the separated family. She thinks G. will be fondest of her, tells mad wife (she's *sick*, I mean, really *sick*) it is of course Anne, feels very clever. Then finds out, when A.'s book is accepted, it is really A., gets furious. Calls up . . . or gets sociologist friend to call up Society for Prevention of Cruelty to Children, never really finds out if they get through. Day in park. Children can't speak, finds herself throwing peanuts to pigeons, etc. Ducks, squirrels, children blank-staring and oblivious. Smell bad, girl urinates on bench. I wouldn't be surprised to read tomorrow in the paper how that little girl was *killed* falling from that roof. Of course she never does read any such thing. Her good will perverted, conditional on pity that would generate from self if G. was her lover, when cheated of that, it becomes nasty busybodiness. THE OLYMPIANS. Poor, married poets in Ritz bar. . . .

Ann Peregrine was as methodical about committing suicide as she was about cleaning house.

Tuesday, June 16. A discovery. I'd already discovered it, but didn't know what it meant. A discovery, a name: SADIE PEREGRINE. I had her being Mrs. Whatsis in the beginnings of my Silver Pie-server story. Suddenly she became the heroine of my novel *Falcon Yard*. Oh, the irony. Oh, the character. In the first place: S.P., my initials. Just thought of this. Then, peregrine falcon. Oh, Oh. Let nobody have thought of this. And Sadie: sadistic. La. Wanderer. She is enough, this Sadie Peregrine, to write the novel at Yaddo while I fish for bass. . . .

OUR THIRD WEDDING ANNIVERSARY TODAY. Ted lost our good umbrella (his first wedding present to me was an umbrella, this lost one a different one, about the third, as we have lost several) yesterday in the Book Store while buying our anniversary present to each other: Will Grohmann's *Paul Klee* book. Superb. *The Seafarer* in full color. . . .

* * *

Saturday, June 20. Everything has gone barren. I am part of the world's ash, something from which nothing can grow, nothing can flower or come to fruit. In the lovely words of 20th century medicine, I can't ovulate. Or don't. Didn't this month, didn't last month. For ten years I may have been having cramps and for nothing. I have worked, bled, knocked my head on walls to break through to where I am now. With the one man in the world right for me, the one man I could love. I would bear children until my change of life if that were possible. I want a house of our children, little animals, flowers, vegetables, fruits. I want to be an Earth Mother in the deepest richest sense. I have turned from being an intellectual, a career woman: all that is ash to me. And what do I meet in myself? Ash. Ash and more ash.

I will enter in to the horrible clinical cycle of diagramming intercourse, rushing to be analyzed when I've had a period, when I've had intercourse. Getting injections of this and that, hormones, thyroid, becoming something other than myself, becoming synthetic. My body a test tube. "People who haven't conceived in six months have a problem, dearie," the doctor said. And, taking out the little stick with cotton on the end from my cervix, held it up to his assistant nurse: "Black as black." If I had ovulated it would be green. Same test, ironically, used to diagnose diabetes. Green, the color of life and eggs and sugar fluid. "He found the exact day I ovulated," the nurse told me. "It's a wonderful test, less expensive, easier." Ha. Suddenly the deep foundations of my being are gnawn. I have come, with great pain and effort, to the point where my desires and emotions and thoughts center around what the normal woman's center around, and what do I find? Barrenness.

Suddenly everything is ominous, ironic, deadly. If I could not have children—and if I do not ovulate how can I?—how can they make me?—I would be dead. Dead to my woman's body. Intercourse would be dead, a dead end. My pleasure no pleasure, a mockery. My writing a hollow and failing substitute for real life, real feeling, instead of a pleasant extra, a bonus flowering and fruiting. Ted should be a patriarch. I a mother. My love for him, to express our love, us, through my body, the doors of my body, utterly thwarted. To say I am abnormally pessimistic about this is to say that any woman should face not ovulating with a cavalier grin. Or "a sense of humor." Ha again.

I see no mailman. A lovely clear morning. I cried and cried. Last night, today. How can I keep Ted wedded to a barren woman? Barren barren. His last poem, the title poem of his book, being a ceremony to make a barren woman fertile: "Flung from the chain of the living, the Past killed in her, the Future plucked out." "Touch this frozen one." My god. And his children's book, on the same day as I went to the doctor, yesterday, getting the long, praising letter from T. S. Eliot. *Meet My Folks!* And no child, not even the beginnings or the hopes of one, to dedicate it to. And my *Bed Book*: not accepted yet, but it will be, whether the cloudy McLeod rejects it or not, and I dedicating it to Marty's adopted twins. My god. This is the one thing in the world I can't face. It is worse than a horrible disease. Esther has multiple sclerosis, but she has children....

During the summer, the Hugheses took a trip across America, Sylvia pregnant. On their return they went to the artists' colony, Yaddo, in Saratoga Springs, New York, where Sylvia wrote nearly a third of her first book of poems, The Colossus. They had earlier made the decision to return to England to live and await the birth of their first child.

YADDO

Wednesday, September 16.... Woke out of a warm dream to hear Ted rustling and moving, getting his fishing things together. Dark, more sleep, then the red sun in my eyes, horizontal beams through the dark pines. The faint, brimming nausea gone, which has troubled me the past days. Air clear enough for angels. The wet dews gleaming on the rusty pine needles underfoot, standing on the looped plant stems in pale drops. The great dining room handsome: the dark-beamed ceiling, the high carved chairs and mammoth tables; the terra-cotta plaster in a frieze about the polished woods. Honey oozing out of the comb, steaming coffee on the hot plate. Boiled eggs and butter. Through the leaded windows the green hills melting into blue, and the frost-white marble statues at the garden fountain. I shall miss this grandeur when we move above the garage—the gilded old velvets of pillows, and the glow of worn rich carpets, the indoor fountain, the stained glass, the oil paintings of the Trask children, the moony sea, George Washington.

A terrible depression yesterday. Visions of my life petering out into a kind of soft-brained stupor from lack of use. Disgust with the 17-page story I just finished: a stiff artificial piece about a man killed by a bear, ostensibly because his wife willed it to happen, but none of the deep emotional undercurrents gone into or developed. As if little hygienic transparent lids shut out the seethe and deep-grounded swell of my experience. Putting up pretty artificial statues. I can't get outside myself. Even in the tattoo story I did better: got an outside world. Poems are nowhere:

Outside the window the wet fern

I said to myself yesterday, reading Arthur Miller in Ted's studio, my foot-soles scorching on the stove. I feel a help-lessness when I think of my writing being nothing, coming to nothing: for I have no other job—not teaching, not publishing. And a guilt grows in me to have all my time my own. I want to store money like a squirrel stores nuts. Yet what would money do? We have elegant dinners here: sweetbreads, sausages, bacon and mushrooms; ham and mealy orange sweet potatoes; chicken and garden beans. I walked in the vegetable garden, beans hanging on the bushes, squash, yellow and orange, fattening in the dapple of leaves, corn, grapes purpling on the vine, parsley, rhubarb. And wondered where the solid, confident purposeful days of my youth vanished. How shall I come into the right, rich full-fruited world of middle-age? Unless I work. And get rid of the accusing, never-satisfied gods who surround me like a crown of thorns. Forget myself, myself. Become a vehicle of the world, a tongue, a voice. Abandon my ego. . . .

In the morning light, all is possible; even becoming a god.

Friday, September 25. Again woke to hear Ted readying for fishing. Foolishly griped at being woken: that's enough to make a man kill his wife. Why should he stay in bed soundless till

I choose to stir? Absurd. Yet I woke from a bad dream. Oh, I'm full of them. Keep them to myself or I'll drive the world morbid. I gave birth, with one large cramp, to a normal-sized baby, only it was not quite a five-months baby. I asked at the counter if it was all right, if anything was wrong, and the nurse said: "Oh, it has nest of uterus in its nose, but nothing is wrong with the heart." How is that? Symbolic of smother in the womb? Image of mother dead with the Eye Bank having cut her eyes out. Not a dream, but a vision. I feel self-repressed again. The old fall disease. I haven't done German since I came. Haven't studied art books. As if I needed a teacher's sanction for it.

Spent an hour or so yesterday writing down notes about Yaddo library, for they will close the magnificent mansion this weekend after all the guests come. The famous Board. John Cheever, Robert Penn Warren. I have nothing to say to them. It would not matter if I had a sort of rich inner life, but that is a blank. Would getting a degree help me? I'd have to know a lot more, study, keep juggling my understandings, but why can't I do this on my own? Where is my willpower? The Idea of a life gets in the way of my life. As if my interest in English had crippled me: yet it supports myriads of professors, and they make a life. Always this desperate need to have a job, a work to steady my sense of purpose.

Yesterday, the great thick tiger cat that always waylays us by the garage and bit at Ted the last time we patted it, bit Mrs. Mansion so badly on the hand that she had to go to the hospital. They are going to kill the cat, I think. It is nowhere in sight. Mrs. A. going to kill hers, too, she announced suddenly at supper: "It's cramped my style. She's lived nine years, that's long enough." A queer cold thing for her to come out with suddenly. . . .

Wrote one good poem so far: an imagist piece on the dead snake. Am working on a rambling memoir or Cornucopia. Will try farm story in character of simple girl next: read Eudora Welty aloud. Much more color and world to her than to Jean Stafford, somehow.

Wasps gather and swarm in skylight, then disappear. My flesh crawls. Sun pure through spaces of pines, bright on needles. Crows caw. Birds warble. List incidents for possible stories. Read for poem subjects. Next to snake poem, my book poems *are* all about ghosts and otherworldly miasmas—R. Frost would not take it, I am sure, but I wish they'd hurry and let me know.

Saturday, September 26. . . . Listened to Schwarzkopf singing Schubert lieder last night in the music room. Immensely moved, "Who is Sylvia?" and *"Mein ruh ist hin"* recognizable, words here and there: a strong sense of my own past, from which I am alienated by ignorance of language which I find difficult to break through.

Reading much Eudora Welty, Jean Stafford, must go through Katharine Anne Porter. Read "A Worn Path," "Livvie," "The Whistle" aloud. That is a way to feel on my tongue what I admire. "The Interior Castle" a lurid, terrifying recreation of intolerable pain. . . .

Must get into deep stories where all experience becomes usable to me. Tell from one person's point of view: start with self and extend outwards: then my life will be fascinating, not a glassed-in cage. If only I could break through in one story. "Johnny Panic" too much a fantasy. If only I could get it real.

A dream last night of my father making an iron statue of a deer, which had a flaw in the casting of the metal. The deer came alive and lay with a broken neck. Had to be shot. Blamed father for killing it, through faulty art. Relation to sick cats around here?

K. A. Porter can't speak or eat with people when she is writing. . . .

A horrid priest came to the back door of the mansion yesterday, raw, bright red face looked to have gone under carrot scraper. Black coat, white neckband. Asked for Jim Shannon. I didn't know where he was. He chewed gum of some sort, harrumphed, rubbed some coins together. Asked me to show him and wife (?) around mansion. I grew cold, said I was not authorized to do so. What are you, a writer? A repulsive ignorant and oddly disgusting man. . . .

. . . I am so impatient. Yet the one important thing is to pile up good work. If, IF I could break into a meaningful prose, that expressed my feelings, I would be free. Free to have a wonderful life. I am desperate when I am verbally repressed. Must lure myself into ways and ways of loquacity. . . . My first job to open my real experience like an old wound; then to extend it; then to invent on the drop of a feather, a whole multicolored bird. Study, study one or two *New Yorker*'s. Like the now-prolific Mavis G.

Tuesday, September 29. A smoggy rainy day. Somnolent bird twitters. A weight upon me of the prose solidity of the professional storytellers: something I haven't come near. A lingering breakfast in the garage room: reminiscent of a private dormitory, an institution, a mental home. The waxed linoleum, the straight strawbacked chairs, the ashtrays and bookcases, and mammoth blue-glass grapes. Looked at the two pages of my Pillars story I wrote yesterday and felt disgust at the thinness of them. The glaze again. Prohibiting the density of feeling getting in. I must be so overconscious of markets and places to send things that I can write nothing honest and really satisfying. My feverish dreams are mere figments; I neither write nor work nor study.

Of course I depend on the mirror of the world. I have one poem I am sure of, the snake one. Other than that, no subjects. The world is a blank page. I don't even know the names of the pine trees, and, worse, make no real effort to learn. Or the stars. Or the flowers. Read May Swenson's book yesterday. Several poems I liked: "Snow by Morning" and a fine imagist piece, "At Breakfast," on the egg. Elegant and clever sound effects, vivid images: but in the poem about artists and their shapes, textures and colors, this seems a mere virtuosity with little root. "Almanac" I liked too, about the world's history measured by the moon a hammer made on a thumbnail.

I write as if an eye were upon me. That is fatal. *The New Yorker* rejected my two exercises: as if they knew that's what they were. Are still "considering" Christmas poem, although I am sure they will not take that. The adrenaline of failure. A black hornet sits on the screen, scratching and polishing its yellowed head. Again the rains fall on rooftops the color of a pool table.

If I could cut from my brain the phantom of competition, the ego-center of self-consciousness, and become a vehicle, a pure vehicle of others, the outer world. My interest in other people is too often one of comparison, not of pure intrigue with the unique otherness of identity. Here, ideally, I should forget the outer world of appearances, publishing, checks, success. And be true to an inner heart. Yet I fight against a simplemindedness, a narcissism, a protective shell against competing, against being found wanting.

To write for itself, to do things for the joy of them. What a gift of the gods.

Create Agatha: a mad, passionate Agatha. Immediately I want her husband to keep bees, and I know nothing of bees. My father knew it all.

How much of life I have known: love, disillusion, madness, hatred, murderous passions.

How to be honest. I see beginnings, flashes, yet how to organize them knowledgeably, to finish them. I will write mad stories. But honest. I know the horror of primal feelings, obsessions. A ten-page diatribe against the Dark Mother. The Mummy. Mother of shadows.

An analysis of the Electra complex.

Wednesday, September 30. When I woke this morning in the dark, humid bedroom, hearing the rain beating down on all sides, it seemed to me I was cured. Cured of the shuddering heartbeat which has plagued these last two days so that I could hardly think, or read, for holding my hand to my heart. A wild bird pulsed there, caught in a cage of bone, about to burst through, shaking my whole body with each throb. I began to want to hit my heart, pierce it, if only to stop that ridiculous throb which seemed to wish to leap out of my chest and be gone to make its own way in the world. I lay, warm, my hand between my breasts, cherishing the surfacing from sleep and the peaceful steady unobtrusive beat of my rested heart. I rose, expecting at every moment to be shaken, and indeed I was not. I have been at rest since waking. . . .

Began, just yesterday, two pages about the Mummy. If I can do this honestly. Twenty-page chapters out of nightmare land. Then I will pile them up and think about weird quarterlies to take them. They are absolutely uncommercial: no story line, no steady grammar like Paul Engle chooses to be Best American [short story]. . . . If I can only get some horror into this mother story.

* * *

Saturday, October 3....No poems. The Mummy story dubious. Is it simply feminine frills, is there any terror in it? Would [there] be more if it were real? Set with real externals? As it is, it is the monologue of a madwoman. [No copy of this story has survived.] Dreams: the night before last, a terrible two-day rush to pack for the ship to leave for Europe: missing Ted here, there, the hour passing and me still stuffing odd sweaters and books in my typewriter case. Last night I lived among Jews. Religious service, drinking milk from a gold chalice & repeating a name: the congregation drank milk also at the same time from little cups, I wished they put honey in it. Sitting with three pregnant women. My mother furious at my pregnancy, mockingly bringing out a huge wraparound skirt to illustrate my grossness. P.D.* in this too. Shaving my legs under table: father, Jewish, at head: you will please not bring your scimitar to table. Very odd....

Sunday, October 4. Marilyn Monroe appeared to me last night in a dream as a kind of fairy godmother. An occasion of "chatting" with audience much as the occasion with Eliot** will turn out, I suppose. I spoke, almost in tears, of how much she and Arthur Miller meant to us, although they could, of course, not know us at all. She gave me an expert manicure. I had not washed my hair, and asked her about hairdressers, saying no matter where I went, they always imposed a horrid cut on me. She invited me to visit her during the Christmas holidays, promising a new, flowering life.

Finished the Mummy story, really a simple account of symbolic and horrid fantasies. Then was electrified this morning, when I made an effort to come out of my lethargy and actually wash a pile of laundry and my hair, to read in Jung case history confirmations of certain images in my story. The child who dreamt of a loving, beautiful mother as a witch or animal: the mother going mad in later life, grunting like pigs, barking like dogs, growling like bears, in a fit of lycanthropy. The word "chessboard" used in an identical situation: of a supposedly

*Peter Davison
**A promised meeting with T. S. Eliot

loving but ambitious mother who manipulated the child on the "chessboard of her egotism"; I had used "chessboard of her desire." Then the image of the eating mother, or grandmother: all mouth, as in Red Riding Hood (and I had used the image of the wolf). All this relates in a most meaningful way my instinctive images with perfectly valid psychological analysis. However, I am the victim, rather than the analyst. My "fiction" is only a naked recreation of what I felt, as a child and later, must be true.

Now, forget salable stories. Write to recreate a mood, an incident. If this is done with color and feeling, it becomes a story. So try recollecting: . . . Not to manipulate the experience but to let it unfold and recreate itself with all the tenuous, peculiar associations the logical mind would short-circuit.

Tuesday, October 6. Yesterday very bad oppressed. Heavy skies, gray, but with no release. Spent the day writing a syllabic exercise in delicacy about Polly's* tree. Coy, but rather fun. Read Pound aloud and was rapt. A religious power given by memorizing. Will try to learn a long and a short each day. Best to read them in the morning first thing, review over lunch and catechize at tea. I would have him as a master. The irrefutable, implacable, uncounted uncontrived line. Statement like a whiplash. God.

Of course Henry Holt rejected my book last night with the most equivocal of letters. I wept, simply because I want to get rid of the book, mummify it in print so that everything I want to write now doesn't get sucked in its maw. Ted suggested: start a new book. All right, I shall start with a snake, and simply send out the old book over and over. Also a wordless, even formless rejection of Max Nix, which does bore me. An inexcusable thing. . . .

. . . Is it because the avenue of memory is so painful that I do not walk down it, gray, laden with sorrow, vanished beauties and dreams? The skies and rooftops of Paris, the green Seine, the frieze of the British Museum in London. Once, once I began, all would be well. One story: shall I set a year to work? Then, if all is not reached, a year after that? One story, and I

---

*A woman on the Yaddo staff; Plath was very fond of her.

would have begun. I flit now from one subject to another: the farm? the Mayos? Spain? Paris? I must choose one. The only stories I can bear to reread are "The Wishing Box," "Johnny Panic," "The Mummy" and "The Tattooist." All the others—the Oxbow, the Cornucopia one, the Fifty-Ninth Bear, and Sweetie Pie and the Hospital one—are duller than tears. Begin, begin.

October 10, Saturday. . . . *The New Yorker* accepted the Winter's Tale poem. Felt pleased, especially after *Harper's* rejection.

Feel oddly barren. My sickness is when words draw in their horns and the physical world refuses to be ordered, recreated, arranged and selected. I am a victim of it then, not a master.

Am reading Elizabeth Bishop with great admiration. Her fine originality, always surprising, never rigid, flowing, juicier than Marianne Moore, who is her godmother. . . .

When will I break into a new line of poetry? Feel trite. If only I could get one good story. I dream too much, work too little. My drawing is gone to pot, yet I must remember I always do bad drawings at the first.

German and French would give me self-respect, why don't I act on this?

October 13, Tuesday. Very depressed today. Unable to write a thing. Menacing gods. I feel outcast on a cold star, unable to feel anything but an awful helpless numbness. I look down into the warm, earthy world. Into a nest of lovers' beds, baby cribs, meal tables, all the solid commerce of life in this earth, and feel apart, enclosed in a wall of glass. Caught between the hope and promise of my work—the one or two stories that seem to catch something, the one or two poems that build a little colored island of words—and the hopeless gap between that promise, and the real world of other people's poems and stories and novels. My shaping spirit of imagination is far from me. At least I have begun my German. Painful, as if "part were cut out of my brain." I am of course at fault. Anesthetizing myself again, and pretending nothing is there. There is the curse of this vanity. My inability to lose myself in a character, a situation. Always myself, myself. What good does it do to be published, if I am producing nothing? If only a group of people were more important to me than the idea of a Novel, I might begin a novel. Little artificial stories that get nothing of the feeling, the drama even of life. When they should be realer, more intense than life. And I am prepared for nothing else. Am dead already. Pretend an interest in astrology, botany, which I never follow up. When I go home I must teach myself the tarot pack, the stars, German conversation. Add French to my studying. This comes so natural to some people. Ted is my salvation. He is so rare, so special, how could anyone else stand me! Of course, otherwise I might get a Ph.D., teach in New York, or work at a career. It is hard, with our unplanned drifting, to do much in this way.

Another thing that horrifies me is the way I forget: I once knew Plato well, James Joyce, and so on and so on. If one doesn't apply knowledge, doesn't review, keep it up, it sinks into a Sargasso and encrusts with barnacles. A job that would plunge me in other lives would be a help. A reporter, a sociologist, anything. Maybe in England I will have some luck. They are, in a sense, less "professional" than we are here. More open to the amateur. At least I think so.

I can't reconcile myself to the small time. How easy it is to get ten dollars here and there from *The Christian Science Monitor* for poems and drawings. Two poems accepted this morning: my "exercises" on Yaddo and Magnolia Shoals. Yet I hunger after nebulous vision of success. Publication of my poetry book, my children's book. As if the old god of love I hunted by winning prizes in childhood has grown more mammoth and unsatiable still. Must stop this. Grow enamored of the orange toadstool, the blue mountain, and feel them solid, make something of them. Keep away from editors and writers: make a life outside the world of professionals from which I work.

. . . Take a lesson from Ted. He works and works. Rewrites, struggles, loses himself. I must work for independence. Make him proud. Keep my sorrows and despairs to myself. Work and work for self-respect: study language, read avidly. Work, not expect miracles to follow on a hastily written nothing.

October 19, 1959, Monday. Most of my trouble is a recession of my old audacity, unself-conscious brazenness. A self-hypnotic state of boldness and vigor annihilates my lugubrious oozings of top-of-the-head matter. I tried Ted's "exercise": deep-breathing, concentration on stream-of-conscious objects, these last days, and wrote two poems that pleased me. One a poem to Nicholas,* and one the old father-worship subject. But different. Weirder. I see a picture, a weather, in these poems. . . . The main thing is to get rid of the idea [that] what I write now is for the old book. That soggy book. So I have three poems for the new, temporarily called *The Colossus and Other Poems*.

Involvement with Mavis Gallant. Her novel on a daughter-mother relation, the daughter committing suicide. A novel, brazen, arrogant, would be a solution to my days, to a year of life. If I did not short-circuit by sitting judgment as I wrote, always rejecting before I open my mouth. The main concern: a character who is not myself—that becomes a stereotype, mournful, narcissistic.

A beautiful blue day. Pure soul weather. Frosty, and my Harcourt form rejection. Ted says: You are so negative. Gets cross, desperate. I am my own master. I am a fool to be jealous of phantoms. Should maunder in my own way. These three new poems are heartening. Yesterday not so good—too linked to the prose vision of the garden in my Mummy story. Must not wait for mail for it ruins the day. Work without vision of world's judgment. I shall do it yet.

Another thing: to stop concern only with own "position" in world. Another phantom. I am. That is enough. I have a good way of looking I can develop if only I forget about an audience.

Ted is the ideal, the one possible person.

Worked on German for two days, then let up when I wrote poems. Must keep on with it. It is hard. So are most things worth doing.

Immerse self in characters, feelings of others—not to look at them through plate glass. Get to the bottom of deceptions, emotions.

The florid cinnamon-scented oil-colored world of St.-John Perse.

Old wish to get reward for elimination. That is evident. Old

---

*The child she was expecting turned out to be Frieda; Nicholas was born two years later.

rivalry with brother. All men are my brothers. And competition is engrained in the world. Separate baby and poem from decay and rot. They are made, living, good-in-themselves, and very keepable. Children might humanize me. But I must rely on them for nothing. Fable of children changing existence and character as absurd as fable of marriage doing it. Here I am, the same old sourdough. Eight years till I am thirty-five; I should work in that time: stories, *New Yorker* or otherwise. A novel. A children's book. With joy and renaissance enthusiasm. It is possible. Up to me.

October 22, Thursday. A walk today before writing, after breakfast. The sheer color of the trees: caves of yellow, red plumes. Deep breaths of still frosty air. A purging, a baptism. I think at times it is possible to get close to the world, to love it. Warm in bed with Ted I feel animal solaces. What is life? For me it is so little ideas. Ideas are tyrants to me: the ideas of my jealous, queen-bitch superego: what I should, what I ought.

Ambitious seeds of a long poem made up of separate sections: Poem on [her] birthday. To be a dwelling on madhouse, nature: meanings of tools, greenhouses, florists shops, tunnels, vivid and disjointed. An adventure. Never over. Developing. Rebirth. Despair. Old women. Block it out.

This paragraph is the origin of Plath's poem "Blue Moles."

Two dead moles in the road. One about ten yards from the other. Dead, chewed of their juices, caskets of shapeless smoke-blue fur, with the white, clawlike hands, the human palms, and the little pointy corkscrew noses sticking up. They fight to the death Ted says. Then a fox chewed them.

The shed of the hydraulic ram. Black, glistening with wet: gouts of water. And the spiderwebs, loops and luminous strings, holding the whole thing up to the rafters. Magic, against principles of physics.

No mail. Who am I? Why should a poet be a novelist? Why not?

Dream, shards of which remain: my father come to life again. My mother having a little son: my confusion: this son of mine is a twin to her son. The uncle of an age with his nephew. My brother of an age with my child. Oh, the tangles of that old bed.

Drew a surgical picture of the greenhouse stove yesterday and a few flowerpots. An amazing consolation. Must get more intimate with it. That greenhouse is a mine of subjects. Watering cans, gourds and squashes and pumpkins. Beheaded cabbages inverted from the rafters, wormy purple outer leaves. Tools: rakes, hoes, brooms, shovels. The superb identity, selfhood of things.

To be honest with what I know and have known. To be true to my own weirdnesses. Record. I used to be able to convey feelings, scenes of youth; life so complicated now. Work at it.

October 23, Friday. Yesterday: an exercise begun, in grimness, turning into a fine, new thing: first of a series of madhouse poems. October in the toolshed. Roethke's influence, yet mine. Ted's criticisms absolutely right. Mentioned publishing poetry to [Malcolm] Cowley last night: his wry, tragic grimace told me: he's seen my book, or heard of it, and rejected or will reject it. Dream of Luke's painting: florid, elegant ballade landscape in silvered blues and greens of peasant Corsican nativity with Adam and Eve leaning out of the long grass to look. A luminous pink-white light on the scalloped and easy leaves, round caverns of pale blue shadow. Fine, welcoming letter from an editor at Heinemann on seeing my *London Magazine* poems, which begin the magazine: hope springs. England offers new comforts. I could write a novel there. So I say, so I say. Without this commercial American superego. My tempo is British. Wet, wet walk with Ted. Blue drippings, dulled green lakes, dim yellow reflections.

November 1, Sunday. A wet, fresh air, gray skies. All the colors of the last weeks dulled to smoke-purple and blunt umbers. Dreamed several nights ago of having a five-months (born at five months?) old blond baby boy named Dennis riding, facing me, my hips, a heavy sweet-smelling child. The double amazement: that he was so beautiful and healthy and so little trouble. Ted claims this is a rebirth of my deep soul. Auspicious. Dreamed last night a confused dream of two youths, juvenile delinquents, on a dark lawn in front of our old Winthrop house, throwing our saucepan of milk out. In a fury, I flew at one and actually started tearing him apart with my teeth and hands. The other had said he was going into the house, and I thought he would ruin it and hurt Mother. (Triggered by seeing the children out for Halloween last night, the gang of adolescents?)

I wonder about the poems I am doing. They seem moving, interesting, but I wonder how deep they are. The absence of a tightly reasoned and rhythmed logic bothers me. Yet frees me. . . .

Feel unlike writing anything today. A horror that I am really at bottom uninterested in people: the reason I don't write stories. Only a few psychological fantasias. Know very little about lives of others. Polly's ghost. The old superintendent standing at the foot of his bed in full moonlight holding a baby. She later finding a picture of him in same posture, holding a lamb.*

Get out big botany book at home. What an inertia has overcome me: a sense of fatality: the difficulty of learning out of school.

Ted's dreams about killing animals: bears, donkeys, kittens. Me or the baby? Starting to type his play. Ill-advised, said yesterday wished it were realistic. Of course, I want a Broadway hit in my cheap surface mind, an easy street. He has revised and really improved the children's book *Meet My Folks!* I feel we must find a publisher here, yet the macabre is so outside our tradition. There again, the real world must give the wonder. My *Bed Book* will probably fail because of no human, or child, interest—no plot. . . .

Wednesday, November 4. Paralysis again. How I waste my days. I feel a terrific blocking and chilling go through me like anesthesia. I wonder, will I ever be rid of Johnny Panic? Ten years from my successful *Seventeen* [publication], and a cold voice says: What have you done, what have you done? When I take an equally cold look, I see that I have studied, thought, and somehow not done anything more than teach a year: my

---

*Babies and lambs were part of Plath's own system of correspondences. At this stage of her pregnancy, she had morning sickness.

mind lies fallow. I don't look forward to a life of reading, and rereading, with no mentor or pupil but myself. I have written one or two unpleasant psychological stories: "Johnny Panic" and "The Mummy," which might well justify printing, a light tour de force about the tattooist, and that is all since Sunday at the Mintons' seven years ago. Where is that fine, free arrogant careless rapture? A cold mizzle of despair settles down on me when I try to think even of a story.

Miraculously I wrote seven poems in my Poem for a Birthday sequence, and the two little ones before it, "The Manor Garden" and "The Colossus," I find colorful and amusing. But my manuscript of my book seems dead to me. So far off, so far gone. It has almost no chance of finding a publisher: just sent it out to the seventh, and unless Dudley Fitts relents this year and gives me the Yale award, which I just missed last year, there is nothing for it but to try to publish it in England and forget prizes, which might well be a good thing. I think I should try the Yales, therefore hope I won't get it accepted as an entry to the Lamont, which I have even less chance of winning—that would cancel both. Comparing it to [Philip] Booth's book, [Ned] O'Gorman's book, etc., and Starbuck's, I do feel I am not without merit.

I shall perish if I can write about no one but myself. Where is my old bawdy vigor and interest in the world around me? I am not meant for this monastery living. Find always traces of passive dependence: on Ted, on people around me. A desire even while I write poems about it, to have someone decide my life, tell me what to do, praise me for doing it. I know this is absurd. Yet what do I do about it?

If I can't build up pleasures in myself: seeing and learning about painting, old civilizations, birds, trees, flowers, French, German—what shall I do? My wanting to write books annihilates the original root impulse that would have me bravely and blunderingly working on them. When Johnny Panic sits on my heart, I can't be witty, or original, or creative.

... Writing is my health; if I could once break through my cold self-consciousness and enjoy things for their own sake, not for what presents and acclaim I may receive. Dr. B. was right: I avoid doing things, because if I do not do them, I can't be said to fail at them. A coward's custard. ...

Pleasant dream of return to London: renting a room with

the bed in a garden of daffodils, waking to soil smells and bright yellow flowers.

November 7, 1959, Saturday. Despair. Impasse. I had a vision last night of our swimming in the Salt Lake: a solid beautiful thing. I thought: this light, this sensation is part of no story. It is a thing in itself and worthy of being worked out in words. If I could do that, get back the old joy, it would not matter what became of it. The problem is not my success, but my joy. A dead thing.

My Mummy story came back from *New World Writing* with a mimeographed rejection. It is a very bitter, often melodramatic story, simply an account. I have built up my old brother-rivalry praise-seeking impulses to something amounting to a great stone god-block. Ten years after my first talent-burst on the world, when everything flowed supplely to my touch. I could create the Mintons* seven years ago because I forgot myself in them.

Dangerous to be so close to Ted day in day out. I have no life separate from his, am likely to become a mere accessory. Important to take German lessons, go out on my own, think, work on my own. Lead separate lives. I must have a life that supports me inside. This place a kind of terrible nunnery for me. I hate our room: the sterile white of it, the beds filling the whole place. Loved the little crowded Boston apartment, even though J. Panic visited me there.

What horrifies me most is the idea of being useless: well-educated, brilliantly promising, and fading out into an indifferent middle-age. Instead of working at writing, I freeze in dreams, unable to take disillusion of rejections. Absurd. I am inclined to go passive, and let Ted be my social self. Simply because we are never apart. Now, for example: the several things I can do apart from him: study German, write, read, walk alone in the woods or go to town. How many couples could stand to be so together? The minute we get to London I must strike out on my own. I'd be better off teaching than writing a couple of mediocre poems a year, a few mad, self-centered stories. Reading, studying, "making your own mind" all by oneself is just not my best way. I need the reality of

---

*Plath's early prize-winning story

other people, work, to fulfill myself. Must never become a mere mother and housewife. Challenge of baby when I am so unformed and unproductive as a writer. A fear for the meaning and purpose of my life. I will hate a child that substitutes itself for my own purpose: so I must make my own. Ted is weary of my talk of astrology and tarot and wanting to learn, and then not bothering to work on my own. I'm tired of it too. And tired of the terrific drifting uncertainty of our lives. Which, I suppose, from his point of view, is not at all uncertain, for his vocation of writing is so much stronger than mine.

My poems pall. A jay swallows my crumbs on the wet porch. My head is a batallion of fixes. I don't even dare open Yeats, Eliot—the old fresh joys—for the pain I have remembering my first bright encounters. Less able to lose myself. And myself is the more suited for quick losing.

Independent, self-possessed M.S. Ageless. Bird-watching before breakfast. What does she find for herself? Chess games. My old admiration for the strong, if lesbian, woman. The relief of limitation as a price for balance and surety....

November 11, Wednesday. I only write here when I am at wits' end, in a cul-de-sac. Never when I am happy. As I am today....

Felt warm in my tweeds, pleasantly fat-stomached. The baby is a pleasure to dream on. My panics are seldom. If only I can get a doctor I trust, firm, capable and kind, and a hospital where I will know what is going on, I shall be all right. It can't last much more than 24 hours. And if the baby is sound and healthy....

Woodpile: cut limbs, heartwood pink as salmon, great fraying shards of bark. Textures of rough and smooth.

I am eager to leave here. 11 weeks is too much. Ted loves it though. If I were writing a novel it would be okay. But even then, I like the bother and stimulus of ordinary life, friends, plays, town-walking, etc. Dry grasses and blue woodsmoke sailing by my window. I'd like to work in London. A novel, a novel. I'd send it to a British publisher first. Feel my first book of poems should be published, however limited. I wrote a good poem this week on our walk Sunday to the burnt-out spa. A second book poem. How it consoles me, the idea of a second book with these new poems: "The Manor Garden," "The Colossus," "The Burnt-out Spa," the seven Birthday poems, and perhaps "Medallion," if I don't stick it in my present book. If I were accepted by a publisher for the Lamont, I would feel a need to throw all my new poems in to bolster the book. For the Yales* I do not feel such a need. Well, three months till the Yales open.

Excited about practical matters of packing and traveling, seeing people. I hate our room here: white, surgical, a hospital. Have, in two months, written three stories, none very satisfactory, about ten or twelve good new poems, a bad, impossible children's book. When I am off alone I become more inhuman. Need width of interests, stimulus, demands. Distractions, yes. The fight to go to two good movies here ridiculous: there is the big station wagon they won't use. To live in city or country. I am excited about England. When I think of living in America, I just can't imagine where: hate suburbs, country too lonely, city too expensive and full of dog turds. I can imagine living in London, in a quiet square, taking children to the fine parks. Moving to country right outside, still being near. Every day life begins anew.

November 12, Thursday. A note only. My optimism rises. No longer do I ask the impossible. I am happy with smaller things, and perhaps that is a sign, a clue.... Last night found out Lehmann accepted my story "This Earth Our Hospital." Have changed the title to "The Daughters of Blossom Street." A much better thing. This is satisfying. The story is amateurish in very many ways, but not too thin in texture. I'm putting my old things, the thin ones, out of circulation. Skipped back from the garage in the blue light of a fuzzy moon, a warmish, windy night. Finished the blue mole poem yesterday to our satisfaction. Every day is a renewed prayer that the god exists, that he will visit with increased force and clarity. I want to write about people, moving situations. If only I could combine the humorous verve of my two recently accepted stories with the serious prose style of the Mintons [story], I should be pleased.... If only I could break through my numb cold glib-

---

*Yale Younger Poets series

ness that comes when I try to make a declarative sentence. Color it up, thicken it.

. . . Keep a notebook of physical events. My visit to the tattoo shop and my job at the hospital supplied me with two good stories. So should my Boston experience. If only I can go deep enough. A party at Agatha's, Starbuck's wife. The gardens. Oh, God, how good to get it all. Slowly, slowly catch the monkey. Small doses of acceptance help. Perhaps telling stories to children will help me do a few books there. . . .

. . . Last night . . . the girls: the elder, ageless, with dark, old-maidish bun, skinny, flat chested, short, with flat black shoes and a nondescript beige dress with maroon velvet belt. . . . Glasses, a bright, luminous face, a speech instructor: "Oh, Mr. Binkerd, the music sets such a *mood*!" The other, younger, arty, quite pretty with delicately heeled blue shoes, a loose fashionable hairdo, blue-shadowed eyes, glasses also, a stylish gray-blue sweater and skirt, a silver Mexican necklace, elaborate, in good taste. Sultry manner. Teaches weaving and jewelry making. May [Swenson] in the other room: freckled, in herself, a tough little nut. I imagined the situation of two lesbians: the one winning a woman with child from an apparently happy marriage. Why is it impossible to think of two women of middle-age living together without lesbianism the solution, the motive?

November 14, Saturday. A good walk this morning. Got up in time for breakfast at 8 and the mail came early as if to reward us. Warm blowy gray weather. Odd elation. Note this. Whenever we are about to move, this stirring and excitement comes, as if the old environment would keep the sludge and inertia of the self, and the bare new self slip shining into a better life. . . .

We walked out on the bland, sandy track. Pale purple and bluish hills melted in the gray distance. The black twiggy thickets of the bare treetops. Leaves rattled in the wind. A black bird flew up to a bow. Burnt corncobs, old corn stalks. A black flapping scarecrow on crossed staves made out of a man's tattered coat and a pair of faded, whitened dungarees. Waved vacant arms.

Saw dogs, two, tongues hanging, exploring a copse of saplings and bracken. The yellow-brown, dessicated color of the land. Found cartridge shells. Fox tracks, deer prints in the soft sand. The green, brilliant underbed of the lakes. Molehills and tunnels webbing the Yaddo lawn. Felt into a hole, both ways, with my finger after breaking into the tunnel.

Wrote an exercise on mushrooms yesterday which Ted likes. And I do too. My absolute lack of judgment when I've written something: whether it's trash or genius.

Exhausted today after several late nights. Fit to write nothing. Dreams last night troubled: Mother and Warren in puritanical, harsh, snoopy poses. I bit her arm (repeat of my biting the delinquent), and she was old, thin, ever-watchful. Warren discovering me about to bed with someone whose name was Partisan Review. Old shames and guilts.

But a sense of joy and eagerness at living in England. Partly, too, because of the recent hospitality my poems, and my story, have found there. Much closer to my mind.

November 15, Sunday. Have had a series of bad, sleepless nights. The coming unsettling? As a result, tired, without force, full of a sour lassitude. Late last night made the mistake of having coffee, thinking it would keep me awake for the movie. We didn't go, and I lay in a morbid twit till the hollow dark of the morning, full of evil dreams of dying in childbirth in a strange hospital unable to see Ted, or having a blue baby, or a deformed baby, which they wouldn't let me see.

My one salvation is to enter into other characters in stories: the only three stories I am prepared to see published are all told in first person. The thing is, to develop other first persons. My Beggars story a travesty: sentimental, stiff, without any interest at all. And the horror is that there *was* danger, interest. Slangy language is one way of breaking my drawing room inhibitions. Have I learned anything since college writing days? Only in poetry. There I have.

Ted's good story on the caning. Very fine, very difficult. He advances, unencumbered by any fake image of what the world expects of him. Last night, consoling, holding me. Loving made my nerves melt and sleep. I woke drained, as after a terrible emotional crisis. Today am good for little. Submerged in reviews of reviews. How good is it to read other people? Of other people? Read their stories, their poems, not reviews.

I am well away from the world of critics and professors. Must root in life itself. Yet Iris Murdoch has a brilliant professorial intellect operating in her work. Mesmerize myself into forgetting the waiting world. The IDEAS kill the little green shoots of the work itself. I have experienced love, sorrow, madness, and if I cannot make these experiences meaningful, no new experience will help me.

A bad day. A bad time. State of mind most important for work. A blithe, itchy eager state where the poem itself, the story itself is supreme.

In December the Hugheses left for England, where they planned to live in London. Frieda Rebecca was born at home in London in April 1960. Plath signed a contract with Heinemann for the publication of her first collection of poems, The Colossus, *and the book was published in October. In early 1961 she suffered a miscarriage and underwent an appendectomy shortly thereafter—her notes on her stay in the hospital have survived as the following piece, "The Inmate."*

THE INMATE

Monday, February 27, 1961. In Hospital. Still whole, I interest nobody. I am not among the cheerful smilers in plaster and bandages or the bubbling moaners behind the glass and pink wood partition. The sad, mustachioed doctor and his bright white starchy students pass me by. This is a religious establishment, great cleansings take place. Everybody has a secret. I watch them from my pillows, already exhausted. The fat girl in glasses walks by, testing her new leg, the noseless old woman, with her foot strung up in "traction," the lady with the sour face, chest and arm in plaster, scratches herself inside with a stick. "My skin's ruckled up." They'll cut her out Thursday. A helpful inmate in a red wool bathrobe brings the flowers back, sweet-lipped as children. All night they've been breathing in the hall, dropping their pollens, daffodils, pink and red tulips, the hot purple and red-eyed anemones. Potted plants for the veterans. Nobody complains or whines. In the black earphones hung on my silver bedstead a tiny voice nags me to listen. They won't unplug him. Immensely cheerful pink, blue and yellow birds distribute themselves among flowers, primarily pink, and simpering greenery on the white bed-curtains. It is like an arbor when they close me in. Last night I got lost in the wet, black Sunday streets of Camden Town, walking resolutely in the wrong direction. I asked an old woman getting out of a car where the St. Pancras Hospital was: she asked her old husband—he said: "It's a bit complicated. I better drive you there." I got into the back seat of the old comfortable car and burst into tears. "I'd rather have a baby," I say, "at least you've got something for it." "That's what we all say," said the woman. The man angled the car through obscure, black glistening streets to the hospital. I stumbled through the rain, my bang in wet hanks plastered to my forehead. The admissions office was shut. I walk down a long brilliantly lit hall and a boy in brown takes me to Ward 1 in the elevator. The nurse asks me questions and fills out a form. I want to answer more questions, I love questions. I feel a blissful slumping into boxes on forms. The lady next to me has a bandage under her neck— they found in a chest X-ray that her thyroid had grown into her lung and cut it out. Now, curtains drawn round her bed, an occupational therapist sounds to be hitting her: a-slap-a-slap-a-slap. All kinds of equipment is ferried by—vacuum cleaners, stepladders, instruments for tipping up one end of the bed, a large aluminum box on wheels which is plugged into the wall—I think it is a hot-box for the steamed lunches. Last night I felt too sick for supper—had only a cup of Ovaltine, got into my nightdress behind flowered curtains. A young, attractively lean Doctor "Cahst" came round and asked me symptom questions. Put an exclamation after the observation that I might be pregnant again. Cold air blows down from the tall window on my head. The thyroid woman coughs dryly behind her curtain. A pretty young sociable woman named Rose came to chat with me last night, introduced me to a lively black-haired lady in diaphanous pale blue nightgown named "Bunny" who had "been in Boston," another bright lady whose husband studied locusts in Africa—they both had malaria; he owns some zoo in South Devon to which he sent animals in pairs. Tried vacantly to read *The Paris Review*. A red and a white pill slowly dragged me into a fog. "Lights out" at nine.

The round globed ward lights switched to red—8 red cutout circles in the twilight—light lingered everywhere. Good night, good night, bedmates said, and reduced themselves to humps. I considered asking that my curtains be drawn, but then shut my eyes and found with surprising pleasure I had my own curtains which I could shut at will. Woken out of a shallow sleep at 5 by a bustle, creaking, running of water and clanking of buckets. At six, in the wan wet gray, the white lights came on. Tea, temperatures, pulse. I washed, swabbed my privates with a blue antiseptic and urinated obligingly in a glass jar. Later they swabbed my nose to see if I was "carrying any germs to infect wounds." Breakfast at 7:30. Thin brown bread scraped penuriously with butter (or some substitute) so only a faint glaze testified to which side was the right side for the orange marmalade; tea, a shallow bowl of smoky saltless gruel, bacon and tomatoes (very good) and more tea. Bad, dreggy fusty coffee midmorning. Paper boy, chocolate and cigarette cart. Green graphs on polished aluminum clipboards hooked to the foot of each bed.

Tuesday, February 28. Today is the day. Amid the chatter and breakfasting of all the other patients I alone am quiet and without food. Yet I feel curiously less worried about losing my appendix than being electrocuted. The gently-spoken gray lady at my right, "Duchess," or "Mrs. Mac," goes home today. She goes to Harrow by ambulance, her frail form stooped now over a bowl of cornflakes in her white crocheted shawl. I feel slightly sick after all this waiting, but here where everyone is amiable with gracious smiles, it is impossible to indulge in mopes or self-pity, a very good thing. Last night a young nurse shaved me with exceedingly scratchy strokes, exposing that old mole that grew on the left when I was pregnant. Today, after a sleeping pill, I woke when the nurse took my temperature and pulse. Had tea and buttered toast at 6:30. Then they took away my water and my milk. "Bunny," "Daisy," Jane, Rose. The goiter lady (her thyroid grew into her lung) on my left had a "pounding" yesterday—her bed raised at the foot and she pummeled "to loosen the phlegm," Daisy said interestedly. I too as the latest operative case, am of interest. Was I shaved? Will I have an enema? And so on. Ted came last night. Precisely one minute after 7.30 a crowd of shabby, short, sweet peering people was let into the ward—they fluxed in familiar directions, bringing a dark-coated handsome shape twice as tall as all of them. I felt as excited and infinitely happy as in the early days of our courtship. His face, which I daily live with, seemed the most kind and beautiful in the world. He brought an air letter from *The New Yorker* for me with a $100 contract for letting them have "first reading" of all my poems for a year! The date of the letter was that of our first meeting at the *Botolph* party 5 years ago. He brought steak sandwiches and apricot tarts and milk and fresh-squeezed orange juice—I felt afterwards that if I said, "For him—he will be on the other side," I could go through anything with courage—or at least reasonable fortitude.

Later—10 A.M.—now I'm really prepared for the slaughter—robed loosely in a pink and maroon striped surgical gown, a gauze turban and a strip of adhesive shuts off the sight of my wedding ring. The lithe nurse was snippy when I asked how long the operation took. Oblivion approaches. Now I'm close enough, I open my arms. I asked to have my flowered curtains left drawn—the privilege of a condemned prisoner—I don't want the curious gossipy well-meaning ladies peering for signs of fear, stupor or whatever. Evidently a lady went out on a trolley a few minutes back—"Was she asleep?" "She looked asleep, she just lay there." Now they've given me the first injection—which will "dry my mouth, make me feel drunk and so I don't care what happens." A handsome lady anesthetist came in and told me about the details of *that*. My arm is swollen—right upper—a bee sting, red and hard to the touch. I feel a bubbly drowsiness take my heart and so shall only write in here after it's over—a letter from Ted reached me—my dear dear love.

Friday, March 3. Three days since my operation and I am myself again: the tough, gossipy, curious enchanting entity I have not been for so long. The life here is made up of details. Petty pleasures and petty annoyances. Tuesday I was so drugged I knew nothing and nothing bothered me. Wednesday the drugs wore off and I felt sick and resentful of the lively health of the ward. Yesterday I felt tired and so-so. Today I threw off my fetters—got up to wash and had my first laborious goat-shit, changed my hospital pink and red flapping jacket which left my bum bare to my frilly pink and white Victorian nightgown. They just wheeled one of the new women by on a stretcher— the muscular lime-green porter loaded her on the trolley—the queer flat shape of a drugged body—the white turban, green blankets, eyes staring up, dumbly. The other night, they say, "Thelma died." I vaguely remember a lady in a yellow gown, youngish, wheeling the tea round. "She died after her op." Outdoors it is sunny, smelling of wet sweet earth. A few stray airs filter in the windows. I remember luxuriating in these blowing airs on my first night when I lay wakeful after a day of sleep yet deeply drugged and invulnerable—it blew sweetly over the sleeping forms and stirred the curtains.

Annoyances & sorrows: The window above my bed was broken—cracked. First, before my op, a cold wet air laid itself on my head like a nasty poultice. Then, the day after my op, two men came to fix the window. My bed was wheeled out into mid-corridor. I felt unsettled, vulnerable. I was bumped. My side hurt. The fat girl in the wheelchair gave my dresser (locker) a great bump which jarred my bed. My side hurt. I slunk deeper into my pillows, exposed to strange peerers at the far end of the ward on all sides. I thought. "Everybody going by bumps me," I said to the nurse after an hour. "I'd rather have the draft. I have to use the bedpan." Chagrined, they had to wheel me back. When the workmen returned they were told to come back at one. They did come in visiting hours & move me out, but Ted was there so I didn't care. *Vacuuming:* They vacuum all day—little frizzy-haired tasty fat lugubrious women mooching up the overnight dust—wooz-wooz. Then the bump and the jingle of *trolleys*—bedpan trolleys, mouthwash trolleys, breakfast trolleys, tea trolleys, medicine trolleys. They thump on the floor & rattle. Then the *typewriter*: Hooknosed witch with the two crooked canes and green dressing gown put out a huge black old-fashioned monster typewriter on the table in front of my bed. Bank-bonk-clatter-clatter, the worst curse— an unsteady typist. "I'm not ready to go back to the office yet," I said. *Snoring*: The worst horror of all. I am next to the ward snorer. The first night she came I was too drugged to hear her, but Wednesday morning a nurse laughingly remarked on it. That night I lay & tossed & ached till midnight: the stentorious roar echoed & magnified itself. The nurse with her flashlight said I couldn't have another sleeping pill so soon—she pulled the flowered curtain, woke the snorer up and turned her over, made me some hot Ovaltine. Then the night sister came round with a second big blue pill which took me away in a warm bliss through all the petty bustle and noise from 5–10 A.M. (Now the stretcher with its two green plastic pillows comes in again for the neighbor of the first woman in Bed 9. Green blankets. She looks just like the other woman—her eyes staring at the ceiling.) Last night I went to sleep before the old woman started to snore but woke with a start before 3 A.M. to hear her roaring. Got up to go to bathroom in a daze and grunted. Nothing happened. They finally made me some Ovaltine and gave me two codeines which cut the sharp pang of my scar and the shooting gripes of wind in my bowels. I put the pillow over my head to shut out the noise and so woke at 7. Another peeve is that there are no bells to ring for the nurses—one has to rise on one elbow—mine are pink and raw from hauling myself up—and shout "Nurse" hoarsely. How a really sick person does, I don't know.

Sunday, March 5. The fifth day after my op. I have been lazy about writing in here. I feel fine now: an old soldier. Still with my stitches in and something to talk about. The stitches pull and twitch ("My mendings itch") but I demand codeine. Rose of the blue robe and white-haired "Granny" with the awful bloodshot crossed eyes, impressively black with iodine or some such when I came in, are going home today. Rose forgot her skirt so keeps her robe on—a Symbol, that of the desire to be "one of us." A dressed person, a person dressed for the street, is a bother here—not "one of us," a sort of masquerader. Rose wheels the trolley of flower vases about and distributes them—each glass vase or china pitcher is numbered with the bed number of the patient on a bit of adhesive. The nurse just walked by with the square white cardboard spittoons. I shall have a story out of this, beginning "Tonight I deserve a blue light, I am one of them"—describing the shock of entering this queer highly rhythmical and ordered society as a stranger, an outsider, attuning oneself to the ward vibrations, undergoing the "initiation"—the real central common yet personal experience, and recovering in harmony. As soon as one is well, too well, one is excluded, "unpopular"—the violet-gowned Miss Stapleton immediately to my left has relapsed. Her thyroid or goiter scar has healed, but she lies mouth open and eyes shut—her leg has swollen and hurts, she has phlebitis. She is going to a convalescent home after this. So is the lady with jaundice three beds down to my left next to Gran. She is bright yellow, has been "opened" innumerable times and is going to Clacton-on-the-Sea—to a convent convalescent home where the nuns bake their own bread and do up tasty dishes. "The Salt air does you good," I say. I face Helga's* pot of tulips and Charles's** dying iris and daffodils. "That yellow stuff's lasted well," Daisy says of Miss Stapleton's bouquet. "For-sigh-thia," drawls Maury with the pain-set face and tart tongue. She told me she'll never be able to move her arm, just her fingers. Now it is 1:40 P.M. Sunday afternoon. I have desperately washed, powdered my sallow bandaged body, combed my greasy hair—feel shoddily in need of a shampoo. Bunny and Joan are talking about the difference between "black African" and "white Afrikaans." The nurses are "tidying" beds before visiting hours. To my own surprise I am allowed to go out and sit on a park bench in the sun with Ted and the pooker [Frieda] as I did yesterday all afternoon; I am immensely fond of all the nurses in their black and white pin-striped dresses, white aprons and hats and black shoes and stockings. Their youth is the chief beauty about them—youth, absolute starched cleanliness and a comforting tidying-up and brow-smoothing air. The routine, even with the quite short night's sleep (about 10–6 if lucky—swimming to it through Mrs. John's snores and clutching it through the nurses' morning bustle and glassy clatter) I feel more fresh and rested than I have for months. I am above the "sick level" of the place so I have an extra advantage—although I slightly cancel it by much bedside visiting and gossiping. I feel so fresh and peaceful now, in spite of a slight shiver at the thought of my stitches coming out—it is like a diverting holiday—my *first* since the baby was born almost a year ago: quite bracing. All morning talked to Jay Wynn across the way about her office and private life and nervous breakdown—cannot congratulate

---

*Helga Huws, wife of Ted's Cambridge friend Daniel Huws
**Charles Montieth, editor at Faber & Faber

myself too much on this confidence because I blabbed about my own breakdown and misapplied shock treatment. Shall outline her account after I come in tonight. Ted is actually having a rougher time than I—poor love sounded quite squashed yesterday: "How do you do it all?... The pooker makes an astonishing amount of pots to wash.... She wets a lot" and "I seem to be eating mostly bread!" I felt needed and very happy and lucky. My life—as I compare it to those in the ward about me—is so fine—everything but money and a house—love and all. A sunny day. HOT. The radiator at my back makes me sweat—I should have listed it among annoyances. The windows—the three bay windows on the far side of the ward— are white and dazzling with sun. Dark green blinds, dulled moonbulbs.

7:45 P.M., twilight. Low voices, sleepy breathers. I was going to sleep till pill-time, but the sight of the old woman's hands clutching the...bow-shaped...pull-up bar on its curiously heavy iron "prison chain" stopped me. Those gnarled white roots of hands. Mrs. Fry was evidently run over by a car on some Friday or other—latest news is that she insisted on being moved to this hospital—nearer her home—from another.... She moans, yells, curses. "You devil! You're trying to murder me"...over pills, or moving down in bed or something. "Mother, Mother...Oh, how I've suffered." She refuses medicine, calls the nurses constantly. I sat tonight (it's now five to nine) with the giggly RADA* girl—all short red hair, pink luminous baby skin and even white teeth and giggles like a froth on champagne about the brain operation, snorting horribly in her nose tubes and skull sock. She told me Mrs. Fry's legs (both broken) were almost mended. Another story said they were just broken. The man who ran her over and his wife came tiptoeing in with flowers; "How are you?" "Very poorly, very poorly," she says with relish. Often, the nurses disappear. The old noseless lady of 82 with the broken leg in traction at the left end of the row facing me yelled for a bedpan earlier: "Nurse"—her sock-face grotesquely leaning forward past the fat jolly dark Italian girl's. I gradually felt it devolve on me, bed by bed, to get a nurse. "Nurse," the old lady yelled. I tried

*Royal Academy of Dramatic Art

to cheer her up this morning by telling her a lady at *least* 10 years her senior with *two* broken legs was in the adjoining ward. "God is Good," the old thing said. Immense camaraderie here. I am in an excellent position for "visiting round." The nurses are absolute angels.

Monday, March 6, 4:20 P.M. In bed after an hour alone in the warm sun of the park reading the late poems of Pasternak— they excited me immensely—the free, lyric tone and terse (though sometimes too fey) idiom. I felt: a new start can be made through these. This is the way back to the music. I wept to lose to my new tough prosiness. Tired after a ghastly night— the woman (Mrs. Fry) with the two white-root hands put on a huge scene—started calling for the police. "Police, policeman, get me out of here"; "Oh, how I suffer." Theatrical wooing groans. "I'll call my doctor in the morning to show how you leave me all night because of your whims. I'll tell your mummies on you." The sister went in to her. "Why won't you take your medicine?" Evidently she had some pills to make her shit and shat all day and thinks they're trying to kill her like this. Some more cursing and I saw the nurse and sister in the lit office-cubicle gleefully preparing a hypodermic. Often she sounds manic—"Ooo, what are those around me? Walls walls walls . . ." "Those are windows," the sister said firmly. "What are those frocks on the chair?" "Those are pillowcases." At about 3 I was woken by a crash and more wooing. She'd thrown a medicine glass down. Evidently on her first day here she hit a doctor with her pocketbook. My stitches pull and snick. I am tired.

•*Notes:* •The pink "bud vases" or antiseptic over each bed our thermometers are kept in.

•The flower bowls on windowsills, the trolleys of valiant but dying flowers.

•The old lady's plastic flesh-colored neckpiece on her table like an extra head—peach-pink with air holes, white straps and silver studs and a lining of yellow sponge and pink-flowered nightgown silk. Her bowl of fruit, C. P. Snow's *New Men*, stubbornness—eats food out of tins her daughter brings.

•Once last night the old lady Fry shouted, "You can laugh. I can laugh. He who laughs last laughs best." I felt guilty, as I had just smothered a snort in the pillow. But the nurses laughed also.

•The sock-head nose-tube lady had water on the brain—snorkles and drools, dull-eyed. Was a district nurse, mannish, efficient—now: "she may go one way or the other—mental."

Bed 1: Joan in a plaster cast from toe to bosom for 4 months knits dark green wool. Has a house on the sea in South Devon. Obvious brave front. Reads *Horse and Hound*. Two sons 16 and 14. Sent to public school at 6. "The only thing." Her entomologist husband, their life in Africa, studying locusts.

Bed 2: The ubiquitous popular Rose, born in Camden Town and married at an early age to the boy round the corner, of Dutch descent and working at the same print factory for 15 years, with one son—is gone.

Bed 3: Mrs. Johns—the neckpiece lady—sits straight as a schoolmarm reading. I guessed right about her—she thinks she's "better"—keeps an utter schoolmarmish reserve which she broke for me yesterday. She is the wife of an elementary-school headmaster, daughter of two country schoolteachers and granddaughter of schoolteachers. Her daughter is a bossy gabby schoolteacher who—not surprisingly—divorced her husband in Africa before the birth of their first baby and she now lectures at the University of London—teaching teachers. She informed me, almost in tears, last night, that her daughter had looked at my books while I was out and said she had "an intellectual next to her." Said she felt "so unfriendly" not talking but she was always in pain, had a TB abscess in her spine. It was treated "wrong"—as neuritis, with exercises—now very bad. She seems to stick to her trouble and has given her doctors and nurses a stiff-neck resistance. Her night snoring and sleeping all day is enough to make us all pitiless.

I found out today who Mrs. Pfaffrath is—that elusive lady whose pool forms keep coming to our house. She is—or was—our dead landlady, and a woman here knew her! I got round to talking to the prim trim North Irish Nelly in the middle bay window as I dried my hair and found she once lived in our district. I asked if she knew Chalcot Square and she said, "I knew the landlady of Number 3." She was married to a French wigmaker. Evidently there was a great demand for men's wigs after the war, as lots of soldiers lost their hair and went bald for one reason or another.

Daisy is the real original. Wish I could overhear her stories. "I could tell she's a Jew," she said triumphantly of wild Mrs. Fry. "She said 'already.' That's what the Jews say." "I say 'already' too," Jay put in gently, but that didn't deter Daisy. "We're all like little animals," she said, "waiting for dinner."

The white-haired Jewess from Hackney in the lavender bed-sweater told me of her pale hardworking teacher-daughter and her marvelous grandsons, who are brilliant, one entering Oxford in geology. Impression of desperate grubbing study. She went to have a badly fitted false leg improved Friday—has come back in because her other foot has "gone bad"—a diabetic—my father's classic case—as the witchy Jewess in the green-arsenic dressing gown told me on my walk—she insisted on coming, but went right in.

In the spring and summer of 1961 Plath was at work on The Bell Jar *with the help of a grant from the Eugene F. Saxton Foundation. According to a note in the margin, she was re-reading the early journals at this point, possibly as source material. By late summer of 1961 the Hugheses had moved to Devon, where their second child, Nicholas, was born in January of 1962.*

The following character sketches of Devon neighbors were done in 1962; they were separate from her regular journals, and are all that survive in prose from this period, though she was also at work on a second novel.

MRS. PLUM AT CRISPENS

A tall, imposing white-haired woman at the back door early on—a sense of her measuring, judging. Invited me to coffee with Frieda [Plath's daughter]. She lives across the street at an angle to the right in a handsome white house with black trim, and a wattle fence protecting her garden beautifully groomed by a retired gardener. With her aged dachshund Pixie. . . . During the war her daughter, Camilla (from where I got the name for Dido in my novel), stayed with her: they had a Victory Garden at the back. Mrs. Plum an eminent woman, admirable. I like her more & more. She "would have been a doctor" if women had been educated in her day. As it is, her granddaughter (Camilla's daughter, I think) is studying medicine at Edinburgh. Virginia (I think) had her 21st birthday this winter—Camilla made a sit-down luncheon for over 40 people. Virginia got hundreds of pounds, records, jewels, etc. I was pleased to tell Mrs. Plum I had gone to Cambridge. That is the sort of thing that she would be pleased at. She seemed very hard of hearing at first, and I dreaded meeting her because I feel very reluctant to raise my voice—it makes everything one says seem rather fatuous because of the unnatural emphasis.

Mrs. P.'s interior: I came in the fall. The long living room with French windows out onto the screened lawn and flower border was jammed with flowers; bunches of huge chrysanthemums and dahlias arranged with no art in clumps of yellow, pink and tawny orange and red. Mrs. P. a marvel with Frieda. Not at all put off or silly as many grown-ups are. Let her go so far, gave her a box with a sixpence in it to shake. Frieda well behaved. A handsome Staffordshire (I think) pot dog on a side table—a wonderful red-orange and white. Pixie, like a patched sausage, dozed at the hearth. A coal fire, perfectly banked, burned like something artificial—one could not imagine that it left ash or clinkers—it was so high & full, glowing rosily. A handsome brick fireplace: copper coal scuttle, a flat, plaited woodbasket, gleaming brass tongs & brush. Mrs. P. has a son too, in Brooke Bond Tea. She lived in India, her husband was a coffee planter. Her tiny immaculate pale blue Morris. The sense of grandeur and expansion behind her. Comfort & the happiness of knowing precisely what she wants and how to achieve it. Very sensible.

Then she came here: sat at tea in the front room and told us of the place before our time—the gardener who kept all the gardens going, the austerities of the old lady with her stone kitchen floors, no electricity or phone. Asked about Ted's writing. Very curious, but benignly so. Brought round a bunch of yellow mimosa when I had Nicholas.

February 6, 1962. Brought Nicholas to see Mrs. P. on his first day out. ("Mrs. P. is dying to see Nicholas," said the midwife on her morning visit.) Waited in cold wintry sun in front alcove, too timid to go in, for Mrs. P. to return from market. She *really* admired Nicholas. Made me take off his white cap so she could see the shape of his head and remarked at the back brain-bulge of it. Her pleasure at his maleness; asked if Frieda was jealous. When I said Ted seemed to be reluctant it was not another girl, she said: I suspect he's jealous for Frieda. Her queer, fine "listening" quality. Something N.T.* for example does not at all have. I tried to notice colors, fabrics. Everything very very rich—deep-blue velvet piled curtains, deep blue & white Orientals, worn, elegant. A polished board floor. A bookcase containing, surprisingly, *The Lord of the Rings*, and, not surprisingly, all of Winston Churchill's books on the war & the English people. A lot of old gardening and travel books. I must look closer sometime to get the thin titles. Mrs. P. made good mugs of Nescafe. "In the north," she said, "we have a custom on the baby's first visit." She went into the kitchen and bustled about getting a paper bag with a match (for a good match), coal (to light the fire), salt for health, a sixpence for wealth, and an egg for I'm not sure what. Said she is flying to the Near East for two weeks with a friend.

February 21: Mrs. P. materialized outside my study this morning: source of a great fratch between Ted & me—my sense of surprise invasion. This is my one symbolic sanctum. Stunned, I asked her in. Ted got a chair, & I & she both realized the awkwardness of it. She had come to say good-bye & see baby before her 2 weeks in Beirut, Rome, etc. I took her to see Nicholas, not before her eyes had taken in the study in such detail as offered—"this was the boys' playroom" (which boys?). The sense that Mrs. P. wanted to see how we lived in the back rooms. She looked at my long unbraided hair as if to take it in, drink the last inch, and make a judgment. I very upset, angry. As if we could be observed, examined at any moment simply because we were too shy or polite to say Nay, or She's working, I'll get her down. Or Please wait here. My anger at Ted for being a mat, not at Mrs. P., really.

* * *

*Probably North Tawton, the local village

May 12: Had not seen Mrs. Plum for three months. Ted met her in town & she suggested I come over this afternoon, Saturday. Stood at the door with the dressed-up baby & Frieda and rang and rang. No sound of Pixie barking. Felt cross and neatened for nothing; then I heard a bumping around upstairs, and knocked very loudly. Mrs. P. finally came to the door. Showed me around the garden first: a blaze of colors, little gravel paths, raised stone walls. One very pink cherry tree over a garden bench. A fire of wallflowers, red, yellow, pumpkin. I began to see the virtue of these common and popular garden creatures. An ornamental pool with a great orange carp. Begonias, peonies, lupins, lots of tulips, giant pansies. Immaculate weedless beds. We had tea. Frieda in a whiny spoilt mood. Carried about a glass ashtray with a provocative naughty look. Ran outside with a little table & put it on the grass. Mrs. P. had caught a chill in Italy. Had seen the pyramids. Loved Rhodes. She was to leave Monday for a fortnight at her daughter's. Admired Nicholas's head, no doubt but that he was a boy, she said. Frieda cried at the clock musical bell. Felt her competition with Nicholas for attention. Indoors, great bouquets of cherry blossom and tulips. Where was Pixie? She had died in Mrs. P.'s absence. A tone of muted grief. Advised me to dig up and burn my tulips, as from the symptoms I described they had fire-disease.

MR. AND MRS. MILFORD

March 1, Thursday. My first visit to the Milfords in the cottage on the corner, adjoining Mary Smith's, and, on the front, the crippled Molly (with the high black boot, humpback and the stuffed fox under glass in her parlor). I wanted to give some return to this crippled couple for their gift of three big, handsome chrysanthemums, one yellow and two mauve, and the pink potted primula they brought after I had Nicholas. So I made and sugared some one-egg cupcakes. Rang, with Frieda. The (I think) blind Mr. Milford answered the door, and I told him who I was. I could not look into his white eyes. He led me into a fearful, dark parlor with dark-brown veneered objects standing about and giving off the depressing smell of old people, varnish and stale upholstery. Let me through a door into a long room with a table and windows looking over (or rather up to) a little garden set on a level halfway up the house, with a well between it and the house, of paving. "It's a pity we've just had tea or you could have some." I sat down, with Frieda on my lap. She looked as if she were going to burst into tears—like a little animal frightened by the darkness and sad smells.

Mrs. Milford came out, took the cakes. I saw she had a handsome fruitcake, with one quarter cut out, on the table, cleared of tea things. Green and red and brown fruit studded the bottom of the yellow slab sides, and it rose to a browned crown. There was also a jar of black currant jelly she had preserved herself. I made conversation.

The Milfords lived in London (Wimbledon) during the bombings. Their windows were out. Mrs. Milford hugged her neighbor (a publican's wife) during the raids as they sat under the stairs. "If we had been killed, we would have died with our arms around each other." They stayed in London because of their son, Ben, who was in the forces. They thought if he was wounded or came home, they would be there for him, holding the home front. I hadn't the heart to ask where Ben was now, for fear he would be dead.

Then they moved to Broadwoodkelly (a few miles from North Tawton). The soil there was poor, nothing like the rich red soil here. They had to work the garden too hard, it was too much for them, three quarters of an acre, so they moved to this cottage. They were waiting for a decorator, a Mr. Delve, to paper their front room, so they did not know when they could come to tea (how are the two related?). Mr. Delve had to fix the wall. Something about a heavy mirror, now in their dining room, that had either been about to fall off the parlor wall, or was shoring up a faulty parlor wall. I couldn't tell. They go to the library . . . for books, but only seldom. The stairs up to the library room are too much for *Mrs*. Milford and Mr. Milford is blind and couldn't read the titles if he went himself. "We're a couple of old crocks." They are Catholics, too. I left with Frieda, horribly eager to get out into the fresh air. The smell of age and crippling a real pain to me. Can't stand it.

Mrs. Milford had taken my cakes carefully off the plate, washed and dried the plate, and handed it back to me. The bushy plants on tall stalks in the garden were, Mr. Milford told me, "greens."

NANCY AXWORTHY AND MISCELLANEOUS INTELLIGENCE

April 25. Nancy has not been to clean all this week. Her mother-in-law was sick again last Tuesday. Nancy's husband, Walter, had gone to a contest of Devon bell-ringers the previous weekend. Then his mother was taken. I met Nancy's friend, the humpbacked Molly who lives in a tiny cottage with a stuffed fox at the bottom of our lane, and she said Nancy was sitting up all night and had to wash four of the old lady's sheets in one day, as she was wetting the bed and vomiting. Then, as Ted & I were going in the early dusk to deliver our great weekly bouquet of daffodils to Jim,* on Friday, Molly came stumping out in her high, black orthopedic boot, called, "Mrs. Hughes, Mr. Hughes." Nancy's mother-in-law had died that afternoon, from a heart attack. I felt an immense relief, that I would not lose my invaluably helpful Nancy for her need to nurse a sick & malingering mother-in-law. So selfish am I. But the old lady was evidently a terrible patient, never doing what the doctor said, and Molly herself said Walter said it was a mercy, if she had to go, that she didn't linger.

The funeral is to be at 2:30 this afternoon. Molly stumped up yesterday morning to ask if she could buy four shillings' worth of daffodils. Of course we said no, we would bring down a big bunch, we had been meaning to bring her a bunch. So last night we picked about 150 daffodils & I went down in the clear pink twilight & knocked. Molly was not home. But this morning the top half of her Dutch door was open & she was waiting. "How much am I in your debt?" Oh, nothing, I said. She said she is going in a week to the holiday for the disabled (who come from as far as Oxfordshire) to Westward Ho! They come every year for two weeks. The Rotary Club takes them out for lunch. They are very high up, in this big place, with a

---

*The local grocer

ballroom. She can see the Isle of Lundy from her bed. I said to send the daffodils with our love. Nancy, she said, will be up to see me tomorrow.

Nancy's husband, Walter, is a big heavy smiling blond man who works for Jim Bennett. He went through a ceiling he was repairing and strained his back. Marjorie Tyrer says when he came to repair their bathtub he broke a scale by stepping on it. He is a bell-ringer, the number seven bell, a big one. He is head of the North Tawton fire department (which has a drill every Wednesday at 7), and teaches woodworking at the local school. I hope to take woodworking this next fall.

MR. WILLIS

July 4. Mr. Willis, said the midwife, had a piano. It looked horrible, she said, but was supposed to be in good tone. We walked round in the heat of the afternoon. Asked at a wrong door first. A smiling white-haired woman directed us to the next house in the street on the steep hill. She had a queer old zombie-dog, pink-gray flesh showing through shorn hair, at her door: it is not mine, it is a farmer's on the hill, it is an ancient sort of sheepdog like they used to use, and it comes to me for scraps. We rang. No answer. She had been listening and came down: I expect he can't hear, he is listening to the wireless. She pounded, went in: there are some young people to see you. A very old, crabbed white-haired man, but somehow lively, met us. He had been sitting in front of a radio, had a tea tray with currant buns on the made-up bed in the sitting room. Led us out back through a dark scabrous kitchen, did away with a bucket (urine?) and showed us a fusty old piano, the veneer peeling. We lifted, hopelessly, the keyboard cover. It was his wife's, who had died four years ago at the age of 74 or so. Hadn't been opened. We tried a few notes. Every other one stuck, motionless, and a substance, matted dust or the decay of the interior, seeped up between the keys.

Then he began to talk. Are those your writings in the window? I asked. I had seen some odd placards with large plain childlike writing about "the scandal of the century" and "would he have left his pram if he did not intend to stay?" and "Water

Board" and "National Assistance Board." A kind of public plaint, indecipherable, written first in pencil, then over again on the same card in ink. One placard was upside down. These, evidently, were his grievances. He had been robbed by his brother and sister of seven fields: property had been left to his brother and his heirs (that's me, isn't it, his heir?) and sold. A doctor in Wales had given him two injections a day, by nurses, and paralyzed his left side, then said he had a stroke. His wife had died—they wouldn't take her into hospital because she was incurable. What had she died of—a broken heart? His son-in-law was a Freemason in Okehampton—the Freemasons were in power, they were robbing him, cheating him. The National Assistance were robbing him. He had written to the Queen. Somebody in a paper had said pink luster cups were worth hundreds of pounds. He showed us four saucers and three cups in pink luster in his cupboard. The man had said he would be in the district & have a look & value them, but of course never came. His wife had fallen from the bed, it was like a butcher shop, and no one came. Her daughter did not come and broke her heart. He had to leave the door unlocked Thursday night for the nurse, and someone might steal the cups. He had china as well, a dinner set and a lovely tea set. There was a desk, with two polished brass candlesticks & a brass bell. Winston Churchill had fallen, and look at the treatment he had. Mr. Willis fell, and was an hour picking himself up by himself. The flood of injustice went on, a great apocalyptic melding of perhaps slights or real small grievances. The policeman walked down the other side of the street, nose in the air, and did not read his complaints in the window, which were there for all to see. We edged out, in distress, telling him to talk to the nurse, she was nice. Yes, the nurses are all good, he admitted, I have had a lot of them. . . . And we went.

MAJOR AND MRS. CRUMP

Whitsun, June 10. Met the Crumps at Charlie Pollard's bee-meeting and were invited to tea. We found the house "small as a postage stamp," on the Eggesford Road. . . . A tiny, cramped brick house all on one floor like a holiday camp, with a glass grape arbor built all along the front overlooking a view of rolling green farmland to Dartmoor, and a kitchen built along the back. An impeccably mown lawn back and front. Beehives, painted pink and white, in a nettly enclosure at the bottom of the front lawn, with lots of big blue cornflowers ("they love those") and red and yellow broom ("three and six a cutting") round about. And a new shed, one of those self-erectable ones with a clean gravel floor, for bee equipment and watching. Infinitely fine vegetable garden—rows of thick, bushy strawberry plants, some with white flowers, some with embryonic green berries beginning: sweetpeas climbing sticks, rhubarb, a weed-grown asparagus patch (the only slovenly corner), Velocity cabbages, goosegog, round and lucent green & hairy, celery, broad beans. The superbly weeded rows. Then a pile of hens in a battery, eggs collected by the Chumleigh man, not the Okehampton man (who was too fussy about washing the eggs). Seedlings set out in myriad tin cans.

Mrs. Olive Crump an amazing & indomitable woman: white short hair, tall, keen blue eyes & pink cheeks. Quite greedy, though fattish, she ate lots of scones & cream & jam for tea. She cans (or bottles) about 200 weight of jam a year. And extracts her own honey. Secretary of the Conservatives in the country. At the end of the afternoon, she brought out her scrapbook of her life in British Guiana. An astounding document. Lots of pictures of waterfalls seen from the air in her three-seater plane; her black silk flying suit, like Amelia Earhart; her handsome pilot; close calls. Pictures of her with short hair, in pants, handsome herself, ordering a cowering black to move some dirt, on horseback, driving a locomotive which she & her engineer built, straightening the 7-mile railway tracks they made to help get the timber to the river. A succession of wood houses, grander & grander, as they made more & more money. They were at first too poor to buy meat; at the end the grant was sold for £180,000. I couldn't understand whether the Major was her first husband, or second. Or whether she & her father built the timber plantation, or she & her husband. At one point, she said she had no children but attended a mother's union, as she had cared for a lot. And then, when she was showing me the pictures of children & weddings in the hall, she seemed to say, "These are *his* children," meaning the Major's? Her father . . . an amazing man of 89 in white linen jacket with that military blue eye who attributes his health to drinking a quart of rum a day all his life, said that when a jaguar was troubling them, she locked up all the dogs, resolved to shoot it. Heard a noise, a scratching, at the house window in the dark. Crept downstairs with rifle & outside: saw a dark shape fall from the window. That's a dog, she thought, that the jaguar has thrown out. I'll save it. She ran & embraced the dark object, which turned out to be the jaguar. It dashed off & hid in the chicken shed. She went over & shot into the shed, then did run. In the morning the natives found the jaguar in there, dead, shot through the lung. So she is a big woman. Very opinionated. Said that these women get multiple sclerosis from worrying over their husbands' bad health and not accepting what God has sent them!

Major Sidney Crump curiously the odd man out. Always making jocular references to his wife's expertise (on bees) & domination: "She has her finger on my jugular." A man of action; can't stand still. His father was a drunkard journalist & potboiler. He started in the ranks of the cavalry himself & worked up to head of the C.I.D. in British Guiana. An immense admiration, sardonic, for lawyers: how they can make monkeys of truths & learned men. He writes all winter: reports. Can't talk standing still: walks round & round the lawn, with a sort of horse-rider's lurch. His blue eye, also, his clipped silver mustache. The old man, his father-in-law, a sort of elderly double of himself. Three things I'll tell you, he said: There is no sentiment in business. There is no honesty in politics. And self-interest makes the world go round. All right, I said. I give you those. Gave Ted a box of little Velocity cabbages in tins & a couple of bunches of very odd cylindrical green celery ("for soup").

. . . The old man was according to his daughter all sorts of wonderful & odd things. He seemed drastically hungry for a listener. Brought out his photograph album with prize-winning photos he had taken: of an old hawker with white hair and wrinkled like Methuselah; a fat little native baby eating dirt; snow on a wire fence ("That's a bee comb," someone guessed, to his delight), hand-colored lily pads like violent green saucers, and moonlight on the big waterfall (Kaieteur?), the highest in the world, in British Guiana. [She] said something about his being a crack marksman, a world champion, & a trick entertainer on a [hunting] party with the king & queen (which?). He brought Ted to his bedroom at the end, to show him little boxes of jewelry he made from loose colored rhinestones & frames which he gave to friends; showed him his watercolors for doing photographs, and his mother and father, an oval black and white portrait of a dark, oppressed little woman & bearded smiling patriarchal man (her parents were killed in the Mutiny; she was married at 14). He prided himself on making the baby smile. Pretended to eat Frieda's parsley & then gave it back, while she made her queer "shy" face, sliding her eyes to one side under her lids. Promised to tell a story of a cockroach. Gave me a sprig of "rosemary for remembrance" as we left. Brought out a Captain Hornblower book, autographed to him from C. S. Forester, whose picture he had taken atop the big falls.

Margaret, a blond, quiet plump-faced sweet-looking girl of 13 was home from boarding school to stay with her grandparents. She brought out her toys, a dog, a doll, to amuse Frieda & played with her; later cuddled and cooed over the baby.

A big tea laid, scones, cream, cherry jelly; a chocolate cake with rich dark frosting; little cut sandwiches. Tea a bit awkward, drafty, in the tiny dining room crammed with sideboards & tables. Two bedrooms, a bath & a tiny front room with a TV made up the interior of the house.

The old man, on showing his photos: "That's the girl who has two children in New Zealand, that's the one with the voice Olive's going to visit next week, that's the boy that's dead, that's the mother of the lot . . ." and a photo of his wife, dead 25 years, with a paper in her lap showing headlines about Hitler.

THE MIDWIFE: WINIFRED DAVIES

First met in Dr. Webb's office last fall at my first checkup. A short, rotundish but not at all fat, capable gray-haired woman with a wise, moral face, in a blue uniform under a round-brimmed blue hat. I felt she would judge, kindly, but without great mercy. Her fine opportunities to visit me and observe the habits and domestic setup of the new arrivals. Very aware that our being undefined "artists," with no provable or ostensible or obvious work, plus me being an American (the stereotype of pampered wealth), which would prejudice a staid English countrywoman against me. Her first judgment in my favor came the first day in the office, when I told her I nursed the baby, Frieda, for 10 months and that Ted was my "home-help." There was some hope for us!

Nurse D. is by some odd linking I have yet to discover, the niece of Mrs. Plum. They are two pillars. They must know everything, or almost everything. Nurse D.'s visits invariably came when I most intuitively suspected them simply because I had been lax about housework to get to my study. Nothing Ted could say could stop her—she would forge up the stairs, he preceding desperately to warn me, and I would see her smiling white head over his shoulder at the study door. I would be in my pink fluffy bathrobe (over my layers of maternity clothes, for warmth), and she would say "artist's outfit," go into the bedroom, find the bed unmade, and I would have hastily thrown a newspaper over the pink plastic pot of violently yellow urine I had not bothered to empty, on the principle that all housework should wait till afternoon. She obviously relished seeing how far and of what sort our house-decorating was— observed our bedroom Indian rug was "very like her own" (the ultimate approval). One morning she seemed all twinkly with news, could hardly wait to say "My son's school friend is a fan of your husband's." By some incredible coincidence, Nurse D.'s only son, Garnett (a family name in the north), had a school friend at the Merchant Taylors' School in London who had written Ted about his book and received an answer postmarked "North Tawton," whereupon he asked Garnett if he knew a Ted Hughes. We were "placed." I felt very pleased.

Nurse D.'s husband is the mystery. Was he killed in the war? Garnett is roughly 19, hers was a "war marriage." She has had to bring up the boy on her own. [Omission.] She raises Pekingese pedigree pups. Had one she doted on. She killed it by accidentally stepping on it. It used to go everywhere with her. A horrible story. As the baby approached in time, Nurse D.'s manner grew sweeter, gentler, more amiable. I felt very glad she would be my midwife, and lucky the baby came not on her day off, and just before she took a "holiday" to tend her sick father at a hotel in South Tawton (a man over 80, with two pneumonia attacks, living with his wife while they had a house built).

Nurse D. came from Lancashire (I think, not Yorkshire), had a wonderful big family (7?), and her mother had lots of help. She had a fine childhood, she said, and a nanny. I forget most of the picture she painted now, alas. She has brothers and sisters scattered about—a brother who was headmaster of a well-known boys public school here and who is now head of one in Australia; a sister, I think, in Canada. She has about 10 dogs, 3 of which are allowed to take turns coming into the house. She gardens. She has an acre or two and wants to raise geese, then sell the geese & buy sheep, then sell the sheep & buy a cow. . . .

May 16. Our second entering wedge. Is it that Mrs. D. disliked the Tyrers & waited till they were gone? At any rate, she invited us to tea to meet a Mrs. Macnamara on her own day off. We climbed the steep hill off the main street opposite the secondary modern school to where Mrs. D.'s new house sat spanking white overlooking the meadows that greenly undulated toward the purple domes of Dartmoor. A flashy blue car parked outside next to the nurse's discreet pale one. Her house all white walls, full of light, big windows overlooking a plateau of close-cropped green lawn and a rather bald display of flowers—heather, tulips, anemones. A great many Pekingese dogs yapping like fur mice from a wire enclosure. Mrs. Macnamara a handsome white-haired woman (descended from Irish farmers), with red lipstick and a feminine blue-figured blouse and silvery suit. Exuded wealth, well-being. Had come round originally to buy a Pekingese. Lived at Cadbury House beyond Crediton. Her husband, Mrs. D. said, was something in ITV, and lived in a flat in London till he was to retire, for Mrs. Macnamara couldn't bear going back to London. She had fallen in love with the house, which had 9 acres and was under repair. She had a lot of cats, one ginger one in shreds, pelt split, eye hanging out, from a fight, which she had to go home to swab. She had a doctor daughter in Washington state, married to a doctor, who was the "highest-earning woman" in the state, according to a tax official. The daughter had two daughters of her own and an adopted child. She had three miscarriages before she had a baby, and lost her baby son, born a Siamese twin with the other twin an embryo in his bowel. Insisted on knowing why his prognosis was only to live 8 hours, bundled up the dying baby & traveled 200 miles by train to where he could be operated on by a friend. Then nursed him ("he was quite blind, and deaf, and his hands could grip nothing, they just lay flat") although she knew he would die in three months, which he did. Ever since she has been impossible, behaved badly, her father won't let her into the house. Ironically, she was a child-specialist, called on all over to diagnose, prescribe. She had an adopted sister, adopted when she was 12 & had polio, and of the same age. Sisters devoted to each other.

We ate tea round a table, a yellow-frosted banana cake with cherries, very good currant buns, dainty tea service. Kitchen in half walled-off area, red counters, big windows overlooking moors. Photographs of places framed in narrow black & hung on white walls. A silver-embroidered Oriental screen in living room, an African violet, a little vase of early lilies of the valley, a sunny window seat, a handsome radio with all the foreign stations. Mrs. Davies in gray, with silver earrings. After Mrs. M. left, she showed us the garden in a high wind, then the upstairs, the stark white rooms, large built-in cupboards, Garnett's room with a beer-bottle lamp & trophies from pubs, a set of literature in matched jackets. Her own room with framed photos of a flat shy boy and a Pekingese, a gas ring by the bed, a telephone. Modern lavatory. Her wired kennel of Pekes, jumping, praying, the babies a fat beary gray, toddling endearingly. Saw just-hatched blackbirds in hedge, a luminous martian green, pulsing like hearts. Arranged for luncheon at Mrs. Macnamara's in a fortnight.

Because only work notes survive from this last section of the journal, it almost gives the impression that Plath died long before she actually did end her life—on February 11, 1963, in her thirtieth year.

In the fall of 1962, just after the end of her marriage, Plath came to write her great work, the poems of Ariel. They were written in a flood of incandescent energy, thirty poems in one month; the first drafts came pouring out, but she worked over each one carefully later. No one else had seen these poems, but she knew with great certainty that she had made the leap. As she wrote to her mother on October 16, 1962, in the middle of her extraordinary month: "I am a genius of a writer; I have it in me. I am writing the best poems of my life; they will make my name...."

Chronology

1932   Born October 27 in Jamaica Plain,
           Massachusetts, to Aurelia and Otto Plath

1935   Brother Warren born

1937   Plath family moves to Winthrop, Massachusetts

1940   Otto Plath dies following a leg amputation
           resulting from a diabetic condition

1942   Plath family moves to Wellesley, Massachusetts

1950   Enters freshman year at Smith College on
           scholarship

1952   August: Publishes a prize-winning story,
           "Sunday at the Mintons'," in *Mademoiselle*

1953   Summer: Guest managing editor at
           Mademoiselle, New York City
           August 24: Suicide attempt in Wellesley,
           Massachusetts, at home

1954   Winter: Returns to Smith for second semester
           Summer: Attends Harvard Summer School

1955   May: Graduates from Smith with prizes for
           poetry
           October: Begins Fulbright year at Newnham

College, Cambridge University
1956 February 25: Meets Ted Hughes
April: Trip to Germany and Italy with Gordon Lameyer
June 16: Marries Ted Hughes
Summer: Long honeymoon in Benidorm, Spain
1956–57 Second Fulbright year
Living in Cambridge
1957 June: Returns to America with Ted Hughes; holiday in Cape Cod, Massachusetts
1957–58 Instructor in English, Smith College
1958–59 Writing and hospital clerical job in Boston; seriously involved in therapy; attending Robert Lowell's poetry class
1959 Summer: Sight-seeing trip across America
Fall: Writing poetry at Yaddo, Saratoga Springs
December: Leaves for England
1960 April 1: Birth of daughter, Frieda Rebecca, at home in London
October: *The Colossus* published in England
1961 February: Miscarriage
March: Appendectomy
August: Moves to Devon
1962 January 17: Birth of son, Nicholas Farrar
May: *The Colossus and Other Poems*, U.S. edition
October: Separates from Ted Hughes
1963 January: *The Bell Jar* published in England under the pseudonym Victoria Lucas
February 11: Suicide in London

ABOUT THE EDITORS

Ted Hughes is one of Britain's major twentieth-century poets. His most recent work is *The New Selected Poems*, published by Harper & Row. Mr. Hughes was married to Sylvia Plath from 1956 until her death in 1963.

Frances McCullough has edited all of Sylvia Plath's posthumously published works. She is presently Senior Editor at The Dial Press.

Index

Aaron, Daniel, 160
Abels, Cyrilly, 86, 195
"Above the Oxbow," 303, 304, 316
"Acrobats," 213
"Aftermath," 299
"Afternoon of a Faun," 105
Aiken, Conrad, 32
"Almanac," 313
"Amedee," 273
"Ancient to Ancients, An," 250
Ariel, xii, xiii, 352
ARTnews, poem for, 187, 188, 195, 199, 205–6, 216
"Arts in Society," 299
Arvin, Newton, 188, 195, 199, 201, 202, 203, 219, 225, 232
"At Breakfast," 313
Atlantic Monthly, The, 160, 171, 207, 244, 258n, 299, 304
Atlantic Press, 299, 306
Auden, W. H., 72, 76, 151, 225
"August Lighthill and the Other Woman," 298
Axworthy, Nancy, 344

"Babysitters, The," 27
Bald Soprano, The, 279
Barnes, Djuna, 203n
Barnhouse, Ruth. *See* Beuscher, Dr. Ruth
Baskin, Esther, 220, 255, 289, 301, 309
Baskin, Leonard, 220, 223, 243, 301
Baudelaire, Charles, 125
Beale, Jimmy, 26–27
Beast in the Jungle, The, 171

Bed Book, The, 298, 299, 306, 309, 322

Bell Jar, The, 11n, 29n, 38n, 86n, 295n, 339

Belmont Hotel, 41, 46–47, 49–50

Benidorm, Spain, 142–45, 250

Bert (Cambridge friend), 109–10, 128–29, 130

Beuscher, Dr. Ruth (R.B.), 86, 194, 230, 263, 266, 268, 269, 270, 272ff., 280, 282, 287, 289ff., 294ff.

"Bird in the House," 249, 258

Bishop, Elizabeth, 187, 317

Blake, William, 124–25

"Blue Moles," 320, 326

Boddy, Michael St. George, 135, 137, 140

Booth, Dr., 214

Booth, Philip, 114, 214, 301, 323

Booths, the, 301

Boston, 200, 217, 220, 235–309

Bradley, F. H., 124

Bragg, Mrs., 214

Bramwell, James, 181, 196, 197–98

Bramwell, Joan, 182, 188, 196, 197–98

Brawner, Phil, 49

Brontë sisters, 145–46

Brooks, Peter, 289

Brown, Marcia (Marty), 27, 63, 82, 83, 84, 184, 213, 274, 287, 309

Browning, Elizabeth Barrett, 209

Bull of Bendylaw. See Devil of the Stairs, The

Burden, Jack, 154

"Burnt-out Spa, The," 325

Burton, Miss, 124, 128

"Button Quarrel, The," 273, 274

Cambridge, England (Newnham College), 86, 87–131, 135, 136, 145, 148–59; dream about, 165–66; fish-and-chip shop, 155–59

Cambridge, Mass. See Harvard

Cantor, Mrs., 170, 213

Cantors, the, 51

Capote, Truman, 273

Carson, Rachel, 54

Cary, Joyce, 154, 155

"Casualty, The," 214

Chairs, The, 279

"Channel Crossing," 127

Chatham, Mass., 51–55

Childhood, 20–21, 178

Children (babies) and pregnancy, 99, 169, 187, 217, 219, 238, 251, 272, 277, 282, 296, 305–6, 309, 318, 324, 325 (See also Hughes, Frieda Rebecca; Hughes, Nicholas), birth of Frieda, 329; birth of Nicholas, 339; dreams about, 315, 321; lack of ovulation and fear of barrenness, 307–9; miscarriage, 329

"Child's Park Stones," 232

Chirico, Giorgio de, 208–9

Chris (Cambridge friend), 97, 99, 131

Christian Science Monitor, The, 53, 103, 298, 318

Chronology, 353–54

"Circus in Three Rings," 191

Cocteau, Jean, 115

Coffee, Mary, 5–6

Cohen, Eddie, 11, 13–16, 66

Colossus, The, 309, 319, 323, 325, 329

Colson, Nancy, 56

Columbia University, 71

"Companionable Ills," 298

Conrad, Al, 214, 215

Cowley, Malcolm, 321

"Creation While You Watch," 207

Crockett (English teacher), 57

Crump, Sidney and Olive, 346–49

Cummings, E. E., 32

Daiches, David, 124

"Dark House," 259

"Dark Marauder," 139

"Daughters of Blossom Street, The" (orig. "This Earth Our Hospital"), 301–2, 303, 304, 326

Davies, Winifred, 349–52

Davison, Peter, 86, 106, 214, 258, 274n, 315

Davy, Dr. (psychiatrist), 98, 108, 129

Death of Ivan Ilyitch, 295

Defoe, Daniel, 260

Dentist, experience with, 8–9

Devil of the Stairs, The (orig. *Bull of Bendylaw*), 300, 302

Devon, England, 339–52

De Vries, Peter, 105, 154

Dickinson, Emily, 209

"Dick Straightup," 258

"Disquieting Muses, The," 208, 216, 217, 272

"Doomsday," 75

Drake, Janet, 132

"Dream, The," 208

Dream Play, 202–3

Drew, Elizabeth, 76, 150

Dryden, John, 74

Eastham, Mass., 159–72

"Electra on Azalea Path," 296, 298

Eliot, George, 218

Eliot, T. S., 32, 215, 219, 224, 248, 309, 315

Emile (boyfriend), 9–11, 52

England, 57, 58, 289, 291, 323, 328, 329–52. *See also* Cambridge, England; London; Withens, Yorkshire

Engle, Paul, 314

Enigma of the Oracle, The, 208

Ethical Studies (Bradley), 124

"Eye Beam One, The," 160

Falcon Yard (novel), 160–61, 178, 183, 184, 196, 197, 218, 221, 226, 307

Fassett, Agatha, 287, 290, 306

Fassett, Stephen, 285, 290, 304

Faulkner, William, 292, 295
"Faunus," 250
Fiddler crabs, 172
"Fifteen Dollar Eagle, The," 303
"Fish & Chips," 155–59
Fisher, Al, 108, 175, 177, 180–81, 182, 201, 228, 230
Fisher, Eddie, 255
Fitts, Dudley, 302, 306, 323
Fleurs du Mal, Les, 125
Forster, E. M., 124
France, 92–94. *See also* Paris
Freud, Sigmund, 276
"Frog Autumn," 291
Full Fathom Five (poem book; orig. *The Earthenware Head*), 191, 196, 211, 220, 241

Gallant, Mavis, 171, 312, 319
Gardner, Isabella, 187, 209
Gauguin, Paul, 187, 188, 199
Gendron, Val, 52–55
Generation of Vipers, 43
Germany, 136
Gibian, George, 108, 181, 201, 221
Gilling, Dick, 101
Giovanni (Italian journalist in Paris), 132–33, 136, 138, 140
"Go Get the Goodly Squab," 75
Gold, Herbert, 273
Goodbye Columbus, 300–301
"Goring, The," 299

Grandfather, 25
Grandmother (Grammy), 24, 25, 126, 141, 264, 289
Granta, 128
Graves, Robert, 219n
Gray, Tony, 133–36, 138
Grohmann, Will, 307
Guggenheims, 205, 232, 293, 297

Hall, Donald, 170, 216
Hamish (boyfriend), 107, 109, 111–12, 128, 129
"Hanging Man," 223
Harcourt, Brace & World, 306, 319
Hardwick, Elizabeth, 288, 290, 306
Hardy, Thomas, 250
Harper's, 75, 78, 150, 151, 171, 199, 244, 317
Harris, Jack, 47
Harvard, 76, 81ff., 86, 203, 212–15, 232, 277, 278, 285n, 294
Haupt, Gary, 124–25, 126, 138, 139, 149, 293
Hawk in the Rain, The, 151
Hawthorne, Nathaniel, 190
Healy, Lou, 149
Hecht, Anthony (Tony), 222, 225
Heinemann (publisher), 321, 329
Herself Surprised, 155
Hill, Charles, 180, 181, 185
Holt, Henry, 306, 316
Holyoke, Mass., 204–5
Hopkins, Ann, 292
Horse's Mouth, The, 154, 284

Houghton Mifflin, 298, 300
Howard, Frances Minturn, 304–5
Hudson Review, 302
Hughes, Frieda Rebecca, 318n, 329, 335–36, 339, 340–41, 342, 349
Hughes, Nicholas, 318, 339, 340ff.
Hughes, Olwyn, 189
Hughes, Ted: in Boston, 238ff., 255ff., 266ff., 274–75ff., 307, 308–9; in Cambridge, 149ff.; on Eastham holiday, 163, 168ff.; Harvard reading, 212–15; in London and Devon, 331–32, 335–36, 341, 344, 349, 350; marriage, honeymoon, 142–45; meets S. P., 110–11; and rage of S. P., 225ff.; at Smith, 172, 173, 176ff., 184, 185ff., 194ff., 207ff., 216ff.; and S. P.'s early romantic dreams of, 128–30, 131, 135, 137, 138, 140; Withens visit, 145–46; in Yaddo, 310, 316, 317ff.
Hunter, Nancy, 149
Hurley, Ben, 204–5
Huws, Dan, 110, 335n
Huws, Helga, 335
Huxley, Aldous, 128

Ilo, 5–7, 51
"Infirmary Blues," 62
"Inmate, The," 329–39
"Interior Castle, The," 312

Ionesco, Eugene, 273, 279–80
Italy, 136, 140

Jack, 279
Jack and Jill, 178, 187
Jacob's Room, 164
James, Henry, 154, 171, 173, 176, 217, 218, 221
Jane (Cambridge friend), 98–99, 125, 149
Job, Book of, 288
John (Cambridge friend), 97, 99, 130
"Johnny Panic and the Bible of Dreams," 272, 273, 287, 303, 312, 316, 322
Johns Hopkins, 71
Journal of the Plague Year, 260
Joyce (Holyoke friend), 204
Joyce, James, 2, 82, 122, 187, 221
Jung, Carl, 315

Kazin, Alfred, 108, 201, 202, 230
Kazin, Ann, 201
Keightley, Philip, 257
Kenyon Review, The, 246
Klee, Paul, 199, 205–6, 208, 307
Knopf, Alfred A., 49, 242, 306
Koffka, Kurt, 70
Kokoschka, Oskar, 215
Kramer, Art, 48, 49, 50
Kroll, Judith, ix
Krook, Dorothea, 124ff., 150, 194, 217

Kumin, Maxine, 300, 306

Kunitz, Stanley, 293

Ladies' Home Journal, 84, 170, 209, 218, 226, 273, 294

"Lady and the Earthenware Head, The," 152, 191, 241

Lady Chatterley's Lover, 194

Lameyer, Gordon, 72, 77n, 86, 100, 118–19, 136–40, 149, 214

Lameyer, Mrs. (Gordon's mother), 126

Lamont award, 306, 323, 325

"Last Words to a Dumb Friend," 250

"Laundromat Affair," 155, 160, 170–71

Lawrence, D. H., 42, 124, 126, 154, 176, 177, 194, 197, 257

Lawrence, Seymour (Sam), 160

Leg, broken, 66, 74, 119

Léger, Fernand, 223

Lehmann, John, 272, 326

Lesson, The, 279

Letters Home, 262

Levin, Mrs. Harry, 213

Lewis, C. S., 124

"Little Mining Town in Colorado, The," 304

"Livvie," 312

London, 141, 324, 329–39

London Magazine, 196, 199, 272n, 321

Lonely Crowd, The, 302

Lookout Farm, 3–8

"Lorelei," 242–43, 245, 272

Lotz, Myron (Mike), 66n, 69, 72–73, 74, 76, 77n, 129

Lowell, Amy, 32, 209

Lowell, Robert, 219, 226, 288ff., 294, 297, 302

Lucretius, 74

Lynes, Russell, 75

McCall's, 209

McCurdy, Marla, 214

McCurdy, Phil, 46–49, 214

McGinley, Phyllis, 209

McLean Hospital, 282

MacLeish, Archibald, 32

McLeod, Emilie, 306, 309

Macmillan, 306

Mademoiselle (Mlle), 39, 49, 53, 78, 80–81, 114, 171, 195, 240

"Mad Girl's Love Song," 129

Mangada, Widow, 142, 143

"Man in Black," 297, 298

"Manor Garden, The," 323, 325

Mansion, Mrs., 311

Man Who Died, The, 126

"Man Who Made Faces, The," 189

Marlies (Smith teacher), 182, 185, 188

Matisse, Henry, 188

"Matisse Chapel, The," 105

"Medallion," 325

Meet My Folks!, 309, 322

Merwin, W. S. and Dido, 187, 188

"Metaphors for a Pregnant Woman," 296

Milford, Mr. and Mrs., 342–43

Millay, Edna St. Vincent, 209

Miller, Arthur, 310, 315

"Miss Henderson's Marriage," 54

Monas (Smith teacher), 182

Monroe, Marilyn, 315

Montieth, Charles, 335

Moon, the, 31–32

Moore, Marianne, 151, 209, 238, 248, 317

Moss, Howard, 217, 240

Mount, Miss, 204, 205

Mourning and Melancholia, 276

Mrs. Dalloway, 150

"Mummy, The," 314, 315, 316, 322, 324

"Mussel Hunter at Rock Harbor," 240, 242, 248, 252

Mutrie, Pat, 47, 49

Myers, Lucas (Luke), 109–10, 128, 131, 198

Nation, The, 151, 257, 291

New Poets of England and America, 183

New World Writing, 221, 273, 324

New York, 80–81, 85; Poetry Center Contest, 195

New Yorker, The, 98, 100, 103, 189, 190, 226, 298, 304, 312, 313; acceptances, 178, 239, 240, 241, 256, 257, 297, 301–2, 317; contract, 332; Mavis Gallant and,

171, 312; rejections, 105, 128, 217, 260, 313

Nielson (Smith president), 181

Nightwood, 203

"Nocturne," 240

Northampton, Mass. *See* Smith College

Norton, Dick, 21n, 29n, 38–39, 40, 43–45, 51, 57–58, 59, 62ff., 66, 67, 77n; and S. P.'s virginity story, 280

Norton, Mr. (Dick's father), 43–44

Norton, Mrs. (Dick's mother), 38n, 43, 281

Norton, Perry, 21, 23, 57

"November Graveyard," 195, 248

O'Connor, Frank, 81, 273, 281

Oedipus, 224, 226

Oesterreich, on possession, 254–55

"Of Cats," 199

O'Gorman, Ned, 323

O'Neill, Eugene, 103

"On the Decline of Oracles," 208, 216

"Owl Over Main Street," 240, 298

Paris, 117, 120, 121, 125, 130, 132–41

Partisan Review, 151, 328

Pasternak, Boris, 337

"Pennines in April," 195

"Perfect Setup," 281

Peron, Evita, 54

Perse, St.–John, 319

Picasso, Pablo, 195
Pierson, Carol, 213
"Pike," 242, 255
Plath, Aurelia (mother), 5,
    26, 35, 40, 49, 81, 101,
    102–3, 114, 127, 141,
    169, 186, 210, 220, 224,
    242, 258, 262, 272, 352;
    arranges Eastham holiday
    for Hugheses, 159; friend
    of Mrs. Norton, 38n; at
    Harvard reading, 214;
    and S. P.'s pregnancy
    dream, 315; and S. P.'s
    therapy and hostility,
    263ff., 272ff., 282, 283,
    286, 301, 302; surgery in
    1955, 86
Plath, Otto (father), 19n,
    25–26, 126–27, 225,
    264, 276, 282, 297, 298,
    312; visit to grave, 295–
    96, visit to grave, poem
    of, 297–98
Plath, Warren (brother), 26,
    49, 100, 193, 218, 253,
    277, 278, 328
Plum, Mrs., 339–42
"Poem for a Birthday," 259,
    263, 323, 325
"Point Shirley, Revisited,"
    289
Porter, Katherine Anne, 312
*Possession: Demoniacal and
    Other*, 254–55
Pound, Ezra, 205, 316
Prouty, Olive Higgins, 59,
    101, 214
"Pursuit," 114, 127

Rainbow, The, 194
"Ravaged Face, The," 295

Redpath (professor), 103,
    127
"Relic," 199
"Return, The," 244, 250
Reynolds, Debbie, 255
Rich, Adrienne (A.C.R.),
    170, 183, 209, 212, 214,
    216, 289, 290–91, 292,
    294
Roche, Clarissa, x, 190,
    206, 207, 222
Roche, Paul, x, 190, 206,
    207, 220, 222, 224, 225,
    226
Rodman, Selden, 247
Roethke, Theodore, 295,
    321
Rogers, Ralph, 204, 206–7
Rosenbergs, the, 80–81
Rosenthal, M. L., 151, 306
Ross, David, 111
Rossetti, Christina, 209
Roth, Philip, 300, 301
Rousseau, Henri, 137, 199,
    206, 208, 217

St. Botolph's Review, 107,
    110
Salinger, J. D., 154, 301
Sanctuary, 292
Sappho, 209
Sassoon, Richard, 86, 89–
    96ff., 105–6, 108, 115–
    23, 125ff., 130, 132,
    133, 137ff., 149, 230,
    287
Saturday Evening Post, The,
    164, 167, 170, 183
Saxton, Eugene F.,
    Foundation, 127, 232,
    239, 248, 339
Scarlet Letter, The, 195

Schwarzkopf, Elizabeth, 311
Scott, Bill, 195
"Sculptor," 299
Seventeen, 22, 53
Sewanee, 257
Sexton, Anne (A.S.), 297,
    298–99, 300, 306–7
Seymour: An Introduction,
    301
"Shadow, The," 303
Shaw, Irwin, 154
Shock treatments, 86, 111,
    282, 295n, 335
"Singing Rider, The," 215
Sitwell, Edith, 209
Skiing, 119. *See also* Leg,
    broken
Smith College
    (Northampton), 16–27,
    34–46, 58–80, 86, 253;
    time of teaching job,
    169ff., 172–234
Smith Quarterly, 84
Smith Review, 41, 75
"Snakecharmer, The," 208,
    258, 272, 311, 313
Snakecharmer (Rousseau),
    137
Snodgrass, W. D., 299
"Snow by Morning," 313
"Sonnet: To Spring?," 33–
    34
Sons and Lovers, 194
Spaulding, Mrs., 163, 249
Spectator, The, 293
Spender, Stephen, 98, 115,
    151
Springfield Daily News, 40
Stafford, Jean, 226, 306,
    311, 312
Starbuck, Agatha, 327
Starbuck, George (G.S.),

298–99, 300, 305, 306–
    7, 323
Stenberg, John, 27
Stevens, Wallace, 125, 252
Strange Interlude, 98
Strindberg, August, 282
"Strumpet Song," 250
Suicide, 58, 80, 98, 124,
    150, 276, 282n, 352
"Suicide off Egg Rock," 292
Sultan, Florence, 252, 301
Sultan, Stanley, 252n, 301
"Summer Place," 209
"Sunday at the Minton's,"
    49, 281, 324
Swampscott, Mass., 27–34
Swedenborg, Emanuel, 74
Sweeney, Jack, 203, 213ff.
Sweeney, Mairé, 213, 214
"Sweetie Pie and the Gutter
    Men," 302, 303, 316
Swenson, May (M.S.), 183,
    209, 313, 325, 327
"System and I, The," 304

"Tattooist, The," 258, 316,
    322
Tattooist shop, 258–59
Taylor, Elizabeth, 255
Teasdale, Sara, 61
Thérèse, St., 281
Thomas, Dylan, 204, 288
"Thought–Fox, The," 213,
    258
Todd, Mike, 255
"To Eva Descending the
    Stair," 75
Tolstoi, Count Leo, 295
"To Paint a Waterlily," 213
To the Lighthouse, 150
"Trouble-Making Mother,

The," 164–65, 167, 170

Truslow, Jane, 274

"Two Gods of Alice Denway, The," 72

"Two Lovers and a Beachcomber," 191

Tyrer, Marjorie, 345

Unfinished Man, The, 198

Untermeyer, Louis, 32

Valley Head Hospital (Carlisle), 295

Van der Poel, Priscilla, 215, 221, 223

Van Voris, Bill, 192, 227ff.

Van Voris, Jacky, 228, 229

Varsity, 128

Verlaine, Paul, 115

"Water Color of Grantchester Meadows," 297

Waves, The, 162

Weeks, Edward, 258

Wellesley, Mass., 8–16, 49–51, 81–86

Welty, Eudora, 311, 312

Wendell (Smith teacher), 185, 190

Whalen, Mrs., 239, 253

What Maisie Knew, 217

Wheelwright, Philip, 227

"When We Dead Awaken," 99

"Whistle, The," 312

White Goddess, The, 219

Wilbur, Richard, 290, 292–93

Williams, Oscar, 224

Willis, Mr., 345–46

Wilson, Sloan, 209

Wings of the Dove, The, 220

"Winter Landscape with Rocks," 104

Winthrop, Mass., 295–96

"Wishing Box, The," 316

Withens, Yorkshire, 145–46, 298, 300

Women in Love, 154, 194

Woolf, Virginia, 61, 150, 162–63, 164, 166, 194, 197, 301, 302–3

World Publishing, 242, 257n

"Worn Path, A," 312

Wuthering Heights, 298

Wylie, Elinor, 32

Wylie, Philip, 43

Wynn, Jay, 335

Yaddo, 297, 309–29

Yale Review, The, 199, 287

Yale Series of Younger Poets, The, 302n, 305, 306, 323, 326

Years, The, 301, 302–3

Yeats, Jack, 215

Yeats, W. B., 2, 74, 75, 215, 216, 222, 225, 295